Selling War

SELLING
WAR

*The British Propaganda Campaign
Against American "Neutrality"
in World War II*

NICHOLAS JOHN CULL

New York   Oxford
OXFORD UNIVERSITY PRESS

Oxford University Press

Oxford   New York
Athens   Auckland   Bangkok   Bogota   Bombay
Buenos Aires   Calcutta   Cape Town   Dar es Salaam
Delhi   Florence   Hong Kong   Istanbul   Karachi
Kuala Lumpur   Madras   Madrid   Melbourne
Mexico City   Nairobi   Paris   Singapore
Taipei   Tokyo   Toronto

and associated companies in
Berlin   Ibadan

Library of Congress Cataloging-in-Publication Data
Cull, Nicholas John.
Selling war: the British propaganda campaign
against American "neutrality" in World War II/
Nicholas John Cull.
p.   cm.
Includes bibliographical references and index.
ISBN 0-19-508566-3 (Cloth)
ISBN 0-19-511150-8 (Pbk.)
1. World War, 1939–1945—Propaganda.
2. Propaganda, British—United States—History—20th century.
3. World War, 1939–1945—United States.
4. Neutrality—United States.
I. Title.
D810.P7G7248   1995   940.54′88—dc20   94-5614

2 4 6 8 9 7 5 3

Printed in the United States of America
on acid-free paper

For my family and Gloria Emerson

Acknowledgments

My chief debt is to Philip M. Taylor of the University of Leeds, who inspired me as an undergraduate and supervised my graduate research. I also owe much to my other teachers at Leeds, especially Roy Bridge, Professor David Dilks, Nicholas Pronay, Owen Hartley and the late Graham Ross; to Professor Donald Cameron Watt of the London School of Economics, for his numerous helpful comments, and to my colleagues in the School of History at the University of Birmingham. For finance I am grateful to the British Academy, to the Harkness Fellowship program of the Commonwealth Fund of New York, and to the Franklin and Eleanor Roosevelt Foundation. For help on the tortuous road to publication, I am grateful to Professor Henry Winkler—a generous reader—and my editor at Oxford University Press, Nancy Lane.

I am indebted to the Departments of History and Religion, and the Program in Afro-American Studies at Princeton University for their hospitality during the American phase of this research, and particularly to Arthur N. Waldron, now of the U.S. Naval War College, Newport, R.I., whose friendship and intellectual enthusiasm sustained me through my bleaker months. I have learned much from my fellow scholars particularly Anthony Aldgate, Ben Alpers, Susan Brewer, Angus Calder, David Carrasco, Robert Cole, David Culbert, Fred Inglis, Fred Krome, Tom Mahl, C. J. Morris, Thomas Troy, and John Young. I am grateful to Harold Evans of Random House, for his encouragement, for employing me as a research assistant, and for allowing some portions of that research to appear here.

The most enjoyable and productive moments of my research have most certainly been my contacts with the survivors of the war years, especially Joan and Geoff Galwey, the late Graham Hutton, John and Brenda Lawler, Hermione MacColl, Peggy Macmillan, Leonard Miall, Janet Murrow, and Chaim Raphael, who were particularly generous with their time, encouragement, and hospitality; also the late George Ball, Sir Maurice Bathurst, Sir Isaiah Berlin, Wallace and Peggy Carroll, Alistair Cooke, Walter Cronkite, David Daiches, Lionel Elvin, Douglas

Fairbanks, Jr., George Forrest, Gizelda Fowler, the late Lord Harmsworth, Lady Harmsworth, Heather Harvey, Sir William Hayter, Robert Heaney, the late Denis Hennessy, Alger Hiss, Harry Hodson, the late Lord Inchyra, Anne King-Hall, Larry Lesuour, the late Drew Middleton, Helen Milbank, Richard Miles, H.G. Nicholas, Jim Orrick, Dick Pear, Lord Perth, Peggy Ratcliffe, James Reston, Wendy Reves, the late Eric Sevareid, Lord Sherfield, Val Stavridi, Frank Thistlethwaite, Ann Thoms, and Stanley Wilson; and to "Mitch" Mitchell and the other witnesses with whom I corresponded.

I am grateful to Sir Edward Cazalet, Lord Lothian, Lord Holderness, the Honorable Hector McDonnell, and Lady Caroline Peake for permission to consult and where necessary to quote from private papers in their possession; to the National Film Board of Canada for permission to quote from documents written by its wartime director, John Grierson; to Turner Entertainment and Castle Hill Productions for permission to reproduce stills from films in their copyright, and to Margaret Gale and the staff of the British Information Services in New York for providing copies of some of the more interesting documents in that organization's archive. The material in this work taken from the BBC Written Archives Centre is copyrighted and appears by kind permission.

I owe much to the staff of the PRO at Kew and of Princeton University's Firestone and Mudd Libraries for all their help, to Verne Newton and his staff at the Roosevelt Library in Hyde Park, New York; to John Taylor and the staff at the National Archives in Washington, D.C.; to Jo Baggins and the staff of the photographic and film sections of the Imperial War Museum in London; to Ben Hopkins at the Hulton-Deutsch collection in London; to Debbie Goodsite at the Bettmann Archives, New York, and to Dr. Janusz Cisek at the Jósef Pilsudski Institute in New York.

The work would have been impossible without extensive traveling and I must thank numerous hosts, especially Clayton Messalt of Madison, Wisconsin, who opened his home to me on the slightest of connections. I also owe a special debt to friends on both sides of the Atlantic, especially Clive Kennedy, Paul Evans, and Kate Morris in Britain; to Victor Anderson, Helen Cho, Catherine Fasbender, Ken Halpern, Richard Kaye, Eric Lowery, Gregory Murphy, Stephanie Sheerin, and Hu Ying in Princeton; and to Judith Farbey, who knows both worlds. I owe much to David Williamson, who read several drafts of this work and in the process patiently taught me to write again, and to Elizabeth Moodey, a supportive friend and a wonderful proofreader. The encouragement and friendship of Gloria Emerson have been beyond price. Finally, I am indebted to my parents (also valiant proofreaders), grandparents, and sister, Hilary Cull, for their support throughout. All judgments and errors are my own.

Contents

Terminology

In accordance with established practice among scholars of mass persuasion, the word *propaganda* is used throughout this work not in the popular pejorative sense, but as a specific term to describe the act of mass persuasion. *Propaganda* cannot be defined by the nature of the material propagated; the definition must rest on the intent underlying the dissemination or, as in the case of censorship, the suppression of the material in question. Although Britain's wartime Ministry of Information and other agents of British propaganda consistently sought to avoid this term in describing their American activities, no other word is appropriate. The success of their endeavors demonstrates the inadequacy of popular notions of propaganda and of barriers against propaganda founded on such preconceptions.

Abbreviations

AFL   American Federation of Labor: One of the two main American trade union confederations.

AIPO   American Institute of Public Opinion: A U.S. polling organization run by George Gallup.

AP   Associated Press: A U.S.-based news agency.

BBC   British Broadcasting Corporation.

BIS   British Information Services: A title first used in 1941 for the Ministry of Information's administrative office in New York, set up to oversee the existing British publicity organizations in the United States. In 1942, the entire British operation amalgamated under this title. The office remains in operation.

BLI   British Library of Information, New York: A British Foreign Office agency founded as a publicity outlet in 1920; amalgamated into BIS in 1942.

BOPS   British Overseas Press Service: An offshoot of the BPS established in the winter of 1940–1941 to feed British news to British publicists in the Empire, in South America, and in Asia.

BPS   British Press Service: A Ministry of Information office founded in October 1940 to channel British information to the American press; amalgamated into BIS in 1942.

BSC   British Security Co-ordination: A British government agency in charge of all British covert operations on the American continent, founded in 1940 under Sir William Stephenson.

CDAAA   Committee to Defend America by Aiding the Allies (also
            known as the William Allen White Committee): A
            moderate U.S. interventionist organization founded
            in 1940.

CIO   Congress of Industrial Organizations: The second
            (and more radically inclined) main American trade
            union confederation.

COI   Office of the Coordinator of Information: A U.S. covert
            operations and propaganda office founded in June 1941
            under Colonel William Donovan. Later becomes the OSS.

ESU   English Speaking Union: An Anglo-American cultural
            organization set up in 1919.

FARA   Foreign Agents Registration Act: A U.S. law, passed in
            1938 and revised in 1942, for controlling foreign
            propaganda.

FFF   Fight For Freedom committee: An extreme intervention-
            ist organization founded in the United States in 1941.

FO   Foreign Office, London.

GPO   British General Post Office: A patron of documentary
            film production through the GPO Film Unit under
            John Grierson.

IAIC   Inter-Allied Information Center and Committee:
            A British-funded organization founded in New York
            in 1940 (with London office from 1941) to facilitate
            "propaganda by the lesser allies." Known as UNIO, and
            under U.S. chairmanship, from 1942 onward.

MEW   Ministry of Economic Warfare, London.

MI5   The British domestic security service.

MI6   The British overseas secret service (also known as SIS).

MI7   Short-lived British War Office propaganda agency,
            1939–1940.

MoI   Ministry of Information, London.

NFB   National Film Board of Canada: Established in 1939.

OEPEC   Overseas Emergency Publicity Expenditure Committee:
            The body controlling the funding for Britain's MoI.

OFF   Office of Facts and Figures: A U.S. government publicity
            agency established in the autumn of 1941.

OSS	Office of Strategic Services: The U.S. covert operations agency; later evolved into the CIA.
OWI	Office of War Information: A U.S. government propaganda agency, founded in 1942.
PID	Political Intelligence Department: A British Foreign Office intelligence department that served as a cover for covert work.
PWE	Political Warfare Executive: The British Foreign Office department for psychological warfare in enemy countries, founded in 1941.
RIIA	Royal Institute of International Affairs: A London-based organization for the study of international relations; also known as Chatham House.
SIS	Secret Intelligence Service: An alternative title for MI6.
SO.1	British Special Operations: The Covert Propaganda Section of SOE from June 1940 until August 1941; split off to become PWE.
SO.2	British Special Operations: The Sabotage Section of SOE.
SOE	Special Operations Executive: British agency founded in June 1940 for sabotage and, until August 1941, propaganda.
UNIO	United Nations Information Organization: Title of the IAIC from November 1942 onward; in 1945 UNIO became the information division of the United Nations organization.
UP	United Press: A U.S.-based news agency.
WRUL	A Boston-based short-wave radio station whose foreign language broadcasts to Europe were subsidized by Britain.

Selling War

Introduction

On February 15, 1942, Winston Churchill broadcast an address to the world. Still flushed with the news of Pearl Harbor and fresh from a visit to Washington, he gloried in the United States' entry into World War II as an event that he had "dreamed of, aimed at, and worked for." The admission was unfortunate. The British ambassador to Washington, Lord Halifax, immediately warned that the words *worked for* were "troublesome" to American ears, giving "the idea that a simple innocent people have been caught asleep by others cleverer than themselves." This was no way to begin the Anglo-American partnership.[1] But as both men knew well, Churchill had spoken the truth. That "work" is the subject of this book.

From the eve of the German invasion of Poland to the moment of Japan's attack on Pearl Harbor, the British government mounted a concerted effort to draw the United States into the war. This work was by no means limited to regular diplomacy. Bitter experience had taught the British that the White House could only be as useful to their interests as the Congress, the press, and public opinion would allow it to be. Seeing that popular isolationism blocked the way to American aid, the British inaugurated a new public relations policy in the United States; by 1941, they had established a sizable propaganda machine on both sides of the Atlantic. The full scale and impact of this activity has never been revealed. The campaign soon sank from view, obscured by British diffidence and the spectacular activities of the Japanese on the morning of December 7, 1941.

During the period of Britain's campaign, American public opinion clearly changed. American foreign policy on the eve of Pearl Harbor stood in radical contrast to the knee-jerk isolationism of the 1930s. In 1935, most Americans were isolationists; indeed, given the course of American history, any other policy would have been surprising. But by 1941, this same public was ready to risk war to aid the Allies and was quite unprepared to allow Germany to dominate the world. Roosevelt directed American foreign policy accordingly.[2]

The transformation of American opinion is an essential component in the story of U.S. entry into World War II. It reflects a road to war as distinct as the familiar tale of diplomatic exchanges with Tokyo and London; a road based not on secret telegrams and grand policy but on the open flow of information from Europe to the great centers of American opinion-making: New York and Hollywood. Its principal characters are not statesmen or diplomats, but journalists and propagandists who attempted to mold public opinion and thereby reset the parameters of high policy. This story transcends national boundaries, but again and again it touches one powerful actor: the British government. It is commonly acknowledged that the gritty radio speeches of Winston Churchill and the stirring coverage by American correspondents of the London Blitz shaped America's perception of the British and their struggle. Yet these broadcasts—and the associated newsreels and press photographs—were not spontaneously generated sparks of actuality, leaping the Atlantic of their own accord. They were individual elements in a concerted British propaganda policy. Not the American broadcasters reporting on the war from Europe, nor the well-born activists of the East Coast interventionist lobby, nor even the proclamations of President Roosevelt himself can be wholly divorced from the work of Britain's publicity machine.

After the war, the British government seems to have tried to destroy the evidence of its war propaganda in the United States. It hoped to avoid the embarrassment that followed exposure of its similar campaign to draw America into World War I.[3] Nevertheless, the story of the British campaign is not unknown. Several participants left memoirs, and the colorful activities of filmmakers and secret agents have attracted a measure of attention, but accounts of these offer only a glimpse of Britain's activities. The full effort, as revealed by public and private archives on both sides of the Atlantic and by the recollections of the survivors, stands as one of the most diverse, extensive, and yet subtle propaganda campaigns ever directed by one sovereign state at another.[4]

The British effort of 1941, however, did not come easily. In fact, throughout most of the preceding decade British policy explicitly forbade any such endeavor in the United States. But as the international scene darkened and Britain looked longingly toward the uncommitted might of America, some policy makers in London began to wonder how they could address the problem of isolationism, and whether they might, through judicious use of propaganda and publicity, be able to undermine U.S. neutrality and somehow sell Britain and a second world war to a skeptical American public.

1

The Gathering Storm:
Britain's American Propaganda Policy,
1937 to 1939

> We must act and state our case in such a way as to retain American
> sympathy at all times.
>
> Robert Vansittart, December 1936[1]

By January 1937, Britain faced its worst international crisis since
the end of World War I. The trouble had begun six years before, when
the Japanese army seized Manchuria. Now the threat of further
Japanese expansion into China had been augmented by growing instability in Europe. While the League of Nations fumbled with the
Abyssinian crisis, Mussolini had drifted toward an alignment with the
new menace of Hitler's Germany. Then, in March 1936, the German
army marched into the Rhineland, shattering the foundations of the
postwar European peace. With the Spanish Civil War beckoning the
dictators to intervene, further conflict seemed inevitable. In London,
the Conservative government of Stanley Baldwin responded with full-
scale rearmament but was fully conscious that Britain could not
muster a credible deterrent before 1939 at the earliest. The French
begged Britain to make a commitment to uphold the European order;
but the British, wary of stretching their reduced naval strength across
three possible theaters of war, felt unable to act without a guarantee of
American support. By 1937, the British had good reason to fear that
this support would never be offered.

In 1935, American foreign policy had taken on a fresh certainty:
strict neutrality was mandated by a set of newly passed Neutrality
Acts. During 1936, these laws had been tightened to prevent all trade
with belligerent powers. Britain watched these developments with
horror. Writing on December 31, 1936, in his end-of-year review, the
Permanent Under Secretary of State for Foreign Affairs, Sir Robert

Vansittart, mourned, "We scrambled through the last war by import-
ing in its early stages some 500 million dollars' worth of American
munitions. To-day, in the event of war we can count on getting
nothing."[2]

But the road to substantial American aid was barred by more than
law. The laws represented just another manifestation of an all-perva-
sive culture of U.S. isolationism: a dynamic impulse to remain aloof
from European politics, long evident in the American public and Congress alike, underpinned by profound regional, ethnic, historical, and
generational forces, and hammered home by the experience of World
War I and the postwar slump. Moreover, American political culture included certain anti-British strains that, although largely inactive in
1937, constituted political traps on the road to Anglo-American cooperation. Whitehall dared not attempt to "roll back" the influence of
isolationism, but neither could it stand by and watch its world crumble
for want of American support.

On the eve of 1937, Vansittart's American policy recommendation
was simple. "We must act," he wrote "and state our case in such a way
as to retain American sympathy at all times."[3] In the best of times this
would have been difficult. But British policy was about to take a turn
for the worse. The new Prime Minister, Neville Chamberlain, had
written off all hope of American aid and was quite unprepared to
shape Whitehall policy to please Peoria. The next two years were to
shake Anglo-American relations to their core, but from this tangle of
needs, fears, and frustrations Britain's wartime propaganda policy in
the United States emerged.

Britain's Dilemma: Britain in American Opinion, 1919 to 1937

> Burn Everything British But Their Coal!
>
> Irish-American banner, 1921[4]

As Vansittart and his colleagues knew only too well, Britain occupied a
paradoxical position in the American mind. Many Americans adored all
things English; but every current of anglophilia seemed to be matched
by a countervailing surge of anglophobia, and even sympathetic
Americans were unprepared to throw off neutrality at Britain's whim.

Some degree of American anglophobia was only to be expected. It
flowed from the historic struggle to be free from tyrannical redcoats
and a profligate king. Moreover, Britain's rigid class system seemed to
represent the epitome of everything America had rejected in 1776. The
scale of such feeling varied from region to region and from community
to community. Some Southerners remembered that England had hon-
ored Confederate ship-building contracts; but other Americans recalled

only wrongs. German- and Irish-Americans had ample reason to despise London and saw themselves as having absolutely no stake in a war to save the British Empire. The farmers of the American interior recognized Britain's role in financing the railroads that bled them dry, and hence the British joined the plutocrats of Wall Street and the White House as central figures in the political demonology of the Prairies. The newer immigrants from Eastern Europe had felt the lash of other empires and were in no hurry to endorse the British version, particularly when isolationist views offered easy proof of Americanism. Even the enemies of Hitler were not necessarily admirers of Britain. American Jews knew who ruled Palestine, and American Communists knew who continued to refuse aid to the Republican side in Spain. Any American untouched by such ethnic or political allegiances could contemplate Britain's failure to pay its war debt or the commercial injustice of its system of imperial preference in trade.[5]

Even so, Britain still had its admirers in the United States. A Gallup poll of April 1937 found that 55 percent of American voters considered Britain to be the "European country" they "liked best"; the closest runner-up was France, with a meager 11 percent.[6] Such a response was no guarantee of wartime aid, but it gave hope to Whitehall. This sentiment also had solid historical roots. At the end of the nineteenth century, Britain and America had discovered a community of interest. As Americans awoke from their dreams of the limitless frontier and embraced instead an urban, industrial future, Britain became a model for the younger nation. Some saw British democracy as the mother of the American way; some admired the maritime supremacy of the Royal Navy; some, including President Theodore Roosevelt, anticipated a glorious shared racial destiny for the "Bold and hardy, cool and intelligent" English-speaking race.[7]

The notion of a joint Anglo-American destiny offered a firm footing amid the shifting sands of the early twentieth century, and it prospered accordingly. It prompted a brassy music-hall lyricist to declare "It's the English-Speaking Race Against the World!"; it drove Rhodes to found his scholarships, and Edward Harkness to reciprocate with the Commonwealth Fund Fellowships. A network of Atlanticist organizations worked within the elites of both countries to promote business and cultural links, the most important of these being the Pilgrims Trust, founded by Harkness at the turn of the century. Other organizations sought to spread Anglo-Americanism to a wider audience. In 1918, Sir Evelyn Wrench, fresh from Britain's campaign to pull the United States into World War I, founded the English Speaking Union to preserve that wartime relationship for the years ahead. The ESU organized a vigorous program of speaking exchanges and published pamphlets on Anglo-American relations; it prospered on both sides of the Atlantic. Similarly, the British and American delegates to the Versailles conference agreed to found parallel bodies to promote knowledge of international affairs and to encourage Anglo-American cooperation in particular. The Council on Foreign Relations and the Royal Institute of International Affairs at Chatham House nurtured this vision of an Atlantic rapprochement throughout the difficult years ahead.[8]

The elites of Britain and the United States set the seal on the spirit of the era with a flurry of intermarriage: Joseph Chamberlain married an American; and both Harold Macmillan and Winston Churchill had American mothers. Similarly, a number of senior British diplomats, including Vansittart and the British ambassador to the United States, Sir Ronald Lindsay, married Americans. American immigrants such as "Chips" Channon and Ronald Tree found their way into the House of Commons, while the Astor family bestrode the ocean as a trans-Atlantic dynasty. In fact, a survey of 132 members of Parliament in 1938 revealed that more than one in ten had family ties to the United States, while one in five had large personal economic interests in that country.[9]

Unique bonds also united the working masses of the two countries. Cultural links flowed naturally from the common language and from ongoing ties of immigration and commerce. Britons and Americans shared common heroes and a common psychological landscape that embraced the fog-shrouded London of Sherlock Holmes, the India of Kipling, and the Mississippi of Mark Twain. It was a world in which Buffalo Bill's Wild West Show played for Queen Victoria, Oscar Wilde lectured to miners in Colorado, and P. G. Wodehouse churned out Bertie Wooster stories for the American *Saturday Evening Post*.

The interwar years strengthened these ties. In the 1920s, the stars of the American stage and screen took the British masses and high society by storm. Conversely, British actors dominated an American theater industry that still lacked its own stage schools. When talking films created a new demand for trained voices, Hollywood naturally looked to Britain, and hardly a major film appeared thereafter without C. Aubrey Smith, Cedric Hardwicke, Charles Laughton, David Niven, Basil Rathbone, Leslie Howard, Robert Donat, Ronald Coleman, Cary Grant, or Claude Raines. Some Britons successfully disguised their origins. Despite his stage name, Boris Karloff was not only British, but also the brother of Foreign Office East Asian expert Sir John Pratt.[10] Hollywood's depiction of English life bore little relation to reality: in American films, England remained a semi-medieval land, populated exclusively by dilettante aristocrats and chirpy cockneys. But Americans would react with great indignation when its cherished world of Jeeves and Wooster began to disappear under German bombs.

The British government did not set much store by the anglophilia of either the masses or the elite in the United States. The British ambassador in Washington feared that, since these sentiments sprang from romantic notions of English life and institutions, Americans would always be disappointed by reality. He warned that the typical American "expects much of England, almost superhuman wisdom; and when something goes wrong, even though it be something which does not affect American interests, he is loud in his condemnation, for 'Whom he loveth he chastiseth.'"[11] The liberal response to British policy during the World War II did much to confirm this observation.

By the late 1930s, the limits of American sympathy were obvious. Americans may have liked British actors, but they loathed British politicians. As the British government defaulted on its debt and scrambled to secure a European peace through "appeasement," Britain's position in the United States seemed doomed to decline. The time had come to act.

The most obvious British response to American isolationism in 1937 would have been to launch a grand public relations campaign. Such campaigns had served Britain's interests well in World War I and became a staple of British interwar policy, culminating with the founding of the British Council for Cultural Relations Abroad, in 1934. But the British government was reluctant to use such methods in the United States, largely because British propagandists had worn out their welcome by successfully bringing the United States into World War I. Americans knew that, throughout the war, the British had shamelessly manipulated war news, had peddled pictures of bloated Prussian beasts, had invented tales of "Hun" atrocities, and had faked the evidence to fit.[12]

Despite its lurid reputation, the earlier British effort included much subtlety, and many of its techniques—particularly the cultivation of American journalists, writers, and other opinion formers—would resurface in World War II. But the United States knew of these methods as well. The director of this work, the Canadian novelist Sir Gilbert Parker, had published his story in *Harper's* in 1918. In 1935, the historian Walter Millis reminded Americans that, throughout the war, Parker's London-based propaganda office had fed American correspondents "articles gratis from such priceless but patriotic pens as those of Kipling, Wells, Galsworthy and . . . George Bernard Shaw." He went on:

> Sir Gilbert arranged propagandist interviews with the leading British statesmen . . . flattering American opinion as he "educated" it. He distributed propaganda . . . to American libraries, educational institutions and periodicals; he was particularly careful to arrange for lectures, letters and articles by pro-Ally Americans rather than by Englishmen; while he himself established relations with influential and eminent people of every profession in the United States . . . . As the war went on and the agony deepened, every possible means of influence was to be exploited by the intelligent directors of Allied publicity.

Millis argued that British propaganda gained its "overwhelming effectiveness" from Britain's monopoly over the trans-Atlantic cable, the passion and conviction of Allied propagandists, and the "predisposition of the Americans to receive the propaganda." His findings sparked a surge of anglophobia and paranoia.[13]

America's disillusionment with World War I merely made matters worse. The press and the academic community raged against British duplicity. In their view, British war propagandists shared war guilt with the financiers of the House of Morgan and with Woodrow Wilson himself. Soon the very concept of mass propaganda became anathema, and a powerful fear of propaganda took root in the popular consciousness. Broader trends buttressed this fear. Had not Freud laid the workings of the human mind open for analysis? Was not advertising the key to business success? Could not an individual learn the mechanics of interpersonal propaganda and thereby "win friends and influence people"? In such a world, what havoc might a foreign power wreak? While George Gallup and Hadley Cantril pioneered the "scientific study" of public opinion, scholars of propaganda formed institutes and set about forewarning the innocent.[14] The spirit of the age sharpened the United States' conviction to be on guard against propaganda "next time," but even so the British dared not entirely abandon their efforts to mold American opinion.

Foundations: British Propaganda in the United States, 1919 to 1937

> This word propaganda seems to have no terrors for the official world . . . . But as you know, it never fails to disturb me because over here it has now only the debased meaning of a sinister activity. It is a good word gone wrong . . . .
>
> Angus Fletcher, 1929[15]

Despite the United States' fear of propaganda, from 1920 onward the British government maintained a small press bureau in New York. This office, known as the British Library of Information, New York (BLI or BLINY), was a small, experimental branch of the Foreign Office News Department, housed within the Consulate General near Battery Park. Its first Director, Charles de Graz, hoped to build on the effective press relations element of Britain's war propaganda and develop it into a full-scale publicity bureau; but London had other ideas. Whitehall was both alarmed by the United States' fear of propaganda and revolted by the Frankenstein's monster it had unleashed on the world during the war. In 1924, the Foreign Office proclaimed that British policy in the United States was to be "to tell the truth, to eschew secrecy except when publicity would prejudice delicate negotiations or do harm to others, and to let the facts speak for themselves."[16] This policy of "No Propaganda" became the starting point for all subsequent discussions of British propaganda in the United States for the next two decades. The BLI evolved accordingly. Its second director, Robert Wilberforce, was a man of high moral character. A great-grandson of William Wilberforce, the renowned British abolitionist, and a convert to Catholicism, he had no desire to use war propaganda methods in peacetime. Wilberforce applauded the British decision merely to "satisfy the existing demand for information on British affairs rather than to create or increase the desire for such information," and he worked toward a long-term "broadening of the general knowledge of British affairs in the United States." Under Wilberforce, the BLI drifted away from its earlier press liaison function to become the American agent for all British government publications and source of reference information on all things British, from royalty to tax law. The only digressions from the BLI's aboveboard activities came with the addition of an annual fund of $2,000 to counter Indian nationalist propaganda in the United States and the introduction of a press survey section to monitor American newspapers. The survey became the British government's principal barometer of American public opinion. It proved its usefulness during the Anglo-American naval crisis of 1927–28. Detailed press reports helped the British Cabinet reach a modus vivendi with the Americans.[17]

Although the library was always available to curious laymen, the BLI consciously aimed its activities at the makers of American public opinion. Its directors sought to "be regarded in all important quarters in the United States as the principal and most accessible source of authoritative information on Great Britain and her policy." To this end, library staff developed their own network of contacts. Unfortunately, these remained rather limited. The library's deputy director from 1922 onward (and co-director from 1928 onward), Angus Fletcher, became a pillar of the Special Libraries Association of America, while Robert Wilberforce developed connections with the Catholic Church and numerous Catholic editors, writers, and universities. Their principal assistant from 1930 onward, a rather dull career diplomat named Alan Dudley, tried to move in literary and film circles. Eventually the BLI left the Battery and moved uptown to 270 Madison Avenue, but any significant expansion of BLI activities remained all but unthinkable. As Fletcher reminded the Foreign Office in 1929, he had no intention of undertaking any propaganda or "special pleading" to promote any issue of British policy, prestige, or interests. He would provide information only as and when it was requested.[18]

While the BLI puttered along in New York, the Foreign Office News Department in London increasingly emphasized propaganda as an appropriate tool of foreign policy. Then, in 1932, the British Broadcasting Corporation began its English-language "Empire Service." Although beamed at Canada, this service consisting of news and talks could also be heard south of the forty-ninth parallel. Broadcasting House soon noticed that it was receiving more correspondence from American listeners than from Canadians, and it assumed that its audience figures matched these proportions. Since the dry content and rigid, Oxford-voiced delivery of the Empire Service were clearly designed for British

Imperial tastes, the BBC felt confident that American listeners did not feel propagandized, but merely felt privileged to eavesdrop on the British Empire talking to itself.[19] It was a small beginning. When an initiative to expand trans-Atlantic broadcasting followed, it came not from Britain but from that center of innovative political broadcasting, the Roosevelt White House.

In 1934, alarmed by British misperceptions of his New Deal, President Roosevelt suggested a regular exchange of radio news commentaries between Britain and the United States over the Columbia Broadcasting System and the BBC. The BBC's Director General Sir John Reith agreed and selected the American journalist Raymond Gram Swing to serve as the BBC's commentator on American affairs. In 1935, Swing began his weekly broadcasts to Britain, which swiftly became a national institution. Despite the misgivings of the Foreign Office, CBS reciprocated by carrying British speakers in regular "Trans-Atlantic Bulletins," which were handled from 1936 onward by the able British broadcaster and journalist Vernon Bartlett.[20]

The advent of trans-Atlantic radio exchanges spawned a supporting bureaucracy. In 1935, the BBC decided to appoint a "North American Representative" to seek out American material from an office in New York, to oversee the exchange of talks, and to advise London on its treatment of American affairs. There were two main candidates for the job. The first to be interviewed was the young BBC film critic, Alistair Cooke. Having studied at Yale and toured the United States as a Commonwealth Fund scholar, Cooke was keen to combat British ignorance of America and had already persuaded the BBC Home Service to institute a weekly *American Half Hour* of talks. His enthusiasm did not help his cause. Cooke bewildered his crusty interview panel by suggesting that he might also cover Canadian politics and learn Spanish to help collect material from Mexico. The job passed instead to a BBC talks producer named Felix Green. Green would eventually disappoint the stuffed shirts at Broadcasting House by becoming a free-thinking guru of the American Far Left, but for the moment he was happy to play the BBC game.

In December 1935, the BBC opened its New York office in the Rockefeller Center's British Empire Building on Fifth Avenue—a prestigious site soon to be shared with the BLI—and Green began a tireless quest for American material to send to Britain. He scoured the country for plays, dance bands, variety acts, and regular speakers. His recruits included Herbert Elliston of the *Christian Science Monitor*, who made a weekly broadcast to Britain on financial affairs, and Alistair Cooke, who had just arrived in New York to work for NBC and write for the London *Times*. Thus Cooke began his long career as an interpreter of America to Britain. It was a modest beginning, but with the practice of broadcast exchanges secure, the BBC had a bridgehead for British broadcasting to America. A new era in peacetime trans-Atlantic communication had commenced. It now fell to the British government to build the same concerns into its preparation for war.[21]

In 1935, Britain began to rearm. This process included plans for wartime propaganda, and the Committee of Imperial Defense duly established a shadow Ministry of Information. The planners, however, soon became preoccupied with internal feuds over the question of domestic propaganda. As a result, they had little time to deliberate on the broad question of overseas publicity, let alone the specific matter of wartime propaganda in the United States. Not until 1938 did the Foreign Office establish a special committee to investigate overseas publicity, under Vansittart.[22] But the question of American publicity did not have to wait so long. The Foreign Secretary, Anthony Eden, took the initiative. In March 1937, he asked the British ambassador in Washington, Ronald Lindsay, to compile a detailed report on how the British might "retain . . . the goodwill of the United States Government and public opinion" in the mounting international crisis. In so doing, he took the first step in constructing Britain's wartime propaganda policy in the United States.[23]

The Awakening: British Planning, 1937 to 1938

> I remember a remark made to me once by one of the cleverest American writers on foreign affairs . . . . He said "Anglo-American relations are foolproof; and they are only in danger when you try to improve them." There is a basis of very profound wisdom in this saying.
>
> Sir Ronald Lindsay, March 1937[24]

Lindsay responded swiftly and thoughtfully to Eden's request. In a long report dated March 22, 1937, he made numerous constructive suggestions for improving American opinion of Britain. He urged the Foreign Office to consider the American public when formulating British economic policy and to woo the American government with a liberal trade in miliary secrets. He acknowledged the importance of the BLI's work, but he emphasized the danger inherent in expanding publicity beyond a few visiting lecturers and feature films. He endorsed the "No Propaganda" policy but nonetheless asserted that Britain could do much within the confines of this policy to win American sympathy. To this end, Lindsay called for a large British contribution to the New York World's Fair of 1939, in the form of an exhibit focusing on Britain's cultural achievements. "We have been asked to pay a compliment," he wrote, "and we shall not be blamed if we pay it handsomely." The Foreign Office worked to ensure that this opportunity did not go to waste. In the event, it provided an invaluable boost to the British cause on the eve of war.[25]

Eden was a ready champion of Lindsay's policy. He had no doubt about the importance of the United States for British diplomacy. "Everything," he declared in January 1938, "must give way to the primary importance of good relations with Roosevelt and America." Unfortunately, Chamberlain disagreed. Convinced that American isolationism had rendered President Roosevelt's sympathy irrelevant, he went behind Eden's back, snubbed a presidential peace initiative, and set his mind on buying off Mussolini. Furious, Eden resigned from the Cabinet and embraced political exile.[26]

Others shared Eden's belief in the need for an Anglo-American rapprochement. Key sections of the British establishment remained attached to the vision of an Anglo-American world order. Some—most notably the Astors and the Rhodes Trust Secretary, Lord Lothian—were prepared to appease Germany in the interim; but many took exception to such ideas. By 1938, a loose pro-American, anti-Chamberlain bloc had formed within the British elite. Its adherents included Eden; Vansittart (who had been promoted into a position of glorious impotence in December 1937); Duff Cooper; Dick Law; Jim Thomas; Lord Cranborne; the American-born Ronald Tree; the head of the Foreign Office News Department, Rex Leeper; the columnist, Robert Bruce Lockhart; and Victor Gordon Lennox, diplomatic correspondent of the *Daily Telegraph*.[27]

This group also overlapped with the Old Guard of Tory dissenters, including Winston Churchill and his young protégé Brendan Bracken, who still held fast to the Anglo-Saxonism of the previous generation. The Old Guard understood the need to retain American sympathy and to convince the U.S. public that not all the British were appeasers, against the day when a more resolute Prime Minister might take residence at Downing Street and request American aid for war. They knew where to begin: with the American press corps in London.

Although the American public clearly desired to remain aloof from the affairs of Europe, they nevertheless wished to know exactly what they were missing, and throughout the 1930s the American press steadily strengthened its representation in Europe. The press had lately been joined by a new breed of journalist: the radio correspondent. A common language, technical convenience, and the pull of such stories as the abdication crisis of 1936 guaranteed London's emergence as the hub for this coverage. Here was a golden opportunity for those in Britain who wished to reach out to America.

While the Prime Minister's office bombarded the American press corps with "unofficial censorship" and outright rudeness, the Foreign Office News Department strove to ensure that the journalists were well supplied with material. The centerpiece of their effort was a daily press briefing given at noon to all British and American journalists. The format was rigid. The journalists would assemble in the briefing room at the Foreign Office; the Deputy Director of the News Department,

Charles Peake, or his junior Tom Dupree (another diplomat with an American wife) would enter and take his place in the window seat; and then, with the morning sun pouring over his shoulder, he would begin: "Gentlemen: you will take down the following." Unwanted questions were easily deflected. Dupree favoured a gentle: "We're not talking about that today." In the afternoon, Rex Leeper, the department head, would be available to answer questions individually. The information was stilted and carefully controlled, but the arrangement marked a beginning.[28]

The American press corps in London did not need educating on the subject of Hitler. Edgar Mowrer and Dorothy Thompson were being expelled from Germany at a time when members of the British elite were still talking about trains running on time. A decade of watching the European peace crumble had confirmed these journalists' fears. The old hands of America's coverage of Europe—distinguished correspondents such as John Gunther, Vincent Sheean, and William Stoneman—had no doubt that Hitler and those (like Chamberlain) who underestimated him had to be stopped.

Most of the American correspondents were otherwise well disposed toward Britain. Many displayed the anglophilia of their class; some had more tangible attachments to Britain. Vincent Sheean had an English wife; Dorothy Thompson of the *New York Herald Tribune* had an English father; and Walter Duranty of the North American Newspaper Alliance had been born in Liverpool and educated at Harrow and Cambridge. Others, however, lacked both the roots and the inclination to love Britain. Drew Middleton of AP confessed himself "skeptical" upon first arriving in Britain; Eric Sevareid of CBS found the nation's "little England" mentality to be quite a match for the isolationism of his native Midwest; and Edward R. Murrow (appointed European director of CBS in 1937) initially thought of Britain as a "pleasant" but relatively unimportant "museum piece." Complaints about British complacency, classism, and cooking abounded. Fortunately, Hitler inspired harsher antagonism, and useful alignments followed.[29]

The American reporters slipped naturally into the anti-Chamberlain set. They needed good stories, and the circle of dissenters around Eden were eager to oblige. Many also shared the internationalism of the British foreign policy elite. Harold Callender of the *New York Times* was sufficiently committed to Anglo-American relations to serve on the English Speaking Union's public affairs committee. Ed Murrow had first seen London in 1935 as a representative of the International Institute of Education, and he took up his CBS job with a network of internationalist connections. Within weeks of arriving in England, he had renewed these links and addressed a meeting at Chatham House.[30]

One American was particularly well connected to the anti-appeasers. Helen Kirkpatick of the *Chicago Daily News* had been a mainstay of the anti-Chamberlain set before joining that paper in 1939. Kirkpatrick moved to England in 1937, after working in Geneva for the Foreign Policy Association, to join Victor Gordon Lennox of the *Daily Telegraph* and the deputy editor of the *Economist*, Graham Hutton, on the anti-Hitler, anti-appeasement news sheet *Whitehall Letter*. She was the letter's only full-time writer. Week after week, the letter revealed the scale of Hitler's ambitions and the folly of Chamberlain's response. It soon built up an avid readership in Britain (including Winston Churchill) and in certain circles in the United States, where Helen Kirkpatrick's brother had arranged for distribution of a cabled edition. Kirkpatrick also contributed material to a string of British papers and produced two substantial books: one for Americans, offering a sympathetic picture of Britain to undermine isolationism; and the other for British readers, demanding a firm stand against Hitler. The Prime Minister was not amused. Conservative Party agents tapped her telephone, and Chamberlain is reputed to have asked W. H. Smith and Sons to remove her British book from their station bookstands.[31]

By 1938, the American journalists had become intimates of the anti-Chamberlain set, and a rich and productive network had developed within it. They met socially with Eden, Vansittart, Duff Cooper, and Lord Cranborne, and they thrashed out the issues of the day over cocktails with Bruce Lockhart at Whites Club. A few members of the American press corps enjoyed contacts at the highest levels of British society. Sheean came to know Churchill on the French Riviera; Helen Kirkpatrick, Herbert Knickerbocker, and John Gunther were regular guests at the home of Ronald Tree. Ed Murrow made a point of developing such links. On arriving in Britain in 1937, he resolved to neglect the substantial American colony in London in favor of the British, and he became a popular guest at all the Atlantic-minded country houses.[32]

This network had far-reaching consequences. Vansittart, Leeper, Lockhart, and their circle dominated the planning of British political warfare during the last days of peace. The innumerable hours of amiable dinner-party conversation they had shared with their friends from the American press would loom large when the time came to plan British war propaganda in that country.

As the British prepared their response to U.S. neutrality, they were able to draw a measure of hope from the first cracks in the isolationist rampart. The United States had been roused by renewed Japanese aggression in China, and American anti-Nazi sentiment seemed to be growing. The American Jewish Congress had been demonstrating against Hitler since March 1933. Now, their boycott of German goods had taken hold; by 1938, an estimated 56 percent of Americans supported the boycott.[33]

By 1938, Hollywood was also throwing off encouraging sparks of unneutrality. These had been slow in coming. The Hays office and Production Code Administration had fought long and hard to keep politics out of the movies, and the Jewish producers who might ordinarily have led the anti-Nazi campaign seemed reluctant to challenge these rules. Meanwhile, such actors as the passionately anglophile Douglas Fairbanks, Jr., who pressed for openly anti-Nazi pictures, encountered a general fear among producers and directors that open opposition to Hitler would produce an anti-Semitic backlash against "Jewish warmongers" in the United States. But there were exceptions. After a studio employee was murdered by the SS in 1936, Warner Brothers introduced a regular twist of anti-totalitarianism into their movies; and the independent producer Walter Wanger became vocal in the cause of anti-fascism.[34] Wanger (an Episcopalian of Jewish parentage, who pronounced his name to rhyme with *danger*) had never sought to avoid controversy. Throughout the 1930s, his films carried a clear political (and usually anti-war) message; his 1938 film on the Spanish Civil War, *Blockade*, mixed opposition to war with a denunciation of fascism that was sufficiently outspoken to earn the film bans in Spain, Italy, Germany, Portugal, Peru, El Salvador, Bulgaria, Yugoslavia, Lithuania, Czechoslovakia, and Poland. Soon thereafter Wanger began actively campaigning for a solid anti-Nazi stance in Hollywood. By 1938, 5,000 Hollywood filmmakers, writers, and technicians—from timid liberals to brash Popular Front Communists—had joined him in the Hollywood Anti-Nazi League. It was only a matter of time before the movies themselves caught up.[35]

The most explicitly anti-Nazi and pro-British films of the era came from the American newsreel *March of Time* (a subsidiary of Henry Luce's *Time* empire). By 1938, under the vigorous direction of Louis de Rochemont, the series had adopted a firm stand on the international crisis. The *March of Time* film "Inside Nazi Germany—1938" became the first anti-Nazi motion picture to gain commercial distribution in the United States.[36] De Rochemont launched a special British edition and opened a London office to ensure a regular supply of "British interest" stories for the British and American editions of the newsreel. Thus, during the final years of peace, the 20 million Americans who watched *March of Time* each month saw more news from Britain than from any country except the United States itself. Although the heroic *March of Time* version of British diplomacy ran somewhat ahead of reality, this did no harm to the cause, and it won de Rochemont friends in Britain.

The London bureau of *March of Time* soon became part of the capital's left/liberal circuit. The company tapped directly into the ideas and approach of the British documentary film movement, hiring John Grierson, whose films for the General Post Office film unit had set new standards in the documentary genre, as a consultant. Grierson was committed to the idea of using film propaganda to show a dynamic and democratic Britain to America. He had failed to persuade the British Council to use his films at the New York World's Fair, but *March of Time* seemed eager to embrace his vision of British life. Soon Grierson's protégés were making films for *March of Time*; one, Edgar Anstey, eventually became foreign editor for the entire series. Back in the United States, the editors of *March of Time* were no less eager for British advice. The producers regularly invited the British Library of Information in New York to preview issues "with a view to securing criticism and comment." Thus a coalition of anglophile Americans and left-wing English filmmakers, armed with the advice of Britain's rump propaganda organization in New York, fashioned the images set to play in movie houses across the United States.[37]

Americans flocked to see British films in ever-increasing numbers. The year 1938 brought *The Citadel*, and 1939 saw substantial audiences for *Pygmalion*, *The Beachcomber*, *Goodbye Mr. Chips*, and Alfred Hitchcock's masterly caper through a thinly veiled Nazi Germany, *The Lady Vanishes*.[38] These successes brought a fresh infusion of British directors into the Hollywood studio system. The Fairbanks clan took up the cause of the Hungarian-born director, Alexander Korda, whose love of England matched their own. They lent him the funds to buy a partnership in United Artists, thereby guaranteeing American distribution and Hollywood budgets for his grand British Empire spectaculars.[39]

Hitchcock arrived in the United States to take up a generous contract with Selznick International Studios. This was a natural career move, but Hitchcock also understood his duty to help the British cause. He had been reminded of this by two senior Conservative Party propagandists: Sir Patrick Gower, the chief publicity officer at the party's central office; and Oliver Bell, director of the British Film Institute and a former Conservative Party press officer. They charged him with a special mission to work for "the better representation of British characters in Hollywood produced films." On arriving in Hollywood, Hitchcock gave full details of this mission to the British Consul General in Los Angeles, including his plans to amend all his screenplays to include "secondary characters whose representation will tend to correct American misconceptions regarding British people."

Hitchcock's task was made easier by his producer. Selznick International seemed eager to have his films treat British themes. Hitchcock swiftly extended his terms of reference, and consulted the British Consulate regarding the possible production by Selznick of Neville Shute's *What Happened to the Cobetts*. Since the screenplay called for scenes of air raids, he was anxious to know of any specific points that the British government might wish to see included. The Consulate duly arranged a private screening of the government film,

The Warning. Although this project came to nothing, the value of Hitchcock's unique position remained.[40]

Despite the first stirrings of anti-Nazi sentiment in Hollywood, a mood of restraint persisted. Most American filmmakers remained unwilling to court controversy at home or overseas, and even Warner Brothers set limits on its partisanship. The company banned *March of Time*'s "Inside Nazi Germany" from its own movie theaters, and even an obviously anti-totalitarian film like its *Adventures of Robin Hood* (1939) contained a nod to the isolationists. Robin (Errol Flynn) pointedly blames England's misfortunes not on the corrupt regent Prince John, but on the rightful King—Richard—and his penchant for "foreign wars."[41] But the producers were wise to exercise such restraint. American fear of foreign propaganda remained extremely high, and in the summer of 1938 it achieved new heights in the person of Congressman Martin Dies of Texas.

In August 1938, the House Committee for the Investigation of Un-American Activities convened under Dies's chairmanship to begin a crusade against all foreign propaganda. The Dies Committee's investigation did not constitute the first such inquiry, but Dies included the British in his brief. He was to be disappointed. Thanks to London's "No Propaganda" policy, he found no evidence of foul play.[42] The deeper threat to British public relations lay elsewhere. Congress had resolved to extend America's neutrality laws and to shackle the demon of war propaganda once and for all.

In June 1938, Congress passed the Foreign Agents Registration Act (FARA), requiring all foreign agents to register with the State Department and all their literature to be formally labeled with its point of origin. Lindsay realized that the FARA threatened even limited British operations in the United States. Fortunately for the British, the effectiveness of the bill hinged on the precise registration criteria adopted, and these rested with the State Department and (more specifically) Assistant Secretary of State George S. Messersmith. No other American official of the era was so well attuned to the danger of Hitler. Like Vansittart in London, he cast himself in the role of Cassandra. Before he finalized the registration criteria, Messersmith had several long talks with Lindsay. The Ambassador confessed his concern for the survival of the BLI, and Messersmith took pains to allay the Ambassador's fears. As Lindsay reported to London: "Messersmith . . . told me in confidence that the State Department never approved the legislation which he himself regards as entirely inept; but that now that it had passed they have of course to do their duty . . . he hinted to me quite strongly that I need have no reason to worry."[43]

The State Department remained true to its word and, in drawing up the terms, gave "a great deal of friendly attention to the British Library of Information." One official even proposed that the BLI be exempted from all registration if the British would pledge only to give information on request. This was already the modus operandi of the BLI, but Lindsay nonetheless felt unable to commit the library to such terms; as Fletcher confirmed, the BLI mailed out unsolicited propaganda to a mailing list based on requests for information about India. Rather than relinquish this activity, Lindsay agreed to register the library. Thus, on October 27, 1938, when the *New York Times* published a State Department list of declared foreign propagandists operating in the United States, the list included both Fletcher and Wilberforce of the BLI. Fortunately, the act had also required the registration of 170 other foreign propagandists and the American public seemed far more interested in the exotic details of Haile Selassie's New York agent than in the news that the dusty BLI had formally identified itself as a propaganda agency.[44]

Despite their interest in organs of publicity, Britain's foreign policy planners did not ignore the potential of conventional diplomatic channels. By the summer of 1938, the British Embassy in Washington had fallen under Foreign Office scrutiny, amid mounting reports of Lindsay's personal failure in the field of public relations. Americans complained of the Embassy's arrogance and aloofness in its dealings with both politicians and journalists, an attitude that had driven Washington to joke about "the British Compound."[45] In London, one Atlanticist resolved to act. In August 1938, Lord Lothian brought the complaints to the attention of the new Foreign Secretary, Lord Halifax. Halifax agreed that a new attitude was needed at the Embassy and, to Lothian's surprise, offered him the job. Given Lothian's record of support for both appeasement and the Anglo-American relationship, he was the logical choice to serve as Chamberlain's ambassador in Washington. The international crisis delayed Lothian's appointment until the following summer. In the interim Lothian busied himself in the cause of Anglo-American relations, undertaking a tour to gauge American opinion and to establish contacts with "people interested in international affairs." "America," he declared on his departure, "really holds the key to the whole future." This conviction led him to become the single most significant figure in the development of British propaganda in the United States.[46]

While Lothian settled into the role of heir apparent to the British Embassy in Washington, the international crisis took a new and depressing turn. On September 12, Hitler declared that he would never abandon the Germans of Czechoslovakia. Within hours, the Germans of the Sudetenland were rioting in the streets. As President Beneš mobilized his army to restore order, war seemed only days away. Then Chamberlain seized the initiative. Two weeks of desperate personal diplomacy bore fruit in a last-minute international conference. On September 29, representatives of Britain, France, Germany, and Italy met at Munich; the compromise that followed would impress political imaginations on both sides of the Atlantic as the epitome of folly. Britain's need for American sympathy had never been greater.

Preparing for the Worst: Britain's American Propaganda Policy, September 1938 to September 1939

> What in history has been more shameful than England and France conferring with Beneš at midnight in Prague while they played Judas to Czechoslovakia? Let England go into the wilderness and perish with her sins. They are all guilty: Germany, France and England. Guilty as dogs!
>
> Senator William E. Borah, 1940[47]

The Munich agreement confirmed the United States' worst suspicions about Britain. This was not Chamberlain's intention. Much in the agreement had seemed likely to appeal to American opinion. Chamberlain had replaced the discredited frontiers of Germany, as dictated at Versailles, with new boundaries, had tied these to solid principles of self-determination by plebiscite, and had dressed them in a mantle of international agreement. If Hitler could be trusted, Chamberlain had preserved the peace. If not, Chamberlain would have war, but with the moral high ground secure.

To reinforce this, the Prime Minister apparently contrived what became the most famous news image of the buildup to war. Before leaving the Munich Conference, he prevailed on Hitler to sign a declaration that Britain and Germany regarded the Munich Agreement as "symbolic of the desire" of their two peoples "never to go to war with one another again." As Chamberlain explained to his private secretary Viscount Dunglass: "If Hitler signed it and kept the bargain, well and good . . . if he broke it, he would demonstrate to all the world that he was totally cynical and untrustworthy . . . this would have its value mobilising public opinion against him, particularly in America."[48] It was this supplementary agreement that Chamberlain emphasized on his return. This was the piece of paper he held aloft at Heston Airport. The newsreel cameras immortalized the scene, but British audiences saw the drama from a skewed perspective. On orders from Downing Street, the best positions had been given to the American newsreel cameras.[49]

Initially, the United States responded well to Chamberlain's gambit. Roosevelt privately congratulated him in the shortest telegram of his career: "Good Man." The British Library of Information reported an initial surge of public sympathy, but feared that this could prove fickle. America's continued support hinged on the success of the settlement. Any return to the crisis of the early autumn promised to produce an anti-British backlash. By January 1939, returning ESU lecturers reported that "anti-Chamberlain feeling" was "intense." The Foreign Office mourned America's failure to understand the necessity of the

British move, and it noted a return to "the only 'traditional' line of foreign policy": isolationism.[50]

The American reaction to Munich gave a fresh impetus to official and unofficial attempts to consolidate Anglo-American relations. A flurry of British concessions produced a long-overdue Anglo-American Trade Agreement on November 17, 1938. Meanwhile, individual enthusiasts pressed the News Department and the ambassador-designate, Lord Lothian, to begin active propaganda in the United States. In November, in a speech heard over NBC, Winston Churchill urged America to rearm and stand shoulder to shoulder with the "English-speaking world." Anglo-American enthusiasts, including Douglas Fairbanks, Jr., scrambled to speak for the British cause in the United States, and the chairman of the ESU proposed a grand Anglo-American conference on the democratic ideal. The Foreign Office declined most of these offers and wished that Churchill had been more circumspect, but it asked the ESU to step up its "ordinary work" discreetly in the field of Anglo-American relations. Britain had to act.[51]

In December 1938, Anthony Eden made a bid to set the record straight; to this end, he accepted an invitation to visit the United States for the first time. In a long speech, broadcast nationally over CBS on December 9, he emphasized that Britain was "neither decadent or faint hearted" in the face of the Nazi threat, and certainly did not seek to "lure others to pull our chestnuts from the fire." But several days of meetings with leading columnists, newspaper proprietors, and Roosevelt himself left him profoundly depressed. "Quite serious people," he noted, imagined Chamberlain to be "a pure fascist," and there was little else to inspire their confidence in the country as a whole. Britain needed to demonstrate its resolve to fight Hitler soon, or it faced being written off by the Americans.[52]

Americans had good reason to be concerned. As of January 1939, the British had offered only fine words and compromise in response to German aggression. This situation infuriated President Roosevelt, whose position in foreign policy was delicate enough without British indecision. He had no desire to see Hitler triumph, and yet he also knew that he was a prisoner of an isolationist public and Congress. Although popular opposition to Hitler gathered momentum in the wake of the *Kristalnacht* pogroms in November 1938, the American public was still in no mood for a military commitment. The best interim solution was for the British to fill the breach and set an example for the United States and the world; and yet, despite Eden's bold words in New York, the British still seemed unwilling to commit themselves to fight for the postwar European order. First, FDR tried gentle reassurance. In October 1938 he informed Colonel Arthur Murray, a go-between from the Prime Minister, that Britain could count on "the industrial resources of the American nation . . . in the event of war with the dictatorships," and that 40 percent of Americans regarded Hitler as a threat to Latin America.[53] By January 1939, however, he had changed his approach. When Lord Lothian urged him to accept the responsibilities of global power and take up "the spear of civilization" in Britain's place, Roosevelt retorted that the British ought to take a "good stiff grog" and get on with the job themselves.[54]

Although aware of Britain's failings, Roosevelt was also eager to boost British stock before the American public. At the height of the Munich Crisis, he renewed an invitation (first made in May 1937) for the new King and Queen to round off their forthcoming tour of Canada with a visit to the United States. This, he assured the King "would be an excellent thing for Anglo-American relations." Roosevelt then stage-managed the visit to reveal the King and his country in the most favorable light possible. Roosevelt insisted on informality. He suggested that the King visit the World's Fair and then enjoy "three or four days of very simple country life" at Hyde Park—his Hudson Valley country home—rather than merely shaking hands in Washington, D.C. A few members of the Foreign Office staff grumbled, but the British government warmed to Roosevelt's initiative, and preparations for the visit began.[55]

While Roosevelt and Eden worked to restore the image of Britain in the United States, official plans for British propaganda in war moved into high gear. During the Munich Crisis, the shadow Ministry of Information had been called prematurely into life, whereupon its shortcomings had become obvious to all. The shambles of those weeks brought a string of personnel changes, including the sacking of the Director General Designate.[56]

More significantly for American propaganda, the crisis brought changes at the Foreign Office News Department, where Rex Leeper had finally gone too far. At the height of the Munich Crisis, he had issued an unauthorized communiqué pledging that, if Germany attacked Czechoslovakia, both Britain and the Soviet Union would "certainly stand by France" and fight back. This was not British policy, and the Prime Minister was not about to have his hand forced by a wayward official. Chamberlain's minions kicked Leeper upstairs to plan the Foreign Office's psychological warfare section, the Political Intelligence Department (PID), and gave all responsibility for contact with the press to Charles Peake, an inveterate crony of the Foreign Secretary (and co-architect of appeasement), Lord Halifax.[57]

While planning PID, Leeper retained his interest in Anglo-American relations. Anticipating that this department would be responsible for wartime propaganda to America, he recruited Sir Frederick Whyte to head an American division. Whyte had served with Leeper in the World War I propaganda machine, and Leeper had contributed to the internationalist journal, *New Europe*, that Whyte had founded and edited; now, as director general of the English Speaking Union, Whyte sat at the hub of English Atlanticism. He had been the Liberal MP for Perth, a private secretary to Churchill, a special political adviser to Chiang Kai-Shek, President of the Indian Legislative Assembly, and an activist in Anglo-American relations for twenty years. As a well-known lecturer in the United States, he had excellent contacts, including the distinguished editor from Kansas William Allen White. The only mystery was how a man of such ability had failed to secure high office. Rumors circulated of a scandal in his past, but such things did not deter Leeper, who considered Whyte the ideal man for the job. Together with Lothian and Fletcher, Sir Frederick Whyte became a dominant force in the development of Britain's American propaganda policy during the final months of peace and beyond.[58]

In December 1938, Leeper's influence over American propaganda came to an abrupt halt. Planners higher up finally decided on a division of labor between the Foreign Office Political Intelligence Department and the independent Ministry of Information: PID would be responsible for propaganda to enemy and enemy-occupied countries; and the MoI would be responsible for propaganda at home, within the British Empire, and to all neutral countries, including the United States.

With the mechanics clear, the planning of overseas propaganda began. This task fell to Iveson MacAdam, the secretary of Britain's sister organization to the Council on Foreign Relations: the Royal Institute of International Affairs at Chatham House. MacAdam naturally recruited many of his fellow members of Chatham House to conduct the research. In early 1939, they began work, hidden away in Chatham House buildings on Chesham Square, funded with British Secret Service money and known as the "International Propaganda and Broadcasting Enquiry"—or "Channels of Publicity Enquiry," for short. Each region had its own subcommittee, with certain additional committees created to plan for particular themes of propaganda, such as religion. Everyone concerned understood the importance of this work, not least because it was evident that these committees would actually become the foreign publicity divisions of the MoI on the outbreak of war. Leeper's original selection, Sir Frederick Whyte, headed the American committee. With the help of Alan Dudley of the BLI and supporting staff brought over from the English Speaking Union, Whyte began his report.[59]

As planning commenced, Whyte and his colleagues had one experience very much in mind: the triumph of American radio news during the Munich Crisis. During the crisis, Edward R. Murrow and the other American foreign correspondents in Europe had become household names across the United States as, night by night, they interrupted regular programming with the latest news flash from Europe.[60] The lesson was not lost on the British. In a report on propaganda written in November 1938, Angus Fletcher of the BLI had suggested that, if the

British government followed the "opposition" and fed "spicy news" to the American broadcasters in London, these men could become an invaluable channel of publicity. "If," Fletcher wrote "someone would take the trouble to cultivate a man like Edward R. Murrow . . . it is expected that he would respond." Fletcher was apparently unaware that Leeper's News Department had itself become what the assistant editor of *The Times* of London called "a centre of anti-Government propaganda"; but given that the British government still offerred only one American press agency access to the House of Commons, his point was sound.[61] Whyte agreed. He immediately recognized that, if Britain could trust the burden of its war news to American broadcasters, it could dodge the United States' fear of propaganda. He drew up British policy accordingly.

This decision was no leap of faith. Whyte knew Murrow well. He was a regular guest at the CBS London bureau, explaining British affairs to American listeners. Moreover, the propaganda planners knew the sentiments of Murrow and his colleagues, thanks to a series of meetings held behind closed doors at Chatham House and the ESU. At these meetings, internationalists, dissenting British journalists and politicians, and Americans—including William Stoneman, Clifford Stark of AP, and Marcel Wallenstein of the *Kansas City Star*—discussed the crisis. Murrow himself provided a keynote address on "The USA and the Post-Munich Situation." When it came to trans-Atlantic propaganda, the ex-head of the FO News Department, Sir Arthur Willert, showed the way: "the people who should explain the English point of view to America were Americans who knew something about England," and Murrow and his colleagues seemed willing and able to do the job.[62]

The Americans' apparent eagerness to cover the war in Britain was not wholly based on dislike for Hitler or high-minded commitment to the cause of democracy. They also expected that the war would make great radio. Moreover, for the sounds of war to have maximum impact, they needed to be heard with a minimum of official interference: live and uncensored. As Ambassador Lindsay wrote in March 1939: "it would be a great mistake not to have as much broadcast from London as may be physically possible . . . . If America ever comes into a European war it will be some violent emotional impulse which will provide the last decisive thrust. Nothing could be so effective as the bombing of London translated by air into the homes of America."[63] To the disappointment of all concerned, Britain's censorship planners soon made it clear that this was exactly the sort of broadcasting they intended to prevent. Their wartime regulations forbade any live relays of actual battle sound; all broadcasts had to be read from precensored scripts and transmitted under a censor's cut-out button.

Murrow was anxious to avoid such regulations. On June 1, he and Clifford Stark received prior warning of these plans at a secret meeting chaired by Whyte, with representatives of the BLI, BBC, and the War

Office on the issue of "Transatlantic Broadcasting." Murrow warned the British that, if the regulations were too restrictive, the U.S. radio chains would quit London for some neutral capital in time of war. The censorship planners were unmoved, but Sir Frederick Whyte demanded that the Americans be regarded as a special case. Thus, from the first moment the broadcasters realized that they would have to fight the British censors, they also knew that they would not have to fight alone.[64]

Although Whyte's call for sensitivity to American opinion did not impress the censors, other authorities had seen the light. By the spring of 1939, such sensitivity was a frequent theme in memos from Lord Halifax, and it rose over the other strains of policy making with the penetrating persistence of a Wagnerian leitmotif. Suddenly, on March 15, the need to impress the United States became acute. Hitler's army entered Czechoslovakia and occupied the Bohemian and Moravian portions of that nation, which had been denied him at the Munich Conference. For two days Chamberlain did nothing. The American press corps laid siege to the Foreign Office News Department and warned the staff that British inactivity was destroying the country's standing in America. Despairing, Vansittart wrote: "if we cannot show more resolution and reprobation than this, we shall certainly lose any possibility of effective cooperation from the United States when our hour comes." On March 17, Chamberlain rose to the challenge. In a speech heard over American radio, he denounced Hitler's coup and gave the first indication that from this point on, Britain would take a firm stand against Germany. Britain had moved one step closer to war.[65]

As the international situation crumbled, Lindsay's gentle propaganda policy of March 1937 suddenly paid a dividend. On April 30, 1939, Franklin Roosevelt proclaimed the New York World's Fair of 1939 open, loosing a flood of eager humanity into what the *New York Herald Tribune* called "the mightiest exposition ever conceived and built by man." Visitors found many wonders. The most popular exhibit was the General Motors "Futurama," which took 28,000 visitors per day on a conveyor-belt ride through a futuristic American landscape of highways and bridges. But one national pavilion challenged Futurama's popularity; and as Lindsay had hoped, it was British. By the end of the summer, the British pavilion had attracted over 14 million visitors. The British, moreover, held a trump card that even General Motors could not match: the royal visit.[66]

The British pavilion was a glory to behold. The finest in British ceramics and textiles could be found next to the latest streamlined locomotive, and works of art by Graham Sutherland, Henry Moore, and Stanley Spencer. A technicolor film of the coronation packed audiences into the pavilion's cinema, while the British Council won rave reviews with concerts featuring specially commissioned works by the finest English composers of the age: Ralph Vaughn Williams, Arnold Bax, and Arthur Bliss.[67]

The centerpiece of the British pavilion was the "Hall of Democracy." Here, the British displayed an original copy of the founding document of Anglo-American liberty: the Magna Carta. On an adjacent panel, visitors could find the pedigree of George Washington, showing his direct descent from King John and several of the signing barons. The British maximized the propaganda potential of the Magna Carta by mailing every school in the United States a translation and brief history of the document, and giving each recipient the option of requesting a full facsimile. Thanks to a sympathetic Congressman, Sol Bloom, Britain did not have to pay the postage for this effort. So long as the envelopes were marked "In commemoration of 150th anniversary of the inauguration of Washington as first President of U.S.A.: New York World's Fair, 1939," they could travel under the postal franking privileges of the U.S. Sesquicentennial Commission. To hammer home the message to adult Americans, the British Library of Information persuaded an old friend at the *New York Times* to produce a magazine feature on the document. The Foreign Office duly proclaimed Magna Carta "a success."[68]

The pavilion took care to portray the British Empire in the best possible light. The ambassador-designate, Lord Lothian, had ensured as much. In a letter to Colonial Secretary Malcolm Macdonald in November 1938, he had objected to the usual "commercial" emphasis of Colonial Office propaganda and demanded "an exhibition of the humanitarian and social services aspect of our Colonial Empire" that could effectively challenge the "constant prejudice in the American mind against British Imperialism." Macdonald successfully redirected the colonial effort, and the Colonial Empire Marketing Board rose to the challenge with a prestigious exhibit that included a "talking" display stand and dramatic photographs of soccer in a Fijian leper colony.[69] To carry the positive image of Britain's "humanitarian" empire farther afield, the Colonial Office also sent a British Empire expert— Sir William McLean—on a national propaganda tour of the United States. McLean had a novel approach. He asserted that Britain had taken on certain portions of its empire as a favor to the rest of the world. For instance, he told audiences in Seattle, that no one else had wanted Palestine in 1919, and indeed the mandate was now "a costly hobby" that "returns nothing but trouble." In a further departure from the usual British line, McLean demonstrated America's own involvement in the British Empire, by thanking the Carnegie and Rockefeller trusts for underwriting welfare schemes. American papers responded with headlines like: "U.S. CASH SAVING NATIVE MASSES IN BRITISH COLONIES." McLean and the Foreign Office in London felt sure that his tour had done much to counter "misunderstandings" of the British Empire. In reality, it probably made little difference. The colonial question was still far from dead; but for the moment, American eyes turned to a rather more decorative aspect of the British Empire: the King.[70]

The arrival of King George VI and Queen Elizabeth in the first week of June 1939 marked the high point of Britain's bid to win American sympathy on the eve of war. The royal couple's visit ignited a firestorm of pro-British sentiment. News of their triumphant tour of Canada had preceded them; tales of their throwing protocol to the wind and meeting the common people face to face had the American press buzzing with talk of "a people's King."[71] The royal train crossed the border to find the United States charmed and ready for conquest. The visit to Washington went like clockwork; then, on June 10, 1939, the King and Queen arrived in New York City. They crossed from New Jersey to Battery Park aboard a destroyer and drove through a six-hour ovation to Flushing Meadows in Queens. They toured the World's Fair to spontaneous choruses of "Land of Hope and Glory" and "Rule Britannia." The King and Queen returned to Manhattan to pay a brief visit to Columbia University and then left the city to spend the weekend with the Roosevelts at Hyde Park. Crowds massed by the roadside as the couple drove northward up the Hudson Valley. Everywhere the air was torn by a cacophony of cheers, horns, and church bells. Stories of the King and Queen relaxing over hot dogs and beer pleased everyone except the Roosevelt's British-born butler, who refused to countenance such indignity and took the weekend off. But behind the spectacle, the King, for one, knew that he had serious business to conduct.[72]

While at Hyde Park, the King and the President spoke at length about the impending war, and the possibilities of American aid for Britain. Roosevelt stressed his sympathy and explained that he was continually trying to alert isolationist regions—in particular, the Midwest—to the dangers of Nazi Germany. He outlined schemes for Anglo-American naval cooperation, including an exchange of American patrols in the Western Atlantic for base rights in the British West Indies. He spoke grandly of shooting German submarines on sight and assured the King that "If London was bombed, the U.S.A. would come in." His words were hasty. The bombing of London did not catapult America into the war, and not until September 1941 did Roosevelt finally order his fleet to fire at German submarines on sight. In all likelihood, FDR exaggerated American sympathy for Britain in order to prod the British toward a firm stand; yet the public response to the royal visit bore out his seeming optimism. Whitehall took courage.[73]

The British government was delighted by America's response to the royal visit. Lindsay reported that American emotions had been "stirred to their very roots" and added that the young King had become "a real political asset." He assured Lord Halifax that "All Americans today feel closer to the Empire than they did a fortnight ago, and this cannot fail to be of immense importance." But he was equally anxious to remind London not to expect an immediate dividend. The warning was astute. While the East Coast cheered the King, a sympathetic revision of the Neutrality Acts was dying on the floor of the Senate. The pro-Allied lobby had bungled its bid to reform the acts. Roosevelt reluctantly asked the Senate to reject the bill and defer discussion until autumn. In London, a senior diplomat mourned that Britain "could no more count on America than on Brazil."[74]

The American isolationists pressed their attack by once again raising the hue and cry against British propaganda. Senators William E. Borah and Gerald P. Nye seized on a British study titled *Propaganda in the Next War*, by British public relations expert Sidney Rogerson, as evidence of "a basic plan to involve us in the next war." Meanwhile, the Dies Committee claimed that America was now in the grip of a war propaganda campaign comparable only to those of 1914–1917.[75] Thus, as Europe slipped into war, Capitol Hill reminded the British both of their desperate need for a fundamental change in American foreign policy and of the severe limits that would restrain any British propaganda to that end. With these strictures in mind, London prepared for war.

On July 20, Sir Frederick Whyte submitted his proposal for British war propaganda in America. It contained few surprises. He upheld the "No Propaganda" principle, arguing:

> the less the British Government attempt by direct propaganda to justify themselves, the better. America will judge the European powers, not by what they say about themselves in foreign propaganda, but by what they do. It is almost certain that American reaction in our favour will arise more from the mistakes of enemy powers, both in policy and in propaganda, than from anything we may say in justification of British action.[76]

By August 1939, the wartime propaganda structure and the policy governing it were complete. The FO News Department would continue to brief the American correspondents, who would also receive help from an American liaison unit in the BBC and from Whyte's small American Division of the MoI. Whyte's division was also intended to maintain links with such Anglo-American organizations as the English Speaking Union and to guide the MoI in producing films and pamphlets suitable for distribution in the United States. Whyte's staff shared his background in prewar Anglo-American organizations. The specialist employed to cultivate external oganizations, Professor Basil Mathews, had been responsible for planning religious propaganda and was already working on a propaganda book for American readers. As a well-known writer and lecturer in the United States, and as chairman of the Literature Committee during World War I, Mathews was no stranger either to America or to propaganda.[77]

Whyte then appointed two old ESU colleagues, Gwyn Barker and Frank Darvall, to cultivate the press. Darvall, formerly the ESU's director of research and discussion, had been a Commonwealth Fund Fellow at Columbia. Unfortunately, his enthusiasm for promoting Anglo-American relations through propaganda outstripped his abilities as a civil servant; and Darvall unknowingly frustrated the Americans and his colleagues with the willowy manners of a classic English Liberal and with an impenetrable memo writing style (known within the department as "Darvallese") that was all his own. Like Whyte and Vernon Bartlett, Darvall had served as a pundit for CBS during the Munich Crisis. His working relationship with Murrow, established at that time, bore fruit later in the war. A pair of research assistants and a dozen typists completed the American Division. Although the parallel publicity divisions for the Empire and for Neutral Europe mustered four times the staff, they had far more territory to contemplate; and as the propaganda war would demonstrate, size was no barrier to significance.[78]

Whyte took care to brief the American broadcasters as to the full extent of British censorship regulations. On August 2, 1939, Ed Murrow of CBS, Fred Bate of NBC, and John Steele of Mutual attended a confidential meeting with representatives of the BBC, the MoI, and the censorship bureau. On the condition that they reveal nothing to their colleagues in the press corps, they were given full advance notice of final wartime censorship regulations. The correspondents heard that they would have to stick to a precensored script and that any "ad-libs" would be subject to the censor's cut-out button. The British apologetically pledged to reconsider the precensoring rule if it proved unworkable. Not everyone objected. John Steele of Mutual (who had a reputation as an anglophile) heartily endorsed the scheme, saying that he had worked under wartime censorship before and preferred "to have the question of what he could and could not publish settled for him." Murrow and Bate, however, were openly disappointed by the ban on live broadcasting of air raids. But the stage was set for further battles on this question. On September 1, 1939, as German tanks rumbled into Poland, Murrow explained to his listeners that censorship meant only "that there are certain matters of a military nature which we shall not be permitted to discuss: it does *not* mean that anyone is telling us what to say." This formula had been agreed upon with the British authorities.[79]

Whyte's plan for propaganda included an expanded BLI and the appointment of a British Embassy press attaché. Lord Lothian, Leeper, and the BLI agreed, but the outgoing Ambassador objected. Reluctantly Lothian postponed any action until he had found his feet in the United States. In the interim, Vansittart made furtive amends by quietly creating two new posts in the United States. His candidates were to have a revolutionary influence on the development of British propaganda in the United States.[80]

First, on June 20, 1939, Vansittart summoned John Wheeler-Bennett to the Foreign Office and mysteriously informed him that Lord

Lothian would shortly be inviting him to become his personal assistant, an offer Vansittart urged him to accept. Wheeler-Bennett was the ideal man to offer Lothian proper guidance on matters of American public opinion. He was the archetypal Anglo-American intellectual—an Oxford don and visiting lecturer at the University of Virginia equally at home at High Table or pacing the battlefields of the American Civil War. He also was a prominent member of the anti-appeasement set, had a unique knowledge of German politics, was a friend of Robert Bruce Lockhart, and regularly contributed to his *Evening Standard* column. He also knew something about providing reliable information on international affairs, having created the information department at Chatham House. Wheeler-Bennett had severe doubts about the suitability of Lothian for the Washington job—the peer's reputation as an apostle of appeasement died hard—but he also understood that Vansittart shared these fears and that, in accepting the job, he might be able to help keep Lothian's former political inclinations in check. As a result, when the Ambassador's invitation arrived in August, Wheeler-Bennett accepted. The appointment represented a backdoor compromise on the press attaché issue, since Wheeler-Bennett was able to perform many of the duties of an attaché. Moreover, as a "man of private means," he had no need to appear formally on the Embassy's diplomatic list.[81]

Next, Vansittart set about bolstering the BLI. The MoI planners had decided to turn the Survey Section of the BLI into a semi-independent press intelligence unit whose assignment was to monitor American public opinion on a daily basis, under the direction of Alan Dudley. To assist with the task, Vansittart recruited a wealthy Welshman, well established in New York, named Aubrey Niel Morgan. Morgan, heir to a Cardiff retail fortune, had married into the family of the American diplomat Dwight W. Morrow on two occasions. Morgan's tragically short marriage to Elizabeth Morrow and his subsequent marriage, several years later, to her sister Constance carried a certain irony: the third Morrow daughter, Anne, had married the aviator Charles Lindbergh, now the self-styled prophet of isolationism. The outbreak of war found Morgan extolling the virtues of British objectivity to his in-laws and predicting that Britain would fight on even if France fell to Germany. Anne Morrow Lindbergh remained unconvinced. Thus the great debate over American neutrality became a Morrow family "difference of opinion." Later, at the height of the British wartime campaign, a *Life* journalist asked Morgan about his relationship with Lindbergh. Morgan rose to the occasion with aplomb. He explained that they regularly engaged in friendly arguments over the issue of war, and pointed to his obvious inability to change Lindbergh's mind as "eternal refutation of the invincibility of British propaganda." Morgan could always be trusted to turn a potentially embarassing question to the benefit of the cause.[82]

Under Morgan and Dudley, the Survey Section developed free from the direct oversight of Angus Fletcher and his increasingly rigid view of the "No Propaganda" policy. This subdividing of BLI marked a vital stage in the development of British publicity in the United States. But for the moment, all thought of Britain's U.S. propaganda policy disappeared in the face of the immediate crisis. In Washington, Lord Lothian finally took his place as the new British ambassador. He began in style, living down the British reputation for stuffiness by posing for photographs outside the White House with a stray black kitten on his shoulder. Lothian then threw himself into negotiations with the President, begging for an alternative to American neutrality, but to no avail. FDR now had no choice but to enforce the neutrality legislation on the outbreak of war.[83] Then it happened. On August 24, 1939, the Soviet Union signed a nonaggression pact with Hitler. The British now knew that war was at hand and that American aid was not.

Early on the morning of September 1, 1939, Germany invaded Poland. Again, Britain's response hung in the balance. While the House of Commons began a series of heated debates, the government threw its contingency plans for war into action and summoned the staff of the MoI to newly commandeered offices in the University of London's Senate House in Bloomsbury.[84] On the evening of September 2, 1939, as German forces pushed deeper into the heart of Poland, Ed Murrow summed up the mood of the hour, asking: "Where stands Britain to-night?"[85] Little could be anticipated of the war that lay ahead, but this much was clear: Britain would need the resources of the United States if it was to sustain a prolonged war with the Germans, and British access to those resources hinged on American public opinion and the leeway that it allowed the President. Despite its "No Propaganda" policy, the British government had to ensure that the United States knew exactly where Britain stood—and why.

2

To War with Words: British Propaganda in the United States during the Phoney War, September 1939 to May 1940

> Both winning the war and the prospects for a stable free world afterwards depend ultimately on whether we win and keep the sympathy of the 130,000,000 Americans.
>
> Lord Lothian, September 1939[1]

At 11:15 on the morning of Sunday, September 3, 1939, Neville Chamberlain broadcast to the people of Britain. In somber tones he delivered the long-dreaded message: Britain was at war with Germany. Moments later, air raid sirens wailed across the city. A German preemptive strike seemed at hand. Inside the Ministry of Information, members of the staff were clustered around office radio sets. At the sound of the siren, they moved en masse into the specially prepared basement shelter. At Broadcasting House, the American correspondents waited, ready for the story that many believed would transform the foreign policy of their country. But the deluge didn't come that day. The siren was a false alarm, and the war at first proved little more substantial. Allied forces assumed their defensive positions in France and waited. In the meantime, Hitler devastated Poland.

London's reprieve gave little respite to the MoI's American specialists. Life could never be easy for a propaganda office pledged to conduct no propaganda. In basing its strategy for wooing American public opinion on a steady flow of news, the Ministry planners had assumed that the war would be worth reporting, but in place of high drama in France the MoI had only the "Bore War." Their American work, moreover, suffered from the lack of a clear objective. The American Division officially worked toward "the creation of general goodwill," while the BBC American Liaison Unit was supposed to be "familiarising American listeners with the situation in this country and thus enlisting their sympathy on our side." Given the vagaries of Chamberlain's policy toward the United States, there seemed little prospect of achieving a more focused approach.[2]

The British officials in the United States fared little better. The British Library of Information held fast to its principle of "information only on demand" and received no inquiries whatsoever on the first day of the war.[3] Yet while the British stood idle, America's isolationists were on the march. Lord Lothian saw the danger. He warned that Britain's fate in war and peace now hinged on "the omnipotent mass" of American public opinion. In a major dispatch to Halifax on September 28, 1939, he explained:

> The American constitution with its division of coordinate powers between executive and legislature makes public opinion the decisive factor in all the more controversial matters of public policy. To an extent unknown under the parliamentary system it is public opinion as revealed in the press, the Gallup polls, the tornado of telegrams addressed to Congress and the ordinary reports of party and political whips and not the responsible view of the executive which decides . . . .[4]

Lothian stressed that "intelligently directed publicity" was essential if Britain was to maintain—let alone advance—its position in the United States. He cautioned the Foreign Secretary that others were at work in the United States. Germany had an active American propaganda policy, but the real danger lay in the gathering strength of domestic U.S. isolationism. Drawing strength from the horror of the blitzkrieg on Poland, the isolationists prepared to defend U.S. neutrality. It is a testament to the vigour of their campaign that this phase of the war gained its name from one of their first salvos; on September 17, 1939, Senator William E. Borah speculated that the standoff in France was just another example of British perfidy and remarked: "There is something phoney about this war . . . ."[5]

The United States and the Phoney War

> This is not our war. We should not make it ours. We should keep out of it . . . . The frontiers of American democracy are not in Europe, Asia or Africa.
>
> *Chicago Tribune*, September 1939[6]

The outbreak of war in Europe produced few surprises in the United States. Roosevelt dutifully pledged to enforce the existing neutrality legislation and then called on Congress to debate the merits of revising the Neutrality Acts in favor of the Allies. The isolationists responded predictably, demonstrating eternal vigilance in the cause of ensuring that America remained aloof from the conflict. The domestic battle lines were drawn. Privately, Roosevelt conceded that his position was precarious.[7] Few Americans displayed any affection for the German cause, but few expressed overt sympathy for the Allies either. Although perhaps not as cynical as Senator Borah, the public certainly refused to see the war as a crusade against the forces of darkness.[8] The regional, ethnic, and ideological impulses toward isolationism and anglophobia developed as expected. One Midwestern wit put it bluntly: "Let God Save the King."[9]

The issue of war produced odd bedfellows. The Molotov–Ribbentrop pact left America's neo-fascists and Stalinists on the same side. Meanwhile, liberals objected to the lack of clear British war aims. As Bruce Bliven, editor and president of the *New Republic* noted in a letter to Borah: "no one has the right to suggest we should aid Britain and France . . . unless we know for what those countries are fighting and whether their war aims and peace terms are such that the American people can endorse."[10] The need for effective British publicity had never been greater; regrettably, the war also provided the final impetus to the United States' propaganda phobia.

As London braced itself for a deluge of German bombs, America awaited a barrage of European propaganda. The absence of a heavy-handed British propaganda effort did not dispel the conviction that such a campaign must be under way. In September 1939, the isolationists' witch-hunt began. Despite London's "No Propaganda" policy, they did not have far to look. The MoI had tried to stem the annual migration of British lecturers to the United States, but did not withhold exit visas, fearing that Americans might assume that Britain had something to hide. A handful of speakers, including the former cabinet minister Alfred Duff Cooper, ignored MoI advice and began a tour. They promptly became the focus of America's propaganda panic. By the time Duff Cooper's tour reached San Francisco, he was met by angry protesters waving giant lollipops emblazoned with the slogan "DON'T BE A SUCKER FOR WAR PROPAGANDA."[11] In Boston, an education expert named Porter Sargent founded a newsletter dedicated to exposing British propaganda. On Chicago's North Side, posters called for "Absolute neutrality—now and forever!" and warned:

> BEWARE THE BRITISH SERPENT!! Once more a boa constrictor—"Perfidious Albion"—is crawling across the American landscape, spewing forth its unctuous lies. Its purpose is to lure this nation into the lair of war to make the world safe for international plunder. More than ever we Americans must now evaluate this intruder into our Garden of Eden, appraising Britain down to the last penny weight of truth.[12]

Meanwhile, in the depths of the New York public library, a fifty-five-year-old electrician named Albert Johnson, systematically defaced all books that he considered too complimentary to England, "to help the next reader read properly."[13]

The Germans lost no chance to play up British activities. Unlike the British, they did not have to swim against the tide of isolationism. As Frank Darvall of the MoI put it, Germany needed only to "confirm

Americans in their own instinctive reactions to the war." Hitler showed little inclination to squander this advantage and promptly ordered his navy to avoid sinking American vessels. The Reich propaganda machine then sprang into life. The German Library of Information in New York produced a steady stream of publications including a volume of captured Polish documents. To the embarassment of the Roosevelt administration these documents included an account of a conversation between the U.S. and Polish ambassadors to Paris, held on the eve of war, in which the American ambassador, William Bullitt, spoke of his government's readiness to support the allies in the event of hostilities. The U.S. isolationist lobby had a field day. In Washington, the German Embassy moved carefully. The chargé, Hans Thomsen, matched London in urging restraint and subtlety in American propaganda. He knew that the key battleground would be the American press, but he reported difficulties in placing articles, as American journalists seemed unwilling to take bribes to publish German material.[14]

Berlin agreed that hard news held the key, and initially it proved far more efficient than London at supplying it. The blitzkrieg on Poland was infinitely more photogenic than scenes of Frenchmen filing into bunkers along the Maginot Line, and German photographs soon outnumbered Allied pictures by a ratio of four to one. The wealth of recent Nazi experience in the business of state propaganda and censorship also paid dividends. The Germans were consistently first with news of Allied shipping losses. Their figures gained acceptance by default and quickly became a serious deterrent to U.S. approval of aid to Britain. Despite American suspicion of German news, both the *New York Times* and the Foreign Office soon conceded that the Hitler was winning the propaganda war in the United States. Meanwhile, British high policy made matters worse.[15]

The Prime Minister did not share Lord Lothian's commitment to Anglo-American cooperation in war and peace. Writing to his sister in January 1940, Chamberlain observed: "Heaven knows I don't want the Americans to fight for us; we should have to pay too dearly for that if they had any right to be in on the peace terms."[16] Chamberlain was not prepared to subordinate British policy to the hope of American aid and was quite prepared to act against the best interests of Anglo-American relations. In February 1940, despite a warning from FDR, Chamberlain refused to commute the death sentences of two members of the Irish Republican Army. To the horror of Irish-Americans throughout the United States, the two were hanged.[17] But British economic warfare policy proved the most consistent irritant. Since the Neutrality Acts required that all war purchases be paid for in cash, Britain sought to conserve its limited currency reserves. The British Treasury slashed American tobacco purchases and cut deeply into the $35 million spent every year on importing Hollywood films. Southern farmers took little solace in knowing that the shortfall in British expenditure on tobacco would be counterbalanced by increased purchases of Yankee munitions.[18]

Britain's naval blockade added insult to injury. In searching neutral vessels for contraband of war and for "obnoxious documents" in the mail, the Royal Navy resuscitated the old issue of the maritime rights of a neutral nation under international law—the cause of the War of 1812 and much tension during the early years of World War I. German propagandists saw the crack and chiseled accordingly. The sinking of a Danish vessel off a contraband control port in the Orkney Islands in January heightened international tension over the blockade. Lothian begged the War Cabinet to examine U.S. shipping in the safety of the port of St John's, Newfoundland. The Foreign Office sent its top economic adviser to Washington to explain the British position, but the issue was not resolved until the German blitzkrieg on Western Europe swept away the assumptions of the Phoney War. Hitler's victory justified Britain's blockade policy, but at a terrible price.[19]

Despite Chamberlain's prejudices, concern over American opinion did shape certain cabinet decisions. In January, the War Cabinet suppressed the Moyne Report on the West Indies on the grounds that its many criticisms of British rule would provoke bad press for the British Empire in the United States. But the West Indians expected its publication in February. The Cabinet knew that news of riots over its suppression would look even worse in the American press. They sidestepped the problem by publishing details of a package of social programs instead, while omitting to say why such reforms were necessary in the first place.[20]

Such concerns also affected military operations. With an eye to the United States, the British Admiralty delayed mining neutral Norwegian waters until it was clearly provoked into doing so by the Germans. The RAF showed similar restraint in its operations over Germany, avoiding all civilian targets. Chamberlain even refused to bomb such key military targets as the Rhine bridges, because he was "apprehensive of the effect . . . on the public opinion of the United States." When the Germans swept westward in the spring of 1940, William Bullitt, the American Ambassador to France, felt obliged to assure the British that the U.S. public would accept a broad definition of "military targets" should the RAF wish to attack the industrial Ruhr. These restraints fit the moral case projected by Chamberlain. In a broadcast on the second day of the war, allegedly made in response to a telegram from the broadcaster Walter Winchell, he had assured the world that Britain had no quarrel with the German people but only with the regime of Adolf Hitler. He said no more on the subject. The burden of developing the British case beyond this fell to an increasingly hard-pressed MoI.[21]

In September 1939, the MoI faced a mighty task in the United States. Britain needed to establish the justice of its cause; to rally the support of its more reticent friends; to convince the United States that the war was genuine and not "phoney"; to counter German propaganda and isolationist attempts to prevent the revision of the Neutrality Acts; and to do all this without inflaming America's propaganda phobia. The stakes were high. Success in the arena of public opinion held the key to victory in any prolonged war. But the risks abounded; and despite the best efforts of the American Division, the inadequacies of the Ministry of Information as a whole added a new layer of difficulty to Britain's war against American neutrality.

Fighting the Phoney War in London: The MoI and the BBC

> If Lord Macmillan's first task was to undo Britain's reputation for cleverness, he could not have done it more brilliantly. Nobody could accuse Britain's propaganda of functioning smoothly . . . it was clumsy, amateurish, slow starting and gave an impression like that of a sincere but badly staged show in which the stagehands dropped things during the big speeches and the curtain came down at the wrong time.
>
> *Time* magazine, September 1939[22]

The early weeks of the war laid bare the defects of the Ministry of Information. The problem lay not with the plan, but with the subsequent intrusion of the Chamberlain government into the process. Chamberlain had given many of the key positions in the MoI to his political allies. His weakest appointment was the Information Minister himself—Lord Macmillan, a lawyer with no publicity experience since 1918. Macmillan was the wrong man to hold the MoI portfolio. His staff saw his appointment as proof that the government did not consider propaganda to be important.[23]

Lord Macmillan was wholly out of touch with his staff. When they complained about their long work hours, he suggested that they try to "keep fresh" and not work quite so late. By contrast, the minister himself seemed underworked. Ronald Tree once caught him surreptitiously reading a novel under his desk. But Macmillan's personal inadequacies paled beside his precarious political position. He had no seat in the War Cabinet or (because he was a peer) in the House of Commons; hence, his department carried no political weight. On top of this, the MoI soon lost its monopoly on the news. Individual ministries established their own press offices and publicity policies. It has been suggested that the Prime Minister emasculated the MoI as a "payoff" to Britain's press barons in thanks for their loyalty during the prewar crisis. Given the news chaos of the early weeks of the war, the "payoff" must have seemed a hollow reward.[24]

The early failures of the MoI became legendary. By October 1939, a virtual open season had been declared on the ministry. Fleet Street pointed to a staff of 999 and blustered about overmanning. The government hurriedly summoned the press baron Lord Camrose to revise the entire structure. As the ministry shrank under Camrose's knife, its staff contemplated impending oblivion. An anonymous MoI official caught the prevailing mood in an "Elegy to the Departed":

> To sift the news, extract, refine,
> We'll start, they say, with nine, nine, nine,
>
> The Fleet St. muttered: news comes late
> Let's get them down to eight, eight, eight.
>
> The Treasury mildly swore to heaven
> They'd soon reduce each eight to seven.
>
> The Commons cried: confound their tricks,
> They can't need more than six, six, six,
> And if they're keen, alert, alive,
> They ought to do with five, five, five,
>
> The public shrieked: more news, much more,
> Reduce your staff to four, four, four,
>
> Lord Camrose spoke: leave this to me,
> I'll run it all on three, three, three.
>
> The pundits wrote: Now this won't do,
> The right amount is two, two, two.
>
> Their task was hardly yet begun
> When lo, they dropped to one, one, one,
> Before they'd done one half they ought
> They quietly dwindled into nought.[25]

Camrose did little to improve the standing of the ministry. Now each Department of State was responsible for issuing its own news, and all censorship functions rested with an independent Press and Censorship Bureau under Sir Walter Monckton. Monckton, at least, represented a great improvement. He was seen as a "Fleet Street man," sympathetic to the American press; and he soon established a close working relationship with Clifford Stark, the AP bureau chief and chairman of the American Correspondents Association in London. By November, officials noted that the American press corps seemed generally "quite satisfied" with the new British censorship system. The crisis had passed.[26]

The American Division escaped unscathed from the attacks on the MoI. The most bitter critic of the ministry, British journalist Norman Riley, actually endorsed their work. Their problems lay elsewhere. Sir Frederick Whyte knew that the United States required more than statements of "Allied strength and the assurance of victory." The MoI had to "stress the energy and determination" of Britain's war effort; "the extent to which the war is real and not Phoney; the extent to which the British Empire has ceased to be 'Imperialistic' in the unpopular

American sense of the term and the liberal character of British war aims."[27] Despite the absence of formal war aims—liberal or otherwise— the American Division set about this task with vigor.

The chief source of day-to-day news for the American correspondents remained the Foreign Office News Department, now formally under Charles Peake. In December 1939, the News Department moved from its old location at the Foreign Office to become a Foreign Office enclave within the MoI building. It officially amalgamated with the News Division of the MoI. Under the new arrangement, Peake acquired the title of Chief Press Advisor to the Ministry of Information. Little else changed. His staff continued their routine of noon briefings and afternoon interviews, as before. The American Division busied itself plugging any gaps in the News Department's work.

Sir Frederick Whyte was an eager advocate for the American journalists' cause in Whitehall. He lost no time easing tensions over censorship procedures and arranged a series of "meet your censor" parties for twenty or so American correspondents and censors.[28] The Americans warmed to these efforts. The generally isolationist *New York Sun* ran an approving interview with Whyte under the headline "Fights for U.S. on news front: Sir Frederick Whyte appointed by British to serve American newspaper men." Whyte, of course, took the opportunity to expound on the "No Propaganda" policy, stressing that: "If America ever does come into this war it will be because of Dr. Goebbels not Freddy Whyte . . . some people tell us that we are leaning over backwards to lose the war of propaganda. That does not bother us. We know our job and will stick to it in spite of busybodies."[29]

Confronted by German domination of war photography, the American Division persuaded the MoI's photographic section to issue all official British war pictures directly to the American photographic agencies and to improve the quality of transmission procedures. By December 1939, the German advantage had been all but nullified, and Whyte turned to a more tenacious adversary: the Whitehall service departments.[30]

The service departments were rarely forthcoming with newsworthy material. The worst offender was the British Admiralty under Winston Churchill. This was only to be expected: the bulk of the war news was being made at sea, and most of it was bad. Churchill coped by returning to his World War I policy of suppressing the bad news until he had a piece of good news to offset the blow. The practice did not suit the new war, however. In a telegram of November 29, 1939, Lothian urged a policy of openness to permit Britain to challenge German claims in a timely fashion. "The best counter propaganda," he wrote, "would be as full information as possible given to the United States correspondents in London." Whyte agreed that "confidence cannot live in a twilight of scepticism which must descend on a country if the Government withhold or varnish the facts." Monckton simply stressed the importance of trusting the people of Britain with the truth. The Admiralty bowed to this cumulative pressure and began to release the statistics, although Churchill's periodic reluctance to own up to losses continued to irritate Lothian. Thus, for instance, Churchill's failure the admit to the loss of HMS *Nelson* and HMS *Barham* in February 1940 drove Ambassador Lothian to write: "I think Winston has made a fool of himself. He is always doing these things. That is why he never becomes Prime Minister."[31]

Victories were as badly presented as defeats. The American press had difficulty covering the sinking of the *Graf Spee* and the pursuit of that ship's service vessel, the *Altmark*. Even though the *Altmark* incident unfolded like a *Boy's Own* story—with a boarding party from HMS *Cossack* leaping onto the Nazi prison ship and shouting to their imprisoned comrades: "The Navy's here!"—the Admiralty still refused to blow its own horn. The MoI and BBC American Liaison Unit looked on in disbelief.[32]

The army and the Royal Air Force did little more in London, but they sent a team of ex-journalist Senior Press Officers to France to guide the press corps though the maze of restraints to news gathering at the front. The Allied and American correspondents in France were well served by two young former *Daily Telegraph* men: Roger Machell and René MacColl. MacColl was particularly suited to the task, having begun his career on the *Baltimore Sun*. A number of American journalists, including Walter Duranty, Bill Henry of the *Los Angeles Times*, and Frank Gervasi of *Collier's Weekly*, reached France only because of MacColl's initiative. He commandeered a tourist plane and flew them directly to the RAF's Advance Air Striking Force, and even provided in-flight "hospitality" on the way. Both he and Machell would leave their mark on British propaganda in America.[33]

Back in London, Whyte's American Division also went the extra mile to help the Americans. They created news by organizing trips to the British fleet and to coastal defenses, each of which yielded a crop of useful articles. The American Division also gave specific help, tailored to the interests of individual correspondents. When a black American journalist named William N. Jones arrived in London in October 1939 to report for a string of black newspapers, the MoI guided him to stories with "black interest" that might help to break down Black American isolationism. First, the MoI introduced Jones to the Colonial Intelligence Department, where he received "priceless material" on the many benevolences of the British Empire in Africa. Next the MoI whisked him off to the Maginot line where "he had a wonderful time in the pill boxes with the Senegalese." Not to be outdone, the MoI Empire Division presented Jones with an exclusive set of photographs of British colonial troops, flown especially from Africa. Jones "went off overflowing with gratitude at having been helped over every obstacle and provided with material in ways he never considered possible." He was given his exit permit and conducted through the final censorship procedures. Unfortunately, the final censor retained material that his colleagues had already approved and Jones only received his material after complaining to the BLI in New York. Despite such hiccups, however, by the spring of 1940, the value of the American Division was clear. American watchdogs of the propaganda war had no doubt that "Freddy" Whyte and his team were winning over the press in London, and they merely questioned whether the "masses" on "Main Street" would also be influenced as a result.[34]

The American Division always gave particular attention to American radio correspondents. They hoped for much in return. The BBC North American Representative even suggested that the radio might prove to be "decisive" in "effecting American participation" in the war. Their efforts were rewarded. Despite the rigid National Association of Broadcasters code of practice requiring neutrality, American broadcasters themselves remained decidedly (if discreetly) partial to the British cause.[35]

The MoI American Division worked closely with the American Liaison section of the BBC to ensure the smooth operation of the BBC's shortwave link that carried all American radio coverage from Europe to the United States. The BBC staff administered their own censorship procedure, which permitted a speed of transmission unmatched by Berlin or Paris. They also monitored American treatment of British issues. Early in the war, command of the American Liaison section fell to Roger Eckersley. Eckersley (a cousin of Aldous Huxley) was an experienced hand at the BBC. He had visited the United States in 1932, during the first flowering of BBC interest in trans-Atlantic broadcasting. No less important, Eckersley had a wry sense of humor, sharpened through practice of that most English of arts: the composition of nonsense verse. His poetic works included such gems as "Virtue" ("Virtue won't hurt you/but vice is nice"). His war work taxed this reserve of humor to the full.[36]

Eckersley spent the Phoney War struggling to provide a steady flow of "good stories" for America. The results amply justified his effort. He found that the American broadcasters, like their colleagues in the press, responded well to organized outings to such sites as a contraband control port and a conscientious objector's trial in Fulham. But Eckersley also knew that no earnest description of a ministry jaunt could match the potency of a broadcast interview with one of the ordinary people caught up in the war, such as American survivors of the torpedoed vessels *Athenia* or *City of Flint*.[37] Eckersley maintained:

> the bringing to the microphone of people who are actually doing the job
> makes a personal appeal to the pro-allied sentiment which is inherent in

most Americans, and consciously or sub-consciously must have its effect. I wish this could really be understood and become part of a definite policy. My Americans are constantly rubbing this into me and they get disheartened when they fail to secure what they know is most wanted.

He argued that, by taking the Americans to the scene of a recent German attack, the British could head off German propaganda claims.[38]

Whitehall provided the usual obstacles. Within days of the outbreak of war, the War Office announced that, although there were three American broadcast chains, only two American radio correspondents would be permitted to join the BEF in France. The three networks drew lots. NBC lost and had no correspondent in France until the BBC and MoI forced the War Office to relent in the first week of October. In France, the BBC's best-known radio correspondent, Richard Dimbleby, worked to ease the problems of broadcasting from the front, acting as the BBC's American Liaison representative and the interim correspondent for NBC. Dimbleby fought to reform the censorship regulations—particularly the ban on unscripted broadcasts.[39]

On occasion the BBC provided service above and beyond the call of duty and the limits of the American broadcasters' code of practice, as in the case of "help" furnished to Mutual in November 1939. Although the code adopted by NBC and CBS forbade them to use recordings in news broadcasting, Mutual made no such promise, and it broadcast the dispatches of Arthur Mann (its correspondent in France) from disks. The BBC helped Mutual in its endeavors. The network was the poor sister to NBC and CBS, the most actively anglophile, and the best customer for rebroadcast BBC material, but there were limits. The problem arose when Mann recorded a talk on the Maginot line. He referred to various noises of the fortification, intending that the gaps in his recording be filled by material already recorded by Dimbleby. After the accidental loss of Dimbleby's material, John Steele of Mutual persuaded the BBC sound effects department to fake the noises necessary to fill the gaps. An angry memo arrived on Eckersley's desk, noting:

> this sort of thing is a fraud on the American listener and one to which the BBC ought not to be a party. We will look extremely cheap if and when it gets out in America that the Diesel engines, electric trains, air raid warnings, and the click-clack of guns being loaded, solemnly listened to over the Mutual network, are the excellent work of George Holt on the fourth floor of Broadcasting House.

Eckersley politely asked Steele to refrain from requesting fakery in the future.[40]

The trust built up between the BBC and the American chains paid a steady dividend. In February 1940, when the German shortwave station alleged that London restricted its American correspondents far

more than Berlin did, Steele promised to note how "kind and sympathetic" Eckersley's staff were in their censoring. Similarly, CBS cabled
New York that:

> In addition to checking remarks that might give 'aid and comfort' to
> Germany, the censor is an advisor, guide and friend. They are all good
> fellows, well informed and capable. They neither try to put over British
> propaganda on us nor do we try to give away their secrets.

CBS then arranged for this statement to appear in a magazine article.[41]

The BBC office in New York completed Britain's structure to support broadcasting of the war, but here the events of September
1939 brought an unforseen crisis. The New York office's head, Felix
Green, proclaimed himself a Quaker and said that he was unable on
religious grounds to play a part in the British war effort. The BBC
found a worthy successor in Gerald Cock, who had overseen the pio-
neering days of British television broadcasting. With the assistance of
his deputy Donovan Rowse, two secretaries, and the part-time services
of Alistair Cooke and Raymond Gram Swing, Cock set about developing the BBC's foothold in the United States. The operation remained
stable until after the fall of France. Soon thereafter it grew beyond all
recognition.[42]

The BBC and the MoI had no monopoly on British efforts to cultivate the American press corps. The senior correspondents continued
to find friends beyond the walls of the MoI or Broadcasting House. The
links between the Anglo-American bloc in the Conservative Party and
the American press continued to operate to mutual advantage. The
Conservative MP Victor Cazalet joined Ronald Tree in the front line of
the wining and dining war. He engineered a dinner party for Eden (the
new Secretary of State for the Colonies), Duff Cooper, Harold Nicolson,
and four of the most important American journalists: Gunther,
Knickerbocker, Duranty, and Stoneman. A wealthy widow, Sybil
Colefax, brought Churchill into play in much the same manner, cajol-
ing him to attend occasional dinner parties with half-a-dozen senior
American journalists.[43] Among the broadcasters, Murrow's star remained ascendent. He strode with ease along the corridors of power
and through many living rooms as well. Despite a punishing schedule,
he always seemed able to find time for a weekend in the country with
Ronald Tree or an evening socializing in St. James's, building connections of an order quite beyond those of his colleagues.[44] The British
returned Murrow's interest, listening carefully to his portrayal of
Britain at war. Generally, they were not disappointed by what they
heard.

Although an intimate of London's high society, Murrow always por-
trayed the war as experienced by the mass of the British people. For
Murrow, the British war effort was socially leveling. By the second day
of the war, he had quoted Marcus Aurelius's maxim that "death put

Alexander of Macedon and his stable boy on a par." He was a master at introducing the telling detail that brought London alive in the minds of his listeners, be it a description of the friendly glow of a cigarette when all else around was cloaked by the blackout, or the simple observation that London was quiet after the evacuation of its children. But despite a sympathetic start, by the end of October 1939 both the MoI and the BBC had noticed a troubling shift in his tone. Frank Darvall noted: "Ed Murrow is getting more cynical in his attitude towards our war effort than he was to begin with, or than he would be even now if less disconnected with life." He attributed the change to worry, overwork, and the Phoney War routine. In response, the BBC liaison team stepped up their news-making exercises. Murrow warmed to their effort with a string of broadcasts that presented an affectionate picture of a crusty liberal Britain muddling through the war, congenitally incapable of efficient propaganda and insistent on preserving the rights of genuine conscientious objectors. On occasion, his broadcasts had a more overt political purpose. On March 10, 1940, for example, he quoted a stinging attack by Harold Nicolson on the increasingly defeatist U.S. Ambassador to Britain, Joseph Kennedy. Murrow's position on the issue of war was clear.[45]

Murrow's friendship with the MoI secretary Iveson MacAdam and his American wife also paid dividends to the British cause. Murrow spent Christmas 1939 as the couple's guest, and in return arranged a live hook-up over CBS so that they could exchange Christmas greetings with their children, evacuated to the West Coast of the United States. As Murrow's biographer observed: "To American listeners on Christmas night the war, for one brief moment, was not a distant quarrel between nations but ordinary people like themselves whose lives had been torn apart."[46] Such broadcasts were propaganda of the most potent kind. Their spontaneity and appearance over the regular channels of American broadcasting placed them far beyond the reach of Goebbels. They may not have produced immediate calls for aid to the Allies; but they nurtured a new picture of Britain, facing the war honestly and without class distinction. For the moment, these ideas existed alongside America's old suspicions of perfidious Albion; but in the wake of the Blitz of 1940, they grew to dominate the American response to Britain and its war.

Recognizing that it could never match the appeal of an American broadcaster to an American audience, the BBC restricted its broadcasts to the United States throughout the Phoney War. Lothian argued that shortwave radio broadcasts could do little to swing American public opinion; by definition, the audience had to be rich enough to afford a shortwave receiver and sufficiently interested in international affairs to have tuned in to a foreign station. Such people, he argued, would already have made up their minds about the war. Other observers feared that Americans would be unimpressed by the BBC Empire Service. The Foreign Office reported that, while Americans warmed to an English accent as spoken on stage or screen, they found the BBC voice "too self conscious" and even "Pansy." Unmoved, the BBC administration refused to drop its "standards" to suit American tastes, and refused to use either North American or British regional accents. In despair, one MoI official wrote:

> The BBC . . . is always emphasising the fact that short-wave programmes are intended chiefly for Empire listeners and that the isolated Englishman in the remoter parts of Empire who is more Blimpish than Col. Blimp himself, would be horrified if the dignity of the BBC were to be exchanged for the snappy radio technique of the Americans.[47]

The BBC achieved its only mass audience in the United States through the rebroadcasting of key British war speeches over the American networks. It was careful not to overuse this privilege, limiting the voices heard in the relays to the Prime Minister, the King and Queen, and Churchill, whose speeches held "a strong entertainment value."[48] By creating the impression that America was merely "listening in" on material directed at the British public, the relays allowed the British to side-step the Americans' fear of propaganda as only another English-speaking nation could. The practice proved invaluable in the summer of 1940.

Although the press and broadcasters carried the great majority of America's war news, the British did not neglect the medium of film. At the most basic level, the MoI assisted U.S. newsreel companies in the same way as it did journalists. It arranged trips to the front and badgered the less enlightened sections of the British government for improved access to news. The American and Films Division of the MoI worked particularly closely with *March of Time*, but all the newsreel companies benefited from their attentions. In January 1940, the Films Division reported: "nearly all the leading producing companies in this country, both British and American, have been persuaded to produce films presenting our war effort in a favourable light."[49]

The MoI improved the London–Lisbon–New York air link in hopes of beating the Germans in the race to the American newsreel screen; it even hired a special courier service to transport important footage to New York in time to meet a release deadline. The BLI monitored America audiences, enabling the British to avoid certain types of material (such as footage of funerals) that American audiences considered too propagandistic.[50]

The ministry's own film production was initially disappointing. The Films Division suffered under the rule of Chamberlain's arch-crony, Sir Joseph Ball, formerly "Director of Research" for the Conservative Party and an inveterate intriguer in the Prime Minister's cause. Ball was hostile to the left-wing documentary film movement. He had little interest in large-scale government film production, preferring instead to lay down his version of the ministry line and entrust wartime publicity to his old allies in the commercial newsreels.

Matters improved after Ball's retirement in the final weeks of 1939. MoI film production moved into full swing under the direction first of Kenneth Clark and then, after Clark's promotion in April 1940, of Jack Beddington, the prewar director of publicity for Shell-Mex. Clark established a three-point agenda for British film propaganda, demanding that it show "I. What Britain is fighting for. II. How Britain fights" and "III. The need for sacrifices if the war is to be won." He embraced the emerging notion that Britain was fighting "a people's war," and he made the films to fit. During January 1940 alone, the ministry commissioned thirty-two propaganda shorts. The American Division provided scenarios suitable for the United States.[51]

The Films Division acquired the services of the distinguished British film entrepreneur and anti-Nazi campaigner Sidney Bernstein. Bernstein knew the United States well. His friends included Walter Wanger and many members of the American press corps in London, including Quentin Reynolds of *Collier's Weekly*. He brought a keen understanding of American needs to MoI film production. The division was also briefly cheered by the presence of the poet John Betjeman, recruited to serve as a script writer. He did not last long. The head of the Empire Division, Harry Hodson, considered Betjeman the ideal candidate for the delicate task of managing British publicity in Ireland. He fancied that Betjeman's quirky disposition, literary flair, and humor would "go down well" in Dublin. Betjeman accepted the job with glee and proved Hodson right.[52]

The spring and early summer of 1940 saw further improvements within the Films Division, as Beddington acquired the services of the entire General Post Office Film Unit for the duration of the war. Working under the direction of Ian Dalrymple, and with the new title of the Crown Film Unit, the unit set to work. The documentary filmmakers needed no prompting to develop a picture of a "people's war," an approach well-suited to a democratically minded American audience. The theme had already surfaced in *The First Days*, a deceptively simple documentary by Harry Watt, Humphrey Jennings, and Pat Jackson that chronicled London's response to the outbreak of war. Shot by the General Post Office unit on their own initiative, this film became the first MoI release of the war. It was a short step from the footage of Londoners resolutely sandbagging their homes beneath home-made signs saying "Let 'em all come" to the scenes of dignity under fire in the autumn of 1940.[53] Yet despite the initiatives of Clark and Beddington, filmmakers continued to encounter problems at the MoI. In August, the documentary filmmaker Basil Wright complained that "there are times when I could scream," while his colleague, Paul

Rotha, noted "the complete failure of the Films Division to have any intelligent understanding of either propaganda or the use of film." Arguably, film remained the weakest element in British propaganda to the United States throughout the war.[54]

Whatever their content, these films could not have had any impact on the United States without adequate distribution. This matter was addressed soon after the outbreak of war by the godfather of the British documentary film movement, John Grierson, who arranged for British participation in New York's International Films Center—a distribution and exhibition point for documentaries from all over the world. In May 1940, the British representative to the International Film Center, Richard Ford, arrived in the United States. He doubled as the film specialist at the British Library of Information. Ford soon set about promoting the distribution of British documentaries on the American lecture and college circuit.[55] But the audience for British documentaries in the United States would always be small. The British knew that only commercial feature films could reach a mass audience. As Vansittart put it:

> Documentaries are all very well in their way, but they appeal to a public that can be counted in thousands, but a big film is a dead loss unless it is seen by a rock bottom minimum of sixty million people . . . . There are plenty of people in Hollywood who would be delighted to make films which work our way if they were provided with the material. Many of the leading actors would give their services for nothing . . . . So far, I repeat, we have made no real use whatever of the most potent means of propaganda.[56]

Fortunately, John Grierson had also begun to build a British beachhead in Hollywood. Grierson spent the first weeks of the war in Hollywood, officially en route to Australia, but busy compiling a report on American film and the war. He was disturbed to see the American film community retreating from the challenge of the war into escapist froth, and he pressed studio heads and the Academy of Motion Picture Arts and Sciences to take a firm stand against Nazism. Warner Brothers, RKO, and MGM appeared receptive to the idea. Grierson also renewed an old acquaintance with Walter Wanger. Staying at Wanger's home, Grierson found him to be "directly interested in doing work which would be valuable." He promised to help the producer with his forthcoming projects, and in particular a war film to be directed by Alfred Hitchcock.[57]

The central problem of using either American or British feature film as propaganda lay in production time. Films usually took at least six months to move from script to screen, which meant that most of the films made during the Phoney War were not seen until long after the Nazi spring offensive had redrawn the map of Europe. The principal exception to this rule came from the British film industry in the person of Alexander Korda. On the outbreak of war Korda halted production of *The Thief of Baghdad*, cashed in his life insurance, and made the propaganda feature *The Lion Has Wings* based on an RAF raid on the Kiel canal. Incredibly, the picture was ready for distribution by the end of October 1939. America was eager to see the result.[58]

Despite a tawdry script, *The Lion Has Wings* had some high points. The opening shots juxtaposed peace-loving Britons riding seaside donkeys with ranks of Nazi's astride their war horses on parade in Berlin, champing at the bit for conquest. Korda confessed that it was "propaganda in the crudest sense of the word," but Americans didn't seem to mind, and they endorsed the movie at the box office. United Artists hurried to release the film worldwide, from South Africa to Japan. The American version of the film included a commentary by veteran foreign correspondent, Lowell Thomas. As the chief commentator for Fox newsreels, Thomas lent authority to the picture. It was not to be the last time that the British employed a distinguished American journalist in this way.[59]

The MoI guided the commercial British film industry toward suitable propaganda subjects, including issues with a direct bearing on the United States, such as the blockade. Michael Powell's film, *Contraband* (shown in the United States as *Blackout*), followed the adventures of a Danish sea captain, forced into a British port for contraband examination only to discover a fiendish Nazi conspiracy to win the war by poisoning Anglo-American relations. The film bristled with propaganda value; the whole plot was a race against time, dictated by the efficiency of British Contraband Control. Early on a British naval officer apologized for any inconvenience but suggested that Britain's blockade policy was, "better than putting a torpedo in you." Powell set his climax in a warehouse stacked high with unsold plaster busts of Neville Chamberlain, which were shot to pieces during a final shoot-out. No American audience could doubt that appeasement was dead.[60]

The most eloquently anti-Nazi film of the Phoney War came from the John and Roy Boulting. *Pastor Hall* was a frank exposé of exactly how Hitler dealt with the "Good Germans." A retelling of the life of the U-boat captain turned pastor and martyr, Martin Niemoller, it included scenes of concentration camps and Nazi atrocities. Although the Boulting brothers acquired the rights to *Pastor Hall* in 1938, reactionary elements among the British Board of Film censors blocked its production until after the outbreak of war. Having experienced such attitudes at home, the Boultings felt qualified to address American isolationism; as Roy Boulting later recalled, "with the enthusiasm of youth" they hoped "that *Pastor Hall* might help them to understand."[61]

The distribution of *Pastor Hall* presented more problems. Two executives of the distributor Grand National crossed the Atlantic to arrange for the release of *Pastor Hall*, with their passage paid by the British Treasury, only to jump ship in New York. The third, Maurice Wilson, found the American film industry—including Walter Wanger— paralysed by self-censorship. With the help of the President's son,

James Roosevelt, Wilson arranged for distribution through United Artists, with the addition of a short introduction written by Robert Sherwood and delivered by Eleanor Roosevelt. *Pastor Hall* opened to critical acclaim in New York City in the summer of 1940. To the delight of the Boultings, the premiere provoked an immediate anti-Nazi riot in Times Square. The City of Chicago promptly banned the film under a by-law prohibiting the display of "depravity, criminality or lack of virtue" in "a class of citizens of any race," although municipal authorities raised no comparable objection to the showing of the German propaganda film *Felzug in Polen*.[62]

By the end of the Phoney War, large-scale British feature film production was well under way. It was only a matter of time before these pictures joined the campaign for American support. Of course, British filmmakers could never rival Hollywood, but they had little need to do so: a vital corner of Hollywood was British already.

The outbreak of war had placed the British colony in Hollywood in an awkward position. Although such actors as C. Aubrey Smith and Sir Cedric Hardwicke were too old for military service, the majority were obviously able-bodied. David Niven actually had military experience. Concerned, the community despatched a delegation led by Sir Cedric Hardwicke to consult the British Embassy in Washington. Lord Lothian bluntly told the actors to stay put:

> The maintenance of a powerful nucleus of older actors in Hollywood is of great importance to our own interests, partly because they are continually championing the British cause in a very volatile community which would otherwise be left to the mercies of German propagandists, and because the continuing production of films with a strong British tone is one of the best and subtlest forms of British propaganda.

Lothian sent the same message to London, reminding Vansittart in September 1940: "It is of the utmost importance to keep British actors in Hollywood, because they do a most effective propaganda piece for Britain during the war and will be invaluable for rebuilding the British film industry when the war is over."[63]

The Hollywood British enforced this policy themselves. Any members of their community who failed to make patriotic films, donations, or noise, were openly criticized. The British press and such patriotic "film people" as Michael Balcon of Ealing Studios condemned the newest British arrivals in Hollywood for having "Gone With the Wind-up." Niven and Olivier eventually "joined up" but the bulk of the British film community performed their war work in Hollywood.[64]

The Hollywood British had little difficulty finding sympathetic projects. By 1939, sound business and sound politics had combined to push the American studios toward the Allied cause. In the final years of peace, the totalitarian world had rejected Hollywood: 1939 brought fresh restrictions on American films in Germany, heavier censorship in Japan, and a complete ban in Italy. Concerned to maximize their remaining markets, the studios adjusted their output. Producers rewrote *Beau Geste* to avoid offending France, Italy, or Belgium (the sadistic villains Boldini and Lejeune were renamed Rasinoff and Markoff) and tactfully shelved plans to film Humphrey Cobb's bitter attack on French martial idiocy: *Paths of Glory*. With the Russian market also closed, producers were free to indulge their anti-totalitarian sentiments to the full. In March 1939, the British Consul General in Los Angeles gleefully reported that Warner Brothers was "quite deliberately flouting German sentiment with their *Confessions of a Nazi Spy*" (an alarming exposure of Nazi intrigue within the United States) and added that "Charles Chaplin's expected burlesque of Hitler *The Great Dictator . . .* is reported likely to be more directly offensive to Germany than even [the] Warner production." Hollywood even managed to give a new propaganda twist to old films. In October 1939, the anti-war classic *All Quiet on the Western Front* reappeared with a new anti-Nazi narration tacked on to redirect the original message.[65]

The politicization of Warner Brothers' output did not stop with *Confessions of a Nazi Spy*. In fact, the studio's willingness to help the cause came as a great surprise to Britain. In the early months of the war, the MoI received word of a remarkable offer from Warner Brothers, transmitted through the equally remarkable channel of Charles Greville, actor and Seventh Earl of Warwick. In the 1930s, Lord Warwick had abandoned his ancestral estates in search of a career in Hollywood, only to spend more time roistering with the Hollywood party set than acting on screen. On the outbreak of war, Warwick "did his bit" for England and began to compile a report on Hollywood for the British Embassy. His inquiries met an astonishing response. Before, Warner Brothers had encouraged Grierson; it now overwhelmed Warwick with its "readiness to produce further anti-Nazi and pro-British films" from any first-class screenplays provided by the Ministry of Information. Ambassador Lothian was enthusiastic, but London remained doubtful. Sir Frederick Whyte had no objection to feeding Hollywood with British scripts, but he stressed that the MoI should only play an informal, coordinating role. Moreover, on the advice of Sidney Kent, president of Twentieth Century Fox, he emphasized that the British government ought to "avoid . . . too close an association with a particular studio." Britain could not afford to lose the goodwill of Warners' competitors. Embarrassed, the MoI chose to defer its decision indefinitely.[66]

When Warners tried again in the spring of 1940, the company's ulterior motives became apparent. The studio engaged the British novelist C. S. Forrester to produce a screenplay based on his highly successful Hornblower novels of navy life in the era of Admiral Nelson. In mid-May 1940, thirteen weeks into a script already bulging with British heroism, Forrester received new instructions, asking that the script be rewritten to increase its pro-British propaganda value. Warner Brothers hoped that, if the film's bias seemed sufficiently ardent, the British Treasury might allow the studio to collect all revenues generated by its British release, instead of the limited return permitted under the wartime export agreement of October 1939. The export market had represented the entire profit element in the studio's prewar revenue, and thus the war had brought hard times to Warners. The MoI welcomed Warner Brothers' new offer, but the Treasury did not. Each big film represented an estimated $5 million in British box office takings, and the revenue could not be spared. Undeterred, Warners continued its anti-Nazi crusade. American isolationists soon attacked the studio for war-mongering on the screen. They did not gain access to the studio's correspondence, however, and thus remained blissfully unaware that only the reticence of a handful of British civil servants had prevented the greatest film studio of the age from transforming itself into an annex of a foreign propaganda machine.[67]

Despite its uneasiness with Warner Brothers, the British government employed an even more unlikely cinematic proxy to undermine America's Phoney War complacency: Joseph Goebbels. In a master stroke of censorship policy, Britain allowed German propaganda films, intercepted by British censors in Bermuda, to continue on their way to the New World. In so doing, they permitted the Germans to commit an appalling policy error. The films included documentaries of the German attack on Poland, produced as a testament to the efficiency of Hitler's blitzkrieg. Goebbels believed that scenes of the Polish army being routed, set to the strains of a jolly German male voice choir, would build an image of the *Wehrmacht*'s invincibility in the Americas. But they did little to impress the people of the United States. The BLI speculated that such films "must have intensified the desire to see Germany defeated." The lesson was not lost on other partisans. In the early summer of 1940 *March of Time* decided to use sequences from the Nazi documentary *Feldzug in Polen* as a powerful climax to their interventionist feature film *The Ramparts We Watch*. The Newsreel Association, long jealous of *March of Time*'s special treatment at the MoI, suspected British help and complained. Walter Monckton assured them that the footage emanated from a source "entirely independent of this Ministry." The source was indeed independent—notoriously so. It was John Grierson, who, as head of the National Film Board of Canada, now enjoyed an option on all German material intercepted in Bermuda.[68]

The MoI used film, radio, and the press to communicate the war to the broad mass of Americans, but it also took care to cultivate the American elite. The ministry began its bid to win over America's opinion makers by recruiting British intellectuals who, it hoped, would be able to challenge the view that the war was rooted in Old World power politics. In September 1939, the MoI approached seventy of the best-known writers in Britain, asking that they volunteer their services. An outraged H. G. Wells refused, but most accepted. An MoI Books Committee then commissioned literature according to the political needs of the hour and fed the completed manuscripts to independent commercial publishing houses. Given America's fear of direct propaganda, the operation proved particularly useful, bringing propaganda to American readers between the bindings not of His Majesty's Stationary Office but of Penguin, Macmillan, Harcourt, Doubleday, and Oxford University Press.[69] On September 24, the American Division reported that:

> Steps have been taken to facilitate the publication privately, under American publishers imprint, of books and articles liable to have a valuable propaganda effect. Contracts have been arranged with Heineman's and Harpers for a book on the European Crisis and the war by Harold Callender of the *New York Times*. A contract is being arranged for publication of the Blue Book of September 21st by American publishers in a popular edition . . . . Negotiations are in progress for the American syndication of articles by J. B. Priestley.[70]

The MoI produced everything from brief pamphlets to sizable books, from small runs to substantial best-sellers, but the message always remained the same: Britain stood resolute in the face of war and intended to win.[71]

The author list of the MoI Literary and Editorial Unit soon included Harold Laski, E. M. Forster, Howard Spring, and such veterans of the Eden bloc as Vernon Bartlett and Harold Nicolson. Several of the American Division's productions looked to a specifically American audience. Norman Angell, America's favorite British pacifist, turned his hand to war propaganda in *For What Do We Fight?*, while *Winston Churchill's Fighting Speeches* took full advantage of Churchill's growing reputation in the United States to display the defiant face of Britain. American historian Allan Nevins and the Labour MP, Josiah Wedgewood, published *Forever Freedom*. The Empire Division commissioned pamphlets to combat Indian nationalist propaganda in the United States, and eventually the MoI produced the *Handbook of the British Empire*, a single volume setting out the full benefits of British imperialism, published in the United States by Dent.[72]

During the course of the Phoney War, British literary propaganda spread its wings. The British Council joined the campaign, working to develop the flow of "cultural writing" to the United States. Meanwhile, as the Books Committee became a fully independent Literary Division, it acquired the services of the great graphic artist E. McKnight Kauffer and a young writer and literary editor of *The Spectator* named Graham Greene. Charged with the task of coordinating the division's output, Greene soon became a familiar figure around the MoI, hurrying through the maze of corridors or pondering a meager portion of curried sausages in the MoI canteen. He contributed his own work to the propaganda effort in America, producing a short story "The Lieutenant Died Last," in which a German parachute attack on an English village is foiled by the timely response of a local poacher. The story, complete with a sympathetic treatment of the German soldiers, was published exclusively in *Collier's Weekly* in June 1940 and resurfaced as the core of the 1942 film *Went the Day Well?*.

But Greene was not blind to the many banalities of life at the MoI. He set down his frustration in a short story, "Men at Work," describing the endless round of fruitless committee meetings in that "high heartless building with complicated lifts and long passages like those of a liner and lavatories where the water never ran hot and the nail-brushes were chained like Bibles." Greene's sketch of the ministry included an American Division request that "certain cuts be made in references to the American War of Independence" in a forthcoming book on the British Empire. It speaks well of his genius that this satire played its own part in the propaganda war. The story appeared in *The New Yorker* in October 1941—a testament to the British capacity for self-criticism. But Greene's stay at the MoI proved brief. In the summer of 1940, he joined British intelligence and left England to become the SIS Head of Station in Freeport, Sierra Leone, a world away from the bureaucrats of Bloomsbury.[73]

As British literary propagandists worked to establish the Empire's moral case, they naturally turned to the subject of religion. The MoI buttressed this enterprise by establishing a Religions Division devoted to the production of this material. The value of this approach for the British case in American was obvious. With the assistance of Basil Mathews, a theology professor attached to the American Division, the Religions Division engaged Catholic and Protestant isolationism in the United States. The ministry organized tours of America by leading British Catholics, instituted a newsletter that was mailed to priests all over the neutral world, and placed pro-British advertisements in Catholic newspapers. It sent 300 "influential" American Catholics complementary copies of an MoI-commissioned book, *Religion and the Reich*, by Michael Power; and even launched its own journal, *The Catholic Bulletin*, which was mailed to Catholic journals and "a considerable number of influential persons" across the United States. With a remarkable disregard for Divine injunctions against "bearing false witness," the MoI carefully concealed the origins of all such material. The *Bulletin* purported to be an offshoot of the English Catholic journal *The Tablet*, and the books arrived as "gifts" from "a neutral friend."[74]

American Protestants received similar treatment. Mathews edited a Protestant journal entitled *Christian Commonwealth*, mailed fortnightly to 10,000 churchmen and editors across America from "an independent address in London." In a similar vein, the MoI commissioned such leading churchmen as the Bishop of York to write articles for Protestant magazines on British war aims, refugee policy, and

British sympathy for the condition of German missionaries. It is ironic that a division dedicated to religion and run by a clergyman named Reverend Hope should have given full rein to the old spirit of British black propaganda, thereby exposing the faithful of the United States to techniques that the British officially practiced only on the citizens of the Third Reich.[75]

The Religions Division did not address America's Jewish community. It did not even acquire a Jewish section until July 1941 and then only to combat British anti-Semitism. The task of addressing American Jews fell to the American Division and to the Foreign Office. It was not a simple job. Although American Jews knew the evils of Nazi anti-Semitism, they felt no automatic sympathy for Great Britain. Memories of the St. James's Palace Agreement and the rigid British-administered quota on Jewish immigration into Palestine died hard. The British had no desire to repeat the errors of the Balfour Declaration of 1917 and therefore refused to make sweeping promises to the Jews. The War Cabinet even shrank from a scheme to raise a regiment of Jewish volunteers in the United States. Moreover, although Nazi anti-Semitism offered an obvious basis for political capital, the issue also evoked memories of World War I. In the autumn of 1939, when the British published their White Paper on Nazi persecution of the Jews, American isolationists denounced it as atrocity propaganda.[76]

Lothian had to act. Before doing so, he consulted Chaim Weizmann, the Zionist leader long resident in Britain. Weizmann assured him that most American Jews were not anti-British and asserted that the rhetoric of the extreme Zionists alienated them from most Americans, both Jewish and Gentile. With this in mind, in February 1940, Lothian sent a stark but sincere message to the American Jewish Congress: "the victory of the Allied powers in this war offers the Jews their only real hope of escaping from the hateful maltreatment of their race, and of renewing their march toward Zionist ideals in concord with the Arab peoples." Privately, Jewish neutrality infuriated Lothian. "I have no objection to their advocating neutrality for [the] USA," he wrote, "But if they do so they have no right to demand that we should bleed for their fellows overseas."[77]

Lothian's message of shared interest was carried through the United States by the chairman of the British Jewish Congress, Rabbi Maurice Perlzweig. Responding to an invitation from the president of the American Jewish Congress, Rabbi Dr. Stephen S. Wise, and well-briefed by the MoI, Rabbi Perlzweig toured the country. He visited twenty cities and made more than 100 speeches at synagogues, dinners, conferences, rallies, and over the radio. He met Americans of all classes, from humble laborers to Supreme Court Justice Felix Frankfurter. Speaking on the theme of "The Jews of Europe," Perlzweig strove to correct what he called the Allied "sins of omission and commission." He set out the full picture, from British appeasement of Arab insurgents to the anti-Semitism of the Polish vice-premiere in exile Kott, who spoke of resettling all Polish Jews in Southern Russia at the war's end. This established his credibility. Finally, after much lobbying behind the scenes, Perlzweig persuaded the Washington Convention of the American Jewish Congress to endorse the Allied cause. In a carefully worded statement, Rabbi Wise declared that: "As between Nazi Germany and Great Britain, we are not neutral. As between democratic France and Bolshevik Russia, we are not neutral." Testaments to Rabbi Perlzweig's persuasive abilities multiplied. The British Consul in Chicago attended a lecture by Rabbi Perlzweig and wrote to the British Embassy in Washington in admiration:

> The message he delivered was immensely inspiring and beneficial and his charming, cultured English voice helped much to put it over. He was given an ovation at the close, and I was left with the feeling that his hundred-odd listeners would be more understanding of our cause, and would go home with a deeper realisation that the Czechs and Poles and Finns and Jews are all in the same boat with Britain and France.

Perlzweig's impassioned plea to listeners to join the struggle against racism overseas was delivered in a small Jewish club. He had hoped to use a larger hall, but America's own brand of anti-Semitism set this venue off limits to Jews. "Such," the Consul noted, was "man's inhumanity to man."[78]

By the end of the Phoney War, concern for American opinion had become a reflex throughout the Ministry of Information. The Empire Division restricted its propaganda in neutral Eire to appease Irish-Americans. Similarly, the MoI Overseas Division recommended that Britain avoid large-scale propaganda in Latin America. The Ministry dodged American "misunderstanding" by hiring the commercial advertising agency J. Walter Thompson to organize British Latin American operations privately. Conversely, E. H. Carr argued that, since the Americans appeared "apt to regard the British policy in China as the touchstone of British good faith," the British should take pains to cultivate China by all means at their disposal. This concern reflected the common sense and tireless industry of Whyte's American Division within the MoI: tireless industry that now propelled the division into an ever-diversifying array of activities.[79]

As planned, the American Division maintained links with such Anglo-American organizations as the English Speaking Union, and it succeeded in eliciting a steady supply of American invitations to send lecturers—essential, since Britain only permitted "propaganda by request." The ministry contacted companies with business in the United States, briefing all commercial representatives due to cross the Atlantic. The area of Commercial Propaganda soon gained its own division, under the supervision of John Rodgers of J. Walter Thompson, and under the direction of Lord Davidson.[80]

Finally the American Division enlisted ordinary British men and women in their campaign. Numerous Britons who regularly corresponded with people in the United States sought the ministry's advice on how they might treat political subjects in their letters. The division replied with regular broadsheets outlining topics that might profitably be discussed; and seemingly innocent British pen-pals joined the propaganda war. American observers naturally remained ignorant of the broadsheets, but they noticed that British mail bound for America had acquired a stamp bearing the flags of the two counties crossed and the legend "BRITAIN AND THE U.S. OF AMERICA, TOGETHER WE STAND: FOR PEACE, HONOUR, SECURITY AND PROGRESS." Had the two nations really stood together, a slogan would not have been necessary.[81]

Although Britain's Phoney War propaganda operation centered on London, this should not obscure the effort in the United States. Even before the end of the Phoney War, Lord Lothian had begun to increase the scope of Britain's publicity apparatus. In so doing, he set the mold for all subsequent developments in British propaganda policy.

Fighting the Phoney War in the United States: The British Embassy and the British Library of Information

> Whilst No Propaganda is still our watch word so far as the United States is concerned, this does not mean that we are not doing our best to make accurate information on our aims and actions available to those who are misinformed.
>
> Lord Lothian, February 1940[82]

Lord Lothian was a master of the American scene. Always accessible and disarmingly frank, he charmed the press corps. Lothian profited from the able counsel of such senior figures in the press world as Walter Lippmann, Arthur Hays Sulzberger, and Helen Ogden Reid; he also enjoyed the able counsel of John Wheeler-Bennett and Keith Officer, an Australian diplomat assigned to advise the ambassador on matters of public opinion. With their advice, he began the work of explaining Britain to America and, no less importantly, America to the British.[83]

From the outset, Lothian determined to stretch the boundaries of the "No Propaganda" policy. Although his predecessor, Lindsay, had urged him to adopt a low profile, he refused to allow the British case to be lost by default, and he spoke to good effect throughout the Phoney War. He began by tackling allegations of propaganda head-on:

contrasting German propaganda and British publicity. As Lothian explained to the Chicago branch of the Council on Foreign Relations in January 1940: "Propaganda is the deliberate attempt to influence your countrymen or other nations to a particular course of action, by lies or half truths or tendentious innuendos. The truth is never propaganda; it is the staff of public life."[84] In point of fact, as the British wartime campaign in the United States would demonstrate, the truth made the best propaganda of all.

Lothian's speeches introduced a series of important themes into British propaganda. He exposed German treachery; he worked to ease Americans' horror of the British Empire by pointing to its development into a commonwealth of freely associated powers. Lothian emphasized the common foundations of democracy in Britain and the United States; he pictured the United States as the inheritor of a precious flame born in Greece, nurtured in Rome, and carried to the New World by Britain. He stressed this theme at a ceremony contrived to touch the nerve of a shared political culture: the depositing of the Lincoln copy of Magna Carta (fresh from the World's Fair) in the Library of Congress. As the Justices of the Supreme Court looked on, Lothian committed the document to a place of safety "alongside its own descendants, the Declaration of Independence and the American Constitution."[85]

Lothian presented the British cause as synonymous with the American way. He drew on American history to support his case. Taking the words of Theodore Roosevelt, Lothian declared: "We stand at Armageddon and we battle for the Lord!" But Lothian owed more than words to statesmen from the age of the first Roosevelt. His assault on the assumptions of isolationism rested squarely on that era's theories of sea power, the intellectual engine that first propelled the United States onto the global stage. Lothian was well-versed in the writings of Alfred T. Mahan and spoke accordingly. He stressed that Britain and the United States were strategically interdependent, and that neither could afford to permit German naval hegemony.[86]

To fine-tune his approach to American opinion, Lothian asked John Wheeler-Bennett to be his "eyes and ears" in the country at large. Wheeler-Bennett began by reporting on Britain's network of consulates in the United States, which he found to be hopelessly outmoded. He also kept discreetly in touch with German anti-Nazis in the United States, including the former Rhodes scholar Adam von Trott, then attached to the Institute of Pacific Relations and later executed for his part in the 1944 bomb plot against Hitler.[87]

Wheeler-Bennett worked from an office at the British Library of Information in New York. He visited the British Embassy in Washington once a week for consultation. He also accepted invitations to lecture farther afield. The Americans, Lothian maintained, were "an ear hungry people." The demand for Wheeler-Bennett's services as a speaker increased dramatically in the early months of 1940. He ranged freely across the country, braving a bewildering succession of meetings with Women's Clubs, Knights of Columbus, Rotary Clubs, Lions, Kiwanis, Elks, and Shriners, delivering the same message of British determination and the justice of the Allied cause. He encountered a predictable array of hot questions and cold luncheons. At his busiest, Wheeler-Bennett spoke eight times in ten days. He stretched the "No Propaganda" rule to its limit and (some felt) beyond.[88]

The main body of the BLI moved more slowly. It seemed out of step with its customers' needs. Hamilton Fish Armstrong—chairman of the Council on Foreign Relations, editor of *Foreign Affairs*, and friend of Wheeler-Bennett—complained: "I don't use the library because it is not of the slightest use to me. I have never got anything I wanted from it." The problem lay with the BLI's director. Angus Fletcher seemed unaware that journalists lived by deadlines. Moreover, since the parent Foreign Office News Department had moved from Whitehall to the MoI building in Bloomsbury, no one knew who was giving the orders. Even so, the BLI began a gentle expansion, building a mailing list of customers that, by February 1940, stood at some 2,500 names. It approached new customers through pamphlets and a low-budget advertising drive in certain technical journals.[89]

There were simple arguments for a full service. As the expansionists on the staff pointed out, by registering the library with the State Department, Britain had confessed to propaganda in America. With this point conceded, it seemed logical to make full use of the BLI machinery. Wheeler-Bennett agreed and proposed a faster service appropriate to the needs of the press. But to his horror, Fletcher rejected his proposal with the words: "This is Teutonic efficiency; this is what we are fighting the war against."[90]

Though never Teutonically efficient, the level of service at the BLI improved during the course of the Phoney War, thanks to an influx of extra staff. The Library drew on the pool of Britons marooned in the United States at the outbreak of war, ranging from Commonwealth Fund students to society heiress Daphne Straight. The recruits included a well-born young poet and painter, Desmond Harmsworth, caught in America on his return from Tahiti. The isolationists failed to notice that the son of the British press baron, Lord Cecil Harmsworth, and nephew of the late Lord Northcliffe (the ultimate bogey of any red-blooded American propaganda-phobe) was now working as an office drudge in the semi-independent BLI Survey Section. On one occasion, however, Fletcher felt obliged to decline the services of a well-connected volunteer. He refused to employ a certain Frau Hitler: the Irish ex-wife of Adolf Hitler's brother. Fletcher feared that having a Hitler in one's propaganda office might be indiscreet.[91]

The BLI Survey Section developed according to plan. Under the leadership of Aubrey Morgan, the section acquired its own premises in

Rockefeller Center and the odd telegraphic address of DIGESTION, New York. There, in a frenzied office nicknamed "the Clip Club," BLI staff collected press cuttings and material mailed from the consulates. A team of writers under Morgan's wife, Constance, then collated this material into reports on general trends and specific issues in the U.S. press. They worked into the small hours of every morning honing the daily mass of material into concise form, ready for transmission to London over the Reuter's line. They joked that the British Cabinet read the previous day's BLI report with the following morning's breakfast. In reality the Cabinet rarely saw the reports, but the BLI survey earned an admiring readership in the British Embassy and in the Foreign Office.[92]

The survey staff also gathered intelligence through personal contacts. Much of this work fell to Major Bill Ormerod, a former financial consultant, who cast himself as a comic-opera Englishman, complete with button hole and top hat. Ormerod charmed his American contacts by fitting all their P. G. Wodehouse expectations. He became the BLI's eyes and ears on Wall Street. Aubrey Morgan himself built links with American journalists and the growing elite pro-interventionist movement. Soon a river of intelligence was flowing into his office. It would be a relatively modest task to switch the direction of this tide and transform the BLI Survey Section from a receiving office for information on public opinion into a full-blown propaganda agency.[93]

The British Embassy also maintained a keen search for fresh avenues of publicity. In early 1940, Lothian's attention turned to Britain's allies, who had far more room to act without offending American sensibilities. Lothian had long suggested that Canada might serve as a valuable proxy propagandist. Others looked to the exiled governments of the Czechs and the Poles, or hoped that the French might share the work. In the event, Canada was too wary of the U.S. propaganda phobia; the Czechs and the Poles simply lacked the financial resources to make a meaningful contribution; and the French in general proved hopelessly inept.

The sole Allied bright spot was the French Information Center in New York. Both its director, Robert Valeur, and his colleague Raoul de Roussy de Sales had excellent instincts for propaganda. As the former "special correspondent" in the United States for *Paris Soir*, de Sales already knew the New York press world. He soon became a central source of information on European affairs for many radio commentators and magazine writers. De Sales also served as the point of contact between the British and French machines, meeting Morgan and Wheeler-Bennett for lunch every Saturday. Encouraged by such contact, Lothian hatched a scheme to outflank Fletcher by establishing a joint Anglo-French Allied Information Agency under de Sales to spearhead a large-scale propaganda drive in the United States. The fall of France destroyed this scheme and de Sales. Sickened at the sight of Vichy, he proclaimed France to be dead and withdrew from the propaganda

battle. But Lothian's idea for an allied propaganda office remained alive
and would resurface later that year.[94]

Despite the scale and variety of the new British propaganda operation, the American isolationists remained fixated with the handful of
British speakers who were lecturing in the United States in defiance
of the new policy. Some lecturers compensated well for the irritation
they caused. The Oxford University Union debate team, led by the
future Conservative Prime Minister Edward Heath, earned the British
Embassy's praise for its work on American campuses.[95] But the friends
of Britain in the United States retained grave doubts about this area of
effort. One of Lothian's internationalist contacts suggested that Britain
"trade off a few gas masks for a few muzzles," while the anglophile
Chicago Daily News concluded an editorial: "call off your lecturers
John Bull, or we will start to think your name means what it says." In a
quaint testament to British ignorance of American idiom, the Foreign
Office clerk reading this last remark felt obliged to pencil a question
mark in the margin.[96]

Such editorials did not greatly trouble Lothian or the Ministry of
Information. The bulk of the British campaign had clearly escaped the
isolationists' notice, and the ministry felt able to expand its activities
within the "No Propaganda" policy with relative safety. The broader developments in American opinion encouraged this course. But as the
expansionists in London and Washington were soon to discover, evad-
ing the isolationists was one thing; dodging the Foreign Office was quite
another.

The Development of American Opinion and British Policy

> American opinion is still . . . almost unanimously anti-Nazi. In ad-
> dition it is now almost more strongly anti-Soviet. It is to a much less
> degree pro-French or pro-British. There are formidable elements
> which are definitely anti-British which take every opportunity to
> misrepresent our motives and attack our methods . . . . I have no
> doubt that the best corrective is the fullest possible publicity from
> England and France through the important and high class American
> correspondents of what the Allies are thinking and doing.
>
> Lord Lothian, December 1939[97]

The development of American opinion in the early months of the war
gave some encouragement to the British. Sir Frederick Whyte saw the
revised Neutrality Act of November 1939 as the "first reward" of British
"prudence." The act made American war material available to the
Allies on a "cash and carry" basis, but this was not the first step on an
inevitable road to American intervention. The new terms were contrived to contain American involvement in the war, and they fitted the

views of many moderate American noninterventionists. Roosevelt's
initiative was double-edged. In helping the Allies, he had also defined
America's diplomatic position. The insistence on hard cash for all purchases ensured that no credit links would be established that might
later draw the United States into war, as had happened in 1917. Moreover, the U.S. ban forbidding all American vessels and passengers to
enter belligerent European waters reduced the risk of a second *Lusi-
tania*. As the columnist Raymond Clapper observed in May 1940, these
measures distanced America from the war. His headline said it all:
"NEUTRALITY ACT WORKS."[98]

The winter of 1939 brought stability to American public opinion.
America settled into an overt hatred of Hitler; and a distinct preference for heroic victims like the Czechs and Poles over the sedentary
British and French. In December 1939, American hearts went out
anew to the Finns, as they defended their homeland against a Soviet
invasion. Standards of press objectivity evaporated as Finland benefited from the very anti-Communism that promoted isolationism elsewhere and reaped the reward for having, alone among World War I
participants, repaid its war debt. As anti-Soviet feeling grew, Lothian
began peppering his speeches with attacks on Marxism, and the MoI
contemplated launching a campaign critical of Bolshevik atrocities in
Finland across the United States.[99]

The East Coast political establishment remained vocally faithful to
Britain. The final year of peace produced a new vogue for Anglo-
American unity, seen in its most extreme form in Clarence Streit's
book of 1939—*Union Now*—urging a formal union between the United
States, Britain, and the remaining democratic nations. More con-
structively, American internationalists rallied into the "Non-partisan
Committee for Peace through the Revision of the Neutrality Law," the
"American Union for Concerted Peace Efforts," and the "Commission
to Study the Organization of Peace," all of which preached that peace
was only possible with an Allied victory. As arch-anglophobe Porter
Sargent noted, the leadership of Professor Nicholas Murray Butler,
James T. Shotwell, Thomas Lamont, Frank Aydelotte, Clarence Streit,
and Clark Eichelberger was a roll call of leading American internationalists and anglophiles.[100]

Sympathetic Americans lost no time in making material contributions to the Allied cause. Teddy Roosevelt's son, Kermit, volunteered
for service in the British army, but his wife warned the Foreign Office
not to read too much into his action. He was not, she explained, a typical American. Others rallied to serve in the American Volunteer
Ambulance Corps in France or to promote the war relief societies organized by men like Thomas Lamont and Douglas Fairbanks, Jr. In
October 1939, the British sent Ronald Tree to the United States to coordinate the aid effort. Tree later claimed that he personally persuaded
Winthrop Aldrich, president of the Chase National Bank, to found a

central French and British War Relief Fund and raise $500,000 for the
Allied cause. The directorate of Aldrich's committee included Mrs.
Dwight Morrow. Thus Mrs. Morrow joined her daughter Constance and
her son-in-law Aubrey Morgan in the fray against her daughter Anne
and her son-in-law Charles Lindbergh. On January 15, 1940, another
new aid organization opened its doors, with Mrs. Winston Churchill as
its honorary sponsor. Dedicated to collecting garments and organizing
knitting circles, this group—Bundles for Britain—became as synonymous with America's wartime culture as a Betty Grable pinup.[101]

The British also received propaganda aid from unexpected quarters.
Publishers of pulp magazines proved to be particularly enthusiastic
supporters. On the outbreak of war, the pulps declared war on Germany en masse. One editor explained:

> We are accepting pulp fiction dealing with the present European war. The
> former ban on anti-German stories has been lifted. For *Air Adventures* we
> would like air story writers to make their heroes English, French or
> American adventurers. For *Fantastic Adventures* and *Amazing Stories*
> we will welcome stories dealing with Nazi intrigue in the United States.

By the spring of 1940, the presses ran hot with tales of RAF gallantry
and of Hunnish plots against America, at a dime apiece. Before the
books had yellowed in their readers' hands, circumstances obliged the
RAF to match the exploits of their fictional colleagues in an all too
genuine "against the odds" battle for air supremacy over England. Pulp
fans across America sat ready and waiting for each new installment.[102]

The United States' propaganda phobia failed to grow at the same
pace as did its partisan sentiment. In the early months of 1940, the
British Library of Information noticed a marked decline of American
concern about propaganda. The hysteria of the early weeks of the war
had produced its own "anti-toxin." More specifically, Dorothy Thompson led a counterattack against the propaganda panic by appropriating
the fear for her own ends, denouncing isolationist propaganda against
propaganda. Thompson's message found an echo in radio news programs sponsored by Ford and General Motors. The BLI concluded that,
despite his notorious personal commitment to American neutrality,
Henry Ford had yielded to fears that the public's sensitivity to foreign
propaganda, if allowed to fester, might develop into a similar rejection
of commercial advertising.[103]

But 1940 presented as many problems as it resolved. German
propaganda and America isolationism remained, and the entire country labored under a mood of complacency, spiced with irritation over
British maritime policy. The root of the problem lay in the United
States' perception of the strategic situation in Europe. Although most
Americans hoped for an Allied victory, few felt that American aid was
necessary to achieve it. Americans simply did not yet view Germany
as a sufficiently grave threat; as Lothian put it: "the United States, like

all other nations, will only act when its own vital interests—which include its ideas—are menaced."[104] The misguided hope for a negotiated
peace between the Allies and Germany compounded American complacency; this hope swelled with Undersecretary of State Sumner
Welles's mission to Europe in March 1940; Britain would receive no
further aid until all such optimism had been crushed.

The need to find a response to break down this complacency split
the British publicity machine. Francis Cowell of the News Department
argued that, since isolationism was grounded in emotion rather than
in reason, point-for-point arguments could achieve little; Britain had
to trust in the emotive force of events. He suggested developing the
image of British fearlessness and exploiting American's liking for the
politician who personified this spirit, Winston Churchill.

In contrast, Alan Dudley of the BLI stressed the intellectual foundation of American isolationism. He demanded propaganda to prove to
America that Allied war aims were not "petty and selfish" and that a
German victory would "threaten the American way of life." Britain's
"problem," he wrote, "is to vitalise and clarify constantly the difference
between the Allies and the Nazis. For years the Americans have demanded that Saint George should fight the dragon, and if now they are
inclined to doubt his sainthood, the need is to remind them." Both men
were right. During the summer of 1940, when Britain tied emotionally
powerful events to a considered message and thereby addressed both
the hearts and heads of America, isolationism began to crumble.[105]

Ronald Tree added his voice to the policy debate. While in the
United States that autumn, he had compiled a report on British publicity. Tree found Americans bored by the "laconic communiqués" of the
Phoney War and rather disappointed not to be hearing "the screams of
the wounded and dying" over their radios. Arguing that Britain was
obliged to give them more to think about, Tree recommended an
immediate expansion of the BLI.[106] He was equally keen to step up propaganda in Britain and recommended the systematic cultivation of all
distinguished American visitors. He saw himself as a key actor in this
campaign, presiding over "politically useful" cocktail parties in London
and flitting between New York and Paris to coordinate Allied propaganda for the United States. Despite this note of self-aggrandizement,
Tree's suggestions were thought "remarkably sound" by Lothian, Whyte,
and the Foreign Office; and although all concerned also urged continued restraint, Tree had earned a job in the MoI. In January 1940, he
became Parliamentary Private Secretary with special responsibility for
American affairs. This was a significant advance. A committed member
of the prewar Atlanticist bloc now sat at the right hand of the Minister
of Information. A marked shift in policy soon followed.[107]

Despite Tree's pressure, the "self-denying ordinance" against
formal propaganda still dominated the MoI's American policy in early
1940. Whyte was particularly unwilling to do anything that might dis-

rupt Roosevelt's probable bid for reelection to an unprecedented third term in office in November 1940. The MoI continued to place its faith in the cultivation of the U.S. press in Britain. Whyte assured Lothian that "the bulk of American pressmen *want us to win* . . . the *net* result of their writing and broadcasting will tell in our favour. That is why I still hold that my little Division in the Ministry is best employed as the 'power behind the scenes' in London working for the Americans here." The objective of Britain's American publicity remained the "promotion of good will." Frank Darvall pressed for more, noting: "Our policy and publicity in relation to America would both be very differ- ent if our secret objective is to get the United States into the war."[108] Initially, further guidelines were not forthcoming, but changes at the top of the ministry would soon begin to challenge the assumptions of the "No Propaganda" policy.

The departure of Lord Macmillan transformed the Ministry of Information. Macmillan had allowed each MoI Divisional head a free hand in executing policy. His successor had other ideas. The new Information Minister was Sir John Reith, the founding Director General of the BBC, a man known for his vigorous administrative style and singular opinions on the subject of communications. Reith had no intention of allowing British policy to drift along in America or else- where. Under Reith, the MoI began to find its feet. He squashed the War Office's rival propaganda unit, MI7; he regained control over cen- sorship and successfully introduced procedures that endured for the remainder of the war. Unfortunately, Reith did not like politicians, and they did not like him. Specifically, he hated Churchill. This did little to enhance the MoI's chances of wringing news from the Admiralty.[109]

Under Reith, the American Division gained a new member of staff. Frank Darvall followed up by proposing that an "editorial officer" join the staff of the BLI in New York to address the American press. The Foreign Office and British Embassy agreed, and Michael Huxley was appointed as a First Secretary "in special charge of press contacts and of the affairs of the British Library of Information." Lothian now had his press attaché. The growth of the British information machine in America had begun.[110]

As the Ministry of Information strained to maximize its output within the "No Propaganda" policy, it paid fresh attention to Britain's own press and institutions. Frank Darvall suggested that the MoI stage a Parliamentary debate on the issue of British propaganda in the United States. He hoped that, if lurid propaganda schemes were proposed only to be rejected in a solemn display of British high-mindedness, Americans might be impressed. Whyte was willing to use "the Mother of Parliaments" as a ventriloquist's dummy, but he feared that Ameri- cans would find the content of the debate too alarming. Still, the underlying principle of allowing the United States to "overhear" the British "talking to each other" was sound; and in April 1940, the MoI began to place material in the British press that could be reproduced to good effect in the United States.[111]

The MoI also knew that, by selling America to the British public, it could reduce Anglo-American misunderstanding and even impress the United States without offending the isolationists. The MoI worked to promote a positive image of the United States through leaflets and a scheme to teach American history in British schools, while the BBC organized broadcasts on American affairs. This work eventually became a major strand in British propaganda policy, generating books, a spate of films about Anglo-American friendship, and even the new academic discipline of American Studies.[112] But—as Lord Reith knew well—such things were no substitute for a solid approach to American opinion.

Reith had no patience for the "No Propaganda" policy. Soon his schemes for a fresh initiative in America bumped up against the Foreign Office with a predictable regularity. In February he suggested using British visitors to the United States for covert propaganda. In March he wanted to send Whyte to the United States to discuss expanding the propaganda machinery.[113] By April he had proposed BLI branches, the adaptation of BBC broadcasts for American tastes, improved coverage of the United States in the British press, and a newsletter for British expatriates. He then surpassed himself by suggesting that the British Secret Service investigate the funding of isolationist pressure groups and release full details of any German support discovered to the American press. The Foreign Office strained to hold him back, but Reith was not alone. Lord Beaverbrook made similar noises in cabinet, and a still stronger call for improved publicity came from the BLI Survey Section in New York.[114]

In March 1940, Alan Dudley called for reform of the BLI. He recommended an ingenious variety of measures, including subsidies for Czech propaganda and use of the German trick of planting news stories in neutral countries in the hope that American news agencies might pick them up. He expressed a preference that these stories be based on fact, but mused that "a story from Mexico City of a monstrous German plot to blow up a ship in the Panama canal would be very effective." In a secret letter to the British Embassy, he proposed taking advantage of the "bandwagon" effect of public opinion polls by planting loaded questions in a "well known poll" in order to remind Americans "that they are opposed to Nazism and that at the same time German propaganda is working unchecked in this country and that the German point of view is being supported by American opinion."[115]

London, however, had other ideas. The Foreign Office preferred a complex plan drawn up by the J. Walter Thompson advertising agency. This plan suggested that Britain emphasize the limited nature of the aid needed from the United States, on the theory that the Americans would be more forthcoming if they knew that their troops would not be required.[116] Other suggestions remained anathema to the Foreign Office, which now dug in for a desperate rear-guard action.

By the end of March, the MoI and Foreign Office were on a collision course. The impact was hardly spectacular. It occurred over lunch on March 21, as Darvall of the MoI begged the wily T. North Whitehead of the FO American Department to allow Reith a "harmless adventure" in American propaganda before he undertook a harmful one. The FO attempted to placate the MoI by giving it full authority over the supply of propaganda material to the BLI, hoping that this and the appointment of an embassy press attaché would satisfy MoI demands until after the November Presidential election. They had not reckoned with the pressure of events.[117]

On April 9, 1940, Germany overran Denmark and lunged north into Norway. The British dispatched an expeditionary force to halt the German advance. A sorry display of military humiliation and inexpert publicity followed. As the British army fell back, pressure for a revised information policy in the United States redoubled. But the vicious acceleration of events in Europe allowed little time for the British publicists to take stock of the results of the policy they had pursued during the Phoney War. In retrospect it seems clear, as Lothian argued in a dispatch of April 10, that the development of American opinion vindicated the "No Propaganda" policy. Britain had built an effective working relationship with the American newsmen. In the industrial Midwest, British war photographs now outnumbered German ones by a ratio of twelve to one, and the worst of the U.S. propaganda phobia seemed to have passed. If the Foreign Office doubted the effectiveness of the MoI, the German Embassy in Washington was full of admiration. When a pro-Allied swing in American public opinion enabled the British to purchase a consignment of American-made aircraft, the German chargé Thomsen wrote: "English propaganda has been rather successful of late in spreading the view that Germany has shown herself to be the enemy of the democracies and capitalism and would therefore in the event of victory jeopardize the American economic system . . . ."[118]

But the Phoney War had also demonstrated the limitations of the "No Propaganda" policy. Britain needed a steady supply of war news to satisfy the American press. Without such news British propaganda withered. Now, however, Hitler's spring offensive furnished the raw news materials and strategic urgency necessary to sweep away the complacent foundations of American isolationist sentiment. In September 1939, a small group of American correspondents had advised the British to pull no punches in releasing news to the United States, because "as soon as the Americans realize that there is a danger of the Allies being defeated, even the isolationists are likely to abandon their present attitude."[119] Hitler swiftly accomplished this and more. Soon Americans began to fear that Britain might not survive long enough to receive their aid.

Whatever the results of British publicity in America during the Phoney War, the future clearly required a higher level of activity, efficiency, and directness. Murrow had urged this as early as April 4. The *Daily Mail*, the *Evening Standard*, and rogue Labour statesman Stafford Cripps all agreed.[120] The pressure to act was doubly keen inside the propaganda machine. On May 2, 1940, the Foreign Office and the MoI met to clarify the status of the British Embassy press officer and to plan a similar appointment for the BLI in New York. The discussion had shifted from whether to expand to how to expand.[121] But changes were also afoot at the highest levels of the British government.

The news from Norway hit the Chamberlain government like a tidal wave and swept away its power base in the House of Commons. On May 9, Chamberlain resigned and the Premiership fell to Winston Churchill. Churchill's accession to power proved to be a watershed event in Anglo-American relations. His coalition Cabinet brought several key figures of the prewar Anglo-American bloc back into power. Eden returned to the front benches as Minister of War. Duff Cooper replaced Reith as Minister of Information, with Harold Nicolson as his Parliamentary Under-Secretary and Ronald Tree as his Parliamentary Private Secretary. Tree also had an informal position. Whenever a full moon exposed Chequers to air attack, the Prime Minister spent the weekend at Tree's country house, Ditchley.[122] Given Churchill's own commitment to the "English-speaking peoples," the reshuffle sounded a death knell for the reticence that had marked Chamberlain's dealings with the United States.

Events confirmed the new cabinet's interest in America. In the early hours of May 10, German panzer divisions crashed west into Holland and Belgium, and thrust onward with sickening swiftness toward the borders of France unprotected by the Maginot line. Allied survival now hinged on American aid.[123] Clearly, Britain had no alternative: there was no chance to win the war by starving Germany into submission, and no question of holding America at arms length to ensure the integrity of the British Empire. The only prospect for the survival of Britain and its way of life lay in the tenacity of the British people and the hope of American support.

3

Their Finest Hour: Projecting the Battle of Britain, May to September 1940

> We shall defend our island whatever the cost may be . . . until, in
> God's good time the New World, with all its power and might steps
> forth to the rescue and liberation of the Old.
>
> Winston Churchill, June 4, 1940[1]

On the morning of May 15, 1940, the German army broke through
French lines at Sedan. Now no Allied forces stood between the Germans and the English Channel. In mounting anxiety, Churchill and the
French Prime Minister, Paul Reynaud, begged Roosevelt to make more
supplies available for purchase. They also requested the loan of fifty
or so destroyers to cover mounting naval losses. FDR agreed to try to
provide more material for sale, but he insisted that Congress would
block any more substantial aid. In place of destroyers, Churchill was
offered "the best of luck." He needed it.[2]

As the British government prepared further pleas for Washington,
Britain's propagandists struggled to maintain the flow of news necessary to rally American opinion behind an active aid policy. Following
the advice of Raymond Gram Swing, the MoI resisted the temptation to
beg. It briefed the British press to be tactful when discussing America's
stand, and it waited for the expected change in U.S. opinion.[3] Meanwhile, in Flanders, the BEF publicity officers worked to support American coverage of the war. The German advance soon complicated their
efforts. Panic swept across the region, and roads were soon choked
with refugees. On May 17, the BEF press liaison unit and their charges
joined the flood, withdrawing from Arras to Amiens and then falling
back on Boulogne. The conducting officers strained to support news
operations throughout the withdrawal. By day, they gathered stories of
the gallant but futile Allied resistance. By night, they sought refuge in
wayside restaurants. Life teetered on the brink of the surreal. One
party came upon a duke in a local hostelry, wounded, drunk, and gig-

gling hysterically. In the midst of the devastation, three British correspondents, including Kim Philby of the London *Times*, asked permission to go golfing, only to find that the course had already fallen to
the Germans. Despite their best efforts, no one could escape the horror
of the hour. The core of the old European order was melting before
their eyes.[4]

On the night of May 19, German dive bombers struck at the heart
of Boulogne. As the American correspondents watched, the press liaison headquarters collapsed into a heap of rubble. Daylight found the
army liaison officer Roger Machell badly wounded in the wreckage;
soon thereafter his RAF colleagues incinerated the office archive on the
quayside. On May 21, the liaison team bowed to the inevitable, pack-
ing the correspondents onto a boat for England, and waiting for their
own evacuation, "momentarily expecting to be bombed to beggary." To
kill time, they broke into the Officers Club Bar and consoled themselves with a "brisk gratis consumption" of its contents.[5]

The American correspondents sailing from Boulogne that morning
drew hope from the behavior of the BEF under fire. Their respect for
the ordinary British soldier redoubled with news of every skirmish
and every perimeter held against the odds. But the view from London seemed wholly black, particularly when seen through the eyes of
American Ambassador Joseph Kennedy. On May 27, 1940, he informed
Secretary of State Hull that "only a miracle" could save the British
army from annihilation.[6] The miracle came at Dunkirk, as the Royal
Navy plucked 220,000 British and 110,000 French troops from the
beaches and harbor. The withdrawal was ignominious in the extreme.
For several days, the British concealed the evacuation from their
French and Belgian allies, for fear that the news might weaken their resistance. But the bravery of the RAF, the Royal Navy, and a handful of
civilian volunteers sparked the British imagination. Perhaps the story
was more cloud than silver lining, but in that desperate summer it was
the only story England had.[7]

With its correspondents safely evacuated, the United States depended on official sources for news from Dunkirk. This threw a heavy
burden on Whitehall. The Canadian High Commissioner in London,
Vincent Massey, warned the War Cabinet that Americans would be
"puzzled and dismayed" by Britain's apparent abandonment of France.
He suggested that Britain might head off the criticism by explaining
that the retreat was preliminary to its rejoining the battle in France
south of the German advance, "even though such a statement might
be an economy with the truth." On May 29, Churchill approved this
approach.[8]

Britain's "economy with the truth" removed an obvious political
breakwater and allowed the first wave of the "Dunkirk Spirit" to break
freely on the United States. On May 31, the *New York Herald Tribune*
declared:

There have been trapped armies before, terrible retreats, perilous embark-
ations, and heroic rearguard actions in the past, but no combination
of them on a scale like this. Defeat sustained with such fortitude is no
disaster . . . . These are soldiers of civilization, enrolling themselves imper-
ishably among those who will save, by suffering, all that makes civilized
life of value.[9]

Not to be outdone, the *New York Times* added: "So long as the English tongue survives, the word Dunkirk will be spoken with reverence.
For in that harbor, in such a hell as never blazed on earth before, at the
end of a lost battle, the rages and blemishes that have hidden the soul
of democracy fell away. There, beaten but unconquered, in shining
splendor she faced the enemy."[10] For these editorial writers, the old
Britain had withered and a new Britain had arisen in its place, re-
deemed by fire and worthy of America's admiration—and aid.

In the days that followed, Britain carefully nurtured the Dunkirk
myth in the United States. Lothian suggested playing up the "little
ships" to excite the American public and subtly direct attention to
U.S. dependence on the survival of British sea power. America's sus-
ceptibility to the Dunkirk story proved an invaluable asset in the years
ahead, ripening into Paul Gallico's novel *The Snow Goose* and the MGM
film *Mrs. Miniver*; but even as the myth took root, British prospects
withered.[11] By June 10, the situation was desperate—desperate enough
to draw the consummate opportunist Mussolini into joining the war.

On June 16, the French Cabinet resolved to capitulate. The British
published the text of a declaration of indissoluble union between
Britain and France. It was a hollow document, published according to
Churchill's private secretary solely "in order that it might have its
effect on U.S. opinion."[12] In reality, the hostility between the British
and the French was now obvious and ugly. As remnants of the British
Army marched into Brest, the townsfolk lined the streets in silence.
Parents pulled back children to prevent their marching beside the
soldiers. A gruff sergeant summed up the mood of the troops. As
he boarded the ship for England, he turned and bellowed: "We'll be
back—you buggers!"[13]

Churchill's public words reflected his private appeals for American
aid. His "fight them on the beaches" speech of June 4 included references to the New World liberating the Old as a last resort. At Sumner
Welles's suggestion, Churchill did not direct his speech to the United
States but to the British Empire and hoped that the Americans would
overhear.[14] His radio address of June 18, displayed the same concern
to involve the United States:

the Battle of France is over. I expect that the Battle of Britain is about to
begin . . . . Hitler knows he will have to break us in this island or lose the
war. If we can stand up to him, all Europe may be free and the life of the
world may move forward into broad, sunlit uplands; but if we fail, then
the whole world, *including the United States*, and all that we have known

and cared for, will sink into the abyss of a new Dark Age made more sinister, and perhaps more protracted, by the lights of a perverted science. Let us therefore brace ourselves to our duty and so bear ourselves that if the British Empire and its Commonwealth last for a thousand years men will still say, "This was their finest hour."[15]

Privately, Churchill's patience was wearing out. On the May 19, the Prime Minister barked to his secretary: "Here's a telegram for those bloody Yankees. Send it off tonight."[16]

Churchill was particularly irritated by Roosevelt's apparent assumption that he would inherit the Royal Navy and stewardship of the British Empire if Britain collapsed. He ordered Lothian to tell FDR that, if Britain should fall "Hitler has a very good chance of ruling the world." In the first week June 1940, Hitler took the next step to that end. On June 10, 1940, the Luftwaffe began the struggle for air supremacy over southern England. Six days later, Hitler signed War Directive 16 and mustered his forces for the invasion of the British Isles. The Battle of Britain had indeed begun.[17]

As Hitler's invasion forces gathered, British propagandists prepared for the battle to win American aid. They soon found that the new strategic situation had some compensations. During the Phoney War, the propaganda effort had foundered for want of a sufficient tide of news; now that tide ran high. The MoI, once beached, now floated free. Watching the drama unfold, the United States forgot its demand for a clear statement of British war aims. Britain's aim was simple—victory—for, as Churchill put it, "without victory there is no survival."[18]

American Opinion in the Summer of 1940

> There is universal admiration here for Winston and the spirit of the country, but as you will say, admiration and sympathy are not much good when one is fighting Hitler in the gate . . . .
>
> Lord Lothian, July 1940[19]

The fall of France shook America to its core. Few things in the world had seemed as eternal and solid as the Paris of leafy boulevards and picture postcard views. Now Paris was German and France was gone. It seemed likely that Britain would be next. Americans immediately took up the question of their country's own position. The great debate over America's response would dominate politics for the next eighteen months. The struggle involved millions of people, but its focus was a single man: President Roosevelt.

Although sympathetic to the Allied cause FDR, like many other Americans, feared a British collapse. If Britain was doomed, any American aid could be turned against the United States by the victorious Nazis within the year. Soon, FDR's personal estimate of Britain's chances of survival fell to as low as one-in-three. Significantly, FDR held back his aid initiative until after Britain had beaten back the first wave of the German air assault. But whatever his personal auguries, he remained a prisoner of the Neutrality Acts, Congressional isolationism, and U.S. public opinion. Still, FDR was at least able to make fresh supplies available for allied purchase by selling government surplus war material back to its manufacturers.

Meanwhile, Roosevelt strengthened America's own defenses. He placed large-scale military appropriations before the House and, in a "fireside chat" of May 26, warned the American people of the "Fifth Column" danger. The Attorney General Robert Jackson (soon to be appointed to the Supreme Court and later to serve as chief U.S. prosecutor at the Nuremberg war crimes trials) muttered of alarmism. On June 10, Roosevelt's support for the Allies reached new heights as he denounced Mussolini's attack on France. He worked to broaden the appeal of his administration, bringing two leading Republicans—Henry Stimson and Frank Knox—into his cabinet, to administer the War and Navy Departments, respectively. He also dispatched the Republican lawyer and war hero Colonel William Donovan on a mission to Britain, to report on the defensive capacity of the islands and to establish a working relationship with British intelligence.[20] The British government took heart from these actions. They were also encouraged by new initiatives from the wider internationalist community.

In May 1940, pro-Allied Americans formed a new, nonpartisan pressure group known as the Committee to Defend America by Aiding the Allies. Although the prime movers in this group were old-style internationalists, they persuaded William Allen White to act as chairman. White—the Republican editor and "Sage of Emporia, Kansas"—represented the antithesis of the East Coast war hawk and was ideally suited to the task of building broad support around a platform of "all aid short of war." The White Committee soon saw results. By the end of May, the American press trumpeted an "Aid For Allies Tide." On May 21, a *Chicago Daily News* editorial quoted White—"Here is a life and death struggle for every principle we cherish in America: For freedom of speech, of religion, of the ballot and of every freedom that upholds the dignity of the human spirit . . . . Here all the rights that the common man has fought for during a thousand years are menaced"—and concluded with its own declaration: "THE TIME HAS COME WHEN WE MUST THROW INTO THE SCALES THE ENTIRE MORAL AND ECONOMIC WEIGHT OF THE UNITED STATES ON THE SIDE OF THE FREE PEOPLES OF WESTERN EUROPE WHO ARE FIGHTING THE BATTLE FOR A CIVILIZED WAY OF LIFE." The White Committee rode high on such feeling. By July 1, it had 300 chapters nationwide. Interventionism was on the march.[21]

On June 10, American newspapers carried an advertisement headed: "A SUMMONS TO SPEAK OUT." It called on the U.S. government to recognize that "a state of war exists between this country and Germany" and to aid the Allies accordingly. Its publication was the first visible act of a smaller group of interventionists, founded by Rhodes Scholars Francis P. Miller and Whitney Shepardson, and known (after their exclusive Manhattan haunt) as the Century Group. An impressive array of public figures answered the "Summons." By the end of July the group included editors, financiers, lawyers, educators, churchmen, and a lone film producer—Walter Wanger.[22] Unlike the White Committee, the Century Group spurned the middle ground; its statement of principle declared that "the survival of the British Commonwealth is an important factor in the preservation of the American way of life," and it called for America to act "in weeks not years"; for American ships to convoy evacuated children and to transport British food; and for war credits, arms exports, and the loan of the U.S. Navy in return for a guarantee that the Royal Navy would not surrender to the Germans. Nor did the Century Group rule out war.[23]

Despite an overlapping membership list, relations between the White Committee and the Century Group were often strained, and the attempt to run a joint newsletter soon broke down. The groups also differed in their methods. The White Committee concentrated on overt publicity in the country at large, whereas the Century Group acted covertly and sought to rally elite opinion in Washington, D.C. These two modes of approach grew out of two very different understandings of the relationship between the President and American public opinion. One was Roosevelt's own view; the other, that of his more zealous colleagues.

White worked with the blessing of the President. As early as December 1939, FDR had asked for his help to "get the American people to think of conceivable consequences" without scaring them "into thinking that they are going to be dragged into this war."[24] Similarly, Roosevelt informed Douglas Fairbanks, Jr., that, although he longed to rally the country behind the Allies, no general could afford to march too far ahead of his troops. He could not risk being denounced as a warmonger. This approach proved its worth during the Senate confirmation hearings for Knox and Stimson. White arranged a deluge of telegrams in support of the nominees from the home states of key senators; then he watched the opposition melt. Awed, White confessed that he felt "like Frankenstein" and "a bit ashamed that one man should have such power."[25]

The Century Group saw Roosevelt not as a general but as a problem, and they actively sought to break his intransigence. During the Phoney War, certain interventionists had discovered that FDR was "susceptible" to "a combination of stories in the press and the coordinated persuasion of people close to him." By discreetly lobbying Eleanor Roosevelt and Harry Hopkins, they had persuaded Roosevelt to allow British evacuees into the United States. Now they prepared to lobby for large-scale aid and trusted that White could mobilize the press on his own. The combination of the two approaches proved highly effective.[26]

But the interventionists were not the only Americans bidding for the ear of the public. The pro-Allied forays drew a counterblast from the usual centers of isolationism, and isolationists also organized. The key development came when the lively nonintervention committee at Yale University attracted the attention of similarly inclined groups of Midwestern businessmen, who approached the chairman of the Yale group, R. Douglas Stuart, and asked if they might use his committee as the core of a national movement to match the White Committee. Stuart agreed and in September 1940 launched the America First Committee. America First swiftly became the heart of the noninterventionist cause, absorbing individual activists and smaller organizations such as the left-wing Keep American Out of War Congress. By April 1941, even "the lone-eagle," Lindbergh, had joined. Among isolationists, only the Communists and the neo-fascists remained outside the fold of America First. Their message was simple. Even the smallest American involvement would escalate into war. As Senator Burton K. Wheeler put it: "You can't put your shirt tail into a clothes wringer and pull it out suddenly when the wringer keeps turning."[27]

The German Embassy watched the growth of organized isolationism with interest. Unbeknown to most of the movement's adherents, the embassy secretly began to provide monetary support for it. Funds flowed, and the German Embassy established a camouflaged literary agent to commission suitable books and articles. German representatives bribed Republican and Democrat Congressmen alike to influence their Presidential conventions toward "no foreign war" platforms, and they continued to promote tired denunciations of British propaganda. But whether German or American, these denunciations offered no new evidence to support their case. Senators were still citing material published in 1937.[28] The lack of evidence did not mean that the British were idle. As Lothian put it in a letter of June 25, 1940: "It is a total misrepresentation to say that there is no British propaganda in the United States, if by that is meant that we allow the situation here to drift without doing anything about it."[29]

Lord Lothian's War: New Initiatives, May to August 1940

> There is now agreement on the principle that the time has come to adopt a more positive policy. There are obvious pitfalls in "propaganda" in America but I do not think anyone is blind to these.
>
> Lord Halifax, July 8, 1940[30]

The collapse of France brought a new focus to British propaganda in the United States. Lord Lothian led the way. Lothian introduced the revised ground rules for British publicity policy that summer, the foremost of these being that British propaganda should complement the work of America's own interventionists. He requested that all official statements on the war in France follow the needs of American opinion, and—after a secret exchange of communications with the White Committee at the end of May—he prevailed on Churchill to pledge that Britain would continue to fight Germany "whatever the issue of the battle in France."[31] Churchill obliged by pledging to "fight on the beaches." He was not always so cooperative.

In contrast to Lothian, Winston Churchill saw only limited value in propaganda. He felt that words were worth nothing without a determined display of resistance. When a War Cabinet colleague urged him to take twenty minutes off to speak to the American press, he angrily replied: "I am sure that only events will serve to turn opinion in the United States. We have a Minister of Information and I cannot consume my limited life and strength in the task you set before me."[32]

Churchill preferred to trust in the two great natural arguments on Britain's side, and he tended to forget that these would be enhanced by proper news coverage. The first argument was the United States' dependence on the Royal Navy, and the second was the intrinsic heroism of the Allied stand. The more heroic the stand, he argued, the greater the Allies' chance of winning American sympathy. Upon rejecting Mussolini's offer to mediate peace, he assured the French Premiere Reynaud that, if Britain and France maintained "stout hearts and confidence," they would strengthen their negotiating position and "draw the admiration and perhaps the material support of the U.S.A."[33]

After the fall of France, Churchill sharpened this argument. On June 20, he informed a secret session of the House of Commons that "nothing" would stir American opinion "like fighting in England" and that the "heroic struggle" offered "the best chance of bringing them in." If Britain could only hold off Hitler until Roosevelt had been reelected, he felt, "the whole English speaking world" would shortly "be in the line together."[34] Lothian refused to be deterred. He laid plans to outflank the isolationists by stressing that "machines not men are the Allies' primary need." The War Cabinet accordingly informed the British dominions that the government was considering this approach and hoped that "by depriving isolationists of their main argument . . . Congress would thus be able to move faster over measures designed to help us." The scheme alarmed the South African Prime Minister. General Smuts saw little reason to discourage full American belligerence at the moment when he believed it to be imminent. Churchill was also reluctant to foreswear an American declaration of war, and not until November 1940 did the British again contemplate a campaign in America based on limited requests for American aid. For the time being, they sent fresh requests for destroyers and waited.[35]

On June 26, Lothian went on the offensive, begging Churchill to broadcast against the "wave of pessimism passing over this country." The War Cabinet shared Lothian's concern and, on June 28, commissioned Lord Halifax to report on the "arrangements for propaganda in the United States." Unimpressed, Churchill grumbled over dinner that evening: "If we smash the Huns here we shall need no propaganda in the United States."[36] He gruffly informed Lothian:

> I don't think words count for much now. Too much attention should not be paid to the eddies of United States opinion. Only force of events can govern them. Up till April they were so sure the Allies would win that they did not think help necessary. Now they are so sure we shall lose that they do not think it possible. I feel good confidence that we can repel invasion and keep alive in the air. Anyhow, we are going to try.[37]

Thus Churchill turned his back on appeals to America and choose to rally his own country to a stand.

Churchill's attitude soon mellowed. On July 7, he urged the MoI to develop its American plans "with all speed."[38] But the initiative in Britain's U.S. propaganda policy remained with Lothian. The British Ambassador focused his work on the theme of sea power. America's dependence on the Royal Navy dominated his public speeches; meanwhile, in "constant private explanations in important and influential quarters," he hammered home the uncomfortable truth that it was "extremely unlikely that either Great Britain or the Dominions would ever hand over the fleet to a neutral America." These "important and influential quarters" included the Century Group. The resulting cooperative campaign vindicated the British policy of using Americans as their proxies in the United States.[39]

Lothian used Aubrey Morgan (whose mother-in-law was a key figure in the movement) as his link to the interventionists. Through Morgan, Lothian met the interventionist theologian Henry P. Van Dusen. Regular contact followed, as Van Dusen arranged a series of four Sunday broadcasts by leading British churchmen. Lothian also renewed his acquaintance with the pro-British writer John Balderston. Thereafter, the two regularly exchanged information to their mutual benefit.[40]

Once in contact, Lothian was able to feed authoritative data on Britain's defenses directly to the interventionists. On July 28, he supplied Whitney Shepardson with a detailed "Private and Confidential Memorandum on British Defense." It painted a bleak picture. Lothian noted that Britain had entered the war with 176 destroyers and that only 70 of these were still afloat. He requested 40 to 100 destroyers and 100 flying boats, and he asked that America's diplomatic status be shifted from neutrality to nonbelligerence, on grounds that this would encourage the British people. Lothian sent the same document to

Henry Luce to help him direct *Time*'s coverage of the crisis. He asked
that all figures be approximated when published, to conceal his hand in
the matter.[41] Through his embassy legal adviser, John Foster, Lothian
also leaked accounts of Churchill's appeals to FDR for aid. This strengthened the Century Group's perception of Roosevelt's intransigence. The
Century Group and sympathetic East Coast press soon began to hum
with energy in the British cause. The isolationists counterattacked in
vain. Bitterly frustrated, the German Embassy reported that "public
opinion is being systematically whipped into a state of panic."[42]

Lothian remained committed to the development of Britain's news
service in New York. His first priority was the immediate appointment
of a press officer for the BLI in New York:

> We can afford to lose no opportunity of reinforcing the present trend of
> opinion towards aiding the Allies as America's first line of defence. Such
> opportunities occur daily and we should be equipped to take every advan-
> tage of them and to cut off each Hydra-head of argument on the other
> side as it appears.

Lothian's attitude alarmed many in the Foreign Office, but it found a
natural echo in the new Minister of Information, Duff Cooper. On July
8, Halifax informed Churchill that they had considered British publicity in the United States and had agreed that "the time has come to
adopt a more positive policy."[43]

Duff Cooper believed in the need for British propaganda in the
United States. He was prepared to finance an expanded campaign, but
he also expected to play a major role in directing the policy. Within a
week of his appointment, he had launched his own bid for an active MoI
role in the United States. On May 14, Duff Cooper had laid his plans
before the Foreign Office. Building on Reith's scheme, he proposed "to
set up in New York a small office under the Ministry of Information, to
get in touch with American journalists and through other sources carry
out the [publicity] work." He suggested that the BLI might be used as
"cover." Halifax acknowledged the need for a new initiative, subject to
the agreement of Lord Lothian. Rumors of a new British initiative soon
abounded. On May 26, Murrow included a call for Britain to retain its
"No Propaganda" policy in his evening news report. Alarmed by this
broadcast, Lothian asked London to confirm that he would be consulted on any new policy.[44]

On June 18, 1940, Duff Cooper sent Lothian an outline of his plan
for a New York press office, with branches to be added eventually in
Chicago and in San Francisco. He insisted that the new office should
fall under his own jurisdiction. Lothian had serious reservations about
this plan. He feared that an MoI office would soon "get at cross purposes" with the British Embassy and the BLI and thus inadvertently
provide ammunition for the isolationists. Fortunately, Lothian was
able to head off the MoI with his own long-planned initiative.[45]

Even before Duff Cooper unveiled his proposals, Lothian had begun campaigning to expand British propaganda in the United States. In May, he dispatched Sir William Wiseman (a cornerstone of Anglo-American intelligence cooperation during World War I) to London to sound out Churchill and the Foreign Office on the matter. When Duff Cooper heard of this he saw his dreams of a propaganda empire in the New World slipping away. He promptly denounced Lothian's scheme as "underhand and indirect work"; planning thus ground to a halt, with the British Embassy and the MoI, respectively, "alarmed" and "gloomy" at the behavior of the other. Each believed that it alone knew how to manage British publicity in the United States.[46]

First blood was drawn by Duff Cooper. In July, he flexed his ministry's muscle and successfully blocked Lothian's nominations for "chief press officer" in New York and for a new U.S. press liaison job in London. In their place, Duff Cooper dipped into the pool of experienced staff left by the breakup of the large British propaganda operation in Paris and commissioned Stephen Lawford Childs (formerly the Paris Embassy's Press Counsellor) to oversee the founding of an MoI office in New York. He then dispatched Viscount Strathallan (who had served in covert propaganda in Paris) to survey opinion among the American elite.[47] The Information Minister's triumph was short-lived, however. Stephen Childs soon proved that, although he traveled under MoI orders, he remained a Foreign Office man at heart. On arriving in the United States, he made contact with Lord Lothian and promptly adopted the ambassador's vision of a British Embassy press agency in New York. It seemed logical, given that Lothian had a lifetime of experience in Anglo-American relations and was only a train ride away from New York. Duff Cooper may have paid Childs's passage, but he was 3,000 miles and five time zones away. Simply put, Lothian was right.[48]

Meanwhile Viscount Strathallan began his six-week mission to survey elite opinion. As the RAF took to the skies to beat back the Luftwaffe, Strathallan plunged into the whirl of the East Coast "Social Register set." He was ideally suited to his task. Through his well-born American wife, he had a wealth of connections. Although officially only an observer, he did not shy away from using the opportunity to correct American misconceptions. When, at a Long Island luncheon party given by Mrs. Pauline Davis, an elderly guest suggested that the Royal Navy had no need for U.S. support, Strathallan leaped forward to set the record straight. He unleashed a barrage of statistics on the true depth of Britain's peril. An argument ensued. After peace had been restored, Strathallan learned that he had just harangued the Chairman of the Senate Naval Committee. He immediately apologized for his manner but not his position. The senator pleaded ignorance. Evidently, in his eagerness to cultivate the interventionist lobbies, Lothian had neglected the Senate Naval Committee. Strathallan alerted the British

Embassy, and within twenty-four hours Lothian had rectified the oversight and telephoned his appreciation to the young peer.[49]

At the end of August, Strathallan returned to London to present his findings to Duff Cooper. He advised him that, although Britain should still entrust the burden of war publicity to American channels, recent events had altered the United States' understanding of both the war and British propaganda. The time was now ripe for a "positive information policy."[50] Stephen Childs brought back the same message. He argued:

> Dr. Goebbels is a successful propagandist not because of his talents and his temperament but because he controls the levers of a machine capable of influencing public opinion in almost every way that has so far been invented for doing this, even including the occasional use of verities . . . . If public opinion in the United States is to be influenced so as to bring about a marked acceptance of Allied needs for the insurance of victory, we must have machinery adapted to the various necessitates of a complex situation.

Rivalries aside, Britain's publicity structure in the United States clearly stood on the verge of a major transformation. London shed no tears over lost innocence, as Childs wrote: "In modern war it is surely the duty of even those belligerents who are hampered by moral scruples to neglect no weapon that may be of service, and nobody who has seen its effects in France and Germany can doubt any longer that propaganda can be made into an instrument of war second to none."[51]

If Churchill seemed reluctant to conduct propaganda himself, others were quick to claim his personal mandate to act. This was certainly true of two men who arrived in the United States during the summer of 1940. Both were destined to leave their mark on Britain's propaganda war in the United States. The first was the film director, Alexander Korda, bound for Hollywood and a leading role in pro-Allied film production. The second was a Canadian industrialist and World War I flying ace named William Stephenson, assigned to direct British Secret Intelligence Service operations in the Western Hemisphere. Their subsequent careers have become legendary to the point of serious distortion.

Korda arrived in Hollywood as the most important addition to the British cause there since Hitchcock stepped ashore in 1939. He had sound business reasons for leaving England. He needed to finish *The Thief of Baghdad*, and his wife, Merle Oberon, had signed a Hollywood studio contract. But Korda also traveled with the blessing of the British government. His family later claimed that he had received his "marching orders" from Churchill's own lips, but the facts of the matter remain unclear. Korda was certainly a great friend of the Prime Minister. He apparently worked with Churchill's private intelligence network and with the "Z" network of the British Secret Service during the 1930s. His arrival in Hollywood promised a solid output of film propaganda and, perhaps, a cover for British agents working in the United States. Whatever the extent of Korda's British Secret Service activities, Churchill certainly appreciated his efforts; and in 1942, he gave Korda a knighthood to prove it.[52]

The arrival of William Stephenson in the United States grew from the obvious need to protect Britain's American munitions purchases from enemy sabotage and from the inadequacy of the existing British intelligence apparatus in the United States. During the interwar years, the British Secret Intelligence Service (SIS) maintained a small office under the cover of the Passport Control Office (PCO) near New York's Battery Park and the British Consulate General. At the outbreak of war, the officer in charge was Captain Sir James Paget, a retired naval officer with an embarrassing record of notoriety with the U.S. Internal Revenue Service. The British avoided intelligence operations in America, leaving such things to the FBI, which they were officially obliged to consult only through the State Department. Although Paget worked informally with the FBI's Manhattan office, neither he nor this mode of operation was suitable for wartime.

Thus, in the spring of 1940, "C," the head of SIS (Major-General Sir Stewart Menzies), dispatched William Stephenson to investigate the possibility of direct contact with the FBI. Like Korda, Stephenson had worked for Churchill and the "Z" network, monitoring German rearmament. He also provided material for the Industrial Intelligence Centre of the Committee of Imperial Defence. Despite his part in a bungled attempt to block the export of Swedish iron ore to Germany in November 1939, his mid-Atlantic position as a Canadian with a rich variety of connections in the United States suited him to the task of serving as intermediary between London and Washington.[53] He did not disappoint his employers. He successfully established direct relations with J. Edgar Hoover and then, apparently with the help of the New York lawyer Ernest Cuneo, obtained Roosevelt's agreement that "there should be the closest possible marriage between the FBI and British Intelligence."[54]

Stephenson advanced with Churchill. By his own account, on the very day when Churchill came to power, the new Prime Minister personally charged him to return to America as the head of British intelligence in New York. Others have noted that the appointment of an agent from outside SIS did not appeal to "C," who initially rejected the plan. After bowing to Churchill's wishes, "C" selected a loyal SIS man as Stephenson's deputy. He should not have bothered. The officer he chose—Major Dick Ellis—later confessed to having sold secrets to both the Russians and the Germans. On the positive side, Ellis was well liked by the Americans, and he helped greatly in establishing America's own intelligence service. One official later recalled: "Ellis instructed me about registry, drops, everything . . . . We couldn't have gotten off the ground without Ellis." Dick Ellis thus achieved the unique distinction of having helped all four of the great intelligence agencies of the age.[55]

Stephenson's brief was vague. According to the official history, he had no formal job description but understood that he would "investigate enemy activities, organise public opinion in favour of aid to Britain." He did much more than this. His ultimate achievements lay in the links he established with the American government and in his role as "chief midwife" at the birth of the Office of Strategic Services.[56] His success in the propaganda field was of a lesser order but apparent nonetheless.

Stephenson arrived in New York on June 21,1940, and established his offices near to the BLI and BBC, on the thirty-sixth floor of Rockefeller Center, 630 Fifth Avenue. Once in place, he became a convenient processing agent for a whole range of British cloak-and-dagger departments. By December 1940, Stephenson represented the Security Division (London's anti-sabotage bureau), the Naval Intelligence Division, and the covert propaganda and "dirty tricks" section: the Special Operations Executive. He was also in touch with the British supply missions in Washington and their parent departments in London. His office was renamed—allegedly at the suggestion of J. Edgar Hoover himself—the British Security Co-ordination. BSC rejoiced in the new cable address INTREPID, New York; and although Stephenson's personal designation was the less glamourous number 48100, he was sufficiently synonymous with the office for colleagues to refer to him as "INTREPID." The name has stuck, but the practice is inaccurate. If all British officials in New York had been known by their cable addresses, Aubrey Morgan would have finished the war as "a man called DIGESTION."[57]

The mission bore immediate fruit. By his own account, Stephenson swiftly obtained some 1 million rifles and 30 million rounds of ammunition. One hundred Flying Fortresses and the Sperry bomb sight followed. Stephenson also began a close and enduring partnership with Roosevelt's new intelligence aide Colonel Bill Donovan (who had just returned from his inspection of Britain's defensive capacity). Donovan and Stephenson then began to lobby for the much-needed fifty destroyers.[58]

Stephenson was equally swift in entering the field of propaganda. He carefully fed American fear of a "Fifth Column" by providing Donovan and the journalist Edgar Ansel Mowrer with secret material on Nazi Fifth Column tactics that soon resurfaced in a series of articles in the *New York Herald Tribune* and a dramatic nationwide radio broadcast by Donovan.[59] Stephenson also exposed the German Embassy's attempts to break the U.S. oil embargo. He supplied the *Herald Tribune* with full details of the one-legged German Commercial Counsellor Dr. Gerhard Alois Westrick and his shady contacts with the U.S. oil industry. Soon, angry Americans were besieging Westrick's house. The

State Department politely asked him to leave the country. Britain's covert campaign to drag America into war was under way.[60]

Duff Cooper's War: New Initiatives in London, May to August 1940

The time has come . . .

Frank Darvall, MoI, July 1940[61]

Although Duff Cooper and Lord Lothian clashed over plans for propaganda in the United States, they were unanimous on the need to expand the MoI in London. Here Duff Cooper had free rein, and his staff rose to the challenge. On July 8, the American Division presented a plan for expansion, observing:

> The time has come to recognise that the American Division must henceforth discharge one of the most important functions of the Ministry. . . . The war has reached a stage when American opinion is of crucial importance; and there are at last real opportunities of influencing that opinion in a direction favourable to us.

The report called for reinforcing the American Division through eight new appointments and, more importantly, for establishing a clear objective for British publicity in the United States.[62] Even before this report had been considered, Duff Cooper had begun his own program of reform.

Duff Cooper understood the needs of the American press. He was, himself, a regular correspondent for the *New York Herald Tribune*. He knew all about deadlines and was not above rewarding friendly journalists by handing out the occasional scoop.[63] In order to attune his ministry to the needs of the American press, he recruited journalists to his staff. This represented a clear break with the Chatham House tradition and proved too progressive for Sir Frederick Whyte. But when Whyte complained, Duff Cooper sacked him. Basil Mathews and the newly appointed Denis Brogan then resigned in disgust.[64] In a letter to Lothian, Whyte philosophically mourned the Information Minister's overconfidence: "You may perhaps recognise in his action an indication that he is suffering from that complaint described by a witty American when he said that no Englishman ought ever to visit the United States for the first time."[65]

Lothian was generous in his reply. The ambassador noted that he "always felt a sense of security" knowing that Whyte headed American operations at the MoI. The loss of Whyte sharpened Lothian's concern that the MoI might become a loose cannon, and it fortified his determination to ensure that the British Embassy controlled all British propaganda within the United States.[66]

Whyte's place was taken by a journalist, Douglas Williams, who had covered the United States for the *Daily Telegraph* for most of the preceding decade. Williams continued the trend toward media professionals, appointing a writer named Charles Hargrove to replace Brogan and tapping the former BEF conducting officer and *Telegraph* journalist Roger Machell to fill Mathews's position, which was now openly described as entailing "propaganda through indirect channels." Machell became the fulcrum of press liaison activities. The reshuffle brought a well-deserved promotion to Gwyn Barker and released Frank Darvall to devote his energies to the deputy directorship of the American Division. Ever an expansionist, Darvall urged his new boss to think on a grand scale. Williams warmed to this and soon demanded that the American Division be "replanned and expanded so as to be more commensurate with the importance of America in the present situation." There was now little sign of the old restraint.[67]

Film also figured in Duff Cooper's campaign. In August 1940, he gave Michael Powell a blank check to make a large-budget propaganda feature aimed directly at the U.S. market. Powell planned a film to "scare the pants off the Americans and bring them into the war sooner." He found the perfect subject in reports of U-boats operating off the Canadian coast. With his producer Emeric Pressburger, Powell devised a script about a U-boat crew shipwrecked in Hudson's Bay and its attempts to escape across the undefended border into neutral America. With the blessing of the Canadian government, Powell and Pressburger began work on *Forty-Ninth Parallel*.

The script consisted of unrelenting propaganda. In it, the escaping Germans encounter a succession of Canadian innocents, including a French-Canadian trapper, a Canadian deserter, and a pacifist aesthete who has sought to avoid war by escaping into the wilderness with a tepee and paintings by Matisse and Picasso. Each of these individuals is bent on personal neutrality; and each is fated to realize the error of his ways on meeting the Nazis in the flesh. With Laurence Olivier as the trapper, Leslie Howard as the pacifist, and music by Ralph Vaughn Williams, the film promised to be a powerful piece of propaganda. Sadly, the production was dogged by problems. The female principal, Elizabeth Bergner, succeeded where the U-boat crew failed and skipped south of the border to begin a new life with her "enemy alien" husband. Such difficulties delayed the release of *Forty-Ninth Parallel* (retitled *The Invaders* for the United States) until after Pearl Harbor. But the film seemed no less apt for America at war; it carried off an Oscar for best screenplay of 1942.[68] But time had once again depleted Britain's film propaganda arsenal at the critical moment. Fortunately for Duff Cooper, less time was needed to inject the new spirit into British shortwave radio broadcasting.

Soon after taking office, Duff Cooper turned his attention to British broadcasts reaching the United States, pressing the BBC to reform the

Empire Service. He received help from an authoritative source. Ed Murrow privately endorsed a scheme to use Americans on the BBC. Significantly, he encouraged the BBC not to be deterred by the small shortwave audience in the United States. This audience, he wrote, was made up of "5,000 class people," and a campaign directed at them would have a snowball effect.[69] Experience confirmed Murrow's assessment. Once the BBC had established the quality of its overseas programming, domestic rebroadcasting followed naturally. Spurred by Duff Cooper and reassured by Murrow, the BBC thus abandoned the old notion of an Empire Service directed at Canada alone and launched a proper North American Service beamed at the entire continent. On the night of May 28, 1940, the broadcasts began.[70]

The new service met the question of propaganda head on. Its inaugural speaker Vernon Bartlett declared: "I am going to talk to you three times a week from a country that is fighting for its life. Inevitably I'm going to get called by that terrifying word 'propagandist.' But of course I'm a propagandist. Passionately I want my ideas—our ideas—of freedom and justice to survive."

The first casualty of the new service was the "BBC accent." At last Broadcasting House resolved to make greater use of the more neutral-accented broadcasters like Bartlett and Stephen King-Hall, and it even permitted the news to be read by a Canadian.[71] But of all the new accents on the air, by far the most significant was the broad West Yorkshire intonation of the playwright and essayist J. B. Priestley, heard regularly on the nightly talk series "Britain Speaks."

The content of Priestley's talks was even more revolutionary than their delivery. As in his Sunday evening postscripts for the BBC Home Service, Priestley painted a dynamic picture of a united Britain engaged in a People's War. He did not shirk from criticizing the old class-ridden England. His heroes were ordinary folk: the community that not only could repulse the Germans but also demanded radical social reform at home when the war was won. Priestley assured his listeners that he was not an official propagandist. He described himself as a mere BBC employee: "just as if I were a pianist or a singer." While his talks were his own affair, he could always count on the MoI for guidance.[72]

Following the Information Ministry line, Priestley avoided direct appeals for U.S. belligerence and sought rather to sharpen the picture of a dynamic Britain preparing to fight alone. He tuned his broadcasts to the American ear by avoiding unnecessary anglicisms; he spoke of streetcars and not trams. He made frequent allusions to the icons American political culture, and on July 4 claimed the very mantle of George Washington for Britain: "Our aim is the independence—of Europe and indeed the whole world from the nightmare of Nazi threats, murderous invasion and slavery."[73]

Priestley did not shy away from confrontation with Americans, Germans, or his own government. He condemned the Americans who left Britain for home as having abandoned their nation's own cause of "Freedom and Liberty"; "the American frontier," he proclaimed, "is the English Channel." He poured scorn on German propaganda and solemnly warned the United States of Hitler's designs on the Western Hemisphere. Unlike Churchill, he proved ready and willing to attack American criticism of the British blockade and to broach the vexing question of British war aims. He would remain a regular speaker on the North American service long after the Churchill government had taken exception to his criticism and brought his Home Service career to an abrupt halt. The BBC North American service had found its voice.[74]

Further innovation followed. On July 7, 1940 the BBC began "live entertainment programmes" on the North American Service. Though initially limited to a fifteen-minute musical slot, this programming was to consist, on the orders of the Deputy Controller of BBC Overseas Services, of "the best possible entertainment with an American appeal."[75] A typical broadcast evening in the summer of 1940, began at 1:30 A.M. London time (early evening on the East Coast of North America) with "Britain Speaks," a talk by Priestley or some other British personality. The news at 2:00 A.M. was followed by a commentary by a prominent British journalist. The final program, "Radio Newsreel," began at 3:30 A.M. "Radio Newsreel" effectively applied the lessons of the Phoney War, making full use of eyewitnesses to flesh out news stories. The formula worked so well that, with a rebroadcast over the U.S. Mutual network, "Radio Newsreel" soon became the flagship program of the North American Service. For John Grierson, "Radio Newsreel" was all that British propaganda ought to be. In August, he wrote:

> England should thank heaven for the BBC. That organization has, within the last few months, been gaining more and more respect with its overseas programmes. Its change of heart and character has been so widely remarked on that nothing in the field of information has created more general confidence in the growing spirit of England.[76]

The use of authentic British voices on the North American Service carried its own problems. Unlike such British speakers as Priestley or the London cabby and raconteur Herbert Hodge, many Britons were not "naturals" for the American airwaves. British voices still sounded effeminate to American ears, and the self-deprecating testimony of eyewitnesses proved peculiarly difficult to understand. The director of the North American Service later recalled: "We would get hold of some commando or paratrooper with a most desperate record, meet him in the studio, finding him an enormous athlete with a face like Victor McLaglen—and then over the microphone would come: 'Oh it's nothing much really,' in a little piping voice."[77] Repeated exposure taught Americans to understand both the accent and the message beneath the British understatement.

The new formula soon proved its worth. By early 1941, Murrow's prediction had been borne out. The volume of mail arriving at the BBC's New York office alone gave evidence of a total audience far in excess of 5,000—so much so that the BBC appealed to its listeners for restraint. Americans had learned that there was more to British broadcasting than cricket scores.[78]

That summer brought new champions to the cause of American publicity. At the Foreign Office News Department, which remained the chief source of news and day-to-day guidance, the new deputy-director, Sir William Ridsdale, became a particular hero of the American press corps. "Rids" brought a new and unfailing frankness to the morning briefings and afternoon consultations. He was respected, trusted, and liked by the Americans. In 1914 he had served as a war correspondent in France for the London *Daily News*, and he understood the needs of working journalists. The Americans were delighted when, in January 1941, he succeeded Charles Peake as director of the FO News Department. The department also acquired the services of the cartoonist, writer, and society wit Osbert Lanchaster, who, with his vast handlebar moustache and inexhaustible supply of bon mots, did much to brighten Bloomsbury press conferences until his departure at the end of 1940. In the MoI censorship section, Cyril Radcliffe seemed able to convince the Americans that material was only stopped for reasons of military security. He would patiently explain the logic of any particular decision challenged by a reporter, and he faithfully reversed overzealous decisions of any subordinate. In Whitehall, the War Office at last provided real help for Americans trying to cover the war, through its press liaison officers Brigadiers Jack Treadwell and Geoffrey Neville. Treadwell, an officer of the Scots Guards, had a particular regard for the Americans. He had an American wife, and later he settled in the United States and took a leading role in the ESU. Drew Middleton of AP found him able to swing entrées to the War Office at a moment's notice. Meanwhile, at the Ministry of Economic Warfare, the press officer David Bowes-Lyon charmed the Americans, which was no easy task considering that he had to explain such matters as the blockade. His popularity owed something to his family connections. King George's wife, Queen Elizabeth, was his sister; and favored correspondents were invited to take tea with her at Buckingham Palace.[79]

By August 1940, the machinery of British propaganda for the United States was alive and humming. The British now had to learn its limitations. Events would prove that it took more than a solid news story inspired by an honest briefing from "Rids" or a hearty radio chat from J. B. Priestley to convince the American people that Britain would survive—or to persuade the U.S. government to part with fifty overage destroyers.

The Battle of Britain and the Destroyer Deal

> It is hardly too much to say that the success or failure of our arms
> may depend on the response of the United States to our appeal.
> Roosevelt and his Administration are anxious to do all they can for
> us but the final say lies with a public opinion which though favour-
> able has not yet wakened up to the need for vigourous action on
> America's part, if she is not to run the risk of facing Germany alone.
> Lord Halifax, June 5, 1940[80]

British publicity during the summer of 1940 focused on two relatively
small groups of people—the U.S. press corps in London, and the interventionists in the United States—and on one relatively small objective:
fifty overage U.S. destroyers. For Sir Frederick Whyte, the successful
acquisition of these destroyers was the ultimate proof of the value of
Britain's publicity policy. For the Minister of Aircraft production, Max
Beaverbrook, the deal owed more to hard bargaining in the face of an
American talent for extortion.[81] Meanwhile, the RAF struggled to hold
the Luftwaffe at bay.

Britain's survival now hinged on this effort. The RAF had everything to prove. Just as many Americans had once overestimated Britain's naval strength, they now underestimated the RAF. If it lost
control of the skies of Southern England, fifty old destroyers could not
prevent an invasion. Nevertheless, the battle for aid continued.

In London, Duff Cooper struggled to throw the British war effort
open to American scrutiny. Whitehall remained obstructive. The Ministry of Home Security even attempted to prevent American journalists
from traveling around the country by car.[82] In the FO News Department, Ridsdale stressed the need to allow the Americans to see the RAF
at work:

> To see British planes getting back, but only just getting back because they
> have been battered and riddled by the enemy, would provide the material
> for an impressive picture of the drain on our resources. These American
> correspondents would know the delicacy of such a position; they would
> not worry weary pilots; they could provide invaluable evidence of our
> spirit and our needs. And they are straining at the leash to give this help,
> which lies within their power, for a cause for which they have intense
> sympathy.[83]

North Whitehead of the FO American Department was even more
blunt:

> we are only likely to win this war if we obtain the whole hearted cooper-
> ation of the United States. We shall not obtain this unless we demonstrate
> in a manner vivid and convincing to the Americans that we can not only
> resist but can also attack. The only way to make our power for offensive
> vivid to Americans is 1) to attack as often and as dramatically as possible,
> and 2) to let the Americans see us doing it through their own country-

men. This involves a constant appreciation of their own importance as political instruments on the part of the fighting services.[84]

Lord Halifax pressed Anthony Eden at the War Office and Archibald Sinclair at the Air Ministry to allow increased American coverage. They replied with a flurry of day trips to barracks and air bases, which produced "an almost embarrassingly large amount of first-rate stories." But stunts were not enough.[85]

The Americans in London felt that the British service ministries had misunderstood the nature of their needs. As the head of the American Correspondents Association in London wrote: "Americans do not want military secrets but human interest accounts of fighting, of crashed aircraft, valor of British Navy in evacuation and so forth, all of which awakens human sympathy."[86] The point was not lost on Lothian. He suggested that human interest might promote American confidence in the RAF. He suggested that "one or two real ace fighters" might visit the United States. He found his candidate in an American pilot named Billy Fiske.

William Fiske III was a 29-year-old pilot officer in an RAF fighter squadron based on the South Coast of England. The son of a leading New York banker, Fiske had followed his father into the trans-Atlantic business community as a partner in Dillon, Read and Company of New York. He had also become a champion tobogganist at St. Moritz. Later he married an Englishwoman, Rose Bingham (the ex-wife of the wayward actor-peer Lord Warwick), and on the eve of war he moved to England. In March 1940, he enlisted in the RAF volunteer reserve. In June the Ambassador requested that he be given leave to visit the United States and speak to "influential Senators, editors and others." The Air Ministry insisted that he see combat first. In July, Fiske was assigned to the 601 City of London Squadron. Combat experience followed swiftly.[87]

On August 13, Goering unleashed the full might of the Luftwaffe against the British Isles in an all-out bid to achieve the air superiority necessary to support an invasion. The Battle of Britain had begun in earnest. The concept of using the Americans in the RAF for propaganda gained momentum accordingly. On August 17, 1940, Sir Maurice Peterson, the MoI's head of overseas publicity, received a secret memo from the Foreign Office praising a rousing BBC broadcast by an American pilot and noting that "publicity of exploits of individual American pilots in our service, even if exaggerated, would have an excellent effect, and would give the hero-worshiping public of the United States a feeling of identity with the conflict; and that interviews, photographs and newsreel shorts etc. might also be followed up."[88] Thus, the British planned to fight Charles Lindbergh with a "lone eagle" of their own making. But the British government had no need to "exaggerate" the ability of Pilot Officer Billy Fiske. Sir Archibald Hope, then a flight lieutenant in his squadron, later recalled him as "unquestionably . . .

the best pilot I've ever known" and "a natural as a fighter pilot." By mid-August he had several enemy kills to his credit and was "hot favourite" to head a projected all-American RAF squadron. Fiske was tough, too. On August 17, he engaged a pack of homebound Junkers 87s, came off the worse, and, although wounded, successfully brought his damaged plane home. Despite serious burns to his wrists and ankles, by the afternoon he was sitting up in his hospital bed wisecracking with his squadron adjutant. As he began his convalescence, Fiske still had no idea that the British Ambassador had cast him as the next dinner guest on the Washington social round and the next hero of every American schoolboy. He never found out. Doctors ascribed his sudden death to post-operative shock. He had flown his last sortie on the very day when the Foreign Office finally endorsed a campaign based on an all-American RAF hero.[89]

Although the British made no attempt to find a replacement for Fiske, an awareness of the propaganda value of the "Yanks" in the RAF survived. When the theme reemerged its focus was not the individual pilots but an institution—the all-American 71 Eagle Squadron of the RAF, operational as of January 1941. In death, Fiske played a small part in the propaganda war. On July 4, 1941 Mutual and NBC broadcast a short service from St. Paul's Cathedral: the unveiling of a small memorial to "An American citizen who died that England might live." One in three of the RAF Eagles would follow him.[90]

The Battle of Britain clarified the British predicament in the United States. Suddenly, Britain's chances of survival could be expressed in a simple statistic: the ratio of the losses of the Luftwaffe to the losses of the RAF. Americans drew comfort from the early "lead" established by the RAF but remained aware of the marked disparities between British and German news reports. Churchill saw no need to answer American doubts by opening Air Ministry calculations to press scrutiny, arguing: "The important thing is to bring the German aircraft down and to win the battle, and the rate at which American correspondents and the American public are convinced that we are winning, stands in a much lower plane. They will find out quite soon enough when the German air attack is plainly shown to be repulsed."[91]

Lothian, in contrast, emphasized the need to establish the credibility of British figures. He knew that officials such as Ed Stettinius of the National Defense Commission in Washington had noted the discrepancy between the losses declared by Britain and their own U.S. Military Intelligence estimates. Lothian's alarm sparked Halifax to write directly to the Air Ministry. "Whatever you can do to give the American correspondents an inside view of your organisation and personnel," he argued, "may, I firmly believe, have the most important influence on the help we get from the United States in the near future." This time, the Air Ministry responded.[92]

In late August, the Air Minister arranged for American correspondents to visit two RAF fighter bases and witness at first hand the compilation of British and German losses. The Americans were impressed to note that the British counted only the "confirmed kills"— the German aircraft actually seen to have crashed in flames.[93] In this way, the British finally convinced the U.S. press corps in London of the accuracy of their figures. A swathe of articles attesting to the reliability of the figures followed. Although American polls continued to show a substantial level of public scepticism towards British communiqués, the British knew that the journalists were convinced, and so long as their audience accepted their analysis of Britain's prospects, public doubt about the raw figures had limited significance.[94] Soon, the Admiralty followed suit, providing the American press and government, for the first time, with reliable statistics on British shipping losses.[95] It now fell to the RAF to finish the job.

By late August 1940, the heroism of the RAF seemed Britain's greatest propaganda asset. The FO urged the Prime Minister to include a formal tribute to their gallantry in his next broadcast to the United States. Churchill did not need prompting to recognize the value of the RAF. The moment came on August 20, 1940, when in a major speech to the House of Commons reviewing the first year of the war, the Prime Minister said of the RAF: "Never in the field of human conflict has so much been owed by so many to so few." Churchill's rhetoric drew a mixed response from the "few" themselves; one flyer quipped; "I thought he was talking about our mess bill." The pilots' cynicism was warranted, inasmuch as words were of little service in the face of an oncoming Messerschmitt; but in the greater battle to present the British cause to the world a volley had found its mark.[96]

Churchill's August 20 speech contained more than praise for the pilots. The Prime Minister had also, at last, addressed the subject of the British blockade of Europe. Lord Lothian and the Foreign Office had both requested this, to counter the campaign headed by former U.S. President Herbert Hoover to allow relief supplies into occupied Europe. Churchill engaged Hoover directly. He noted that Germany denied the need for such aid, and he stressed that occupied Europe was well-stocked with food for the winter ahead. Other matters— including Britain's war aims—remained veiled in silence.[97]

Throughout the Battle of Britain, the MoI searched for fresh channels for American publicity. During August and September, MoI officials became excited by the prospect of using British children evacuated to the United States as just such a channel. The appeal of these innocents to the American public already seemed clear, and a drive to increase the number of British children allowed into the United States had already begun, under the leadership of the anglophile Chicago retail millionaire Marshall Field (who also happened to be related to

Ronald Tree). By late August, the arrival of each evacuee ship had become a British propaganda event in its own right.[98] The MoI planned to mobilize the evacuees by sending each one a bi-weekly newsletter on the progress of the war, in the hope that the newsletter would also be read by the evacuee's host family. To widen the letter's appeal, the MoI resolved to recruit A. A. Milne, author of *Winnie-the-Pooh* (and now eager to atone for his interwar pacifism) to write the copy, while E. H. Shepard, *Punch* cartoonist and illustrator of the Pooh books and of Kenneth Grahame's *The Wind in the Willows*, was to be invited to provide the art work. Ministry officials hoped that older evacuees might contribute their own articles, and they felt sure that, with proper supervision, the young propagandists could easily produce work of a literary standard "comparable with *Time*" magazine. With J. Walter Thompson engaged to manage the advertising, the MoI anticipated that the newsletter might in due course become self-financing. Stephen Childs added that the newsletter would require its own office in New York, and that this could serve as cover for wider British propaganda activities. British propagandists rubbed their hands at the cleverness of their latter-day amalgamation of the Trojan Horse with the Children's Crusade.[99]

Then it happened. On September 17, a U-boat sank the evacuation ship *City of Benares* en route to Canada. Sickened by the loss of young life and suspecting that exporting children compromised the picture of British resolve, Churchill ordered all overseas evacuations to be halted. The Cabinet Defence Committee agreed, and Marshall Field ended his campaign forthwith. For a few weeks, a window stood open to allow Milne, Shepard, and the evacuees themselves to play a part in rallying American opinion. The scheme held a peculiar potency, for the works of Shepard and Milne were as dear to the living children of the United States as they had once been to the dead children of the *Benares*. Now, however, that window had snapped shut.

Nonetheless, others recognized the value of Britain's youngest ambassadors. By October, the White Committee had launched its own evacuee newsletter. The most potent use of the evacuees came in a weekly Anglo-American radio show—*Children Calling Home*—carried on the BBC, NBC, and CBS. The program linked British parents with their distant offspring in the United States, just as Murrow had linked MacAdam with his children at Christmas 1939. The result, as one BBC executive later put it, was "a weekly tear compeller."[100]

The British made good use of the 1940 season of the New York World's Fair, adapting their exhibition of 1939 to carry a "more definite war flavour." Visitors to the British pavilion could now consult an on-the-spot inquiry desk of the BLI and visit an exhibition of art and artifacts illustrating Britain at war. The British cinema showed a solid diet of war documentaries and reportedly became "easily the most popular feature" at the Fair. When the British pavilion closed for good at the end of the 1940 season, it did so on a note of unprecedented triumph.[101]

For all the success of the British effort at the World's Fair, the most dramatic reminder of the conflict was not contrived by the British, but directed against them. At 3:15 on the holiday afternoon of July 4, an American employee of the British pavilion noticed an unattended suitcase in the fan room. He alerted the staff, who moved the case to a deserted lot behind the Polish building for examination by the New York Police Department bomb squad. At 5:20 p.m., the suitcase exploded. Detectives Joseph J. Lynch and Ferdinand A. Socha died instantly. Four of their colleagues were seriously wounded. Had the 20 pounds of explosives detonated where originally set, the pavilion's main roof supports would have been blown away like matchsticks. New York City Police Commissioner Lew Valentine estimated that the blast could have claimed over 1,000 lives. Police investigations were inconclusive, but with news of two previous bombs in New York and a discovered plot to blow up the Democratic Presidential Convention, public concern ran high. The British sent medals to the policemen and civilians involved. For the first time, World War II had scorched American soil.[102]

The British Council also did its best "to carry on" British "cultural propaganda, in spite of Mr. Hitler." They sent the British art displayed at the World's Fair on a tour of American cities that included such centers of isolationism as Chicago, Boston, and Toledo, Ohio.[103]

The MoI, for its part, mounted an impressive show at Manhattan's Museum of Modern Art. The exhibition included photographs of Britain at war; sketches of bomb damage and a battleship propeller; and works by Henry Moore. The show even boasted a poem by the American-born high priest of all things English, T. S. Eliot. This was not Eliot's first sally into trans-Atlantic propaganda; he had long supported "Books Across the Water," a small organization dedicated to developing an Anglo-American literary axis. Now, at the request of his friend at the MoI, E. McKnight Kauffer, he provided "Defense of the Islands"—a short piece of free verse presenting the war as a continuation of England's historic struggles, with England's fighting men "changing nothing of their ancestors' ways but the weapons" and stepping into the breach "in obedience to instructions." Although the poem was not particularly good or widely circulated, this same fusion of the war with Britain's past would blossom memorably into Eliot's 1943 clarion call of "Little Gidding": "History is now and England."[104] But as Lothian and the British negotiators in Washington were discovering, history and heroism could not be traded for destroyers.

The closing of the destroyer deal hinged on more than well-managed interventionist propaganda. Realizing that extraordinary aid could be obtained only through extraordinary concessions, Lothian proposed that Britain offer the United States long-term leases on naval bases in empire territory in exchange for the ships. The generosity of the British offer undoubtedly made it more attractive on Capitol Hill. Roosevelt was encouraged by the accumulating evidence of Britain's will to fight. Harry Hopkins later noted that the President was particularly impressed by the display of Nelsonian grit in Britain's destruction of much of the Vichy French fleet at Oran, Algeria. Roosevelt was always especially swayed by naval matters. By mid-August, he was willing and able to push for further aid for Britain.[105]

Negotiating from a position of strength, the Americans drove a hard bargain. Roosevelt insisted on assurances that the British Navy would not be allowed to fall into German hands. By August 15, Churchill had acceded to the terms, and final negotiations for a quid pro quo exchange of ninety-nine-year base leases for fifty overage destroyers began. Even so, at the conclusion of the agreement, many of Britain's auxiliary needs remained unmet.[106] Churchill broke the news of the agreement to the House on August 20, 1940, and gloried in the promise of cooperation to come:

> Undoubtedly this process means that these two great organisations of the English-speaking democracies, the British Empire and the United States, will have to be somewhat mixed up together in some of their affairs for mutual and general advantage. For my own part, looking out upon the future, I do not view the process with any misgivings. I could not stop it if I wished; no one can stop it. Like the Mississippi, it just keeps rolling along. Let it roll. Let it roll on full flood, inexorable, irresistible, benignant, to broader lands and better days.[107]

The BLI reported "unanimous enthusiasm" for the destroyer exchange and "a distinct but not yet developed tendency to endorse Churchill's declarations that the British Empire and United States interests are inexorably fused." Roosevelt formally announced the terms of the deal on September 3, 1940.[108]

The deal made excellent propaganda at home and abroad, particularly after the Admiralty decided to name the destroyers after towns common to both countries.[109] But it was many months before the destroyers were ready for active service; and in the meantime, Britain's needs remained dire. Moreover, as Arthur Purvis of the British purchasing commission in Washington now realized, there was little hope of further American aid that year.

The acquisition of bases strengthened Roosevelt's program of "hemisphere defense." This could be taken either as preparation for war or as strengthening of the ramparts for peace. In August 1940, FDR established the Office of the Coordinator of Inter-American Affairs under Nelson Rockefeller, with the implicit objective of heading off German commercial and political penetration in Latin America. American propaganda work followed.[110] FDR also introduced legislation that would allow him to call up the National Guard and to draft new recruits as necessary. On September 15, 1940, after a bumpy ride through the Congress, the Selective Service Act—the first peace-time conscription measure in American history—passed into law.

FDR had now pushed his mandate to the limit, and he knew it. Thus, as the danger of a German invasion of Britain approached its peak, evidence of American support for Britain appeared to level off. In the great Wilsonian tradition, Roosevelt dusted off his "No foreign wars" alter ego to fight the election. Ironically, the cooling of Roosevelt's ardor to aid Britain coincided with a new burst of isolationist reaction against his earlier beneficence. Roused and ready, the isolationists had returned to the offensive.[111] On September 5, one day after the signing of the destroyer deal, America First stepped onto the national stage. Unbeknown to the British Embassy, the British also faced attack from an unexpected quarter. If Lothian hoped to offset America First with British propaganda, certain State Department officials had other ideas. As far as the Assistant Secretary of State for Latin American Affairs, Adolf A. Berle, was concerned, the days of British propaganda in American were numbered.

It all began on the eve of the fall of France. President Roosevelt, worried by the activities of the German Library of Information, asked Berle to investigate.[112] As Berle's staff searched for an excuse to close the library, they hit against an obvious problem: the Germans had 162 registered agents, of whom 34 worked in propaganda; but the British fielded 247 registered agents, 132 of whom were certified propagandists.[113] It would be difficult to justify restricting one operation without touching the other. The office formulated a simple solution: "close up all of the existing foreign propaganda offices."[114] In the days of Assistant Secretary of State Messersmith, the initiative would have come to nothing, but he had been transferred to Havana. Berle seized on the idea of a complete ban, writing: "I see no reason why we should allow any of this. British, German or other."[115]

While many of Berle's subordinates regretted the perceived need to close the BLI, Berle did not. He was an American liberal. He had served as a New Deal brain truster; he had championed the cause of the poor, worked to better the lot of the American Indians, and attempted to build links with the Latin American republics. Unfortunately, his dislikes were no less heartfelt. He loathed big business, European wars, and unpaid war debts. By some accounts, he hated Jews; by all accounts, he detested the British.[116] Berle delighted in twisting the lion's tail. One of his diary entries read:

> To the British Embassy to dinner—dull. The wife of the Naval Attaché was presiding . . . and she persisted in talking about "out here"—the typical Country Englishman's method of referring to the United States as though it were a place much like Egypt. I finally got irritated and said emphatically, six times that when I was "out in London" I noticed there were

some odd things, and finally the truth began to dawn and then I said, quite bluntly, that you should not say "out here" when you were in an American capital. Generally speaking, I made myself disagreeable through the dinner.[117]

The British Embassy knew that Berle was no friend, and it usually blamed him for any adverse turn of State Department policy. He was the only senior State Department official who still believed that Britain intended to work mischief with its propaganda machine. He did his best to shape policy accordingly.[118]

On August 28, 1940, Berle asked Secretary of State Hull for authority to lay the question of "liquidating" the two foreign libraries before their respective embassies. He assured Hull that the free flow of news from Britain made the BLI redundant; the sacrifice was necessary to clear the way for a seemingly even-handed removal of the dangerous German operation. Hull agreed and sent the Attorney General a copy of Berle's "draft bill to make unlawful the distribution or publication of matter of a political nature by agents of foreign governments in this country." He also commissioned a report on all foreign propaganda activity. A legislative time bomb had begun to tick.[119] But the British had more tangible problems. On September 7, the Nazis began their Blitz on London.

4

"London Can Take It": British Propaganda and the Blitz, September to December 1940

> A bomb has its limitations; it can only destroy buildings and kill people. It cannot kill the unconquerable courage and spirit of the people of London. London can take it.
>
> Quentin Reynolds, October 1940[1]

On the afternoon of September 7, 1940, approximately 200 German bombers took off from airfields in Belgium and Northern France. They assumed formation over the English Channel and set course for London. That night, and for the fifty-seven nights that followed, the Luftwaffe pounded the capital without mercy. Many German bombs found their mark. The Surrey Docks erupted into flames, drawing the raiders to London's densely populated East End. Firemen struggled to contain the blaze, but it seemed to them that "the whole bloody world" was on fire. The scale of the attack carried an obvious message. The War Cabinet issued the "invasion imminent" signal and then waited. But the invasion never came, and London held firm. On September 10, London hit back. As the Germans approached, searchlights swept across the darkness, and anti-aircraft batteries began to fire. Londoners heard this noise—their noise—and took heart. But the raids continued unabated, by night and day. It was going to be a long campaign.[2]

London had long feared the German bombardment, but Churchill had come to attach considerable hopes to the attack. He believed that the bombing of British cities could bring the United States into the war. Roosevelt had said as much to the King in 1939. By mid-August 1940, however, the Prime Minister's anticipation had bubbled over into impatience. Charles de Gaulle caught him cursing the Germans for staying away. Churchill explained that "the bombing of Oxford,

Coventry and Canterbury, will cause such a wave of indignation in the United States that they'll come into the war!"[3]

In the event, Churchill was to be disappointed. Rather than rallying American opinion, the German bombs merely threatened the confidence won during the Battle of Britain. The failure of the Allied assault on Dakar deepened the pessimism of observers such as Ambassador Joseph Kennedy. Moreover, as dollar reserves dwindled, Britain faced the limit of its war purchases. Churchill grew increasingly angry at American attempts to wring further concessions from the British Treasury. He instructed his negotiators to adopt a "stiffer attitude" and refused to send technical data as a "sweetener" for further aid. But Britain's bargaining position was unenviable.[4] The War Cabinet now acknowledged that the war could not be won without full American belligerence.[5]

In reality, the strategic situation was not quite as dire as Britain imagined. In turning against London, Germany had missed its chance to wipe out the RAF fighter command. As a result, the RAF still barred the way to an invasion; and on September 17, Hitler postponed Operation Sealion indefinitely.

The Battle of Britain had been won. Hitler decided to bomb Britain into irrelevance and seek his total victory elsewhere. On September 28, 1940 he gave orders to prepare for war with the Soviet Union.[6] Meanwhile, diplomatic developments offered a fresh basis for hope of American intervention. On September 27, Japan signed the Axis Pact, which included, Churchill noted gleefully, several clauses "aimed plumb at the United States." Now Roosevelt would be forced to clarify his policy in Asia. The pact gave Britain a vested interest in escalating U.S.–Japanese tension. Churchill immediately stopped appeasing Japan, reopened the Burma Road (which had been closed on July 18) on October 18, and renewed aid to Chiang Kai-Shek. He warned FDR that this could provoke a Japanese declaration of war and suggested that the U.S. Navy pay a courtesy call on Singapore. The Americans declined but welcomed the offer of full use of the Singapore naval base in wartime. Thus, at the very moment when Churchill had abandoned his hope that the bombing of London would bring America into the war, he acquired a new scenario for American belligerence. The timing rested with Tokyo; but for the moment, Tokyo preferred to wait. Meanwhile Britain fought on alone and prayed that this spectacle might still stir America.[7]

The Blitz on London shifted the burden of the war onto the civilian population. This created new publicity needs. The Blitz was a human story and required a sympathetic human eye to capture it. Britain's need for its resident American journalists had never been greater. The working relationships between the Americans and British propagandists became a key factor in securing aid and hence in ensuring

Britain's survival. Fortunately, Murrow and his colleagues stood ready to rise to the challenge.

The Overture: Preparing for the Blitz

> They can take what is coming . . . .
>
> Ed Murrow, August 18, 1940[8]

The American coverage of the Blitz did not materialize overnight. Its practices were well tried and its themes were in place long before the bombs began to fall. Neither the themes nor the practices of the Blitz can be separated by national origin. The British and the Americans shared a common pool of ideas that summer, and the interpretations of each influenced the other in a spiral of cooperation and shared metaphors that would culminate in their coverage of the autumn's epic siege.

By the early summer of 1940, the idea of national and social regeneration had become fundamental to some British and most American commentaries on the war. The American correspondents seemed to accept that Britain had cast off its old ways and was now fighting a "People's War."[9] The war news itself supported this. Little holiday steamers had plucked the British Army from French beaches; old men had rallied to form the Home Guard; and all across the country, the ordinary folk of England were moving into the front lines. The common experience of suffering and endurance during the Blitz confirmed this. The associated notion of national regeneration provided a persuasive framework for understanding this experience. It gave a positive shape to events that might otherwise have seemed unbearable. As the second Fire of London raged, it seemed natural for "purgatorial fire" to be the dominant metaphor in both British literature and American reportage. The formula of national death and glorious resurrection promised much for the British cause in America. It side-stepped doubts over the historical unworthiness of Britain. Britain no longer needed to deny its heritage of imperialism, debt defaulting, and appeasement. Now, it could point to the ongoing example of London under fire and cry: "That was then; this is now."

The theme of regeneration had an obvious appeal to the British left, but it also figured in the rhetoric of dyed-in-the-wool Tories like John Wheeler-Bennett. Wheeler-Bennett's extemporaneous speech at the University of Virginia on June 17, 1940, stands as a fine example of this "resurrection" model for presenting the Blitz. He spoke directly to the hope of a new Britain arising from the ruins of the old, and illustrated his point with Milton's vision of England at the height of its Civil War:

> not degenerated or drooping to a final decay, but casting off the old and wrinkled skin of corruption, to outlive these pangs and wax young again,

entering into the truth of prosperous virtue, destined to become great and honourable in these later ages. Methinks I see in my mind a noble and puissant nation rousing herself like a strong man after sleep and shaking her invincible locks.

Wheeler-Bennett claimed these words for Britain. "I am confident," he declared "that Britain will survive and that this spirit, deepened and purified by the struggle, will outlast the war, be the result defeat or victory!"[10] Three months later Churchill cast the Blitz in similar terms:

> What he [Hitler] has done is to kindle a fire in British hearts, here and all over the world, which will glow long after all traces of the conflagration which he caused have been removed. He has lighted a fire which will burn with a steady consuming flame until the last vestiges of Nazi tyranny have been burnt out of Europe, and until the Old World—and the New—can join hands to rebuild the temples of man's freedom and man's honour, upon foundations which will not soon or easily be overthrown.[11]

The Americans absorbed these themes to varying extents. Writing in the United States, Dorothy Thompson latched onto the vision of the historic, noble England of the past, reborn and facing the trial of the present. By the end of September 1940, she developed her ideas in a three-part essay entitled "The Example of England." Dunkirk, she claimed, had been the moment of death and resurrection, when "one Britain lost the war" and "another Britain was born." The evacuation had been a miracle of Biblical proportions, conducted by civilians "from every village and hamlet on the coast of England," and it heralded a greater rebirth:

> A nation belongs to the people who will die to save it. At Dunkerque was demonstrated that the little men of England would die to save it. Great Britain has not belonged to the people. That beautiful hierarchy of title and wealth and commoners was a political democracy but no social democracy. But Dunkerque is almost an allegory for a strange sort of social revolution.

Thompson's interpretation of the Blitz hinged on this concept of social revolution; everywhere, she reported signs of the People's War.[12] A visit to Britain in the summer of 1941 more than confirmed the interpretation she had formed in New York: "What I saw," she wrote, "was so beautiful, so noble that I shall never doubt again. I have come back reborn, because I have seen a reborn nation."[13] At the other end of the scale, Murrow was more circumspect. He told his listeners in August 1940 that "Britain is still ruled by a class." But he believed nonetheless that the people of Britain would hold together. Observation suggested as much.[14]

Well before the Blitz, the American correspondents had decided that Britain would be able to stand up to the bombs. In the spring of 1939, *March of Time* had found signs reading "Bomb proof" amid the begonias of suburban London. Now their faith in popular bravado could be measured against actual reactions to German bomb damage. Murrow watched public response to the first attacks and predicted that the British could "take what is coming to them." He promised America that "the defense of Britain will be something of which men will speak with awe and admiration so long as the English language survives."[15]

As Murrow whetted American appetites with CBS coverage of the defense of Britain, he was working with the BBC to ease restrictions on his broadcasts. There were now few conflicts. The regulations had softened; and as Britain's need deepened, the Americans seemed increasingly tolerant of the remaining regulations. As Eric Sevareid put it, the secret to good press relations in London was simple: "Most American correspondents were prejudiced; we wanted Hitler to lose."[16] By September 1940, most of them explicitly wanted Britain to triumph. With the conjunction of British need and American sympathy, it was only a matter of time before the Americans were allowed access to bomb sites and freedom to broadcast live commentaries on the Blitz. But Whitehall being Whitehall, the new heights of Anglo-American cooperation were reached via a tortuous trail of memoranda.

By the late summer of 1940, Murrow's British allies were on the offensive. Roger Eckersley (now the BBC's chief censor) declared that the cultivation of American broadcasters represented "the finest form of propaganda of which we can avail ourselves."[17] Angered by inflexible regulations, Eckersley asked that the Americans be given access to the wrecks of downed German planes and the scenes of air-raid damage. He stressed the unique potential of radio for "impinging on American consciousness what air raids really mean." After Eckersley made a direct appeal to the Home Secretary, Whitehall agreed to allow the broadcasters access to all bomb damage other than that of military significance.[18] The Foreign Office obtained similar privileges for the staff of the American Embassy. All British officials now accepted that, whatever the scale of the damage, it was better not to leave matters to the American imagination.[19]

At the very moment when Britain opened its civilian war damage to American scrutiny, the radio networks acquired the manpower for detailed coverage of British affairs. With the influx of correspondents formerly attached to the Allied armies in France, the networks suddenly had a surfeit of battle-hardened broadcasters on their hands. CBS celebrated this concentration of talent by posting its crack commentators—including Vincent Sheean, Larry Lesueur, and Eric Sevareid—at strategic points around the British coast and broadcasting a "round Britain hook-up" on the evening of July 21, 1940. The BBC reported that the program convincingly countered German claims and scored an "outstanding success with the American public."[20]

As the summer wore on, Ministry of Information officials did their best to help the Americans in any way they could. Sometimes this help was personal; Janet Murrow spent much of the summer of 1940 living in the country as a guest of Mrs. Frank Darvall.[21] But all sides knew what was really needed. The Americans still longed for spontaneous running commentaries on raids, but rather than challenging the British ruling against such coverage, they turned to a softer target: their own codes of practice. In August 1940, NBC and CBS declared an interest in broadcasting from recordings. The MoI and BBC immediately arranged for them to record dogfights over Dover. On the first attempt, the Germans stayed away, leaving Murrow, Bate, and Mann standing atop Shakespeare Cliffs with nothing to talk about. When the Germans actually did turn up, the results were hardly spectacular. An engineer forgot to turn up the volume on the recording equipment, and the playback sounded like nothing more than a succession of inoffensive pops.[22]

The BBC scored the first success for itself. The Home and North American Services carried a blow-by-blow account of an air battle over the Channel, delivered by Charles Gardner with all the gusto of a sportscaster doing play-by-play: "Someone's hit a German and he's coming down in a long streak, coming down completely out of control, a long streak of smoke . . . . He's going flat into the sea . . . there he goes! SMA-A-A-ASH!"[23]

CBS soon matched this. Inspired by the success of its "round-Britain hook-up," the network planned a sound montage of London for the night of August 24, with British, Canadian, and American broadcasters speaking live from locations across the capital. The result, "London After Dark," was a triumph. As Murrow opened, live from Trafalgar Square, the air-raid siren sounded. Radios across the United States hummed with an unscripted eloquence to which the censors could not object. Murrow simply held out his microphone and caught the banging doors and hurrying footsteps of a city moving for shelter "like ghosts shod with steel shoes." The censor turned a deaf ear as Murrow ad-libbed around his planned talk. It was the sound of war, live, and as Eric Sevareid recalled, it "chilled the spine of America."[24]

The success of "London After Dark" fueled pressure for a final reform of procedure in London. On August 28, 1940, Darvall reported that the Americans were "anxious" for permission to "broadcast an eye-witness account of an air raid in progress, done, say, from the roof of Broadcasting House." He assured the BBC that the broadcasters could be relied on to respect security and "taste." Darvall and Eckersley agreed to request special uncensored broadcasting privileges for one representative of each chain. Whitehall wavered, but only to the extent of allowing Murrow to record a series of practice commentaries. After six nights spent cutting disks on the roof of Broadcasting House, Murrow convinced Whitehall that he could be trusted. On September 19, 1940, Walter Monckton, director general of the MoI finally granted permission for an unscripted broadcast.[25] With the themes and broadcasting procedures ready, the news from Britain would now have the greatest possible impact. The British could only hope that, when Murrow took to the roof, the Germans would oblige with an attack.

"This Is London": *The Co-projection of the Blitz on Britain*

> I am a neutral reporter. I have watched the people of London live and die . . . . I can assure you there is no panic, no fear, no despair in London town.
>
> Quentin Reynolds, October 1940[26]

On the night of September 21, 1940, Ed Murrow stepped out onto the roof of Broadcasting House and prepared to deliver a live commentary on an air raid. German bombers droned overhead. Anti-aircraft fire leaped skyward from batteries nearby. The circuit snapped into life, but as Murrow began to speak the raiders rumbled out of earshot. The effect was no less dramatic:

> I'm standing on a rooftop looking out over London. At the moment everything is quiet. For reasons of national as well as personal security, I'm unable to tell you the exact location from which I'm speaking. Off to my left, far away in the distance, I can see just that faint red angry snap of anti-aircraft bursts against the steel-blue sky . . . . The lights are swinging over in this general direction now. You'll hear two explosions. There they are! That was the explosion, not overhead, not the guns themselves. I should think in a few minutes there may be a bit of shrapnel around here . . . .

The next morning the American press proclaimed: "Murrow ducks bombs in London." The American people sat up and listened.[27] The weeks of broadcasting that followed would bring some tension between the MoI and the Americans; but for the most part, the depiction of the Blitz became a truly cooperative effort. This was the co-projection of Britain at war.

The Blitz brought fresh irritants in ministry procedure. No one liked the MoI's practice of identifying bomb sites only as "a well loved church" or "a Georgian terrace." But the American correspondents soon accepted this institutional vagueness. They knew that Britain would tell the worst when necessary.[28] The British soon learned how to manipulate specific instances of bomb damage. The bombing of Buckingham Palace on September 13, 1940, enabled the MoI to call in the capital from the royal visit to North America. Churchill ordered maximum publicity. The MoI News Division arranged for journalists to inspect the damage and promote the theme of the "King with his People in the front line together." Stirred by the blind democracy of the bombs, American indignation flared on the King's behalf.[29] On a larger scale, Churchill also demanded extensive publicity for the devastating raid on Coventry on November 15, 1940. He later informed the War

Cabinet that "the effect had been considerable . . . in the United States."[30]

Meanwhile, Murrow and the BBC had reached a final accord over broadcasting procedure. Murrow conceded that he would always be required to speak under the censor's cut-out button.[31] He now knew the limits of British lenience, and the relationship between the government and the Americans was free to develop within these limits. Eckersley and Darvall busied themselves arranging trips to visit Bow Street Police Court, to accompany a night river patrol, and to witness the arrival of a convoy in Liverpool. Murrow asked them to send a CBS correspondent to Iceland as "a couple of talks from the one area successfully invaded by Britain would have a salubrious effect on our audience." The MoI arranged a passage for Lesueur.[32] But the days of taking Americans to the war had passed. Now the war came to them.

The personal involvement of the American broadcasters in the Blitz became central to their coverage. They sympathized with Londoners under fire because they had become Londoners under fire. In the spring of 1939, MoI planners had fought to ensure that London remained the center of American coverage of the European war. Now the value of the American presence became clear. As weeks of bombing dragged into months, the American journalists came to think like Londoners. They developed the same instincts—dodging into doorways on an impulse, moments before a bomb blast. They learned the same fatalism; Murrow became contemptuous of the dangers and earned a shrapnel dent on his tin helmet to prove it. They took their turn in rooftop fire-watches; on the nights when he wasn't working late at the UP office, Wallace Carroll became adept at dousing incendiary bombs with sand. Like the poor Londoners, they drew deep satisfaction from the roar of British anti-aircraft guns. Like wealthy Londoners they also leaned on more tangible crutches—not least the well-stocked bar at the Savoy. In recognition of this, Douglas Williams moved the MoI's nightly press briefings to the Savoy, which he duly delivered, cocktail in hand, clad in a Noël Coward–style dressing gown. As Drew Middleton recalled, the American press corps agreed with Osbert Lanchaster that it was the crowning mercy of the war that the shortage of liquor did not coincide with the Blitz.[33]

The Americans shared London's burden of loss. When bombs flattened the Devonshire Arms near Broadcasting House, everyone lost friends. CBS lost its offices, and Lesueur was bombed out of his apartment and forced to move in with the Murrows. Then, in early November 1940, Broadcasting House sustained a direct hit. Fred Bate of NBC caught the blast in the middle of Langham Place. A Canadian colleague found him struggling to get into Broadcasting House to deliver his address to America as usual. His ankle tendons were severed, and one ear hung loose. Bate was promptly shipped back to America. The blast wrecked their studio, but the BBC technicians immediately returned to work amid tangled cables and floodwaters rising from a fractured main. Somehow an engineer nursed the equipment back to life in time for Mildred Boutwood to speak in Bate's place. She did not mention the bomb. She had no desire to act as a spotter for the Luftwaffe.[34]

All of this gave the broadcasters' work an emotional edge. When, in the late autumn of 1940, Eric Sevareid made his final broadcast from London, his voice audibly wavered as he said: "When this is all over, in the days to come, men will speak of this war and they will say: I was a soldier or I was a sailor, or I was a pilot; and others will say with equal pride: I was a citizen of London."[35] Sevareid and his colleagues had earned the same honor.

American sympathy for the British cause brought a measure of self-censorship, most obviously in coverage of government shelter policy. The rich had disproportionate access to shelters. The East End was particularly badly served; and to make matters worse, the government had closed the underground railway stations, fearing that a "deep shelter mentality" might otherwise prevent London from "carrying on." This story was not suppressed by the British government and was well-known to the Americans; indeed, its most famous incident occurred under their very noses. On the evening of September 15, a smartly dressed Englishman walked into the lobby of the Savoy and asked if he might inspect the air-raid shelter on behalf of an American businessman who wished to stay at the Savoy. As the maître d' showed him into the basement, he opened a side door onto the Embankment. In poured some eighty East Enders of all ages and two dogs. The man was Phil Piratin, a Communist counsellor from Stepney who had fought the Black Shirts in his streets and the fascists in Spain; now he was commandeering shelter space for the ordinary people of London. As the sirens sounded, Piratin explained his case. The police could do nothing. The newcomers had a legal right to shelter for the duration of the raid, so they ordered tea (for which they insisted on paying only the East End price) and settled in for the night. At dawn the all-clear sounded; and the protesters left as swiftly as they came, leaving their sheltermates nonplussed.[36]

This incident challenged the assumptions of American coverage of the Blitz. But instead of addressing it, the news agencies reported the usual story. AP led with St. Paul's Cathedral "saved from a ½ ton time bomb," UP reported "Nazis crash into London Streets: Crowds dance and cheer RAF on," and even the *Chicago Tribune* mentioned only the RAF successes.[37] Yet numerous American correspondents saw the affair; many lived at the Savoy and few ventured out at night. The AP correspondent Drew Middleton recalled the incident in his memoirs. Quite simply, this and other incidents did not fit with the

American press corps' understanding of Britain's war experience. Moreover, no one wished to feed ammunition to Britain's enemies. Murrow did deal with the broader shelter issue, but only James Reston of the *New York Times* covered the story in depth. His account was framed by the British government's plan to house the homeless in "empty West End apartments," but he acknowledged the legitimacy of the Communist case. Faced with similar dispatches in the now markedly less deferential British press, the War Cabinet took notice.[38]

On the afternoon of Tuesday, September 17, Piratin and his comrades broke open the Goodge Street underground station and marshaled the crowds to safety. But the War Cabinet had already resolved to open the underground stations. With this move, the embarrassment of the Savoy incident melted into a new wartime image as potent as a Spitfire or as the little ships of Dunkirk: the world-turned-upside-down picture of Londoners living underground. Now that the shelter policy matched America's image, it received particular attention. Although only 4 percent of the city's population sought refuge on the underground, this aspect of life during the Blitz dominated America's picture of British civil defense. The underground became an integral part of the correspondents's own war experience. Lesueur visited his local station so frequently that he came to recognize the individual shelterers by sight—the same families in the same spot, night after night. Six months into the Blitz, he realized that the children camped under the Cadbury's machine had grown visibly since he first saw them in September. Even on a railway platform, life went on.[39]

The British publicity structure maintained a steady flow of propaganda throughout the Blitz. On the BBC North American Service, Priestley provided stirring descriptions of London "carrying on," but he was swift to rebuke the American headlines describing London as "hell on earth." London, he averred, was not a "hell on earth"; he had seen action on the Somme in World War I and knew the difference.[40] Meanwhile, "Radio Newsreel" brought ordinary Londoners to the microphone. In one program, three small East End boys described being buried alive under bomb debris; another program carried an account of a bombing raid over Berlin. But the real strength of British propaganda now lay not in individual programs but in the way in which the campaign merged seamlessly with America's own news activity. Radio coverage of the Blitz was an Anglo-American co-production. The BBC and CBS teamed up to produce a new feature, "London Carries On," and to bring the sounds of Britain at war into American homes. It became impossible to say where CBS or NBC productions began and the BBC or MoI work stopped.[41]

The hidden hand of the MoI was also present in the field of war photography. The MoI's newly strengthened Photographic Section fed the news-hungry magazines of America a steady stream of images of the Blitz, including Bill Brandt's unforgettable studies of London shelter life.[42] In the summer of 1940, the MoI hired Cecil Beaton—America's favorite British society photographer—to assist in this effort. Beaton became the ministry's most prolific photographer, taking 10,000 pictures during the course of the war. His pictures of cheery pilots, smoldering monuments, and humming factories took America's news magazines by storm. Two pictures proved particularly powerful. The first showed a three-year-old child, Ellen Dunne, who had been wounded by a shrapnel splinter, clutching her teddy bear in a hospital bed. "Her face," Beaton wrote, "so babylike, had suddenly grown old and pale"; she looked at the camera "in a trance of trustful misery." The MoI soon put this simple image to work. On September 23, 1940, it appeared on the cover of *Life* magazine, and it soon became a poster for the White Committee. The second photograph, taken in December, was a portrait of the Prime Minister seated in the Cabinet Rooms at 10 Downing Street, glowering into the camera, "like a bull dog guarding its kennel."[43]

The Information Ministry also worked to bring film of the war to American screens. The spirit of cooperation with Americans reached its apogee in the work of the MoI Crown Film Unit, culminating in the most famous British documentary of life during the Blitz, *London Can Take It*, made in October 1940. From conception to distribution, this film was Anglo-American. The MoI Films Division conceived the film specifically to move America. The division wanted British authorship to be unobtrusive and decided that an American should provide the commentary. Sidney Bernstein duly recruited the veteran correspondent Quentin Reynolds of *Collier's Weekly*. The film's directors, Harry Watt and Humphrey Jennings, were initially unimpressed by Reynolds. He refused to leave the basement of the Savoy to report on night raids and, moreover, had a booming voice and no microphone experience. The MoI team overcame these problems by bringing their microphone to the Savoy bar, all but sticking it down his throat, and making him whisper the commentary. Reynolds repaid them by delivering an electrifying commentary and thinking up the title. Watt and Jennings then assembled suitable pictures of the Blitz from Movitone newsreels.[44] The result was the first really useful MoI film contribution to the propaganda effort in America.

London Can Take It opens with a night raid on the capital. In a grave, urgent whisper, Reynolds notes: "These are not Hollywood sound effects. This is the music they play every night in London." The film then shows the scene the next morning, as Londoners pick their way to work through the ruins. The film appropriates all the stock themes of the Blitz: the People's War, the King and Queen, and damaged monuments of the English-speaking world. One shot shows a statue of Richard the Lionheart, his sword raised, defiant, in front of a bomb-damaged House of Commons. Audiences could hardly mistake the film's message: the people of London "would rather stand and face death than kneel down and face the kind of existence the conqueror would impose on them."[45]

The distribution of *London Can Take It* provided further evidence of trans-Atlantic cooperation. The British cashed in the long-standing promise of support from Warner Brothers by asking that studio to arrange its release. Warners pledged all profits to the British War Relief fund and rushed 600 prints into national distribution in the first week of November 1940. Eight theaters carried the first run in downtown New York alone. Within a few months, the film had been shown at 12,000 American cinemas and had been seen by an estimated 60 million Americans. The U.S. release print of *London Can Take It* credited only Quentin Reynolds. Jennings, Watt, and the MoI went unmentioned. As Watt later recalled: "all America imagined that this was an unbiased, personal report made by one of their own people." Reynolds was happy to retain the outward credentials of "a neutral reporter."[46]

London Can Take It opened the way for further British films. The MoI immediately commissioned a sequel "to make the American public uncomfortable while they celebrate Christmas"; Watt and Reynolds obliged with *Christmas Under Fire*. The new film supplemented the defiance of the previous picture with a moving display of faith in adversity. With an emphasis on Britain's "Christmas underground," the film challenged the complacent peace of Christmas in neutral America. Reynolds growled that this year Britain prayed for bad weather at Christmas—bad enough to hold off the German bombers—as "a stormy night is an ally of England, a non-belligerent that demands no rules of Cash and Carry." He continued:

> There is no reason for America to feel sorry for England this Christmas. England doesn't feel sorry for herself . . . . Destiny gave her the torch of liberty to hold and she has not dropped it . . . she is thankful that when the test came she had the high courage to meet it, and today England stands unbeaten, unconquered, unafraid.[47]

The final moments of the film appealed shamelessly to the sentimental heart of middle America. As choirboys gathered to "worship the Prince of Peace," there could hardly have been a dry eye in the house.

Thus the Blitz on Britain wore on with Anglo-American cooperation as the order of the day. By Christmas, Murrow's flat had become a second Piccadilly Circus, with a steady stream of British politicians, Whitehall officials, and BBC staff dropping by at all hours. Murrow would sit up into the night, discussing everything from postwar reform to the generals of the American Civil War.[48] The correspondents had thrown their lot in with the British, and they had not been disappointed. But one question remained. Britain had stood firm, and they had reported the story; but what did the American public think, and would they respond with aid?

The Impact of the Blitz: American Sympathy and Its Limits

> You spoke, you said, in London . . . . But it was not in London
> really that you spoke. It was in the back kitchens and the front
> living rooms and the moving automobiles and the hot dog stands
> and the observation cars of another country that your voice was
> truly speaking. And what you did was this: You made real and
> urgent and present to the men and women of those comfortable
> rooms, those safe enclosures, what the men and women had not
> known was present there or real. You burned the city of London
> in our houses and we felt the flames that burnt it. You laid the
> dead of London at our doors and we knew the dead were our
> dead—were all men's dead—were mankind's dead and ours.
>
> Archibald MacLeish to Murrow, December 1941[49]

The Americans reporting the Blitz on Britain were quite unable to
judge the impact of their efforts. Their only regular indication of the
United States' mood came in daily, hurried contact with their New York
headquarters over the service line, tempered by a steady stream of isolationist hate mail. Murrow cherished a letter addressed to Mr. Edward
R. Moron. The wider public response could only be guessed. In November 1940, Eric Sevareid became the first of the correspondents to
return home. He was amazed to find that he and his colleagues had
become national heroes. The United States was following the war in
Europe day-by-day, hour-by-hour, on the radio and was deeply moved
by what it heard.[50]

The nation's old dislike of Hitler had now become an overt sympathy for the British people. The United States admired the "magnifi-
cence" of Britain's progress from defiant retreat, to victory in the air, to
courage under bombardment. Each successive phase eroded the old
images of the British Empire. The figure of Winston Churchill towered
over all. Drew Middleton returned home to find a marked change in his
family in South Orange, New Jersey. Although never previously anglophile, they now lay under the Prime Minister's spell. Churchill's
appearance on the radio plunged his welcome-home dinner into silence.
No one spoke until the speech had finished. An old uncle broke the silence: "What a great man." The others echoed: "What a great people."[51]

The opinion polls bore out this change. In November, when Gallup
asked "Do you think the United States should keep out of war or do
everything possible to help England even at the risk of getting into war
ourselves?" American opinion divided evenly on the question. By
December, a full 60 percent were willing to risk war. The previous May,
a similar majority had favored isolation.[52] The British noticed the
change. Lothian reported "an overwhelming sentiment for giving us all
immediate assistance short of war." On October 21, Lord Halifax informed the War Cabinet of "an almost miraculous change of opinion in
the United States after it had become clear that the country was effec-

tively resisting the German air attack." Once pessimistic American journalists now openly expressed the "hope and belief" that the United States would be involved in the war by the autumn of 1941 "at the latest."[53]

Much of the credit for the "miracle" lay with the medium of radio. The Blitz had allowed a powerful medium and a powerful message to converge. This point was eloquently made by Archibald MacLeish. At a dinner in Murrow's honor held on December 2, 1941, he told the broadcaster:

> you destroyed in the minds of many men and women in this country the superstition that what is done beyond three thousand miles of water is not really done at all: the ignorant superstition that violence and lies and murder on another continent are not violence and lies and murder here; the cowardly and brutal superstition that the enslavement of mankind in a country where the sun rises at midnight by our clocks is not enslavement by the time we live by; the black stifling superstition that what we cannot see and hear and touch can have no meaning for us.[54]

But the United States' response also owed much to years of trans-Atlantic cultural interchange. The German bombs did not fall on some unknown corner of the globe but on a city and nation whose landmarks and inhabitants were well-known to all Americans—a familiar place that existed inside the head of any American who had ever read *Oliver Twist* or seen *Goodbye Mr. Chips*. No other country held such sway over the American imagination. Strengthened by its apparent rebirth, Britain appealed directly to American anglophilia. Hitler had given America something to hate; now Britain provided something for America to love.

American popular culture digested the sounds and images of the Blitz and glowed with sympathetic sentiment. Although many U.S. radio stations banned war songs (NBC refused to play certain Gracie Fields records), British patriotic music seemed to be everywhere.[55] In December 1940, Ridsdale reported: "There is such a marked sweep of pro-British feeling running through the States that even strip-tease dancers discard their brassières and what-have-yous to the tune of 'There'll always be an England.' This seems to me not only physically, but psychologically, suggestive and perhaps a tribute to our national virility."[56]

A long poem, "The White Cliffs," by Alice Duer Miller, achieved phenomenal success. It told of an American's love for England—its villages, people, and history—and of her willingness to send her only son to die to preserve it. The poem ended with the lines:

> I am an American bred,
> I have seen much to hate here—much to forgive,
>   But in a world where England is finished and dead,
> I do not wish to live.

Published in August 1940, the poem sold 300,000 copies in the United States. Millions more came to know it through broadcast readings and a best-selling musical version performed by Jimmy Dorsey. It became an archetypal work of anglophilia.[57]

Churchill was prepared to accommodate the American fantasy of village England. In October 1940, when *Life* magazine carried a photo feature on the Prime Minister's namesake village in Somerset, he provided a personal message:

> I have enjoyed looking at *Life* magazine's pictures of Churchill in Somerset. Such villages exist throughout the length and breadth of Britain and I commend these pictures to the readers of *Life*, for they may give a better idea of what Britain is fighting for and how she is meeting the challenge [of Germany] than words can say.[58]

Others saw the pitfalls of this view of England. J. B. Priestley scorned "The White Cliffs": "This isn't the England that is fighting the war. The Christmas card caricature of England couldn't fight this war for a couple of days . . . they don't make 16-inch guns or Hurricanes or Spitfires down on the old family place in Devon."[59] In time, British propaganda would try to correct these illusions; but the United States, like one in love, preferred its fantasy.

The dramatic news from Britain coincided with a new wave of interventionist films. The most significant of these was Walter Wanger's co-production with Alfred Hitchcock of *Foreign Correspondent*, released in the final week of August. This film rode the crest of public admiration that had been building for Murrow and his colleagues in Europe. The opening titles read:

> To the intrepid ones who went across the seas to be the eyes and ears of America. To those forthright ones who early saw the clouds of war while many of us at home were seeing rainbows. To those clear-headed ones who now stand like recording angels among the dead and the dying. To the Foreign Correspondents this motion picture is dedicated.[60]

Hitchcock had abandoned his original plan to film Vincent Sheean's memoirs. Instead, he launched a fictional journalist Huntley Haverstock (played by Joel McCrea) on a roller-coaster ride through a Europe tumbling into war. Haverstock, a humble New York crime reporter, has a keen sense of morality but is wholly ignorant of European affairs until his paper sends him to cover the "crime" of Europe's return to war. He finds a world of German spies, frantic diplomacy for peace, assassinations, chases, and spy-infested windmills. He faces murder in Westminster Cathedral and a plane crash in the mid-Atlantic. The movie's message was never far below the surface. At the climax of the film, after viewers have shared Haverstock's journey from parochialism to wholehearted commitment to the anti-Nazi cause, Hitchcock confronts them with their government's own position. Haverstock is rescued at sea by a rigidly neutral U.S. Navy captain who forbids his filing the big story while on board. American neutrality thus becomes Haverstock's problem.

Foreign Correspondent ends in a crescendo of propaganda, as Huntley Haverstock broadcasts to the United States from London:

> Hello America. I've been watching a part of the world being blown to pieces. A part of the world as nice as Vermont, Ohio, Virginia, California, and Illinois lies ripped up and bleeding like a steer in a slaughterhouse. I've seen things that make the history of the savages read like pollyanna legend.

An air-raid siren interrupts. In the background Londoners move calmly towards their shelters. Bombs explode. Lights flicker. Haverstock continues:

> I can't read the rest of this speech because the lights have gone out. So I'll just have to talk off the cuff. All that noise you hear isn't static, it's death coming to London. Yes, they're coming here now. You can hear the bombs falling on the streets and homes. Don't tune me out—hang on—this is a big story—and you're part of it. It's too late now to do anything except stand in the dark and let them come as if the lights are all out everywhere except in America. Keep those lights burning, cover them with guns, build a canopy of battleships and bombing planes around them and, hello, America, hang on to your lights, they're the only lights left in the world.

Music swells under the words; it is "The Star Spangled Banner." The credits then roll over Wanger's American eagle logo.

The completed film impressed even unsympathetic observers. Goebbels called it "a masterpiece of propaganda."[61] Wanger and Hitchcock also avoided some obvious pitfalls. The final plea spoke only of a defense of America's "lights" and not of intervention to rekindle the lights of Europe. The message was thus closer to the interventionism of William Allen White than to that of Wanger's Century Group. *Foreign Correspondent* was perfect for the moment: it anticipated Reynolds's *London Can Take It*, opened during the same week that Murrow made his live broadcast from Trafalgar Square, and reached theaters exactly as the Germans began their Blitz on London. Fact and fiction collided in one persuasive blur.

Walter Wanger also squeezed an anti-Nazi message into *The Long Voyage Home*, directed by John Ford. The film starred John Wayne as a lovable Swedish sailor whose wish to "goo hoom" is tragically confounded by a German torpedo.[62] Other producers proved equally partisan. In Warner Brothers' Elizabethan epic, *The Sea Hawk*, Errol Flynn thwarts turncoats at home, defeats Spaniards on the high seas, and rouses England to build the fleet necessary to frustrate Spain's dream of an empire stretching "to the Urals." Flora Robson as Queen Elizabeth concluded the proceedings by extolling the virtues of rearmament and proclaiming: "Freedom is the deed and title to the soil on which we exist." "Count on Warners," commented the *New York Times*, "to inject a note of contemporary significance."[63] Then, in September 1940, *March of Time* released *The Ramparts We Watch*, a feature film tracing the World War I experiences of a small New England town. The film undermined the isolationist view of World War I by criticizing the war fever and spy hysteria while still upholding the justice of the Allied cause. German footage of the Nazi bombing of Poland, supplied by Grierson, provided a pointed climax—especially since, at that very moment, the same bombers had appeared in the skies over London.[64]

Twentieth Century Fox offered two anti-Nazi pictures that autumn: *I Married a Nazi* and *Four Sons*, a tale of life in occupied Czechoslovakia, produced by Darryl F. Zanuck. MGM added *Escape*, the story of an American's struggle to free his mother from a concentration camp, and *The Mortal Storm*, which dealt with a German academic's resistance to Hitler's racial doctrines. But none of these pictures matched the impact of the big picture of that autumn: Charlie Chaplin's *The Great Dictator*. Chaplin's tale of a Jewish barber mistaken for the European dictator "Adenoid Heinkel" transformed Hitler and Mussolini into strutting buffoons. Although the absurdities of fascism had long been apparent to most Americans, the cinema now caught up with public attitudes, and Chaplin scored a runaway box office success. The *New York Times* declared the film "perhaps the most significant motion picture ever produced."[65]

The British made their own contribution to the season, with the stiff-upper-lip heroics of Michael Balcon's *Convoy*, and Carol Reed's spirited sequel to *The Lady Vanishes*, titled *Night Train*. Reed's film starred matinée idol Rex Harrison as a British secret agent at large in Nazi Germany. Basil Radford and Naunton Wayne added comic relief at the expense of Hitler, with exchanges such as: "Did you know that every German couple is given a copy of *Mein Kampf* on their wedding day?" "Goodness . . . I had no idea it was *that* sort of book." Walter Wanger adored the film and tried to poach Reed to direct his next war picture, but Reed remained in Britain, overworked and under contract.[66] Some British films proved too idiosyncratic for America. In October, the *New York Times* struggled gamely to welcome the latest George Formby vehicle as "evidence of the Britishers' incorrigible 'Thumbs Up' attitude in the face of mortal danger," but it found *Let George Do It* "only sporadically funny" and speculated that the cast may have been "half listening for air raid sirens."[67]

Whether British or American in origin, these films provided a fertile cultural environment for the news reports from Britain. Audiences watched such movies with the latest newsreel from London fresh in their minds, and they returned home to hear the same war live on the 9:00 news. No better environment for nurturing aid to Britain could have been imagined, and the public gave accordingly. On September

18, the *New York Herald Tribune* reported that "U.S. Red Cross aid to England" was nearing $5 million, and that Bundles for Britain had designated September 29 as "Britain Sunday." But the U.S. government sent no new aid of its own.

The British blamed Roosevelt's reticence on the impending election, but they also noted the limits of the American public's understanding of the war. The United States clearly grasped only the rawest elements in Britain's experience and seemed unsure what Britain would do next beyond "taking" further punishment from the Nazis. Some portion of the blame lay with the lack of British war aims; but for its part, the American press seemed to have forgotten the broader issues of the war. Lothian saw this as a side effect of the liberal reporting restrictions. The license to cover the Blitz and the experience of being caught up in it had ensured that the Americans were "so obsessed with the bombing of London . . . that they cable about nothing else." He concluded: "It gives a wonderful reputation for courage but tends to put the war out of perspective."[68] John Grierson agreed. He remained bitterly critical of British film propaganda in the United States and told the MoI:

> Sympathy is only a second-class propaganda gambit and doesn't create participation. It doesn't create confidence. *London Can Take It* though . . . had I think the wrong secondary effect. "Boy I was sorry for London last night!" Tear dropped, job over. Ditto, it seems for *Christmas Under Fire*. Someone writes to say it is nothing but *London Can Still Take It* and like a Landseer painting of a noble stag bleeding to death on a Scottish moor, but mutely asking no one to be sorry for it, because it is still "Monarch of the Glen."[69]

The American correspondents confirmed this. Larry Lesueur insisted that the MoI could not use the "Britain can take it" line indefinitely. Britain could take it, but only until it was in a position to strike back at the Germans. Lesueur had seen boxers fight bravely for money, and he had seen them fight bravely just to win, but he'd never seen anyone win just because he could "take it." It therefore came as no surprise when, on January 2, 1941, the MoI informed the BBC as follows:

> At the last meeting of the planning committee it was agreed that the phrase "Britain Can Take It" and the other members of the "Can Take It" family had become ineffectual and therefore undesirable. We should be glad therefore if you would discourage the use of such phrases in broadcasting.[70]

A brilliant propaganda device had outlived its usefulness, and in the meantime the battle had shifted to the United States. On November 5, 1940, FDR won an unprecedented third term in the White House. Now, at last, Britain's best friend enjoyed the political security necessary to extend large-scale aid, and the way was clear for a new era of British propaganda in America. Neither of these developments proved wholly straightforward.

Beyond the Blitz: Building New Propaganda Machinery in the United States

> The whole country has sunk back into a post-election reaction. The feeling for Great Britain is as strong and friendly as ever but public opinion is still inclined to live in complacency derived from the failure of Hitler's attempt at invasion of Britain this autumn, while nothing has happened on the international front to revive American anxiety about its own security.
>
> Lord Lothian, November 1940[71]

On November 6, Churchill wrote to congratulate the President on his victory. He did not mention his need for American aid, but hoped that FDR might reply with a new initiative. To the Prime Minister's surprise, Roosevelt failed to answer this message and remained silent on the question of aid to Britain. On December 2, 1940, Churchill told the War Cabinet that he felt "chilled" by Roosevelt's attitude since the election. He assumed that FDR must be waiting for the post-election atmosphere to disperse. Britain, however, could not wait; the country's dollar reserves were all but exhausted. The British Treasury prepared to liquidate all British assets in the United States, but Britain's survival now depended on war credit. Such a radical revision of neutrality law required the sympathy and confidence of both the American government and the American public. But once again American confidence wavered.

In the second week of November 1940, the British noted a sudden loss of American faith in their shipping reports. Certain sections of the press alleged that the British were concealing the scale of U-boat successes, which offered an obvious index of Britain's chances of survival. Germany lost no time in exploiting this line of attack, and thus the Battle of the Atlantic, like the Battle of Britain before it, became a battle for the American headlines. The Foreign Office prescribed openness, but the Admiralty dragged its feet. The MoI made do with some stirring broadcasts and press conferences and helped *March of Time* produce a film on the British Merchant Navy.[72]

Meanwhile, Ronald Tree sought to address the larger problems of British propaganda. In a letter to Duff Cooper of November 20, 1940, he called for clear propaganda objectives so that the MoI could "educate people" in the United States "to help us along specific lines." He argued that the root of Britain's problem was the President. FDR's "refusal to come out and tell the truth" about the war had left the United

States "utterly uneducated as to the seriousness of our position."[73] Tree knew that only action at the highest level could apply the necessary pressure to Whitehall and the White House alike. Fortunately, Churchill was now thinking along similar lines.

On October 20, Lothian returned to Britain for a much-needed rest. He took the opportunity to urge Churchill to broach the question of American aid with Roosevelt. The Prime Minister agreed and resolved to address the President in the strongest possible terms, outlining the true depth of Britain's need. But Churchill did not want to rush; he preferred to wait for the right moment to send his request to FDR.[74] Lothian had other ideas. On November 23, 1940, he landed at LaGuardia Airport in New York City. Reading from a brief unauthorized statement, Lothian presented assembled reporters with a grim picture: "England will be grateful for any help. England needs planes, munitions, ships and perhaps a little financial help." In response to questions, he hinted at an imminent British financial collapse. The *Chicago Tribune* screeched "Envoy Lothian claims Britain is going broke." In the folk memory of Britain's propagandists Lothian had said "Well boys, Britain's bust. It's your money we want!"[75]

Lothian's candor effectively punctured American complacency. The Foreign Office News Department saw its chance and rushed into the breach, calling for the War Cabinet to set clear propaganda objectives in the United States. Charles Peake put the matter bluntly in a letter to Duff Cooper: "We know very well how delicate is the ground upon which we tread. But so long as we are not told how far we can go, what risks we may take, and above all what the Prime Minister expects and wants, we can only nibble at American propaganda and the time is too urgent for nibbling."[76]

At the Foreign Office, North Whitehead predicted a vigourous American debate over intervention. He underlined that: "On the outcome of this discussion our chances of victory largely depend and the result will be guided by public opinion at the time. It is of the utmost importance that we should do what we can to influence that opinion in our favour." He therefore prepared a cabinet paper on British propaganda in the United States. "Briefly," he wrote, "our objective is to obtain the utmost assistance from the United States as quickly as possible, not excluding direct participation in the war."[77]

Duff Cooper heartily endorsed this assessment and begged Churchill to issue a "directive on which to base our propaganda effort." Churchill seemed sympathetic. He asked only that any new British campaign be delayed until Roosevelt replied to his impending appeal for aid.[78] In cabinet, on December 2, 1940, Churchill underlined the need for a considered approach to American opinion. He argued: "If the picture was painted too darkly, elements in the United States would say that it was useless to help us, for such help would be wasted and thrown away. If too bright a picture was painted, there might be a tendency to withhold

assistance." On the night of December 7, 1940, Churchill sent his request for aid to Roosevelt. The State Department forwarded the note to
the President, who was then on a Caribbean fishing trip aboard the USS
Tuscaloosa.[79] With Churchill open to the notion of full-scale British
propaganda in the United States, no barrier remained to prevent an all-
out campaign. Activity merely awaited FDR's reply.

Developments elsewhere heightened Britain's need for effective
publicity. When Jewish refugees scuttled the SS *Patria* off Haifa
rather than be redirected to East Africa, 1,555 survivors found themselves in a British concentration camp. Britain was left in the difficult
position of having to explain an unpopular and seemingly repressive
policy to American Jews and gentiles alike.[80] Meanwhile the isolationists had found the soft underbelly of the American interventionist
movement. They spent the month hammering away at the highly
charged issue of American belligerence. Their initiative wrought
havoc in the interventionist camp, laying bare the split between
the Century Group hawks and William Allen White's "all aid short of
war" policy. In late December, in an interview to the Scripps-Howard
chain, White denounced the radical line and declared "the Yankees
won't come": "America would only play into the hands of Hitler if she
should enter the war actively; the shipment of American war supplies
to England on American merchant ships and the protection of convoys to England is not permissible in any circumstances."[81] The British had tried to put a brave face on the rivalries between the various
aid committees, but this was different. The need for a British propaganda initiative had never been greater. Fortunately, the discussions
over the expansion of the British publicity in the United States had
produced dramatic structural developments. Yet even at this critical
moment, the gremlin of interdepartmental rivalry lurked beneath the
surface.

The prolonged policy wrangles of the summer had pointed to the
need for more British publicity in the United States. Now Britain created the necessary machinery. Lord Lothian led the way by launching
the Inter-Allied Information Committee (IAIC), a body created to fund
and direct the American propaganda efforts of the smaller Allied nations. The new committee brought fresh voices onto the American
stage. The Czechs and Poles had previously had no money to spend on
U.S. publicity, and the German conquests of the spring had silenced
the remaining European powers. The IAIC also offset a new danger.
Lothian had noted the establishment of a French section within the
German Consulate in New York, and he suspected that Britain's erst-
while allies would soon be reading from a German script. In reply, he
proposed that Britain direct Free French news and propaganda in the
United States through the IAIC. The IAIC promised to be the perfect
puppet propaganda machine, not least because the puppets themselves were eager to participate.[82]

This initiative drew a mixed reception in London. Duff Cooper still felt that he should control all such activity, and Halifax was rather appalled by the notion of collaborating with the Free French; but the Foreign Office approved. The leadership of the committee fell to Michael Huxley, formerly the British Embassy press attaché, who now realized that this post would be superceded by the expansion of British publicity.[83] The Inter-Allied Information Committee convened on September 24, 1940, with Huxley at the helm and with a share of the MoI money brought by Childs in its campaign chest. The governments-in-exile of Czechoslovakia, the Netherlands, and Norway, as well as observers from Belgium and Luxembourg, all participated; Robert Valeur (formerly of the French Information Bureau in New York) represented the "France Forever" committee. Valeur would later become the organization's director of publications. By the second meeting, the emigré Poles had joined, and the committee was preparing to draw representatives of the remaining Allies into the fold. The committee operated through its own Inter-Allied Information Center located close to the other British propaganda offices on the third floor of 610 Fifth Avenue, Rockefeller Center, New York. It soon surprised even its creators with its ambitiousness and vitality.[84]

Lothian had originally hoped to use the Allied representatives to address their own national minorities within the United States, thus quietly turning the Polish-Americans of Pittsburgh, for example, into a fifth column for the British cause. But Huxley preferred to build a sturdy public news office. The international character of the IAIC's output highlighted a common experience of Nazi tyranny; it also created a natural environment for the member states to address their common concerns for the future and, most importantly, for postwar international cooperation. Thus, on October 30, the Foreign Office noted: "Mr. Huxley has converted the intended activities of this committee from those of underground propaganda to various U.S. national groups into a 'high grade' information bureau and centre for the discussion of future aims for Europe."[85] The Inter-Allied Information Committee had clearly developed a life of its own. Even as it began work, however, Britain prepared a new tier of propaganda operations in the United States.

As the Blitz on London began, the Ministry of Information was still debating Stephen Childs's scheme for a British propaganda bureau in New York. Duff Cooper presided and Wheeler-Bennett flew in from New York to represent Lothian in the process. Under Lothian's hand, the plan had developed into a two-pronged attack. He had appointed Childs to head an expanded British Embassy press office to handle the embassy's dealings with the MoI in London and with Washington columnists. Now, he sought to launch the long-awaited British publicity office in New York. Lothian held all the cards. He had hijacked Duff Cooper's emissary and used his funds to set up the Inter-Allied machinery. He commanded the loyalty of Wheeler-Bennett and the expansionist faction in the BLI. With the budget of the British Embassy and its press office at his disposal, he did not need any further funding from London. He could take his next step alone. Duff Cooper could only sit back and watch Lothian play his hand.[86]

Lothian planned to use the New York press office as the nerve center of British publicity in the United States. It would cultivate American press and radio commentators, issue "hot news" and features, refute enemy propaganda, and even build links with religious organizations and organized labor. Lothian took care that even the title of the new organization fit these objectives. He avoided the word *relations*, which he said reminded Americans of their own government's rash of "public relations" departments, and he could of course not use the obscene word *propaganda*. In triumph, he hit on the word *service*, writing: "the word 'Service' produces a benevolent reaction in America. We do not wish to be accused of making overt plans to 'influence' the press; although of course it is quite understood that the organisation will specialise in 'relations' rather than acting as a spot news agency."[87] Thus the title British Press Service was born.

In deference to the imminent U.S. elections, work began cautiously. Lothian promised that the BPS would avoid secret service–style whispering campaigns (the practice whereby British agents "mingled in bars and thoroughfares" and introduced subversive rumors into the population at large). The BPS scheme included plans for regional diversification, but not, as yet, for separate regional branches. It would also be responsible for surveying the American press. This was hardly surprising, since Lothian used the old BLI Survey Section as the core of the BPS. He recruited the survey staff wholesale, and assigned Aubrey Morgan and John Wheeler-Bennett to assist in administering the new office. Lothian appointed Alan Dudley, the BLI's survey chief, as acting director. Dudley lacked the charisma of Morgan or Wheeler-Bennett, but his unassuming character served Lothian's present purpose well. Like Morgan and Wheeler-Bennett, Dudley was well known in the New York press world, and the array of familiar faces disguised the degree to which this office represented a new departure in British policy. British propaganda had, at last, broken free from the suffocating rigidity of Angus Fletcher and the BLI. This, Wheeler-Bennett wrote, was "the first step toward creating a 'popular' institution for the conduct of British public relations; an organisation which aimed to serve the curious many rather than the enquiring few, and which was based upon the principle of creating an ever growing demand for its services."[88]

The BPS found office space on the forty-fourth floor of the RCA building, 30 Rockefeller Plaza, close to the British Library of Information. The offices of NBC were in the same complex; CBS and a slew of New York newspapers lay within easy reach. The budget was sub-

stantial—Lothian requested $14,000 per month for the New York
office alone—but other facilities were sparse. The reference section
initially consisted of little more than several willing hands, a well-
thumbed British *Who's Who*, and a ragged selection of books from
Wheeler-Bennett's own shelves. During the early days, Sir William
Wiseman, a ghostly presence from the previous war, drifted in and out
to offer his advice. He held no formal appointment, however, and soon
slipped into the background.[89]

The office scrambled to hire the necessary staff. Some officers recruited their friends. The stranded British student Frank Thistlethwaite
brought in his sympathetic American college friend John Lawler. Lawler had worked on the *Des Moines Register* and brought an intimate
knowledge of American journalism and the American Midwest. He
gained ample reward for his service, meeting his British wife on the
staff; in later years he would joke that he married her in lieu of a
knighthood. For the clerical posts, the BPS followed usual diplomatic practice and hired staff at the local employment exchange. The
telephone operator, New York native "Mitch" Mitchell, joined without
knowing the nature of the office's business; his only clues were the ini-
tials BPS over the door. He used only the number when answering the
telephone. His colleagues seemed equally vague. The office wit, Alan
Judson, steadfastly maintained that he had first entered believing that
this was the British Pornographic Society. Despite the reticence of
their employers when the BPS and British Embassy press office opened
for business in mid-October 1940, the new recruits found no shortage
of work.[90]

From the first, the British Press Service sought to provide a steady
stream of reference material within the deadlines required by working
journalists. They offered a rapid and accurate reference service for editors, correspondents, and radio commentators situated as far west as
Chicago. The BPS prepared information bulletins based on MoI "Hot
News" material, and it arranged transport to the British Isles for
Americans seeking to cover the war. No less important, the office
served as the main point of contact between the British government
and the American interventionist movement. Morgan and Wheeler-
Bennett maintained close relations with their opposite numbers in the
Century Group (soon to become the Fight For Freedom committee).
Through their offices, the interventionists received a steady supply of
BPS news releases. The Century Group leaders, Ulric Bell and Peter
Cusick, were in touch with Morgan or Wheeler-Bennett by telephone at
least once a week and, when events dictated, enjoyed personal confidential briefings on the latest material from London. This did not
require much effort. Fight For Freedom operated from the twenty-
second floor of the same building.[91]

The BPS did not shy away from such sensitive issues as the food
blockade of occupied Europe. The first BPS bulletins, issued to the

American press and the interventionists in early November 1940, included an authoritative response to Herbert Hoover's campaign on this subject, digests of statistics, and a speech by the Minister of Economic Warfare, Hugh Dalton. Thereafter, the BPS allowed the Century Group to push the British line on the blockade, and turned its attention to the task of convincing the United States that Britain could "take" the Nazi Blitz.[92]

Even though Lothian had established the BPS in consultation with Angus Fletcher of the BLI and Duff Cooper, neither of these men was entirely happy with the new office. Fletcher did not appreciate being outflanked by the ambassador and refused to help the new office. This threw the entire burden of press relations onto Wheeler-Bennett and his colleagues. They found themselves working sixteen to eighteen hours a day, and their phenomenal success merely made matters worse. Their work load grew with their reputation. Morgan and Wheeler-Bennett did not forget Fletcher's attitude. As their influence grew, it became clear that Fletcher's days at the BLI were numbered. In January 1941, he received a knighthood for his long service in New York. In August 1941, he was dismissed.[93]

Fletcher represented the ancien régime, but Lothian soon learned that revolutionaries could be no less troublesome. Duff Cooper and his new American Division director Douglas Williams still hoped to have an active voice in the application of propaganda policy in the United States. Since the MoI had financed the BPS, the IAIC, and the British Embassy Press Office, their interest was not wholly unreasonable. The problem lay in the question of who should have ultimate authority. Duff Cooper still wanted to run policy from London and, if necessary, impose his view on the "local representatives." North Whitehead noted that George III had made the same mistake. Even before Lothian had set up the BPS, Duff Cooper moved to bring the entire operation under his own control. He saw his chance in the vacant post of permanent director of the New York office. In late September 1940, Williams wired the British Embassy to say that he had dispatched "certain journalists" to New York to "direct press contacts." Lothian was not reassured to learn that this envoy should have been identified in the singular.[94]

The appointment of a "certain journalist" to the New York position reflected Duff Cooper's bid to professionalize the MoI, as well as his disdain for the men who had borne the burden of British publicity to that point. Morgan and Wheeler-Bennett were stung to discover that he considered them no more than "monied amateurs." Yet Duff Cooper's candidate for the job, René MacColl, was undoubtedly well-chosen. He was a veteran of the *Baltimore Sun*, the *Daily Telegraph*, and the RAF press relations unit in France. Armed with letters of introduction, MacColl prepared to take passage to the United States. On the morning of October 4, 1940, the front page of the *New York Herald Tribune* announced MacColl's appointment as "Chief British Press Relations Officer in the United States." Once again Lothian shuddered at the tactlessness of the MoI and prepared a volley of angry telegrams. His anger increased when, that same morning, he received a telegram un-coded and en clair from Douglas Williams, requesting that the ambassador approach William Allen White in order to establish a tele-phone link between his committee and the Information Ministry. Lothian wired back: "It would be most disastrous to the William Allen White Committee were it ever to be established that it was communi-cating and collaborating with any branch of His Majesty's Govern-ment." Ominously, Lothian pledged to take "certain measures to avoid further possible damage" to British publicity. Lothian asked that the MoI postpone MacColl's arrival until after the U.S. election and that he accept duties under Dudley's direction. Unfortunately, this did not fit the instructions MacColl had in hand on November 19, 1940, when he finally landed on American soil.[95]

René MacColl arrived in New York believing himself empowered to take charge of the BPS. He promptly discovered that the staff of the BPS did not acknowledge Duff Cooper's authority to have appointed him. MacColl was thus an innocent victim of his minister's "Byzantine Intrigue" to gain control of propaganda in America.[96] Lothian saw MacColl as a threat to the BPS. On November 30, he gruffly informed the MoI:

> I now feel very strongly that press and publicity questions are at this juncture so important that it would be unwise to do anything to disturb the smooth working of the BPS and its satisfactory development. It would not . . . be part of wisdom to confide its direction to a new arrival, how-ever brilliant his journalistic gifts, who had not in my view had the administrative experience to enable him to take full charge of this organ-isation.[97]

MacColl endured a fortnight of frustration during which his col-leagues withheld telegraphic traffic addressed to him as "director of the BPS." The mutiny did not last long. Duff Cooper conceded defeat and accepted MacColl's appointment as assistant director of the BPS with responsibility for the supply of hot news to American press and broad-cast networks. MacColl immediately set about the task of building a dizzying array of connections with the New York press world. Despite being a Ministry of Information appointee, he displayed all the qualities of the old hands in New York. His commitment to the BPS, his humor, and his healthy disregard for Foreign Office procedure soon won him the hearts of his New York officemates. He outraged the career diplo-mats at the British Embassy in Washington by introducing such snappy expressions as "Hot Cat!" into his file minutes. British relations with the New York press prospered as they never had before.[98]

By mid-December 1940, the BPS was stable and poised to challenge Roosevelt's intransigence. Then came the news. On December 12, Alistair Cooke, special correspondent of the London *Times*, called at the British Embassy to interview Lord Lothian. The butler responded to the visitor with solemn composure: "I'm terribly sorry, Sir, that will be quite impossible. The Ambassador died early this morning."[99] Lothian's death was a severe blow. His illness—a kidney infection—had been sudden, and its gravity known only to a few. Lothian's Christian Science beliefs had complicated matters. The ambassador's personal staff—his secretary, his driver, and his deputy, Neville Butler—were also Christian Scientists and had reinforced his resolve to refuse conventional medical attention. Lothian's head of Chancery, Derek Hoyer-Millar, together with John Wheeler-Bennett and the senior diplomatic staff, tried to approach him to argue the case for a doctor, but they found their way blocked. Lothian's co-religionists insisted that he was responding to Christian Science treatment.[100] Yet even from his sick-bed, Lothian had led the British attack.

On December 11, Neville Butler read an address prepared by Lothian to the American Farm Bureau Federation in Baltimore. It was Lothian's first full-length speech in five months. Lothian declared that the war had become a revolutionary struggle between Hitler's totalitarian world and democracy. He had no doubt that British democracy would emerge from the war even stronger than before; but with his final words, he placed the burden of the future firmly on the American people:

> We are, I believe, doing all we can. Since May there is no challenge we have evaded, no challenge we have refused. If you back us you won't be backing a quitter. The issue now depends largely on what you decide to do. Nobody can share the responsibility with you. It is the great strength of democracy that it brings responsibility down squarely on every citizen and every nation. And before the judgement seat of God each must answer for his own actions.[101]

The post-mortem recorded Lothian's death the next day as being due to uremic poisoning. Lord Halifax preferred to note "another victim for Christian Science."[102]

Washington mourned Lord Lothian's passing. The State Department arranged for his temporary interment, attended by an honor guard, in Arlington National Cemetery. Lothian's remains were placed beneath the mast of the battleship *Maine*, whose mysterious sinking in Havana Harbor in 1898 had pitched the United States headlong into the Spanish-American war. Given Lothian's desire to accomplish much the same feat, it was a fitting spot.[103] But the ceremony provided scant compensation for the loss. This single blow shattered the cornerstone of British propaganda in the United States. Never had the office held such importance. Now, the future of Anglo-American diplomacy hung in the balance.

The vacancy on Massachusetts Avenue triggered an immediate flurry of speculation as to a suitable successor. Raymond Gram Swing advised Churchill, "Urgently remember that liberals won the election here so Ambassador must be Liberal." He added "No old school tie also must not be appeasement."[104] But the Prime Minister's choice flew directly in the face this advice. Churchill selected an arch-Tory, an old Etonian, and a peer with an unrivaled reputation as an appeaser: the Foreign Secretary, Lord Halifax. Halifax reeled at the suggestion. He had known enough of American to appoint Lothian, and he understood that, as a former viceroy of India, he was not a suitable successor. Halifax was the six-foot-six-inch, living, breathing personification of every negative stereotype that Americans nurtured with regard to Britain—the very antithesis of the dynamic new nation of Spitfires and the Dunkirk spirit. But Churchill insisted that the appointment of the Foreign Secretary could not fail to impress the Americans, and he called on Halifax to accept "This high and perilous charge . . . on which our whole future depends."[105]

Churchill stood to gain much from Halifax's departure from London. At the death of Chamberlain in October 1940, Halifax had inherited the mantle of Munich and thus had become a political liability. Besides, since Halifax had already appeased Gandhi, Mussolini, and Hitler, it seemed logical to trust him to appease America. Few in Whitehall missed the deeper reasons for Churchill's choice. The appointment enabled Churchill to consolidate his hold on the War Cabinet, moving Anthony Eden back into the Foreign Office and assuming the War Office himself.[106] Halifax fought valiantly to change Churchill's mind, but to no avail. When the offer was sweetened by an arrangement whereby he retained a seat in the War Cabinet, he accepted the job.

The news of the appointment fell heavily on American journalists and British propagandists alike. Murrow confessed himself appalled. René MacColl simply recorded in his diary: "22 December 1940 . . . Halifax is Ambassador. Christ."[107] Despite his own misgivings, Halifax determined to make the best of his new circumstances. Sadly for Britain, his initial performance in the post suggested that his best would be inadequate.

As the year 1940 drew to a close, the future of British propaganda in the United States appeared especially uncertain. While Halifax packed his bags, Duff Cooper took advantage of the Embassy interregnum and lunged to snatch control of British propaganda in the United States. Sir David Scott, head of the Foreign Office American Department, regarded his attempt to capitalize on the death of Lothian as "unworthy of a third-rate sensational newspaper editor . . . indecent and disgusting" and blocked his move.[108] But Churchill had no interest in such matters.

He fixed his gaze on the absence of American aid and waited. Then, suddenly, Roosevelt broke his silence. In a press conference on December 16, he announced that he planned to "get rid of the silly, foolish old dollar sign" from the question of aid to Britain. Roosevelt put the case in terms of homely common sense: "Suppose my neighbor's home catches fire, and I have a length of garden hose . . . ." Churchill remained unimpressed. On December 21, 1940, he reminded Halifax that: "We have not had anything from the Americans that we have not paid for and what we have had has not played an essential part in our resistance."[109] Meanwhile the Blitz raged on.

The night of December 29 brought unprecedented destruction to central London. As incendiary bombs rained down on the city, firemen fought back to the best of their ability. It was not they who failed London, but its river. Their hose-ends soon flopped, flaccid and useless, in shallow pools on the empty bed of the Thames. That night produced one of the most enduring propaganda images of the war: the dome of St. Paul's Cathedral, alone, surrounded by a sea of fire. St. Paul's survived, but the Guildhall and eight Wren churches perished. Sir Alexander Cadogan recorded the cabinet's response in his diary: "decided to advertise attack on City . . . . This may help us enormously in America at a most critical moment."[110] Yet December 29 also brought new hope for the future; for while London burned, Roosevelt delivered his most outspoken public statement since June. In a fireside chat, FDR declared that the interests of the Allies and of the United States were now one and the same. America would become, he pledged, "the great arsenal of democracy." At last, large-scale American aid was on the way.

5

"Give Us the Tools . . .":
British Propaganda and American Aid,
January to August 1941

> Here is the answer that I will give to President Roosevelt: Put your
> confidence in us. Give us your faith and your blessing, and, under
> Providence, all will be well . . . . Give us the tools and we will
> finish the job.
>
> Winston Churchill, February 9, 1941[1]

The first weeks of 1941 brought a new dawn in Anglo-American relations. On January 6, 1941, Roosevelt publicly pledged himself to an
"all inclusive national defense" and "full support" for the Allied cause.
Congress replied with the Lend-Lease bill. Britain breathed a sigh of
relief. There were also signs of a new era in Anglo-American diplomacy.
Joseph Kennedy resigned from the American Embassy in London and
was replaced by the internationalist John Gilbert Winant. Roosevelt
also sent his trusted aide Harry Hopkins on a six-week mission to
Britain. The British pulled out all the stops to impress their guest.
Charmed, Hopkins assured Washington that it could work well with the
Churchill government.[2] Unfortunately, Britain's chief new arrival in
Washington proved rather less successful.

Lord Halifax began his mission to Washington in style, steaming
into Chesapeake Bay aboard the Royal Navy's newest battleship, *King
George V*. From this point, however, his mission went rapidly downhill.
He was baffled by his new surroundings, and a frost fell over his dealings
with the U.S. government. Ill-considered remarks and an incautious
visit to Congress soon set isolationist alarm bells clanging. Startled,
Halifax retreated into "Political Purdah" until the Lend-Lease bill had
passed. Other British arrivals fared better. A delegation from the British
Chiefs of Staff began vigorous talks with their American counterparts

that, in two months, produced a plan for Anglo-American military cooperation in the event of a war between the United States and Germany. They fixed Germany as the "first" enemy, even if Japan also entered the war. But contingency plans alone were not enough.[3]

Britain knew that American isolationism remained strong; the passage of Lend-Lease was by no means a foregone conclusion. The need for a concerted British publicity policy in the United States remained strong. The British possessed the necessary structure, but they needed a new theme to replace the stale "Britain can take it" line of the Blitz. Churchill provided the necessary inspiration. On February 9, 1941, the Prime Minister addressed Britain and the world. He reviewed the progress of the war since September 1940, building up to the recent victories in North Africa. He painted a picture of a country not simply "taking it" but fighting back. Churchill took care to respect the United States' desire to avoid war. He stressed: "we do not need the gallant armies which are forming throughout the American Union. We do not need them this year, nor next year that I can foresee." He concluded: "Give us the tools and we will finish the job." These words became the new keynote of Britain's approach to America in 1941.[4] Of course, Churchill hoped for more than "tools." He may not have needed "the gallant armies" that year, but he certainly needed the gallant navies. Britain's campaign of 1941 was thus founded on a distortion. It took six more months of shipping losses to force British publicity into line with the truth.

New York: Winning the War from Rockefeller Center

> My brief was to drag the Americans into the war.
>   Isaiah Berlin, on his job in 1941[5]

British propagandists entered 1941 ready to address America as never before. The feud between the British Embassy and the MoI had lapsed into an uneasy ceasefire as, in late December 1940, Duff Cooper - commissioned a report on the entire British publicity structure in the United States as a prelude to appointing an overall Director General. He entrusted this work to Charles Peake, the former deputy director of the MoI News Department, who now advised Lord Halifax on his dealings with the U.S. press. Since Peake was a close personal friend of the new ambassador, it seemed certain that his report would be acceptable to the British Embassy. In the spring of 1941, Peake began his work. He found the British offices at Rockefeller Center alive with fresh activity. The British Press Service led the way.[6]

By early 1941, the British Press Service had come into its own. On the forty-fourth floor of the RCA building, Dudley, Morgan, MacColl, and Wheeler-Bennett labored night and day to build a unique network of contacts. Morgan worked with the interventionists, while Wheeler-Bennett cultivated academics and maintained shadowy links with German refugees. René MacColl courted the senior figures of the American press. His diary records lunch meetings with *PM* editor Ralph Ingersoll and *Time* vice-president Allen Glover, and it includes such notes as: "talked to Raymond Gram Swing on the phone and gave him some air raid material which was later incorporated into his radio talk." At a lower level, Major Bill Ormerod toured press bars, cornering columnists with carefully memorized tidbits from MacColl and urging them all to "keep in touch." To his colleagues he was a standing joke, but the American journalists loved him. He became an integral part of the New York press world for the rest of the decade. Now no press lunch or dinner party in New York was complete without the cheery presence of a British propagandist.[7]

MacColl's Press and Radio Division worked like a news agency, providing reliable, free, and frequent British stories and photographs; MacColl also contributed pieces under his own name to such magazines as *Current History* and *Atlantic Monthly*. MacColl tailored his press service to fit his customers' needs. To sharpen this output, he engaged an experienced American journalist as a news editor: an old *New York Herald Tribune* man named Carl Johnson. With Johnson's help, MacColl devised a system whereby incoming MoI news and features were divided into material suitable for a national wire "slugging" and items to hold back for release to a single paper. MacColl knew that an exclusive feature given to the right newspaper could command particular attention. The system lasted longer than its co-architect. One evening late in the winter, Johnson disappeared. His wife found him the following morning, fast asleep in a snowdrift at the terminus of his subway line. His availability for British war work had been related to a long-term drink problem, and the stress of work at the BPS had driven him back to the bottle. He never returned to the office, but he had done his job. MacColl did not replace him.[8]

In February 1941, MacColl scored his first major propaganda coup. His diary recorded the sequence of events. On February 10, MacColl met John Pepper of British Security Co-ordination and the old French propagandist de Sales to discuss plans for photographic propaganda. The following day, MacColl put these plans into action. Over lunch at the Artists and Writer's restaurant with Powell, the Inter-Allied Informatic Committee's photographic officer, MacColl produced a packet of photographs from occupied Poland showing graphic scenes of Nazi butchery. He did not record in his diary how these came into his possession, but he noted: "slipped Powell the Polish horror pictures." The IAIC office passed the pictures on to their final desination: the liberal newspaper *PM*. On February 14, MacColl wrote in triumph, "*PM* splashed the Polish pictures."[9]

The paper made full use of its exclusive. The cover carried a grisly photograph of a German firing squad. The caption proclaimed: "These are Poles being shot by Germans in 'The New Order in Europe.' A German aviator liked this picture so well that he carried it with him. That's how it happens to be here, found in his pocket with four others when he was shot down in England." The others pictures covered an inside page and the centerfold. They showed prisoners marching to their deaths; a second firing squad; Poles (apparently Jews) digging a mass grave surrounded by piles of dead bodies; and two corpses dangling from a street lamp. The story of the pilot was almost certainly a fabrication—a convenient "paper clip" contrived to link pictures assembled by MacColl from material smuggled out of Poland by the Sixth Division of the Polish Home Army and passed by it to either the British Ministry of Information or the Secret Service. But the impact of the photographs outweighed all questions of their origin. With the help of an obliging American paper, MacColl had provided pictures with all the impact of a Great War atrocity story but within the new boundaries of "propaganda with fact."[10]

The BPS staff threw everything they had into their work. Even letters from home had propaganda value. When MacColl's assistant Joan Skipsey received a particularly vivid letter from a friend in the women's army auxiliary, she immediately passed it on to the *New York Post*. The work was personal; the staff knew the "research girls" at *Time* and *Newsweek* by their nicknames. It was also powerful; BPS writers regularly spotted their material in the columns of Walter Lippmann, although it was seldom credited. The *New York Sun* ran BPS articles verbatim, under the by-line "Our Special Correspondent." When Charles Peake asked radio commentators about the BPS, Raymond Gram Swing, George Fielding Eliot, and Johannes Steel assured him that they were "constantly" in touch with the office for "news, and opinions, and guidance." This, Peake concluded, meant that the BPS had acquired "some influence" over daily radio audiences consisting of from 40 to 50 million Americans.[11]

As the BPS grew, new experts joined the staff, including, in January 1941, the young Oxford philosopher Isaiah Berlin. Berlin had first joined the campaign the previous summer when stranded en route to the British Embassy in Moscow. At that time, he had compiled a report for the BLI on anti-British strains in AP dispatches from occupied Europe; then he had returned to Britain. Now he was back, assigned to cultivate American Jews, Blacks, "minor Christian denominations," and (in the absence of an embassy labor attaché) the organized labor movement.[12] He was not alone in his bid to win over American Jews. In 1941, the great Zionist leader Chaim Weizmann toured America at the request of the British government. Weizmann found American Jews actively raising money for the Allies, but the community still resented British policy in Palestine. Isaiah Berlin faced a formidable task.[13]

The BPS also acquired the services of the mysterious Jack Rennie. A wartime recruit to the Baltimore consulate, Rennie now operated a small radio-monitoring office. He hinted at a murky cloak-and-dagger past and claimed to suffer from an exotic and debilitating illness. The illness turned out to be varicose veins, and his murky past consisted of a career in radio advertising in New York. His cloak-and-dagger days lay ahead of him. After the war, he headed Britain's Cold War propaganda outfit, the Foreign Office Information Research Department, and eventually MI6. His work in 1941 was less spectacular but still useful. His radio interceptions provided the latest British news. He also managed to pick up the German domestic news service, where the Reich's propaganda ministry gave its rumors their first airing. He would then brief Major Ormerod with a counter-story, and Ormerod would trot off on his daily round of cocktail parties, scotching the rumors as he went.[14]

Finally, Paul Scott-Rankine took over the press survey. He brought with him a repertoire of comic impersonations (including impressions of Hitler and Mussolini) and a slobbery pet bulldog. No one minded having a dog living in the office; after all, he was called Winston.[15]

The other British offices in Rockefeller Center were equally lively. The Inter-Allied Information Committee, now under Donald Hall, continued to promote postwar internationalism. It also played its part in the battle for American aid, defusing the image of Britain fighting alone and for its empire. With Allied help, Britain seemed rather more able to "finish the job." In February 1941, Lord Halifax wrote to the MoI praising the office. He singled out the success of its photographic section and publications, which now included a weekly, *Inter-Allied Review*, with a circulation of 150,000 and a smaller "clip sheet" of "propaganda" circulated to 1,750 "smaller newspapers."[16]

During the spring of 1941, the IAIC grew to include representatives of Denmark, Australia, and China. It provided a widening stream of information on the resistance movements in Europe and worked directly with the interventionists, helping the Committee to Defend America to launch its own news service devoted to Allied issues. On Easter Day 1941, the IAIC staged an award-winning radio spectacular on "The Resurrection of Europe." Broadcasts celebrating Magna Carta and Bastille Day followed. Lord Lothian's proxy propaganda agency was now an efficient reality.[17]

By the time of Peake's visit, yet another British office had sprung up at Rockefeller Center. Known as the British Overseas Press Service, it collected British bulletins and American clippings to supply to British publicists in Latin America, Asia, Europe, and the colonies. War shortages made this work easier to do from New York than from London, even though the office did not address the U.S. public. Its work confirmed the need for a single official to head Britain's burgeoning propaganda bureaucracy in the United States.[18]

Peake encountered only one major problem in New York: the British Library of Information. While the BPS forged ahead, the library remained a backwater. The problem lay in its leadership: Angus Fletcher still opposed expansion of the library's field of operations. Peake hoped that a new Director General could remove him.

In early April 1941, Peake presented his report. He ruled out intermediate control from London and suggested that British publicity be integrated into a single structure under an executive office in New York, staffed by MoI employees but under the authority of the British Embassy in Washington. The officer in charge would hold the diplomatic rank of minister and the title of Director General of British Information Services. From that moment onward, all British propaganda organizations in New York were known collectively by this name. The British Information Services or BIS had been born.[19]

Duff Cooper did not have to look far for a suitable Director General for the BIS. On Halifax's recommendation, he offered the job to Sir Gerald Campbell, a diplomat well known in the United States from his long service as Consul General in Philadelphia, San Francisco, and New York. He seemed the ideal man to front a friendly propaganda office, but Campbell hesitated before accepting the post. He understood the depth of America's fear of foreign propaganda and asked that his appointment first be cleared with the Secretary of State. When Hull proclaimed himself delighted, Campbell quietly took the job.[20] But Campbell did not have a monopoly on British propaganda in the United States; elsewhere in Rockefeller Center, a second, and rather less respectable campaign was underway.

The year 1941 had brought new responsibilities to Stephenson's British Security Co-ordination. In January, BSC became the North American office for Britain's internal security service, MI5. BSC also included a branch of "SO.1," the covert propaganda wing of London's Special Operations Executive; and in his capacity as head of this office, Stephenson began his assault on U.S. isolationism.[21] Like the BIS, BSC encompassed an eclectic array of talent. The staff included Oxford dons Bill Deakin, Alfred Ayer, and Gilbert Highet; advertising genius David Ogilvy; playwright and future Labour MP Ben Levy; Eric Maschwitz, the composer of "A Nightingale Sung in Berkeley Square," and eventually Noel Langley, the co-author of the screenplay for *The Wizard of Oz*.[22] Stephenson originally hoped that Noël Coward might direct his propaganda, but London quashed the appointment. Apparently Coward had made a rude remark about Randolph Churchill at a recent dinner party and was considered a security risk. BSC propaganda work remained under the direction of two journalists: Sidney Morrell and Christopher Wren.[23]

In July 1941, the SO.1 departments of SOE in London became a separate Political Warfare Executive under the Foreign Office. Suddenly, Stephenson's hold on covert propaganda in the United States seemed shaky. The Foreign Office summoned Morrell to England to give an account of his work. In response, he compiled a detailed report of all BSC's covert propaganda operations, which survives in the Foreign Office archives. Morrell began dramatically:

> The activities of SO.1 in New York are three-fold:
>   (1) Subversive propaganda in the United States for the exposure and destruction of enemy propaganda in the United States; countering iso-lationist and appeasement propaganda which is rapidly taking on the shape of a Fascist movement, conscious or unconscious.
>   (2) The use of America's prestige and neutrality by directing osten-sibly American propaganda towards the three Axis powers and enemy-occupied territories.
>   (3) Subversive propaganda in South American countries as in (1) above.

The operations described were simple and direct. In the attempt to distribute "subversive propaganda," the office had established a net-work of middlemen (or "cut-outs"), seemingly unconnected with the British, to place stories and some twenty rumors each day with the "leading home reporters on the New York and Chicago papers" and such commentators as Dorothy Thompson, Walter Winchell, and Edgar Ansel Mowrer. Contact with Winchell was probably maintained via Stephenson's friend (and Winchell's ghost writer) Ernest Cuneo, who also linked both to the White House.[24]

BSC's rumors usually concerned Nazi oppression in enemy and enemy-occupied territory. To ensure their credibility, they were based on letters intercepted by British censors in the Caribbean. Material not fed to the New York tabloids was placed in the U.S. foreign-language press through the Overseas News Agency (formerly a branch of the Jewish Telegraph Agency), over which SO.1 now claimed "effective control." These stories were then "confirmed" by "underground reports from Europe," obligingly issued by the Czech Consulate. The BSC also had an understanding with C. R. V. Thompson, New York corre-spondent of the *Daily Express*, to include the rumors in his dispatches to London. He would cite rumors printed in the American press as European news "obtained by American correspondents." SO.1 then developed the *Daily Express* stories into fresh rumors and fed them back to New York. In this way, every rumor grew by "snowball effect." Morrell did not cite any particular rumors, but he mentioned that the agent who wrote them—code number G124—was "a free-lance journalist" with "close working contact with such publications as *PM*, *The Nation*, *The New Republic* and *The Postal Service Monitor* [sic]."[25]

Morrell scattered his stories widely and made good use of overt British channels:

If a story is considered less important, different angles of it are fed to a variety of press contacts on the theory that the natural inquisitiveness of newspapermen will lead them to ferret out further facts. In some cases, information is handed to the British Press Services and the British Library of Information, or to friendly correspondents of British newspapers in New York.[26]

René MacColl was happy to help. Within days of MacColl's arrival, Morrell had visited the office and had begun feeding the U.S. press with intelligence on German finances in the United States provided by Major John Pepper, BSC's resident economic warfare expert.[27]

The BIS and BSC also cooperated in subsidizing the Boston-based shortwave radio station—WRUL—for its foreign-language broadcasts to occupied Europe. The British Embassy press office funded the daily French, German, and Serbo-Croat broadcasts; the Inter-Allied Information Committee office provided material; and BSC added a secret subsidy of $400 a month. BSC also funded WRUL broadcasts by the Italian Mazzini Society and the France Forever Committee, and claimed to have "formed a committee" of American broadcasters, including Dorothy Thompson and William Shirer, ready to advise the U.S. government on shortwave broadcasting in the event of a need for emergency federal control.[28] A secret history of BSC, written at the end of the war, claimed that BSC had little difficulty in subverting the neutrality of WRUL. BSC funds arrived through inconspicuous "cut-outs." BSC also "recruited foreign news editors, translators, and announcers" for WRUL; supplied news; and prepared entire scripts for commentaries. Although WRUL refused to broadcast material that had not appeared in the American press, the office "got around this by inserting its own material in friendly newspapers, and then quoting it."[29] Yet the secret British role in WRUL transmissions was the least of BSC's operations.

Like the BIS, BSC developed links with the interventionist lobby. Morrell claimed that a number of interventionist organizations had either been formed by SO.1 or been "acquired" through large British funding. His list was extensive:

(i) *The Non-Sectarian Anti-Nazi League*. Used for the vehement exposure of enemy agents and isolationists . . . .

(ii) *The League for Human Rights*. A subsidiary organisation of the American Federation of Labour . . . .

(iii) *Friends of Democracy*.

(iv) *Fight for Freedom Committee*. Both this and (iii) above are militant interventionist organisations whose aim is to provide Roosevelt with evidence that the U.S. public is eager for action.

(v) *American Labour Committee to Aid British Labour*. Another branch organisation of the American Federation of Labour . . . .

(vi) *Committee for Inter-American Co-operation.* Used this for sponsoring SO.1 work in Central and South America . . . .

(vii) *America Last.* A purely provocative experiment started in San Francisco in an attempt to sting America into a fighting mood.

Morrell noted that these organizations were "unaware of British influence, since this is maintained through a permanent official in each organisation, who in turn, is in touch with a cut-out—and never with us direct."

The text was full of exaggerations and typographical errors; however, it had not been written for posterity, but rather to serve the cause of BSC in imminent negotiations in London. Morrell hoped that BSC might become the core of a unified "nation-wide campaign for an American declaration of war" and not only to retain control over covert propaganda but to do the work of the overt British Information Services as well. But Bill Stephenson was a late entrant in the game; his bid came far too late to pose any serious challenge to the newly appointed Sir Gerald Campbell.[30]

The biggest failing of British public relations in 1941 was not in the efforts of BSC or the BIS but at the British Embassy in Washington. By May, it had become clear that the new ambassador was a liability. Lord Halifax knew that he was not suited for service in the United States and had engaged Peake to manage his dealings with the American press.[31] Unfortunately, Peake's work in New York left him little time to help. Moreover, Peake himself was out of his depth in Washington and tended to indulge the ambassador against the advice of wiser heads. While Morgan and Wheeler-Bennett looked on in horror, Peake and Halifax stumbled through a series of avoidable errors.

On March 29, 1941, with Peake's approval, Halifax joined a landed Pennsylvania family to engage in his favourite aristocratic pastime: the fox hunt. While London burned and American workers labored overtime to meet Allied orders, Halifax cavorted on horseback with the social register set. The poet Carl Sandberg denounced his insensitivity in *The Nation* and longed for a return to the democratic days of Lord Lothian.[32] Then Halifax visited Chicago and, in a genuflection to populism, decided to attend a baseball game. Regrettably, he informed reporters that "This is a bit like cricket, except we don't question the Umpire's decision so much in England." He departed before the game was over and, worse still, left a hot dog, forlorn and uneaten, on his seat. Isolationist cameras snapped the image for posterity. Halifax had managed to slight two American institutions in one day. It seemed as though everything haughty and effete and undemocratic about the British aristocracy had taken human form and ridden forth as Britain's special representative to abuse the down-home culture of middle America.[33] Fortunately, the situation in London was a bit more encouraging.

Winston Churchill, master of radio propaganda, addresses a joint session of Congress and a vast radio audience in December 1941. Imperial War Museum, London.

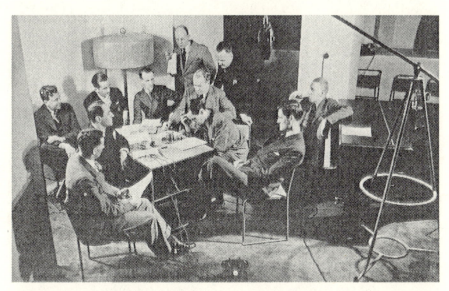

Broadcasting the Blitz: BBC and CBS broadcasters plan "London After Dark," August 1940. Seated, left to right: Vaughn Thomas, BBC; Larry Lesueur, CBS; Bob Bowman, Canadian Broadcasting Corporation; Ed Murrow, CBS; Cecil Madden, BBC; Vincent Sheean, CBS; Michael Standing, BBC; Eric Sevareid, CBS; Sandy MacPherson, BBC organist. Standing: Gerry Wilmot, CBC announcer, and R. H. Wood, BBC Engineer. Picture © BBC, London.

The spirit of "the few": a young RAF pilot, photographed by Cecil Beaton in 1940. Imperial War Museum, London.

A propagandist in death: the funeral of RAF Pilot Officer Billy Fiske. Chosen by the British government to tour the United States as a propagandist, he instead became the first American killed in action in World War II. The Bettmann Archive, New York.

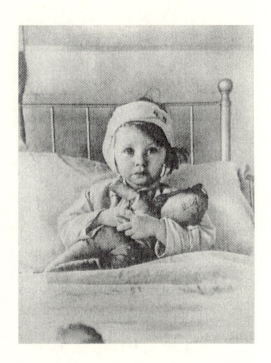

Beaton's photograph of Ellen
Dunne, victim of a Nazi bomb,
widely circulated in the United
States as a *Life* magazine cover and
interventionist poster. Imperial
War Museum, London.

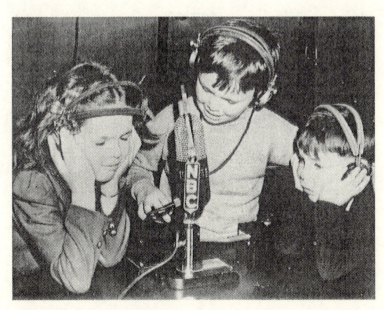

"A weekly tear compeller": British evacuees in the U.S. speak to their families
in beleaguered Britain in the NBC/BBC program "Children Calling Home." Hulton-
Deutsch Collection, London.

The Blitz spirit in a typical news photograph from 1940. The Bettmann Archive, New York.

The war as social leveler: the King and Queen inspect bomb damage in September 1940. Imperial War Museum, London.

"Street scene" in Coventry after the fire-raid of November 1940. Such pictures were withheld from the British public, but the censors allowed UP to send this picture to the United States on December 9, 1940. The Bettmann Archive, New York.

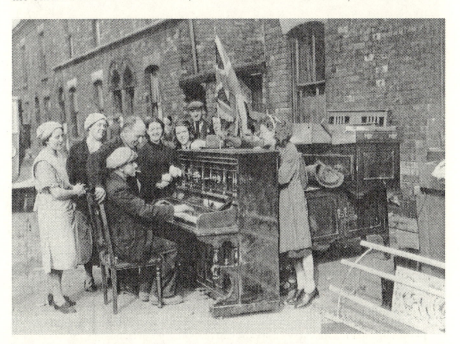

The Blitz spirit in Northwest England, 1941: one day after a raid, bomb victims and clean-up workers gather for a patriotic sing-along around a salvaged piano. The Bettmann Archive, New York.

The Blitz as imagined in MGM's *Mrs. Miniver*, 1942, starring Greer Garson and Walter Pidgeon, and scripted in 1941 with the advice of Britain's Ministry of Information. British Film Institute, London, stills collection, © 1940/ Turner Entertainment Co. All Rights Reserved.

Huntley Haverstock (Joel McCrea, shown here with Laraine Day) broadcasts to the U.S. during a raid on London in the climax of Walter Wanger and Alfred Hitchcock's 1940 propaganda masterpiece, *Foreign Correspondent*. Wisconsin Center for Film and Theater Research, stills collection, © 1939 Walter Wanger Productions Inc. and Castle Hill Productions Inc. New York.

After the raid: a scene from Humphrey Jennings and Harry Watt's 1940 propaganda documentary *London Can Take It*, released in the United States by Warner Brothers. Imperial War Museum, London.

Britain gives it back: an RAF bombardier takes aim over Germany in Harry Watt's 1941 documentary *Target for Tonight*, also released in the United States by Warner

"The Polish horror pictures," as placed in the U.S. press in February 1941 by the British Press Service

Poles murdered by Nazis, published in *PM*, February 14, 1941 under the headline "Germany demanded living space in Poland . . . this is how she is getting it." Jósef Pilsudski Institute, New York.

The front page picture: a German firing squad in Poland. Jósef Pilsudski Institute, New York.

London: British Broadcasting and Film, and the Greek Intervention

> To Hell with whether what I say is propaganda or not. I have never
> stopped to figure it out and I don't think it matters anymore.
>   Leslie Howard, December 16, 1940[34]

London echoed Peake's call for stronger propaganda in the United
States. In the FO Political Intelligence Department, Graham Hutton
proposed a chain of new information offices and subconsulates across
the United States, dedicated to bringing America into the war. Walter
Monckton detected in this a Foreign Office scheme to snatch the entire
U.S. propaganda apparatus from the MoI, so he squelched the plan.
Hutton's moment would come later.[35] More significantly, Churchill now
seemed sympathetic to the propaganda effort. In December, he gave his
blessing to his friend and publisher, the Hungarian emigré Emery
Reves, to join the propaganda war in New York. Reves secured offices
in the RCA building and began to publish anti-Nazi material.[36] In
February, Churchill ordered a warm welcome for a delegation of American Legion war veterans. His speeches continued to show his desire to
rouse the United States. Ronald Tree surmised that Churchill was not
adverse to propaganda per se, but only to any propagandist other than
himself.[37]

The MoI began the year by founding a new internal advisory committee under Lord Davidson to exploit Britain's business contacts with
the United States. Meanwhile, Williams and Darvall pressed for the
Foreign Office to abandon the "No Propaganda" policy completely.[38]
But irrespective of policy, the propaganda makers of the MoI and the
BBC were now operating at full capacity, pumping out propaganda on
the new theme of "Give Us the Tools."

The front line of British broadcast propaganda was the news. The
microphones of the BBC North American Service brought Britain's war
news from the battlefield directly to the American people; and as the
year turned, the news was good. British and Australian troops burst
westward along the desert rim of North Africa, and the BBC correspondent Richard Dimbleby went with them. In succeeding months,
the BBC carried news—good and bad—from battlefronts in Ethiopia,
Syria, and Greece. Britain was giving "it" back, and any American
with a shortwave set could hear it being described in his living room.[39]

The BBC also worked to capture the American ear through entertainment. To this end, it hit on the idea of a propaganda soap opera.
The BBC in New York hoped that this might be valuable channel for
reaching a traditionally noninterventionist group: American women.
In early 1941, the BBC launched "Front Line Family" a daily "serial
story dealing with the adventures of an ordinary family in wartime
conditions." It was a bold move. The high-minded BBC had never pro-

duced a soap opera before. Now the corporation swallowed its pride
and set its sights on "the enormous public for family serials in the
United States and Canada."[40]

The BBC aimed shamelessly for the lowest common denominator.
It instructed the series' writer, Alan Melville, that: "This material must
appeal to an audience of relatively limited mentality, an audience who
believes in thrilleresque, is not squeamish, and is almost completely
credulous." The serial also matched Britain's American propaganda
policy. Frank Darvall was script consultant, and a genuine Canadian
soldier, Private John McLaren, added an authentic North American
accent to the cast. In deference to American tastes, the producers forbade all "cussing" on the air and decided to respect Canadian
convention by making no mention of pubs or of the sale of alcohol. The
result was an entertaining but rather skewed picture of wartime
London. The first episode aired on April 27, 1941, on the BBC North
American Service. The audience response was sufficiently impressive
to enable the BBC to sell the serial to a number of independent stations
for rebroadcast within the United States; and four months later, domestic U.S. transmission of "Front Line Family" began.[41]

The advent of soap at the BBC was the first of many changes. In
early 1941, the former *Radio Times* editor, Maurice Gorham, became
director of the North American Service. Working to satisfy the motto
"British in content but American in appeal," he built up the service
schedule to a full 7 ½ hours a day. The BBC then established its own intelligence unit to survey American opinion and to fine-tune the content
of its programming. The BBC office in New York grew, and it acquired a
new head, Lindsay Wellington on whom Broadcasting House thoughtfully conferred the grand rank of Director; such things ensured that he
would be able to hold his own when dealing with the top brass at the
British Information Services. The move paid off. Soon the two Rockefeller Center offices were cooperating to their mutual advantage.[42]

Recognizing the power of Murrow's live coverage of air raids, the
BBC now sought to go one better. In October, the Overseas Service
Producer Cecil Madden decided that live entertainment "under Blitz
conditions," with such "effects from outside" as sirens, bomb blasts,
and buildings collapsing, would capture a substantial American audience. He had high hopes for the midnight shows at London's Player's
Theatre. But by the late autumn, the Germans could no longer be
relied on to provide the necessary "noises-off." Consequently, the
United States only heard raids if the BBC outside broadcast unit could
get to the scene in time.[43]

Meanwhile, the BBC increased the formal propaganda content of
its North American Service broadcasts. "Listening Post" offered analysis of German propaganda, while "The Stones Cry Out," surveyed
bomb damage to Britain's historic buildings.[44] Other programs nurtured
the idea of a trans-Atlantic community. The BBC emphasized the role

of American volunteers in the British forces with programs such as the "Eagle Club Show," a weekly live broadcast from the American servicemen's club on Charing Cross Road; and "Answering You" allowed British "experts" (from housewives to the Speaker of the House of Commons) to answer American questions about Britain's war. Like "Radio Newsreel," "Answering You" was rebroadcast over the Mutual network. The system worked so well that the BBC launched similar cooperative projects with CBS and NBC: "Trans-Atlantic Call" and "Atlantic Spotlight," respectively.[45]

The BBC's most obvious piece of "Hands Across the Sea" propaganda dated from March 1941, when Gerald Cock suggested that the BBC carry greetings from British towns like Cambridge, Richmond, and Plymouth to their namesakes in the United States, to promote an awareness of a common heritage. The series began impressively. On September 28, "London Calling" included a message from Boston, Lincolnshire, to Boston, Massachusetts. But the BBC soon ran out of well-known namesakes; and by the end of November the program was reduced to recording a message from the small Middlesex town of Sunbury-on-Thames for the dubious benefit of the citizens of Sunbury, Pennsylvania. Although a pleasant little town, Sunbury-on-Thames provided scant material for the propagandist. The high point of the broadcast came when an ancient resident recalled punting into the bar of the Flower Pot public house during the Thames flood of 1894. A fine propaganda idea had been exhausted, and the BBC knew it.[46]

Sunbury notwithstanding, 1941 brought victory upon victory for British radio in America. As of December 7, 1941, the service stood ready to work for Anglo-American understanding in the war and (no less importantly) the peace ahead. As ever, however, the achievement of the MoI Films Division was less clearcut.

Despite the success of *London Can Take It*, the MoI Films Division entered 1941 keenly aware of the need for a fresh approach. Even before "Give Us the Tools . . . ," Harry Watt pressed for a more aggressive representation of the war effort. In November 1940, he began work on an appropriate documentary, titled *Target for Tonight*, recounting an RAF bomber raid on Germany. Watt's project matched the needs of the MoI. *Target for Tonight* told the story of a single British bomber named "F for Freddie." Through the artful use of real RAF personnel and a spare Wellington fuselage, Watt created a stunning piece of propaganda. His success was evident from the first preview, at which, for the first time in the history of British cinema, the critics demanded an encore. In August 1941, the MoI sent Sidney Bernstein to New York to arrange for distribution; to his delight, Warner Brothers snapped up the film. The American version (redubbed to avoid the problem of unintelligibly authentic accents) won public acclaim and an Oscar in 1942. This success would have amused the crew of "F for Freddie," but none lived long enough to see it. Such were the losses in RAF Bomber Command.[47]

Most British feature films of 1941 had less to offer. Britain's "supporting features" included probably the worst British propaganda film of the war, David MacDonald's pageant of English history "as told" to an American reporter: *This England*.[48] The MoI's documentary output struggled to compensate for these deficiencies. As of January 1941, the British believed that the most useful MoI film in America was *Britain on Guard*, written and narrated by J. B. Priestley (released in Britain as *Britain at Bay*). With stirring footage of the people's war and a climax based on Churchill's "Fight them on the beaches" speech, *Britain on Guard* provided a powerful vision of a war fought both to preserve old values and to build a better world. The BLI noted the importance of Priestley's "constructive attitude" in "explaining not only what we are fighting *against* but what we are fighting for." The same themes figured in the Boulting brothers' *Dawn Guard*, a short film in which two Home Guard soldiers described their hopes for peace. Such films were important, particularly since the Prime Minister still had not made a formal declaration of British war aims.[49]

Humphrey Jennings best captured the new "Give Us the Tools" spirit. His new documentary, *The Heart of Britain*, concentrated on the industrial midlands and north, showing that region's defiance and determination to strike back at Nazi Germany. The film had an Anglo-American flavor. Ed Murrow narrated an American version, retitled with his trademark phrase, *This Is England*. The film moved swiftly from shots of Britain at peace to tough footage of life and death in blitzed Coventry. Then Jennings cut to a northern choral society roaring forth the Hallelujah Chorus. As the music swelled, shots of the charred shell of Coventry Cathedral gave way to British bombers rumbling off into the night to blast Germany. The commentary continued:

> People who can sing like that in times like these cannot be beaten. These people are slow to anger, not easily roused. Now they and their mates, their wives and their children, have been subjected to the most savage ordeal ever inflicted upon human beings. But these people have the power to hit back. And they are going to hit back, with all the skill in their hands, the tradition of their crafts, and the fire in their hearts. Out of the valleys of Power and the rivers of Industry will come an answer to the German challenge, and the Nazis will learn once and for all—that no one with impunity troubles the heart of Britain.[50]

This Is England crossed the Atlantic in the capable hands of Harry Hopkins. It opened to acclaim and played in 200 New York movie theaters in its first week of release alone.[51]

Humphrey Jennings's next documentary, *Words for Battle*, linked Britain's past glories with its present trial. In a short, lyrical film, he set stirring passages from English literature, read by Laurence Olivier, against images of the war effort. From Shakespeare through Blake,

Browning, and Kipling, Jennings unrolled a picture of a nation living up to its literature. An interest in America shone out in the final sequences of the film. First, Jennings juxtaposed images of England's inviolate coastline with Churchill's pledge to "fight them on the beaches . . . until the new world . . . sets forth to the liberation of the old." Then, as tanks rolled past the statue of Abraham Lincoln in London's Parliament Square, Olivier read the Gettysburg Address. Lincoln's call for a "new birth of freedom" seemed perfectly tailored to Britain's cause and America's susceptibilities.[52]

The MoI made only one film exclusively for American audiences. Titled *We Won't Forget*, it was a thank-you for American aid. The film moved from the aftermath of an air raid to scenes of battered Londoners eating at American canteen trucks and receiving American clothes, blankets, and blood plasma. It showed a plastic surgeon from New York at work on an injured bus driver, and panned across rest centres bulging with American supplies. In the final moments, a fire fighter, a grandmother, a workman, and a young mother each faced the camera and thanked America for its help. Churchill hated this film and asked that it not be sent. He was ignored, and the BLI immediately passed the film on to the various aid-to-Britain agencies.[53]

Britain's film propagandists understood that their work was nothing without an audience. They sought to build up their U.S. distribution through the British office at the International Film Center, in New York. The IFC operation overlapped naturally with the film office at the BLI: Richard Ford occupied both jobs. The BLI also published its own catalogue and soon built up a tidy distribution network on the educational circuit.[54] Nevertheless, Britain's film publicists knew that the nontheatrical film circuit could only reach an American elite already sympathetic to their cause. British films required mass distribution, and achieving this required hard work in the United States.

London Can Take It had revolutionized British film propaganda in the United States. It proved that propaganda could make money. The MoI moved swiftly to consolidate its success and decided to open an office in Hollywood. In the late autumn of 1940, the Films Division dispatched the distinguished British film executive A. W. Jarratt to develop the necessary links with the studios. Jarratt arrived to find that Alexander Korda had assumed the role of British Ambassador to Hollywood. Korda immediately summoned the Hollywood moguls to a grand dinner to meet the MoI representative and to hear about Britain's propaganda needs at first hand. The guests included the Warner brothers; Darryl F. Zanuck and Sidney Kent from Fox; Sam Goldwyn from MGM; Murray Silverstone and Arthur Kelly from United Artists; Harry Cohn from Columbia; Hal Roach; and representatives from Universal, RKO, and Paramount. Walt Disney had a prior engagement with the opening of *Fantasia*, but the British had no doubt of his sympathy. He had already designed propaganda cartoon characters for the MoI.[55]

After a speech of welcome from Louis B. Mayer, Jarratt outlined the sort of film material he thought would be most useful to the MoI. Mayer replied that Britain could "count on the producers of Holly-wood" to do "everything possible to help the great cause." Although encouraged, Jarratt knew that the filmmakers hoped for British reve-nues, British actors, and better British newsreel footage in return. But the Americans soon fulfilled their pledges of support. Hearst and Fox newsreels promised to stop using German footage; and not to be out-done, Warner Brothers offered to distribute a special "British Review" newsreel. The future of the British cause in Hollywood seemed secure. By the time of Jarratt's mission, several studios had followed Warners and agreed to distribute MoI films. Fox took *Men of the Lightship*, a re-enactment of the German attack on the East Dudgeon lightship, and Columbia accepted two MoI films on the RAF. Other contracts fol-lowed. Soon, Jarratt felt sufficiently confident to assure the ministry that the American market could support one new British documen-tary every month, provided that it carried entertainment value. He suggested creating a New York branch of the MoI Films Division and appointing a film expert to the staff of the British Consulate in Los Angeles. On May 9, 1941, the British Treasury approved his scheme; it only remained for the new Director of the British Infor-mation Services, Sir Gerald Campbell, to complete his review of the structure in June.[56]

While Jarratt and the moguls talked, the BLI in New York and the Hollywood British worked hard to prepare MoI films for American distribution. Alfred Hitchcock overcame the barrier of the regional dialects so dear to the hearts of documentary filmmakers. He redubbed *Merchant Seaman* and then redubbed and reedited *Men of the Light-ship*, tacking on a prologue by Robert Sherwood.[57] Meanwhile, the BLI film officer, Richard Ford, advised London about the United States' newsreel needs. Ford called for more war footage, more film of the royal family, and more coverage of the Labour Party Cabinet minis-ters. Irritated by his persistent requests, the MoI's deputy secretary, Colonel Scorgie, suggested sending:

> A newsreel of Mr. Bevin, Mr. Morrison, and the Prime Minister jointly and severally beating the quarter-mile amateur record eastward from the White Cliffs of Dover with a German tank in chase, background Canter-bury Cathedral blitzed, with archbishop holding a service in the ruins supported by Cardinal Hinsley and the Chief Rabbi, foreground a cheer-ing crowd of acceptable Princesses also Royal Duchesses . . . especially wearing trousers.[58]

The MoI Films Division did not stand alone in its battle for the American screen. From Canada, John Grierson opened a second front. Grierson had always believed that Canada could be Britain's bridge to American opinion. By November 1939, he had a plan to accomplish this through a Canadian version of *March of Time*. By 1941, Grierson had launched two film series: *Canada Carries On* and *World in Action*.

Both had U.S. distribution. *Canada Carries On* covered subjects from Canada's war at sea to Roosevelt's "Four Freedoms." The issue on "Children from Overseas" told the story of Britain's young evacuees. The innocents proved to be admirable propagandists. Wide-eyed at the New World, they planned to become cowboys and mistook police sirens for an air-raid warning. Nine-year-old Billy Bishop stole the show by announcing that Canada was nice, but "not as good as ol' Middlesbrough." Grierson never fell into the *London Can Take It* trap of self-pity. The 1941 *World in Action* film "Churchill's Island" bristled with defiance, presenting Britain's "silent wartime revolution" and "inner-strength . . . which bombs and fire and steel cannot pierce." The message to Hitler was blunt: "Come if you dare!"[59]

Grierson soon caught America's eye. Some 7,000 American theaters showed *World in Action*, and as many as 15,000 theaters regularly carried material produced by the National Film Board of Canada. Some films enjoyed particular success. "Churchill's Island" won an Academy Award, and "War Clouds in the Pacific"—a *Canada Carries On* exposé of Japanese militarism—"scooped" all the U.S. newsreels at the time of Pearl Harbor and earned more than $70,000. Grierson had plugged a gap in British film propaganda. He was certainly not a pillar of the MoI, but (as Churchill said of his own relationship to the church) he made a fine buttress, supporting its often rickety structure from the outside. By 1941, he had masterfully shown London how film propaganda should be done.[60]

By the end of March 1941, Britain's propagandists had been rewarded by the smooth passage of the Lend-Lease bill into law. It now fell to the British to "finish the job" and fulfill the words and images of Churchill's speeches, BBC radio programs, and MoI films in solid achievements on the battlefield. The government required a display of Britain's determination to defend democracy, in order to impress America. Britain's fighting forces performed accordingly, but at a terrible price.

The drama was acted out in the Balkans that spring. As German forces massed on the Bulgarian frontier, the British pondered their response. The Greeks were unpromising partners, but the question of American public opinion tipped the balance. Greece was more than an ally in a strategic location. Greece was the cradle of the Anglo-American way, the source of the flame of democracy that had been passed from Athens to Rome to England and delivered safely into the hands of the American Founding Fathers. With this in mind, Britain prepared to commit 60,000 troops from its forces in North Africa to the defense of Greece.

The British knew that the Greek cause was desperate, and from the first they presented their decision as moral rather than strategic. Churchill described the move to FDR in a telegram heavy with noblesse oblige: "I must tell you what we have resolved about Greece. Although it was no doubt tempting to push on from Benghazi to Tripoli . . . we have felt it our duty to stand with the Greeks, who have declared to us their resolve, even alone, to resist the German invader."[61] Lest FDR miss the point, the actual decision was taken in the presence of White House envoy Colonel Bill Donovan. Meanwhile, Duff Cooper ordered the MoI to stress that Greece was an ally and as such had to be aided; but, anticipating defeat, he added that, since Hitler had hoped to conquer the country through infiltration, Britain would at least have forced him to fight.[62]

The United States was seen as the only important audience for the news from Greece. Duff Cooper's aide Sammy Hood saw no need to send out guidance telegrams on the story to British missions elsewhere, because the "U.S.A. is all that really matters and U.S. correspondents will be given the line here." Duff Cooper did send a cable, but his instructions included an American angle:

> It is unthinkable that His Majesty's government should leave Greece to face these odds alone. To abandon her to her fate would violate all the principles for which we stand. Accordingly, in the spirit so eloquently expressed by President Roosevelt of extending aid to all those defending their independence against aggression, we have sent fresh assistance to Greece.[63]

In London, Eden broke the news to the British and American press corps with the words "We are pledged to defend democracy"; privately, the MoI warned the BBC that victory was not "a foregone conclusion." It was an honest, but ominous message.[64]

On April 6, the blow fell. German tanks surged across the Greek frontier, while Allied forces struggled to slow their advance. On 24 April the Greek government surrendered. The remaining British and Commonwealth units were evacuated to Crete, which they hoped to hold as a naval base. A German airborne assault beginning on May 20 killed this hope at the loss of 13,000 allied troops. It was yet another bitter defeat; but as Churchill emphasized in his speech of April 27, the Allies had done their duty. In later years, Churchill maintained that his gamble had worked and that Britain's stand "appealed profoundly to the United States, and above all to the great men who led them." Roosevelt did admire the stand; but as Churchill soon realized, he remained reluctant to provide any further aid.[65]

Washington: Friends, Enemies, and the Supply Crisis

Here is Churchill's latest appeal to Roosevelt:
Frankie, Frankie, Give me your answer do,
I'm half crazy, waiting for news from you,
Britannia won't have a carriage,
For the Anglo-American marriage,

> If you don't send on the Lease and Lend,
> A ship-load of Dollars too!
>
> German propaganda song, circa April 1941[66]

By April 1941, Britain faced a new supply crisis. American aid had escaped the internal blockade of the isolationists, but it still had to navigate the North Atlantic. German U-boats were now sinking British vessels faster than its shipbuilders could launch them. In February, Britain lost 400,000 tons of shipping; in March, 500,000 tons; in April, 700,000 tons. As Hitler extended his declared Atlantic "War Zone," Churchill warned Harry Hopkins: "the strain at sea on our naval resources is too great for us . . . we simply have not got the escorts to go round and fight at the same time." Without American naval support Britain could be starved into submission. The U.S. Navy already patrolled the western North Atlantic, but Britain needed it to do more. Churchill appealed, but FDR did nothing.[67]

Frustration mounted in Washington. British and American officials struggled to rationalize the President's inaction. Lord Halifax complained that FDR was "ultra respectful of public opinion." Harry Hopkins muttered that he would "rather follow public opinion than lead it." But Roosevelt was unmoved. He had lived with U.S. public opinion all his political life. He knew how to monitor its changes and, when the climate seemed right, how to lead it. His critics scorned his approach. "Every great leader," Clare Boothe Luce observed, had his "typical gesture": Hitler had the upraised arm, and Churchill had the V sign; but Roosevelt's gesture was a single wetted finger, raised to determine which way the wind was blowing.[68]

On May 16, Roosevelt broke his silence and declared that the United States stood by "the principle of the Freedom of the Seas." Then, in a Fireside Chat of May 27, he proclaimed "an Unlimited National Emergency." The country supported his move. Gallup reported that 70 percent of Americans now wanted British supply convoys to be protected by the U.S. Navy and that 85 percent thought that a war with Germany was inevitable.[69] But even so, it was many weeks before Roosevelt extended further naval aid; in lieu of this, he took certain institutional steps to advance the cause.

In November 1940, a Washington Cabinet Committee had called for development of a formal propaganda campaign in support of the national defense effort. In late May 1941, Roosevelt embarked on this policy. The British were both its beneficiaries and its model. First, FDR established the Office of Civilian Defense, under Fiorello LaGuardia. This office included a publicity section, the Bureau of Facts and Figures, to promote preparation for war. LaGuardia lobbied for this bureau to become an office in its own right, and he nominated the interventionist poet Archibald MacLeish to become its director. When the appointment seemed likely to be made, MacLeish turned to the British for advice. On October 10, 1941, he wrote to Sir Angus Fletcher: "I

shall need to talk to you very badly if this thing goes through."
Fletcher's reply is lost, but when the Office of Facts and Figures opened
its doors on October 26, MacLeish promised a "strategy of truth"
with no "balley-hoo" methods. His words might have been spoken by
Fletcher himself. Unfortunately, the agency also emulated Fletcher's
lackluster performance. Frustrated journalists dubbed the new venture
the "Office of Fun and Frolic."[70]

The British also aided America's first forays into the fields of covert
propaganda and intelligence. Inspired by his contact with William
Stephenson, Colonel Bill Donovan transformed FDR's initial plan to
monitor isolationists at home into a proposal for an international intelligence agency. Stephenson promised his full assistance and supported the scheme through discreet lobbying in Washington.[71] In mid-
June of 1941, the British and American military intelligence staffs
agreed to exchange information and established a joint intelligence
committee. Stephenson pressed for more. On June 27, Ian Fleming of
BSC's Naval Intelligence contingent sent Donovan a proposal for an integrated intelligence and propaganda machine that could be ready "to
meet war before Christmas."[72] On July 11, Roosevelt moved again,
establishing the office of the Coordinator of Information (COI) under
Donovan. Donovan in turn set up a Foreign Information Service under
Robert Sherwood to oversee shortwave broadcasting. The BBC in New
York provided fraternal advice and arranged for Donovan and Sherwood to visit Broadcasting House in London in September 1941.[73] In
the space of two months, the Roosevelt administration had, with British
help, planted the seeds of the Central Intelligence Agency and the Voice
of America.

Roosevelt also became interested in British publicity. When Rudolf
Hess parachuted into Scotland, FDR wrote to Churchill to emphasize
the propaganda value of the story:

> If Hess is talking . . . it would be very valuable for public opinion over
> here if he can be persuaded to tell your people what Hitler has said about
> the United States . . . . I can assure you that the Hess flight has captured
> the American imagination and the story should be kept alive for just as
> many days even weeks as possible.[74]

But London said nothing. For a month, the British maintained complete silence over the Hess story. He had not provided any information
suitable for public consumption. FDR was disappointed, and anti-
British editors speculated that Britain might yet strike a deal with
Hitler. Far from providing a propaganda coup, the Hess story had
pointed up a vital flaw in British war publicity. Britain still needed a
clear program of war aims.[75]

While FDR wished that Britain would say more, others in Washington worked to silence British propaganda once and for all. Most
significantly, Assistant Secretary of State Adolf A. Berle continued to
use the U.S. government's anti-Nazi measures as an entering wedge for

his campaign against the British propaganda apparatus in the United States. On January 27, 1941, the State Department committee investigating foreign propaganda presented its findings, and the details of the growth in British activity in late 1940 made disturbing reading. The reported activities of the Inter-Allied Information Committee inflamed fears that foreigners might stir up America's linguistic minorities. A crop of memoranda with such titles as "Foreign Political Propaganda in the United States: Measures for Terminating the Same" followed.[76]

Despite Bill Stephenson's cooperation with Donovan, Berle singled out British Security Co-ordination as the principal malefactor. In March 1941, he informed Sumner Welles:

> William S. Stephenson . . . is, nominally, in charge of providing protection for British ships, supplies, etc. But in fact, a full size secret police and intelligence service is rapidly evolving. There are, or about to be, district officers at Boston, New York City, Philadelphia, Baltimore, Charleston, New Orleans, Houston, San Francisco, Portland and probably Seattle. We know that to the existing offices there are now reporting a very considerable number of regularly employed secret agents and a much larger number of informers, etc. We likewise know that the information is by no means limited to the work of safeguarding ships and munitions, but enters into the whole field of political, financial, industrial, and probably military intelligence . . . . I have reason to believe that a good many things being done are probably in violation of our espionage acts.

Berle warned that British and American interests did not always overlap. "There is always," he concluded, "a temptation to use this sort of machinery to influence strictly American decisions." His solution was simple: ask the British either to dissolve the BSC or to transfer the network into American hands. In June 1941, Berle and the Justice Department began work on laws to put the British propagandists out of business for good.[77] The British remained unaware of his plans. They would doubtless have been appalled by the news, but at the time they were more concerned with interdepartmental troubles of their own. London was preoccupied with its worst news crisis since the Phoney War and enmeshed in a struggle over propaganda policy that came to be known as the Battle of Bloomsbury.

London: The Battle of Bloomsbury

> The situation vis-a-vis the press and public opinion has entered a new phase in which our ability to present our case and influence authoritative opinion sufficiently well may play a vital part within the next few weeks or months in determining the role America is to play in supporting us. We have to face a new situation which demands an organised drive at once.
>
> Charles Peake and Lord Halifax, April 25, 1941[78]

By April 1941, all Whitehall agreed that the time was right for a concerted effort to win American public opinion; unfortunately, while the
British Embassy and MoI were prepared to accomplish this by expanding the BIS, the Foreign Office still clung to the old "No Propaganda"
line and reverently produced Lord Lothian's telegrams of September
1939 as their gospel.[79] Meanwhile, the Prime Minister and the Admiralty used American opinion as an excuse to suppress information
about British shipping losses. They argued that bad news would de-
press America and good news would make them complacent. The
result was, in Halifax's words, a "conspicuous success" for "Dr. Goebbels." A hundred senior American journalists agreed. Friends and
enemies alike assured the British Embassy that Britain was failing to
provide enough news.[80] As London sank into a "news crisis," the struggle to settle the issue of American publicity began.

The debate began in mid-April, when Lord Beaverbrook proposed
to the War Cabinet that the depressing news from the U-boat war be
used to awaken America. The Admiralty ignored him, and the crisis
deepened.[81] The MoI made the next move, sending Ronald Tree to the
United States to survey the problem. Before he left, Churchill asked
Tree to "ram home" the direct threat to the United States—specifically
the danger of Hitler overrunning Africa and then making "the short
hop across the Atlantic to the bulge of Brazil." Thus primed, Tree
began a six-week visit. He met the staff of the BIS, the New York press
and interventionists, and even General Wood of America First and
Robert McCormick of the *Chicago Tribune*. Tree found Wood unimpressed by visions of Nazis on the Rio Grande; the General cut Tree's
prophecy short, suggesting that a German victory might actually be
good for the world. He had a much easier time at the *Tribune*, where
McCormick quizzed him to find out whether his London correspondent was ill or just malingering. Tree distilled these experiences into yet
another report. He called for the creation of branches of the BIS in the
American interior; for more lecturers; for a regular exchange of staff
between the BIS and MoI; and for an improved flow of news from
London.[82] But the supply of news dwindled regardless.

During May 1941, the propaganda war became harder to fight. The
Blitz on London ended on May 10, and the war in the Mediterranean
offered nothing to rouse America. In North Africa, Rommel's Afrika
Korps had recaptured all of Libya, while on Crete the remnant of the
British Expeditionary Force to Greece lay under German bombardment, awaiting yet another evacuation—this time to Cyprus and
Egypt. In late May, a small group of American journalists approached
Beaverbrook to express their concern about the British government's
handling of press relations during this phase of the war. Some objected
to censorship, claiming that a photograph of a child killed in an air
raid had been held back; all condemned the military service departments for sitting on news. They threatened to quit the country unless

things improved.[83] At the same time, the two most senior Americans in Britain, Ambassador Winant and special envoy Averell Harriman, urged the British government to release more news, to stir not the American people but their President.[84] At last, the War Cabinet moved.

On May 19, 1941, the War Cabinet Defence Committee met to consider the crisis. Beaverbrook and Eden called for action to "stimulate the United States in the right direction" and news to "make the Americans afraid for their own safety." They suggested that good news be played down, to increase alarm in the United States. Churchill would not go this far, but he knew that American policy had to change. Now no one shrank from the word *propaganda*. The committee asked Beaverbrook, Eden, and Duff Cooper to prepare "practical proposals for a propaganda campaign with the object of influencing American opinion towards an early participation in the war." Beaverbrook submitted their proposals on May 22.

The resulting proposals included a recommendation that the Foreign Secretary and military service ministers each hold a weekly press conference for the Americans, based on questions rather than on prepared statements. Beaverbrook, Eden, and Duff Cooper asserted that no picture of a dead child or any other atrocity had ever been stopped en route to the United States (and that the MoI often gave the Americans pictures thought unsuitable for "home consumption"), but they nevertheless recommended that the Information Ministry be authorized to relax censorship on photographs sent overseas and to give the Americans "photographs revealing the murder of little children." Churchill agreed to the relaxed level of censorship but insisted that the Americans make do with meeting one minister a week. Beaverbrook accepted this compromise. Eden did not; he continued to cultivate the Americans on his own. As Wallace Carroll recalled, that very week he took six American correspondents into his confidence and, asking only that they not give Britain as their source, informed them that he was now certain that Hitler was about to invade the Soviet Union. Leaving the briefing, the Americans were skeptical. None ran the story.[85]

On May 23, Churchill cabled Roosevelt "with the object of bringing along American opinion." He had decided to inform Roosevelt along the lines suggested by Winant and Harriman. He listed the thirty-four merchant vessels lost in the previous twenty-two days, together with further losses off Crete; he asked for a wider U.S. Navy patrol; and finally he delivered stirring news that the Royal Navy was now in pursuit of the German battleships *Bismarck* and *Prinz Eugen*. Churchill asked for U.S. intelligence to pinpoint the Nazi ships: "give us the news," he wrote "and we'll finish them off." In the event, the *Prinz Eugen* escaped, and the Navy caught up with the *Bismarck*.[86]

Roosevelt did not reply as Churchill had hoped. On May 27, he declared an Unlimited National Emergency, but he kept the U.S. Navy at

home. Disappointed, Churchill ordered the MoI to arrange an enthusiastic reaction to the American developments from the British press.
FDR's response to the sinking of the American merchant vessel *Robin
Moor* was similarly restrained. His order to freeze all Axis assets and
to close all German agencies in the United States struck the British as
long overdue.[87]

While Roosevelt played for time, the War Cabinet turned on the
MoI. On one side, the military service ministries defied its requests for
news. On the other, Beaverbrook bellowed "expand or disband," and
by some accounts added "Root hog or die . . . . Pee or get off the pot!"
Duff Cooper despaired, but on July 18, Churchill engineered a fresh
shake-up. He upheld the right of the service departments to issue their
own news, and he packed Duff Cooper off to Singapore as his personal
representative.[88] With a snide cry of "Goodbye Mr. Duff Cooper!"
Berlin's propaganda bandleader "Charlie" marked the occasion with
his own version of "After You've Gone":

> After you've gone and through with lying,
> After you've gone there's no denying,
> You're a snob,
> You've been a flop,
> Your propaganda's been the bottom not the top,
> It's really time you stopped your drinking,
> That'll be the time when you start thinking,
> Goodbye Duffy don't feel so lonely,
> You might get another break as Hate Minister only,
> Now that you've gone who'll bluff the USA?[89]

The job of "bluffing the USA" passed to Brendan Bracken. Churchill never made a better appointment. Bracken transformed the Ministry of Information. Since he was a close friend of Churchill, his ministry
was not susceptible to being ignored in Whitehall or Downing Street.
Moreover, as owner of the *Financial Times*, he knew the newspaper
business from the inside. At last the MoI had the minister it deserved.
With the help of his new Director General, Cyril Radcliffe, Bracken
led the MoI into glorious unobtrusiveness. Soon thereafter Bracken
declared in triumph "We are now less exciting than the British Museum."[90]

As the Battle of Bloomsbury raged, Sir Gerald Campbell worked to
consolidate the British propaganda structure in the United States. His
appointment as Director General of the British Information Services
in New York was still not publicly known. On May 31, a leak to Helen
Kirkpatrick of the *Chicago Daily News* changed this. On June 2, the
British papers also printed the story. One reader was particularly
angry at the news: unbelievably, Winston Churchill knew nothing of
the BIS until he opened his paper over breakfast that morning. Once
he had swallowed his fury, he made a public statement clarifying the

news. The British Embassy had already agreed on a suitable formula
with the State Department; and on July 3, Churchill announced:

> In response to the increasing demand in the United States for fuller and
> more complete information regarding Britain's war effort and for the im-
> provement of the supply of news from British sources, it has been decided
> to entrust the direction of existing British Information Services in the
> United States to Sir Gerald Campbell . . . .[91]

Once officially "in existence," Sir Gerald and John Wheeler-
Bennett traveled to London to argue for the expansion of their apparatus. They arrived at a propitious moment and offered a concrete answer to the great question of the hour: American opinion held the key
to Britain's survival. The expected opposition melted. The MoI meekly
agreed to British Embassy control of the BIS; the Foreign Office accepted that the organization should incorporate the old BLI; and the
British Treasury offered to fund it all. Campbell realized the strength
of his position and decided to request a special fund of $1 million to
be spent at his own discretion. Just before he presented his request,
Wheeler-Bennett persuaded him to trust his winning streak and amend
this amount to £1 million sterling. The Treasury approved this request
without question. Given the state of the exchequer, it was a remarkable
gesture. It now fell to Campbell to spend his winnings wisely.[92]

Campbell began by recruiting a small core of advisers. Unsur-
prisingly, he selected Morgan and Wheeler-Bennett to serve as special
assistants. His other advisers were D. J. Hall of the IAIC operation,
British Embassy legal adviser John Foster, the novelist C. S. Forrester,
and an army captain named Humphrey Cotton-Minchin. He could not
have asked for finer lieutenants.[93] He began his institutional expansion
by approving Angus Fletcher's only initiative of that year: a new
Speakers Section at the library under the dramatist Harley Granville-
Barker.[94] Campbell then added a "Market Research and Commercial
Information" section to the British Press Service, to establish liaison
with American polling organizations and to develop links with the New
York advertising industry, within which certain agencies were "able
to provide indirect propaganda." This section was headed by Keith
Fowler, an old BLI hand whose American wife happened to work for
J. Walter Thompson, New York.[95]

Next, Campbell sought to reach neglected corners of American
opinion. He proposed creating officers to deal with labor, "women's
issues," and economic warfare; branches in Washington, D.C., Chicago, and San Francisco; and information officers at the Atlanta and
Denver consulates. The Washington and Chicago offices had priority.[96]
At the suggestion of the British Consul in Chicago, Campbell offered
the Chicago job to Graham Hutton. Hutton had visited the United
States in May on behalf of the FO Political Intelligence Department,
and recommended a regional propaganda campaign based on an ex-

panded network of consulates. He knew the Midwest well and, as the former foreign editor of the *Economist*, was well connected with the Chicago press and business worlds. Although thunderstruck by the responsibility of launching a propaganda and information office to influence the 42 million Americans of the heartland, Hutton accepted, packed his bags, and sailed for the United States.[97]

Campbell appointed R. J. Shaw, formerly a *Times* of London editorial writer, to direct the BPS Washington office. He recruited the great Labour intellectual R. H. Tawney to advise the British Embassy "on Social and Politico-Economic Affairs" and to "liaise with the New Deal element in Washington."[98] Thereafter, he drew a blank. The BPS still needed a permanent director. Campbell and Halifax settled on David Bowes-Lyon, who had so charmed Americans as press officer for the Ministry of Economic Warfare; but the Foreign Office objected in the strongest terms. The arrival in Washington of the Queen's brother would certainly draw attention to BIS.[99] Campbell then approached the broadcaster and MP, Vernon Bartlett. Unfortunately, on the eve of Bartlett's departure, the Hearst press launched a "venomous campaign" against BIS. Concerned, Harry Hopkins suggested a "go slow" approach, and Churchill thereupon blocked the appointment. It would be many months before Campbell found a director for the BPS.[100]

Now only one major staffing problem remained: Sir Angus Fletcher still ran the British Library of Information. In discussing this problem with the Foreign Office, Campbell recalled that Fletcher had been feeling unwell and suggested he be given a spell of sick leave. Sir Alexander Cadogan seized the chance to write to Fletcher, thanking him for his long service and regretting that his health had forced him to retire. Fletcher was shocked by the letter, since he was in good health and was ineligible for either a pension or sick pay. Unmoved, the Foreign Office sacked him anyway. In 1943, it belatedly found him a quiet job as consul in Buffalo, New York.[101] To replace Fletcher, Campbell appointed Sir Charles Webster, who had been running the American desk at the Chatham House intelligence unit at Oxford. It was not a good appointment. Webster was too bookish and puritanical for New York, and he was particularly appalled to be working with Charles Lindbergh's brother-in-law. But at least the way was open for an expanded library.[102]

Before Sir Gerald left the country, the King and Queen invited him to lunch. As Wheeler-Bennett recalled, Campbell's visit now "had all the appearance of the return of a successful commander from a major battlefront." Given the importance of American opinion, the BIS campaign was indeed a major battle front. Campbell had merely to provide the victory.[103]

Campbell returned to New York to find the news situation greatly improved. Moreover, to the relief of all concerned, Lord Halifax seemed to have found his feet. The responsibility for this propaganda bonus lay with the ambassador's cousin, a Falstaffian Irishman named Angus McDonnell. In late May, Peake had suggested that Halifax employ McDonnell as his personal adviser. McDonnell understood both Halifax and the United States. As a young man building railroads for the Langhornes, McDonnell had learned that you could accomplish as much with cigars and whiskey as with picks and dynamite. He used similar tools to introduce Halifax to America.[104]

McDonnell understood that, unlike Lord Lothian, Halifax hated crowds; so he acquired a studio flat in Washington where he could entertain small groups of journalists and politicians and display Halifax at his best. He invited key figures over for drinks and arranged for Halifax to drop in as if by accident. McDonnell also took charge of the Ambassador's tours. He traveled ahead of the party, briefing the groups of editors and local dignitaries; then, after the tour was done, he forced the ambassador to write personal letters of thanks. He soon made expressing thanks the core of Halifax's tours; thus, in July 1941, with rousing speeches at the ready, Halifax embarked on a thank-you visit to the shipyards and film studios of America's West Coast. Halifax moved from factory to factory speaking to vast assemblies of workers. At a Lockheed plant, a rally of 11,000 roared their support; and at the strike-ridden North American Aircraft plant, workers burst into a spontaneous chorus of "God Save the King." At his final stop, Consolidated Aircraft, Halifax surpassed himself. He assumed the Churchillian mantle and launched into the rhetoric of a regenerated Britain. He made "V for victory" signs and chalked a message on the tail of a bomber: "To Mr. Churchill . . . There are hundreds more like this to help you finish the job." Lord Halifax was now holding his own in the battle for American opinion.[105]

Even as Halifax made his tour, the British government realized that it had now outgrown the "Give Us the Tools . . ." line. Britain clearly needed the U.S. Navy to help it "finish the job," but more important it had to clarify its wider objectives. A sharp shock hastened this realization. On the morning of June 22, 1941, Adolf Hitler invaded the Soviet Union.

Joseph Stalin was not Churchill's first choice as a political bedfellow, but in the summer of 1941 Churchill was in no position to choose. On the evening of June 22, he assured the world: "The Russian danger is therefore our danger, and the danger of the United States, just as the cause for any Russian fighting for his hearth and home is the cause of free men and free peoples in every quarter of the globe." This was a substantial coup. With this broadcast, Churchill had set the agenda for American discussion of the events. The next few days underlined the value of the speech: Paramount played Churchill's words over its newsreels of the German attack.[106]

The war in Russia also brought new concerns. Sir Gerald Campbell asked the MoI to play down the "international communism" angle, inasmuch as a photograph of Londoners greeting Russian diplomats with the clenched-fist Communist salute had alarmed some Americans. He also asked the MoI to stockpile publicity on the RAF, to fill the breach with positive news in the event of a Soviet collapse. For his part, Duff Cooper feared that the United States might be glad to see the demise of Stalin, and he urged BIS to stress that a German victory would create an economic super-bloc in the East and shut the United States out of the European market forever. Anthony Eden shared these concerns. Before he concluded the Anglo-Soviet agreement to make no separate peace with the Nazis, he checked with Ambassador Winant at the American Embassy in London that American Catholics would not take offense. Britain need not have worried. The United States had forgotten its previous admiration for gallant little Finland (now poised to become a staging area for German attacks on Russia's northern frontier). The danger lay closer to home. A Nazi victory in the Soviet Union would bring a new German peace offensive in Europe. Britain needed to be prepared to outline its own vision of a "New Order" for the world.[107]

Roosevelt had already engaged the issue of war aims. In January 1941, he had pledged the United States to defend the "Four Freedoms." His next step was to review the lessons of the past, and to this end, in February 1941, he asked Adolph Berle to "go over President Wilson's speeches from April 1917 on." Berle thereupon immersed himself in study of Wilson's rhetoric of democracy, disarmament, and international organization.[108]

But FDR could not plan Allied ideology in isolation—particularly since the United States was not an Ally. He pressed the British for some clear statement of their national aims. In early June, John Maynard Keynes showed the President a draft speech on war aims to be delivered later that month by Anthony Eden. FDR advised Eden to concentrate on broad objectives that "we could all agree on."[109] Meanwhile Berle, ever suspicious of the British, urged the White House to move before Churchill made any secret commitments that might limit the United States' postwar plans.[110] The need for an exchange of ideas at the highest level was obvious. Roosevelt invited Churchill to meet him off the coast of Canada, and the former naval person set sail.

Between August 9 and August 12, 1941, Roosevelt and Churchill met and talked in Placentia Bay, Newfoundland. The MoI knew the propaganda value of the meeting and, to FDR's chagrin, invited a film unit and two authors—H. V. Morton and Howard Spring—to record the proceedings.[111] But Churchill expected more than propaganda. He hoped that Roosevelt might be ready to declare war. Instead, FDR pushed Churchill to address British war aims so that he could rally the United States to support a well-defined war effort. After many long hours of hard talking, the two delegations agreed on a joint statement of "common principles" expressing their "hopes for a better future for the world." Each point was calculated to undermine Germany and en-

noble the Allied cause. They declared that they sought "no aggrandize-
ment, territorial or other." They promised to respect rights of self-
determination; to restore sovereignty to the conquered peoples of the
world; to open the natural resources of the world to all; to work for the
economic prosperity of all; to open the seas to free trade and safe navi-
gation; and finally, to work for disarmament and a "permanent system
of general security."[112] Here was the egalitarian, humanistic ideology of
Woodrow Wilson and Lord Lothian—the proof that the interests of the
United States and Britain were one and the same, the long-awaited
assurance that Britain fought for more than empire. FDR expected a
propaganda triumph. He was to be disappointed.

The Atlantic Charter did not capture the imagination of the
United States, but it marked a critical moment in the development of
British propaganda. By demanding an articulation of British war aims,
Roosevelt removed the last main obstacle hindering British propaganda in the U.S. The Charter did not answer the question of the
future of the British Empire, but it did defer the debate for fourteen
months. Moreover, as Churchill steamed home, he had much to be
grateful for. In signing the Charter, Roosevelt had taken another step
closer to war. FDR was ready to get tough with Japan, and he had
promised to escort Allied convoys as far as 25° west and to attack U-
boats "even . . . 200–300 miles away from a convoy." Roosevelt had
promised to "wage war, but not declare it." The United States would
"become more and more provocative" and "if the Germans did not
like it, they could attack American forces." "Everything," he pledged,
"was to be done to force an incident." Here, Churchill hoped, was a
recipe for war and for victory.[113]

6

War Comes to America: The Road to Pearl Harbor, August to December 1941

> We have sought no shooting war with Hitler. We do not seek it
> now . . . . But when you see a rattlesnake poised to strike, you do
> not wait until he has struck before you crush him.
> > Franklin D. Roosevelt, September 11, 1941[1]

On September 4, 1941 a British aircraft on patrol over the North
Atlantic spotted a German U-boat. The crew alerted a nearby American destroyer, USS *Greer*, dropped four depth charges and left the
Greer to give chase alone. The U-boat, turned on its new pursuer and,
not knowing the vessel's nationality, fired a torpedo. Undamaged, the
destroyer replied with eight depth charges. The U-boat fired a second
salvo, and then ran. Three-and-a-half hours and eleven depth charges
later the *Greer* broke off the chase. It was an ambiguous incident, but
it gave FDR an excuse to escalate his naval commitment to the Allies.
On September 11, he broke the news to America; a German submarine
had fired "first" and "without warning" on an American destroyer. This
act of "piracy" was evidence of the "Nazi design to abolish the freedom
of the seas." Henceforth the U.S. Navy would seek out all German and
Italian raiders in what Roosevelt vaguely described as "waters, the protection of which is necessary for American defense," and "shoot on
sight." This, in all but name, was a declaration of naval war.[2]

Polls suggested that 62 percent of Americans supported Roosevelt's
action. Few changed their minds when the facts of the *Greer* incident became clear. Roosevelt immediately put this support to work.
From September 16 onward, British convoys traveled with U.S. naval
escorts.[3] The public also pressed for action in East Asia, but here Roosevelt was less eager to provoke conflict. Japanese–American relations
ground toward war regardless.

By September 1941, Japan and the United States were set on a collision course. Japan had embarked on a spiral of conquest in China, but

victory brought new territorial burdens and the heightened enmity of the West. Now, the Japanese Empire faced a critical choice. It could renounce its latest conquests in favor of frontiers that were defensible with its existing resources, or it could strike south and capture the material to fight on. The stakes were high, and time was running out. By 1941, foreign sanctions had bitten deep into the Japanese economy. Rice was already being rationed, and in April 1941 general rationing was imposed on Japan's six largest cities. In July 1941, the Japanese took control of bases in Vichy Indo-China. The Japanese Empire now had a springboard for the conquest of all Southeast Asia and a means to revitalize its war effort. But the move demanded an American response.[4]

Roosevelt pondered his reaction with care. American opinion would not countenance appeasement; but he also knew that full American sanctions could force the Japanese to seize an oil supply in the Dutch East Indies and precipitate a wider war. To avoid a crisis, he ordered a limited embargo against Japan; to retain leverage, he left certain grades of oil off the list of embargoed items. Unfortunately for his strategy, zealous junior officials withheld export licenses of their own volition. By the time FDR realized this, it was too late to reverse the policy. Japan could now survive only through conquest or compromise. The United States had moved a step closer to war in Asia.[5]

By September 1941, most Americans seemed to prefer risking war to passively watching a German or Japanese victory, but isolationism was not quite dead. America First rallied for a last effort behind Charles Lindbergh. As peace slipped away, however, the broad movement of 1940 fragmented. Isolationist pronouncements became more extreme. In panic, the opponents of intervention railed against the old demons of the Prairie stump: White House, Whitehall, and Wall Street, with a sinister new twist. On September 11, 1941, in a nationally broadcast speech, Lindbergh alleged that "the three most important groups . . . pressing this country toward war are the British, the Jews and the Roosevelt administration." The Jews, he argued, posed a particular threat because of their "ownership and influence in our motion pictures, our press, our radio, and our Government." Isolationism had turned ugly, and the movement suffered as a result. Watching from the sidelines, the British were exultant. Heartened by this split in the enemy camp and a rising tide of American sympathy, they prepared their final assault on U.S. neutrality.[6]

The Orchestra of Propaganda: Britain's Overt Campaign in the Autumn of 1941

> It is . . . essential that our machinery should be able to bring into play all the instruments of modern propaganda . . . . Action must be taken through news . . . the film, the radio, the sermon, the

> photograph, the whispered rumour, the Ambassador's press con-
> ference, the special interview, the declaration at home, the
> repercussion of articles in the English press, the voices of our
> Allies—all these must be used and harmonized in our orchestra.
> Though the score may be written at home, it must be interpreted
> by the conductor in this country. And the orchestra must be nu-
> merous, disciplined and efficient.
>
> Sir Gerald Campbell, June 1941[7]

"America," wrote Sir Gerald Campbell in June 1941, "remains the only important non-belligerent country where public opinion can, and does, affect the policies of the Government." FDR's aid to Britain proved as much. At each stage, Campbell argued, Roosevelt had needed the support of "carefully mobilised public opinion" to act. Now Campbell proposed to settle the matter for good. First, he sought to clarify British policy:

> It is the policy of His Majesty's government to use all its influence towards the encouragement of U.S. entry into the war as soon as possible.
>
> I. To present the British case and the allied cause.
>
> II. To assist our friends and friendly groups in stimulating American opinion towards the desired goal.
>
> III. To encourage unity in America and support for the administration's foreign policy . . . .
>
> IV. To contact and influence in the right direction groups already organized so as to sway the opinion of their members—e.g., churches; labour; American Legion; etcetera.
>
> V. To offset the anti-British activities of America First and other isolationist groups.

Campbell understood the need to maintain discretion. He insisted that American channels be used to the full. "None but American instruments and methods" he wrote "must govern American decisions and policy." This showed a vestige of restraint, but few isolationists would have been impressed.[8]

The Ministry of Information laid down groundrules for BIS New York. These were explicitly dedicated to bringing the United States into war:

> (a) never say that we do NOT want America to come into the war.
>
> (b) never say officially [that] we want an American expeditionary force but do not discourage Americans from preparing public opinion for the idea this may be necessary.
>
> (c) stress that this is America's war as much as ours and that it would be impossible for her to come to terms with Hitler in the event of a British defeat.[9]

The British did not pass news of this policy change on to the Americans. Whitehall knew from Harry Hopkins that the U.S. government was not entirely happy with the prospect of large-scale British propaganda.[10] With this in mind, Churchill began to tell the Americans less than the whole truth. On September 10, 1941, he sent American Ambassador Winant a copy of a telegram from the South African Premier General Jan Smuts, crammed with sound strategic arguments for American entry into the war. But Winant did not receive the entire cable. Churchill deleted the lines "American opinion has to be hastened to the inevitable decision by intensive propaganda in addition to diplomatic pressure." He asked that no ellipses be left to indicate an omission.[11]

With the policy settled, the British propagandists made haste to apply it. The autumn of 1941 brought a series of initiatives, as the BIS, now 200 strong, reached out to new regions and new groups in American society. But success also required a solid diplomatic effort by the British Embassy, discreet covert action by the British Security Coordination, and effective support from the MoI in London. Fortunately, all three were now forthcoming.

In London, the American Division of the MoI was ready for the final push. In early 1941, the division acquired the services of the Yorkshire novelist Phyllis Bentley to act as a "Women's Specialist," producing feature material for the American press on the role of women in the war effort.[12] In April, Averell Harriman's aide, Major Dwight Whitney, advised the American Division to inject "a more aggressive note" into all its propaganda, and the division began a major structural readjustment. First it recruited the publisher Hamish Hamilton to supervise "long term publicity," which generally meant entertaining American visitors in London; and an Oxford don, H. G. Nicholas, to collate survey material sent back by the BPS and to brief speakers prior to their departure for the United States. By the autumn, the American Division also had a lend-lease desk and, briefly, a section for disseminating propaganda to German-Americans.[13]

Roger Machell continued to direct the division's press liaison work. With the help of Gwyn Barker and Joan Skipsey (newly transferred from BPS) Machell provided feature material and hospitality, usually at Olivelli's restaurant on Store Street. Their approach paid dividends. Joan Skipsey tamed Eric Noderer of the *Chicago Tribune* by introducing him to her flatmate. Noderer's articles duly acquired a pro-British bias, and he acquired an English wife. The MoI staff did not go uncompensated. They never ran short of nylons or theater tickets. Joan Skipsey inherited Bill Stoneman's furniture and a newspaper job in Topeka, Kansas, when the war ended. Gwyn Barker fared even better. In 1945, Quentin Reynolds hired her to work for the London bureau of *Collier's Weekly*; another American journalist and his wife liked her so much they named their home "Gwyn Manor" on returning to the United States.[14]

The arrival of Brendan Bracken at the MoI bolstered the work of the American Division. His sole directive was to "draw the Americans into the war"; beyond this, Bracken trusted the staff to use their initiative, and he conferred his sanction "after the event." Bracken himself maintained links with senior American correspondents; and in November 1941, Walter Graebner of *Life* wrote to thank him for his trouble. In reply, Bracken asked him to help by "nailing any lies about Britain" when he returned to the United States, and he added "Tell everyone you meet what a grand nation we are!"[15]

Bracken brought a welcome change at the top of the American Division. He replaced the division's director Douglas Williams with Robin Cruickshank, editor of the London *Star* and a veteran U.S. correspondent for the *News Chronicle*. Cruickshank brought with him what Wheeler-Bennett described as a "warm-hearted nature and remarkable powers of persuasion." For the U.S. press corps, his appointment marked the beginning of a golden age of cooperation. Bracken used Cruickshank to bridge the gap between the MoI in London and BIS New York, sending him to New York to fill the long-vacant position of Director of the British Press Service for six months. Cruickshank proved to be no less effective in this interim role as Sir Gerald Campbell's deputy.[16]

Cruickshank played an extremely active role in New York; for although Sir Gerald signed his name to all BIS orders and to the policy papers, he was only a figurehead. To the irritation of the new BLI director, Charles Webster, the initiative and power rested with Campbell's advisers—particularly John Wheeler-Bennett and Aubrey Morgan.[17] The staff privately acknowledged that Sir Gerald was "a nice old codger" but "not terribly bright." Of course, this was thought to be a great advantage. Campbell became a "typically British" puppet of his advisers, but the American public could not see the strings and clamored for his services as a speaker.[18]

Wheeler-Bennett and his colleagues soon realized that Campbell would say—and his audience cheer—whatever they wrote for him. To prove this, Wheeler-Bennett accepted a bet from an office mate to insert a silly phrase into one of Sir Gerald's speeches without either Campbell or his audience noticing. Presented with the phrase "nothing is so ferocious as a cornered sheep," Wheeler-Bennett went to work. The day came, and the staff of BIS tuned in to the radio to hear their boss give his speech. With a Churchillian sweep he built to his climax. He warned that, although Hitler might think that he had beaten the British into a corner and might dismiss the British people as so many sheep, Hitler should remember that "nothing is so ferocious as a cornered sheep." The audience erupted into an ovation and Wheeler-Bennett collected his winnings.[19]

Whatever Campbell's role, there was no disputing the improvement in British propaganda. In the case of the British Library of Information, the improvement was dramatic. Sir Angus Fletcher had built a solid machine, but the library needed his successor to remove the brakes; once that occurred, the library assumed complete responsibility for all telephone inquiries to BIS. With press queries already running at 500 in a six-hour period and with a steady stream of additional questions from the public, the BLI Information and Research Department never ran short of work. Volunteers manned the switchboards and information desk around the clock, answering 1,900 separate public inquiries during November 1941 alone (of which only 412 were in writing).

The public inquiries fell into a familiar pattern. Americans seemed fascinated by the Royal Family and convinced that Britain had a superior tax system. The library staff attempted to answer all questions, irrespective of the questioner's motive. They soon learned that a gruff voice demanding to know "How can you guys justify doing ———— in India?" probably wouldn't wait for an answer. One caller asked whether it was true that, if the apes left Gibraltar, the British would follow; on being told that this was a legend and not formal British policy, he let out a tremendous cheer. He confessed that he was calling from a bar and had just won a bet on the subject. Other questions defeated the BLI staff. Later in the war, when *Time* magazine called to ask the color of General Montgomery's eyes for a cover portrait, the library found the MoI and Foreign Office experts divided on the subject. One said green; the other said blue. *Time* took its pick.[20]

This direct contact with the American public did much for the British cause. The BLI information desk became the front line of British representation in the United States. Most customers carried no more political muscle than their vote and their anecdotal influence on friends. Some didn't even have a vote, like the children who badgered the inquiry desk for "phamplits." Some were crazy. A gunman—convinced that Churchill meant "ill of the church"—attempted to hold up BIS Chicago and accidentally shot a *Chicago Tribune* man in the process. The telephone brought a similar mix of callers. "Mitch" on the switchboard received a steady stream of calls from New York's night people assuring him that the war would end if only Britain would broadcast such-and-such a piece of holy writ. Other customers had a more obvious importance for BIS. On one occasion, Dorothy Thompson harangued the duty officer Frank Thistlethwaite over the phone for an hour-and-a-half about some idiocy of British foreign policy. He didn't mind. He knew such sentiments were better vented in his ear that in the *New York Herald Tribune*.[21]

The BLI extended its influence across the country through touring exhibitions and lecturers. Both innovations had begun under Fletcher. In his final months at the BLI, Sir Angus established an exhibitions division, using material left over from the New York World's Fair, and the Speakers Section under Harley Granville-Barker and an experienced lecture manager named Barbara Hayes. Working with the MoI in London, they produced a list of speakers that included the writer Sir Philip Gibbs, poet Alfred Noyes, and Labour politician Margaret Bondfield. The BIS added its own C. S. Forrester; women's affairs expert Professor Winifred Cullis; and a resident Indian Affairs speaker, Miss M. E. Herrington, who defused American criticism of the Raj by offering assurances that the subcontinent would be granted independence as soon as the war was over.[22]

Similar improvements in BLI publications also stemmed from Fletcher's tenure at the library. All of the major titles published under Charles Webster had been launched under Fletcher. Webster merely appointed a publications director: Vernon Mackenzie, a professor of journalism from the University of Washington, Seattle, to improve circulation and oversee editorial policy. The BLI list included a sober weekly newsletter *Bulletins from Britain* launched in the autumn of 1940 and composed of reprinted speeches, editorials, and concise factual features provided by the library's experts. *Bulletins from Britain* made particular use of the BLI's resident military expert, Brigadier Horace Sewell, a Jamaican who had overcome prejudice against his youth and African descent to become the youngest cavalry general of World War I. Sewell had an uncanny knack for making war forecasts that later came true. Later, the State Department, disturbed by the accuracy of his predictions for the Pacific Theater, politely requested restraint.[23]

The BLI distributed propaganda magazines from Britain, including *Britain Today* and *The War in Pictures*. It provided a newsletter for private evacuees and carried a full range of MoI pamphlets.[24] The library also acted as an agent for the commercial sale of British books and did a brisk trade in British government titles; its best seller in November 1941 was a volume on air-raid precautions. With a mailing list of 50,000 and a monthly output of 259,882 separate items of mail, the BLI had at last come into its own as a propaganda agency. The isolationist predictions of 1939 had at last been fulfilled. It was a testament to the scale of American sympathy for Britain that the isolationists' clairvoyance now did them no good.[25]

The autumn of 1941 saw an extension of the BIS network. The process began in June with the opening of a British Press Service office in Washington, D.C., located not at the British Embassy but in the heart of downtown Washington at 1317 F Street, close to the National Press Club. At the request of the State Department's Current Information Department, the office opened quietly so as not to alarm the isolationists. During his first two weeks there, the director R. J. Shaw did little more than recruit staff. He hoped that a public confession of inefficiency would set isolationist minds to rest; so, on July 17, he informed the press that although the office remained unprepared to function on a full scale, he felt duty-bound to cease withholding its limited resources from the demands of the Washington press corps. He begged the press to forgive his failure to publish an opening announcement and asked the papers to make no mention of his office, in order to avoid swamping the service with too many requests for information. The Washington press corps, anxious that their new source should not be overworked, complied. The papers carried no announcement, and Congress seemed not to notice.

BPS Washington developed along the same lines as BPS New York. Shaw recruited an able staff, including Jack Winocour (later editor of the *Jerusalem Post*) and Charles Campbell, a veteran British journalist lately employed in New Orleans, who worked the downtown press bars, winning friends and spreading the gospel according to Brendan Bracken.[26]

The BPS office in Chicago opened with rather more flair. Hutton arrived in the city on the very day on which Churchill and Roosevelt signed the Atlantic Charter. With a sizable staff and an office at 360 North Michigan Avenue, he immediately set to work transforming his network of contacts in the region into conduits for British propaganda. Rather than moving quietly, Hutton rapped at the front door of American isolationism—that of his old acquaintance Colonel Robert McCormick, owner and editor of the *Chicago Tribune*.

On Hutton's earlier visit to Chicago in the late 1930s, McCormick had been his first host. Hutton felt he could hardly ignore the colonel on his return. At 1:00 P.M. on August 24, 1941, he entered the lion's den of American isolationism, high in the gothic Tribune Tower. He passed through a massive riveted door and found McCormick brooding behind his vast desk. In front lay a large German shepherd dog. As Hutton sat down, the dog advanced, licking his chops. Hutton gently lowered a hand for the dog to smell, and the animal withdrew with a satisfied wag of its tail. Since the dog usually growled at all his visitors, McCormick was most impressed. He accepted the animal's verdict and welcomed Hutton with a warmth that endured for the rest of the war. Thereafter, the Englishman enjoyed the rare privilege of instant access to the uncrowned King of Chicago and Midwestern isolationism.[27]

Hutton put his privilege to excellent use. He found McCormick willing to correct factual errors in *Tribune* coverage of the British case, which, as Hutton later recalled, were generally the work of Irish-Americans on his staff. The two men soon progressed to a broader dialogue on the differences between the British and isolationist positions. They agreed that the British people were as ignorant of the United States as the Americans were of Britain; so, to promote an exchange of views, Hutton arranged for McCormick to contribute an article to the *Daily Sketch* outlining his position. The piece appeared on November 19, 1941. McCormick's interest in this dialogue increased after America's entry into the war. Later, he even planned a London edition of the *Chicago Tribune*.[28]

On one occasion, McCormick provided more practical help. In the early autumn of 1941, Hutton accepted an invitation to address a gathering of America Firsters and Bundists at the downtown Bismark

Hotel. McCormick suspected that the Bundists would attack the platform and urged Hutton not to go. When Hutton insisted, McCormick guaranteed auxiliary police protection. It was a necessary precaution. As Hutton rose to speak, a riot broke out. A mob advanced on the rostrum, bellowing obscenities against Roosevelt. Fortunately, the extra police held back the surge and conducted Hutton to safety. McCormick accepted the Englishman's gratitude nonchalantly. "Mayor Kelly," he said, "does what I tell him to do in these matters."[29]

With the goodwill of Colonel McCormick secure, Hutton approached the Press Committee of Illinois, offering it a supply of British photographs and an information service. He found most papers receptive and some actively pro-British. Hutton had friendly links with Bill Waymack of the *Des Moines Register*; Carroll Binder, foreign editor of the *Chicago Daily News*; Clifton Utley, the region's leading radio commentator; and Adlai Stevenson, chairman of the Chicago branch of the Council on Foreign Relations and a leading light in the Illinois Fight For Freedom and White Committees. Hutton worked hard to build a network that covered the entire region. He regularly spent three or four nights a week sleeping on trains, traveling as far west as Denver, Colorado, building links with the newspapers and British subconsulates as he went. As BIS speakers began to appear at venues ranging from the University of Chicago to the smallest lodge societies of the prairies, the battle for the Midwest commenced.[30]

By November, Hutton reported considerable progress. He told his parents "the influence of our little office grows incessantly and its usefulness is glowingly described to us by our American friends on the papers, radio stations etc." He noted an unprecedented demand for British information: "a general sharp increase in goodwill for us and a decrease of isolationist power in Chicago."[31] Hutton's success accelerated plans to open BIS offices in Los Angeles and San Francisco, but the British propaganda effort needed more than regional branches. It needed a high policy expressed in terms suitable to the moral tastes of the American people; here, the Atlantic Charter proved its worth.

Although the American public was never deeply impressed by the Atlantic Charter, it provided a valuable framework for British publicity. Once the other Allies had endorsed it, it also provided a basis for coordinated Allied propaganda. With the charter as a point of reference, British broadcasters spoke openly of war aims. In November 1941, the BBC North America Service launched "Freedom Forum" for "forward-looking free discussion" of the postwar world. Regular participants included the Tory G. M. Young, Harold Laski for the Left, and Ed Murrow as the American representative. Its chairman was the battered pioneer of propaganda to the United States, Sir Frederick Whyte.[32]

In New York, the Inter-Allied Information Committee waxed lyrical on the Atlantic Charter and on postwar planning. In October, the

IAIC formed a subcommittee specifically dedicated to coordinating Allied publicity on this issue and working with American internationalists. Improvements in the committee structure aided this task. The IAIC also opened a London office to work with the Allied governments in exile. Thereafter, the propaganda flowed freely.[33]

The British placed particular emphasis on the moral dimension of their cause in their propaganda aimed at American churches. They stressed that Britain fought for Christian civilisation against an enemy bent on restoring the heathen pantheon of Wagnerian fantasy. The MoI sent British clergymen to the United States, brought American clergymen to Britain, and invited a succession of bishops to speak over the BBC. The MoI Religions Division continued to distribute its house religious journals, adding a *Bulletin on the Spiritual Issues of the War*. The Pope's denunciation of the German offensive of 1940 offered the division an obvious opening to American Catholics. It was a small matter to increase the circulation of the papal encyclical through British reprints and a discreet subsidy to Harcourt Brace to extend the review list for *The Pope Speaks*.[34]

Robert Wilberforce of the BLI managed contacts with the American Catholic community in New York. He had no Protestant opposite number, however, because Britain dealt directly with the interventionist cleric Henry P. Van Dusen. Van Dusen drew up a mailing list for the MoI's *Christian Newsletter*, "an extremely valuable piece of propaganda" sent from a seemingly independent address to senior American churchmen. With Van Dusen on its side, the Information Ministry saw no need for a Protestant representative in New York.[35] Meanwhile, in the British Embassy, Lord Halifax came into his own. His well-known piety made a pleasing contrast to Nazi godlessness, and he received a steady stream of religious "fan mail" to prove it.[36]

BIS also continued its approach to the Jewish community. By November 1941, it had persuaded the Chief Rabbi's Emergency Committee to distribute British propaganda material. Isaiah Berlin recruited an assistant to help in this work—a young Oxford don named Chaim Raphael, who had arrived in New York to arrange entry into the United States of Jewish refugees, but whose work had been rendered purposeless when the Assistant Secretary of State for emergency war matters, Breckenridge Long, squashed the scheme. Raphael's knowledge of Jewish affairs and of wartime London made him a perfect catch for the BIS. But once he had been recruited, his knowledge of politics and economics proved even more useful; and soon he and Berlin were preoccupied with arguably the largest neglected area of American opinion: organized labor.[37]

In 1941, American labor beckoned the attention of the BIS. The labor movement remained deeply divided over the issue of war. A substantial bloc of unions—largely belonging to the left-wing Congress of

Industrial Organizations (CIO)—had rallied behind the isolationist miners' leader John L. Lewis, fearing that a new war would
bring working-class casualties on the battlefield and government-
enforced no-strike rules in the workplace. On the other side, the leaders of the American Federation of Labor (AFL), led by William Green,
were prominent members of the interventionist lobby. The British also
knew that American organized labor possessed an educational structure of its own that could be used to carry the Allied cause to uncommitted portions of the American working class.

Britain's interest in American labor increased with the passage of
the Lend-Lease Act. Britain now needed the goodwill of American
workers, especially as a wave of strikes rocked Ford, General Motors,
and the other giants of American industry. In the course of 1941, 2.3
million workers took part in 4,200 strikes at a cost of 23 million man-
hours of production. As the labor isolationists struck back, the need
for a British response became overwhelming.[38]

The obvious group to spearhead Britain's appeal to American
workers was the British labor movement. As early as February 1,
1939, Ed Murrow had urged the British to send Labour Party speakers
to America, but neither the Conservative government nor the traditionally anti-American British labor movement was eager to oblige.
The British Trade Union Congress (TUC) was shy of opening links
with the AFL, for fear of souring all dealings with the CIO. Despite
this, in the autumn of 1939, the veteran dockers' leader Ben Tillett
and Liberal peer Lord Astor pressed for formal British links with the
AFL. Downing Street refused. Lord Lothian showed more understanding. In December 1939, he suggested that "two or three really sensible
and intelligent labour leaders" might usefully tour the United States to
"find out what American labour is thinking and doing and . . . discuss
with them the kind of world that Labour wants to see developed at the
end of this war." His advice was ignored.[39]

Following the fall of France, Lothian again called for a British trade
unionist to visit the United States. An interventionist named Spencer
Miller, Jr.—a member of the League of Nations Association and director of the AFL's Workers Education Bureau—arranged the necessary
invitation. On July 10, 1940, William Green, president of the AFL,
formally invited the British unions to send a speaker. The General Secretary of the TUC, Sir Walter Citrine, accepted; and once Roosevelt
had been safely reelected, Citrine set sail for the United States.[40] He
carried with him detailed propaganda "suggestions" from the Foreign
Office, recommending that he emphasize:

> 1) The extent to which the working men of Great Britain are behind the
> present policy of the government. The degree to which they . . . are re-
> sponsible for it and for the men who are now leading His Majesty's
> government.

2) The particular ways in which organised labour is contributing to the war effort . . . .

3) The morale of the country under war conditions and especially but not exclusively, under air attack. [With] special reference to the poorer parts of London . . . .

4) The social structure of England, with special reference to the underlying solidarity between various sections of the population . . . . [41]

Britain's interest in American labor was reciprocated in 1940. Spencer Miller toured labor conventions promoting the cause of British workers, and he assured his friend Ernest Bevin of "a unanimous feeling of renewed confidence" in the British cause and a deepened "sense of solidarity between American and British workers." Miller mobilized the Worker's Education Bureau to distribute British material, and he personally arranged for a letter from Bevin to appear in an anthology, *War Letters from Britain.*[42]

This trend continued despite the strikes of 1941. In the spring, the engravers' leader Matthew Woll founded the AFL's "American Labor Committee to Aid British Labor." Within a few weeks, the group had raised $325,000. The AFL news service urged members to contribute "all we can spare" and show British workers that "we accept our role in this struggle against darkness and decay, against the Nazi, Fascist and Communist system of life." Members did not know that Britain had already replied in kind. Their committee was secretly funded by British intelligence.[43]

By the summer of 1941, the CIO had matched AFL work with its own "Committee for British and Allied Relief." Now, CIO workers on the shop floor rallied to the cause and reportedly refused to allow strike action to disrupt defense contracts. In Chicago, the representatives of rival unions formed a "Coordinating Committee for Defense." As the committee's chairman explained, the "Nazi menace" and "common cause with Britain" had produced a "unity hitherto unknown" between the CIO and the AFL. "The period of strikes," he added, "is over." The German attack on the Soviet Union removed the final barrier to large-scale labor interventionism. Previously hostile U.S. Communist Party publicists like Mike Quin—and other firebrands—now reversed themselves to line up with the interventionists. It only remained for Britain to consolidate its position.[44]

Campbell had hoped that the new Embassy labor specialist, Professor R. H. Tawney, would direct Britain's approach to American labor but Tawney proved rather too cerebral for the task. While he prepared a perspicacious report on American labor, Berlin and Raphael of the BPS carried the burden of the propaganda work. By late 1941, they were joined by a young British lawyer, Maurice Bathurst, who had been stranded at Columbia but now took on the responsibility of explaining

British employment law.[45] They worked through personal contact. Berlin and Raphael had particularly friendly dealings with executives of the International Ladies Garment Workers Union—especially with its president, David Dubinsky, and vice-president, Julius Hochman. Hochman was an eccentric but useful ally. He lived in the Chelsea Hotel in New York, surrounded by books on Freudian psychology; but as chairman of the ILGWU education committee, he gladly opened the union's speakers programs and summer schools to British speakers.[46] Britain's "firm friends" in the CIO included Philip Murray, the Scottish-born president of the United Steel Workers and, eventually, the entire CIO; Sidney Hillman of the Amalgamated Clothing Workers of America; CIO secretary and treasurer Jim Carey of the United Electrical, Radio and Machine Workers of America (who also led an "Americans for World Organization" committee); and Richard Frankensteen of the United Automobile Workers, the CIO's director of aircraft production.[47]

BIS's labor work soon overflowed. When the Fight For Freedom committee founded a Labor News Service to encourage labor interventionism, BIS provided the bulk of the material, citing the British example to demonstrate that war need not annihilate social progress and the German case to warn of the alternative. The approach worked. Union men flocked to the Fight For Freedom banner. By October 1941, twenty-one senior labour leaders were included on the FFF sponsor list and an estimated 1,600 shop stewards worked for the committee at the grass-roots level. With British help, Fight For Freedom had mounted its most successful sectional appeal.[48]

British lecturers pressed home this campaign. Speakers included Josiah Wedgewood, Jenny Lee, Aneurin Bevan, and the Welsh miner and writer Jack Jones. Not everyone saw the value of such work. Despite a request from Wendell Willkie, Churchill refused to spare his junior Minister for Fire Prevention, Ellen Wilkinson, for an American tour.[49]

The MoI had one further asset in its approach to American labor: the burly ex-docker and veteran union activist who now served as Minister of Labour, Ernest Bevin. His speeches were reprinted in their thousands, and when the MoI brought American labor leaders to Britain, an audience with Bevin always served as the climax.[50] Bevin was happy to lend his efforts to the struggle. In September, he marked the United States' Labor Day with a trans-Atlantic radio address calling for "united effort, mutual sacrifice and unremitting production." He was also keen to ease labor's worries over the British Empire. He reassured his listeners that "Britain would not fight an imperialist war." Privately, he had his doubts. In June, he had suggested instituting dramatic reforms in India specifically to impress "American labour opinion."[51]

But the approach to the American unions could not be left to Bevin alone. By virtue of his position, the aristocratic Lord Halifax was also obliged to represent industrial Britain. Encouraged by the success of his summer tour, he actively participated in the effort. His aide, Angus McDonnell, carefully scheduled meetings with CIO leaders for Halifax's visit to the Midwest that autumn, while Isaiah Berlin prepared a speech suitable for CIO ears. In the event, Halifax met the CIO leaders but abandoned Berlin's text when faced with the crowd, and talked about God instead.[52] But the spiritual path to labor's heart paid an unexpected dividend. While in Detroit, Halifax dropped in on his old friend, the Catholic Archbishop Mooney, who counted half the region's workforce in his see. At the cleric's door, angry isolationist "Mothers of America" pelted the ambassador with rotten tomatoes and eggs. Halifax retained his composure, telling his guards to "let them have a good time for their money." The BPS in New York immediately flashed the story around the country, with a rewritten ending. The BPS reported that, when asked how he felt, Halifax had replied "My feeling is one of envy that people have eggs and tomatoes to throw about. In England these are very scarce." The publicized version of the incident transformed his reputation. Now Halifax passed from triumph to triumph. Gatherings of CIO workmen and Ohio realtors alike cheered him to the rafters, and even the black laborers on the Washington reservoir, stopped work to applaud his morning stroll. It was, the bewildered ambassador observed, "the most curious mixture of Viceroy and Political Candidate."[53]

Britain's dealings with the American unions carried an infinite capacity for misunderstanding; but as Isaiah Berlin discovered, the Americans were happy to guide BIS through the minefield of taboos. In the autumn of 1941, Berlin traveled to Buffalo to deliver a message of fraternal greetings from Herbert Morrison of the British Labour Party to the 1941 convention of the UAW. He had just checked into his hotel when a member of the union's public relations staff called up to his room. The man dashed into Berlin's room, disconnected his telephone and pulled him onto the street to talk. He explained that Jay Lovestone, an anti-Soviet communist was running for office at the convention and that the British message might be taken as an endorsement of his candidacy. This could open the door to isolationist mischief. Berlin agreed to cancel the message, and his allies assured him that disaster had been averted.

Others were not so careful. In July, Duff Cooper foolishly declared that he was exploring "the possibilities of exploiting trade union movements in the United States" for publicity. Spencer Miller begged the British to avoid such references to its "information activities in American Labour" in the future.[54]

Despite their many successes, British propagandists remained wary of CIO isolationism. In November 1941, the BBC canceled plans for a special broadcast to the CIO annual convention for fear of undermining their allies in the union.[55] For the same reason, officially, no British delegates or officials attended the convention. Unbeknownst to Britain's enemies, however, a delegation from British Security Co-ordination arrived in secret to help the Fight For Freedom committee undermine the isolationists. Their chosen tool was a rigged opinion poll of delegates. According to one account: "Great care was taken beforehand to make certain that the poll results would turn out as desired," and the questions were contrived "to steer the delegates' opinion towards support of Britain and the war." The results rewarded the effort:

> 96 percent thought defeating Hitler was more important than keeping the U.S.A. out of the war; 95 percent said they would advocate keeping the Japanese out of British possessions in Asia; 90 percent said they would fight at once if it seemed certain that Hitler would defeat Britain. Lindbergh was voted U.S. Fascist Number One . . . .

This was only the beginning of Britain's wartime dealings with the American unions. It was also only the least of BSC's contributions to the propaganda effort in the autumn of 1941.[56]

British Covert Propaganda in the Autumn of 1941

> British Intelligence probably has been giving attention to creating as many "incidents" as possible to affect public opinion here.
>   Adolf Berle, September 1941[57]

By the summer of 1941, Bill Stephenson had a slick system for fighting his secret war. His agents would uncover material damaging to the Axis or isolationist cause and leak it to either the press or the U.S. government. Some of the information was unreliable, but most Americans in a position to know (other than Adolf Berle or J. Edgar Hoover) didn't seem worried by this. As for the public at large, most Americans were happy to believe the worst of the Germans and of their own isolationists.

BSC continued to expose Germany's penetration of American industry and its attempts to avoid the blockade, in one instance by unmasking an agent named Kurt Reith. Once again the *New York Herald Tribune* carried news of German skullduggery: "NAZI AGENT IS HERE ON SECRET MISSION . . . SEEKS OIL HOLDINGS . . . Second Errand is to fight British Aid." The U.S. government deported Reith and prepared for further action. According to the official historian of the British blockade, such revelations spurred Roosevelt to freeze all Axis assets.[58]

Stephenson used similar tactics to blunt Vichy French propaganda. After extensive surveillance, BSC gave the *New York Herald Tribune* full details of Vichy agent Jean Musa, special assistant to French Ambassador Henri-Haye. In an astonishing series of articles published from August 31 to September 4, 1941, the *Herald Tribune* exposed a whole string of Vichy schemes, from a plan to purchase a controlling interest in the manufacture of Bren guns to a plot to construct a propaganda radio station on the Vichy French island of St. Pierre, off Newfoundland. The U.S. government moved to prosecute Musa.[59]

BSC carefully probed America First's links with the German Embassy and recruited a number of Americans to penetrate the committee. The agents included Donald Downes, an activist in the Free World Association, who swiftly established a sizable espionage network. His targets included Axis diplomats, leading isolationists, "an ex-officer in the Czarist secret police named Boris . . . , a retired General of the United States Army" and "two officials of the export division of General Motors."[60] Downes's detailed report was not completed until December 1941, but in the interim other British agents had produced plentiful evidence of Germany's secret support for the isolationist lobby. One agent befriended the woman who ran America First's New York lecture bureau, and thereby acquired details of Nazi funding, including German checks made out to Congressman Hamilton Fish. Armed with this information, Fight For Freedom interrupted a public address by Fish to present him with a card that read "Der Führer thanks you for your loyalty." Fish survived the revelation, but the credibility of the isolationist movement suffered.

BSC also exposed isolationist abuse of Congressional franking privileges and exposed the unregistered activities of German-American propagandist George Sylvester Viereck.[61]

Stephenson's plans to frustrate America First did not always succeed. In October 1941, BSC attempted to disrupt a rally at Madison Square Garden by issuing counterfeit tickets. According to Montgomery Hyde, this stratagem merely presented Lindbergh with a substantial audience for what otherwise would have been a poorly attended meeting. But this recollection misrepresents the popularity of America First. Lindbergh's diary speaks of a successful meeting with 20,000 people inside the Garden and the same number supporting the cause outside. The only opposition was an obvious agent provocateur shouting "Hang Roosevelt." It was a very damp squib.[62]

Other BSC operations bordered on the outlandish, as in the summer of 1941, when BSC hired the Hungarian-born astrologer, Louis de Wohl. This man's talents had once commanded the interest of Adolf Hitler himself. Now, British intelligence hoped to stir the United States with his prophesies of imminent Nazi defeat. On August 6, 1941 de Wohl unveiled his predictions. Credulous Americans gasped, and then gasped again as his forecasts were echoed (by BSC arrangement) in the reported prognostications of an Egyptian sheikh and a Nigerian witch doctor—and then fulfilled. De Wohl had predicted that one of Hitler's allies would become insane; BSC then arranged for revelation of the "news" of the mental instability of the Vichy French governor of Martinique. With his celebrity status secure, de Wohl spent the next six months auguring the Nazis' doom and, presumably, provoking politically useful murmurs somewhere along the way.[63]

With astrology enlisted in the cause, no potential source of influence seemed too obscure for BSC. Late in 1941, the office even lent a helping hand to a Broadway show. When a New York theater decided to produce Lesley Storm's *Heart of the City*—a tribute to the courage of London's theater folk during the Blitz—BSC provided authentic air-raid sound effects, specially recorded on the roof of Broadcasting House. When the show opened in 1942, the result was devastating. Ethel Barrymore, performing next door in *The Corn Is Green*, was obliged to ask that the sound be turned down.[64]

The office did not neglect more serious matters, such as the direct Nazi threat to Latin America. In September 1941, the American press published a letter written by the Bolivian military attaché in Berlin, Major Elias Belmonte, to the German minister in La Paz, Ernst Wendler, that included plans for a coup in Bolivia. The coup was thereby averted and Wendler was expelled. In London, Hugh Dalton triumphantly claimed the deed for BSC. He informed Churchill that "this document was abstracted from the German diplomatic bag and given by our representative to the American authorities."[65] In reality the mission was more complicated. The BSC agent had actually obtained only a transcript of the letter. He then asked the U.S. Ambassador to La Paz, Spruille Braden, to intercept the original. Braden refused; so BSC faked an "original" for publication. The deception went undetected in the press, and the lesson was not lost on BSC. Within the month, a second faked letter had been used to poison Axis dealings with Brazil.[66] Stephenson then applied this British talent for forgery to pull off his greatest propaganda coup. This time his mouthpiece was not a Latin American newspaper, nor even the *New York Herald Tribune*, but President Roosevelt himself.

On October 27, 1941, during his Navy Day speech, Roosevelt made an astonishing claim: "I have in my possession a secret map, made in Germany by Hitler's government, by planners of the new world order. It is a map of South America and part of Central America as Hitler proposes to organize it." The map illustrated plans to reorganize the fourteen countries of the region into five vassal states, bringing the entire South American continent (up to and including the Panama Canal Zone) under the direct or indirect rule of Hitler. Roosevelt claimed that the map made clear "the Nazi design, not only against South America but against the United States itself." To this, he added details of Nazi plans to abolish the Christian religion within the Reich. Germany was as startled by the speech as was the United States. Ribbentrop declared that the accusations were "ludicrous" and denounced the documents as "forgeries of the crudest and most brazen kind."[67] The American press clamored for further details, but FDR refused to produce the map. It carried, he said, certain handwritten annotations and could not be published without jeopardizing the source.[68] That source was BSC.

The map was fed to Roosevelt via Colonel Donovan in early October. The exact date of transmittal is unclear, but it rests in Roosevelt's files between two other British intelligence documents on Nazi Germany, dated October 1 and October 3, 1941. It shows the major air routes and boundaries for the projected United States of South America, with handwritten notes on the location of fuel installations.[69] The route by which BSC obtained the map is rather less clear. Bill Stephenson claimed that his agents stole the map. In 1974, he told an internal CIA historian that his agents had picked it up in South America where "plenty of slippery-fingered persons, especially in the police" were eager to help. In 1975, however, a BSC employee, Ivar Bryce, claimed to have drawn the map himself. Neither version is the whole truth.[70]

Stephenson's story of a theft is upheld by his biographers. In 1962, H. Montgomery Hyde stated that BSC stole the map from the German Embassy in Brazil and that, after an investigation, the Germans blamed the loss on a certain Gottfried Sandstede (head of the Nazi *Auslandsorganisation* in Argentina). The unreliable William Stevenson added that Sandstede was murdered for his error.[71] As John Bratzel and Leslie Rout have shown, however, this story is untrue; first, Sandstede's map was not secret; and second, he was not punished for its loss. Moreover, the map leaked to the FDR could not have been a serious German diplomatic document.

Sandstede's office in Buenos Aires did possess a map showing plans for revised South American boundaries. It was a propaganda device drawn up to tempt the larger Latin American countries toward Hitler's New Order. According to this map, Argentina would be given southern Bolivia, Paraguay, Uruguay, and the Falkland Islands; Brazil, Venezuela, Colombia, and Peru could also look forward to territorial rewards. To ensure that these countries knew of Germany's plans, Sandstede hung a massive copy of this map in the lobby of the Nazi Party office in Buenos Aires. In March 1941, the U.S. military attaché in Buenos Aires reported its existence to Washington, adding that the Argentine government seemed favorably impressed.[72]

In contrast, the map in Roosevelt's files shows a very different redistribution of territory. The boundaries seem contrived to irritate most of Hitler's potential allies in Latin America. Ecuador, Bolivia, Paraguay, and Uruguay disappeared under both plans, but the BSC map also gave larger states reason to disapprove. Apparently Peru would have disappeared into a massively enlarged Chile, which would also have received portions of Northern Bolivia previously promised by Sandstede to Brazil. Brazil also lost the Guianas to Vichy-controlled French Guiana. Argentina prospered under the BSC plan, but the suggestion that Colombia, Panama, and Venezuela would become the super-state *Neuspanien* guaranteed dissension among three states jealous of their independence. There was a world of difference between

Sandstede's promises and FDR's grim talk of "five vassal states" in Latin America—let alone the map's cryptic reference to *Vereinigten Staaten Süd-Amerikas* with no accompanying comment on how this Union of South American States might be reconciled with existing constitutional arrangements. Either BSC had stolen a different map from Sandstede or the document had undergone major alterations before reaching the White House archive.

According to Ivar Bryce, the map began not in Latin America but on his office blotter. During the summer of 1941, he became eager to awaken the United States to the Nazi threat in South America. He sketched maps of the continent as "readjusted" after Nazi conquest until he "came up with one . . . that would appeal to Berlin." Bryce recalled: "It was very convincing: The more I studied it the more sense it made . . . . It made me feel the heady power of king-makers, and I drew most carefully a detailed extension of the idea, as it would appeal to Hitler, for submission to the powers that be, to wit, Bill Stephenson." According to Bryce, Stephenson decided to leak the map to the U.S. government and arranged that the FBI should stumble upon the map during a raid on a German safe-house on the south coast of Cuba. Stephenson turned Bryce's map over to BSC's forgery experts. Forty-eight hours later the forgers had produced it: "slightly travel stained with use . . . . An authentic German map, from the highest, most top secret, archives." Bryce thought no more of his map until he tuned in to Roosevelt's Navy Day address.[73]

The map described by Bryce matches key details of the White House map, most prominently in the division of Chile, but the differences are equally obvious. It would seem that BSC's forgery experts combined ideas from Bryce and Sandstede into a third map. The key to the matter may lie in the annotations. Neither Bryce nor Stephenson—nor FDR himself—commented on the air routes and manuscript annotations so prominent on the White House map. These may have been intended to add verisimilitude, but more probably they indicate a second purpose behind the document. At the time of its presumed forgery, the BSC was also busy producing documents to "prove" intrigue on the part of the Italian airline LATI and Germany's Lufthansa in Brazil. The annotations would suggest that the map was originally conceived as a component in this campaign, and it might even have been passed to Donovan in the hope that he would make the air-routes public.[74]

Whatever the exact origin of the map, the most striking feature of the episode was the complicity of the President of the United States in perpetrating the fraud. According to James R. Murphy, Donovan's executive assistant, who delivered the map to the White House, neither the COI nor the President had any idea that it might not be genuine.[75] This may be true, but others in Washington knew of Stephenson's penchant for forgery and had warned their superiors to beware of British attempts to pass fake documents on to the administration. In early August, BSC had asked the U.S. Embassy in Bogotá to plant forged documents that would blame recent riots there on the German Embassy. This and contemporaneous British intrigue in Dutch Guiana worried Adolf Berle. On September 5, 1941, he warned Cordell Hull that "British intelligence has been very active in making things appear dangerous" in South America. "We have," he added, "to be a little on our guard against false scares."[76]

In late September, Sumner Welles informed Berle of a document provided by British intelligence that hinted at Spanish ambitions in the Philippines. Berle's response was unequivocal. The British had "given us documents which they had forged and on one occasion had approached our people to collaborate on other forgeries." FBI policy, he noted, was to regard "all British intelligence information of this kind as being subject to check." Berle had the measure of Stephenson:

> Without going into a mess of detail, I believe that the British Intelligence probably has been giving attention to creating as many "incidents" as possible to affect public opinion here. When they work up such an incident they apparently use the *New York Tribune* as the means of publication, much the same as they used to use the *Providence Journal* in the [First] World War.[77]

Given such forewarning, the White House ought to have had good reason to doubt the authenticity of the map.

It may be that even the President had his reservations. In the second draft of his Navy Day speech, he spoke of "a secret map of undoubted authenticity, made in Germany. . . ." On the third draft, for accuracy or art, a firm hand had struck out the words "undoubted authenticity."[78] In any case, the document scored propaganda points for the interventionist side. Like Britain's publication of the Zimmermann telegram of 1917, the map tweaked the sensitive nerve of the Monroe Doctrine and accelerated American fears of German ambition in the Western Hemisphere. Roosevelt deployed the map at a vital moment. He spoke just as the Senate was beginning its debate on the revision of the Neutrality Acts, and he needed all the leverage he could muster. FDR made his speech and won his Senate vote. Thereafter, the map slipped from view—until December 11, when Germany recalled the incident as evidence of American provocation, in the text of its declaration of war.

Berle's warnings against British fakery were a symptom of his mounting irritation with British Security Co-ordination. J. Edgar Hoover concurred. Their anger grew not from the forgeries but from BSC's dealings with Donovan. Hoover was jealous of Donovan's challenge to the FBI's hegemony in intelligence matters. At one time, he had cooperated with and learned from Stephenson; now BSC favored only the COI.[79] Stephenson had agitated for the founding of the COI. Now he trained

Donovan's agents, supplied them with choice morsels of intelligence, and (as his minister put it) gave "a great deal of assistance" to Donovan's anti-Nazi operations.[80]

Berle intimated even more. On September 27, he informed Sumner Welles that:

> the really active head of the intelligence section in Donovan's group is Mr. Elliott, who is assistant to Mr. Stevenson [sic]. In other words, Stevenson's assistant in the British intelligence is running Donovan's intelligence service.[81]

Stephenson's day-to-day operations riled Hoover further. During his surveillance of the Vichy French Embassy, he had used unauthorized wiretaps and taken Hoover's acquiescence for granted. Instead, Hoover took offense.[82] Even Welles was appalled when BSC dealt with the problem of Danish sailors who had gone absent without leave in Baltimore, by touring the downtown bars in hired trucks and rounding them up with an ad hoc press gang.[83] The old reminders of FBI cooperation with BSC became a thorn in Hoover's flesh. He had once made a shortwave radio transmitter available for British use. Now he complained to Roosevelt that the British would not allow the FBI to read their traffic.[84] FDR did nothing, but Berle was ready to act. In November 1941, his plan to end all foreign propaganda by revising the Foreign Agents Registration Act of 1938 finally reached the floor of the Senate.

The impending revision of the FARA did not worry the British. The act was due for renewal, and it seemed unthinkable to them that the Americans would disrupt their cozy dealings with British intelligence. BIS gave little thought to the renewed State Department interest in their work. Thus, in the early autumn, when Keith Kane (a former Rhodes Scholar) of the State Department asked the British Embassy's legal adviser, John Foster, for details of British working practices in New York, Foster gave him full details of the press operation. Kane then passed the information straight to Berle, who altered the bill specifically to confound BIS. By requiring that each piece of foreign propaganda be registered before its publication in the United States, the bill could destroy René MacColl's "hot news" service. But Britain still did not see the danger and continued with business as usual.[85]

On November 17, 1941, Senator Kenneth McKellar introduced bill number S.2060. Under the proposed new act, the administration of the FARA would be transferred to the Justice Department, where it would lie within Hoover's reach. The new act would require that all personnel be registered by name and address, all propaganda be labeled, and all files be open for inspection. Rigid enforcement of these provisions would wreak havoc with all foreign publicity and security operations.[86] Even so the British seemed unperturbed. BSC simply drew up a new list of its agents and waited for its usual dispensations. Berle was not reassured. On receiving the list of British personnel, he proclaimed himself committed to the "departure of all the British intelligence outfit."[87] At this point the penny dropped at the British Embassy. Foster belatedly warned that the proposed new law was "unsympathetic." BSC responded by assigning an agent, Dennis Paine, to scour Washington in search of any "dirt" on Berle—dirt black enough to end his troublesome career once and for all.[88]

BIS and BSC might be forgiven for missing the significance of the new act. It went against the main thrust of American foreign policy that autumn. At that time, the Senate was debating whether to end of the neutrality legislation, and Roosevelt seemed hard at work—with public support—building the machinery of global power. British publicity seemed to be everywhere both in the original and in the reflection. When Florsheim shoes advertised their footwear arranged in the shape of the letter V, with the slogan: "V also stands for value," who could doubt the scale of American sympathy? Madison Avenue now saw profit in associating its clients with the British war effort. The United States' culture of belligerence had arrived.[89]

Victory: The United States' Culture of Belligerence

> Herr Hitler, I haff killed an old man and crippled a little boy . . . .
> It iss so eassy beating these Yankee pigs!
> "Captain Nazi," March 1941[90]

By the late summer of 1941, American popular culture bore the stamp of war. The old perspectives of isolation had given way to a new mood of anglophilia, anti-Germanism, and preparedness. The interventionist culture reigned all but unchallenged: the British publicists and their American allies had won the day.[91] As the fires of belligerence took hold, British officials stood back and watched the blaze.

The new mood was obvious from a single glance at the comic books of 1941. In 1938, Superman had fought against the international arms trade; now America's superheroes battled Nazi villains. In late 1940, *Super-Mystery Comics* introduced a Nazi saboteur named "the Clown." *Master Comics* followed by pitting Captain Marvel against the fiendish Captain Nazi.[92] March 1941 saw the American defense effort personified in the launch of *Captain America*, "born of the courage of America" and destined to lead the nation "out of a raging inferno of terror and sabotage." Captain America's opponents personified the German threat; his principal adversary, the Red Skull, wore a Nazi uniform. Inside the comic, the Captain's Boy Scout sidekick invited children to become "Sentinels of Liberty" and join the "war against the spies and enemies in our midst who threaten our very independence." By pledging to assist Captain America "in his war against spies in the U.S.A." (and sending in 10 cents) a reader could acquire a small membership card and badge. By September 1941, 20,000 Sentinels of Liberty had signed up.

Captain America's adventures pandered to the popular mood. In August 1941, he fought "the Killers" of the German-American Bund; then he moved into the Pacific Theater where he saved the U.S. Pacific fleet from an evil Asiatic plot to sink it at anchor by detonating a volcano. When the Japanese accomplished this by more conventional methods, *Master Comics* introduced a new villain: Captain Nippon.[93]

The politicization of American comics did not proceed wholly without the intervention of the British. As Isaiah Berlin recalled, the British Embassy took a hand in the case of Joe Palooka. During the 1930s, an estimated 50 million Americans followed the doings of the kind-hearted but dim boxer. Many emulated him. Thus, when Palooka appeared on a Coast Guard recruiting poster, enlistments to the service doubled; and when he announced that he trained on a diet of cheese, the surge in sales won his creator the title of National Cheese Institute "Cheese King of 1937." Palooka's creator, Ham Fisher, mixed factual characters and situations into his strip. At various times, Palooka met Jack Dempsey, Fiorello LaGuardia, and (by special permission) Franklin Roosevelt. Fisher was a firm supporter of Roosevelt's defense policy, and in 1940 he had Palooka enlist in the U.S. Army to do his bit.[94] Unfortunately, his sympathy did not extend to Britain. When Joe visited England he found it a land of effete appeasers sporting monocles. Fearing that Palooka's endorsement might do for anglophobia what it had once done for cheese, the British Embassy dispatched an officer of the British military mission to correct the cartoonist's perceptions. His attentions flattered Fisher, who responded by introducing a series of pro-British scenarios forthwith; thereafter, a heroic Briton always seemed to be on hand to rescue Joe in his hour of need.[95]

The book trade reflected exactly the same trends. The best-sellers of 1941 were either by anglophile Americans or by British writers themselves. American reportage and comment jostled with British polemics, letters, fact, and fiction for a place in the booksellers' windows. American war literature remained rare, although the year did bring Paul Gallico's contribution to the Dunkirk myth—his novella, *The Snow Goose*. More typical were the numerous volumes by journalists and diplomats on the virtues of Britain and the evils of Germany. Ben Robinson of *PM* provided *I Saw England*; a selection of Ed Murrow's broadcasts appeared under the title *This Is London*; and an Eagle Squadron pilot named Arthur Donahue wrote *Tally-Ho! Yankee in a Spitfire*; a rousing memoir that mixed tales of Nazi brutality with a polemic against American neutrality. William Shirer's exposé of Hitler's Germany, *Berlin Diary*, became the runaway nonfiction success of the autumn.[96]

The crop of American books on the Blitz owed much to the ongoing policy of openness in London. The Foreign Office decision to permit scrutiny of air-raid damage by U.S. Embassy officials paid dividends with the publication of an eyewitness account of the Blitz by a former economic attaché, Harvey Klemmer, entitled *They'll Never Quit*.[97] Klemmer returned to the United States before writing his book and claimed that his "uncensored" record represented a "true picture of the Blitzkrieg," but the text was explicit as to his sympathies. He concluded his first chapter:

> The British will never yield this city. They may yield a pile of ashes, a hole in the ground, but they will never surrender London. The English are sentimental about old things, but they will allow their capital to be destroyed rather than have it fall into the hands of the Nazis . . . . The English will fight on to the last man and the last stone. They'll never quit.

He went beyond the "Britain can take it" line to discuss the iniquities of British air-raid shelter policy and the horror of the bombs themselves. His description of the carnage left by a direct hit on a public shelter left no sight or smell to the imagination, but his picture of British morale followed the usual path. Klemmer ended by stressing that Britain could not survive without American aid. He left his readers in no doubt about where their duty lay.[98]

At a certain threshold, propaganda-colored "fact" melts into out-and-out fiction. Unbeknown to thousands of American readers, this threshold was crossed in 1941 by *My Sister and I*. Purportedly the diary of a twelve-year-old Dutch boy, Dirk van der Heide, *My Sister and I* offerred a child's-eye view of the suffering of the Netherlands and the nobility of their British allies. It proved a runaway success, inspiring a song and selling 52,000 copies before finally going out of print in 1948. But as Professor Paul Fussell revealed fifty years later, young Dirk was in reality Stanley Preston Young, an editor at Harcourt, Brace & Co., apparently working at the suggestion of his fanatically anglophile colleague Frank Morley. Whether the Rhodes Scholar Morley was, as Fussell claims, also in league with William Stephenson is less clear. As the other titles published that autumn show, Americans did not need British prompting to produce pro-British propaganda.[99]

On top of this wealth of American writing about the war, the British added their own material. Americans could read anthologies of war pieces by the British-born *New Yorker* correspondent Mollie Panter-Downes, talks by J. B. Priestley, and numerous volumes of letters from Britons under fire. *War Letters from Britain* included contributions from the Archbishop of York, Myra Hess, John Gielgud, and ordinary British people who spoke of accepting air raids "the way we do our meals" and of fighting evil "to make the world a better place." The British offered stirring history (Arthur Bryant's *Pageant of England*), bi-

ography (General Wavell's study of Allenby), and such topical memoirs
as Phyllis Moir's book *I Was Winston Churchill's Secretary*. Some of the
British titles were aimed squarely at a "Bundles for Britain" market.
John Masefield's essay on Dunkirk, *The Nine Days Wonder*, sold for
$125, in aid of war relief.[100]

British nonfiction never matched the sales of the United States'
own offerings, but British fiction led the field. Britain entered 1941
with a best-seller on its hands: a collection of stories by Jan Struther
entitled *Mrs. Miniver*, based on a column in the London *Times*, recounting episodes in the life of an upper-middle-class Englishwoman.
Mrs. Miniver had a house in Chelsea, a cottage in the country, an archi-
tect husband, two children at home, one son at Eton, and generous
thoughts on love, marriage, and English life in general. She was kind
to her servants, scathing of snobbery, but addicted to life on the fringe
of England's shooting-party classes. She confessed that she found their
blood sports "indefensible, but irresistible," and the United States
warmed to her way of life in the same way. By August 1941, the *Saturday Review of Literature* reported that Americans were buying 1,500
copies of the book each day.[101]

The *Mrs. Miniver* pieces bore the stamp of their times. The threat
of war passed like a shadow across the later portions of the book, as
Mrs. Miniver acquired gas masks for her children and gave thanks that
the war would be fought against an idea and not a nation. The book
predated the ideas of the Dunkirk spirit and of the people's war, but
these themes later figured prominently in MGM's cinematic version of
the book. Meanwhile, other works kept the spirit of Britain before the
American reading public.

In the early summer of 1941, three books dominated American
lists, and all three were British. The first was an anthology of Churchill's speeches, and the other two were novels: *Random Harvest*, by
James Hilton (author of *Lost Horizon* and *Good-bye Mr. Chips*), and
This Above All, by Eric Knight, an expatriate Yorkshire writer best
known as the author of *Lassie Come Home*.[102] Like *Mrs. Miniver*, *Random Harvest* played to traditional American notions of Britain, but
spiced the imagery with patriotic passages. The novel told the story of
a shell-shocked Great War veteran and the selfless woman who nursed
him through the critical phase of his condition only to be forgotten
in a memory lapse. American readers swooned and dragged the book
through thirteen printings between January and October of 1941.[103]

Knight's *This Above All* had more direct propaganda value. Set in
England during the summer of 1940, it was the story of a romance
between a deserter and a young army transport "girl." He is haunted by
the horrors of Dunkirk and is determined to see a better Britain
emerge from the ashes of war. She believes in the old England of
"Shakespeare—and thatched roofs" and "the Magna Carta . . . and the
freedom of the common man that sprang from it." At the end of the

novel, the heroine is left alone and pregnant but determined to fight on for the England of the past and the future. She declares to her unborn child: "We'll win this war because—because we can stick it. And then, God help us, we'll win the peace, too. You'll live in a better England . . . because you deserve it! Everyone deserves it!" As Knight explained to his friend Paul Rotha at the MoI, he wrote this book to cement Anglo-American understanding. To his delight, *This Above All* went through four editions and topped the best-seller lists for weeks. Knight promptly followed up his triumph with a humorous short story based on the Rudolf Hess incident and then returned to Britain to gather material for a propaganda lecture series in support of American intervention.[104]

The final British fiction success of 1941 was actually written by the wife of a BSC agent. Helen MacInnes, author of the thriller *Above Suspicion*, was in reality Helen Highet, wife of BSC agent and Columbia classicist, Gilbert Highet. In the spring of 1940, she and her husband had sent a plan for British propaganda in the United States to the MoI. Now she lent her own talents to this campaign. *Above Suspicion* took a heroic academic and his wife on a hair-raising journey into the heart of the Reich, where the Gestapo beat enemies to death in back alleys and Nazi master-spies conspire in gothic castles. With the help of an American journalist who sees the error of neutrality, justice is done.[105]

Pro-British themes and explicit British influence were even more apparent in the American cinema. Alexander Korda led the new initiative in late 1940 with *That Hamilton Woman*, a potent cocktail of romance and historic resistance to tyranny, based the life of Admiral Nelson's mistress, Lady Hamilton, and starring Laurence Olivier and Vivien Leigh.[106] Korda stressed the story's contemporary relevance in an article published in the *New York Herald Tribune*:

> It is a haunting thing how the times of Lord Nelson so closely parallel those of today. All Europe was ruled by a mighty dictator. England was being blockaded mercilessly and in turn was enforcing a counter blockade. Napoleon with a huge army openly declared "Give me six hours as master of the English Channel and I will be master of the world."[107]

The screenplay highlighted this notion that history was repeating itself. Nelson tells the isolationist Court of Naples: "If you value your freedom, stir yourselves," and warns his own Admiralty: "Napoleon can never be master of the world until he has smashed us up—and believe me gentlemen, he means to be master of the world. You cannot make peace with dictators, you have to destroy them, wipe them out!" Korda's family claimed that Churchill actually wrote this speech. This seems fanciful, but the Prime Minister certainly loved the finished product—a feeling the American public shared. *That Hamilton Woman* grossed $100,000 in its first three weeks alone.[108]

Korda also financed similarly useful projects. In 1941, he and Walter Wanger joined forces to fund Ernst Lubitsch's anti-Nazi comedy

To Be or Not to Be, destined on its appearance in the first weeks of
1942 to mount the most effective cinematic assault on the Hitler-myth
since Chaplin's *Great Dictator*.[109]

American producers followed Korda's example. Recognizing the
propaganda value of the Eagle Squadron, Darryl F. Zanuck began work
on *A Yank in the RAF*, writing the story himself under a pseudonym.
He worked with the blessing of the MoI, granted in November 1940 on
condition that Tyrone Power's character survive the picture. Sidney
Bernstein of the Films Division felt that the sight of Americans dying
in the RAF might not predispose other Americans to follow them to
war.[110] During the course of 1941, Zanuck was also preparing a film version of *This Above All*; meanwhile, his studio, Twentieth Century Fox,
released a second British Napoleonic war allegory, *Young Mr. Pitt* and
produced two war pictures of its own: *Confirm or Deny* and *Man Hunt*.

Both of these films came from anti-Nazi directors (Archie Mayo
and Fritz Lang), and both were set in the Hollywood England of fish-
and-chips and chirpy cockneys. Essentially the same plot developed in
each—a neutral (American reporter in one case, British aristocrat in
the other) rises to the meet the responsibilities of the British cause—
and both films featured Walter Wanger's wife Joan Bennett and child
actor Roddie McDowall. In *Confirm or Deny*, an American foreign correspondent has the chance to broadcast an uncensored scoop on the
impending invasion of Britain. His censor is dead and the circuit is
open to address the world, but he refuses the temptation and censors
himself. In *Man Hunt* (based on the British thriller *Rogue Male*, by
Geoffrey Household), an English big-game hunter stalks Hitler with an
empty rifle for sport, but is then pursued by Nazis who seek to use his
escapade as a justification for war. After a chase across England, he finally overcomes both his pursuers and his former diffidence, and
resumes his hunt for Hitler for real. Britain could not have asked for
more.[111]

Warner Brothers was similarly helpful. The studio put its own
Yank—Ronald Reagan—into the RAF in *International Squadron*; and
it mounted a spectacular allegory of the transition from pacifism to
belligerence in *Sergeant York*, a retelling of the life of the World War I
hero, starring Gary Cooper. Warners then offered *Underground*, a tale
of the "good German" resistance to Hitler. This set the seal on Britain's
gratitude. On August 18, 1941, the MoI Films Division sent a message
of thanks to the studio.[112]

Roosevelt was equally pleased by Hollywood's support for his defense policy. In a radio address of February 27, 1941, to the annual
banquet of the Motion Picture Academy (at the request of the Academy's president, Wanger), Roosevelt thanked the film industry for its
"splendid cooperation."[113] The industry responded with a fresh batch of
celluloid recruiting posters, including *I Wanted Wings* and *Dive Bomber*. Abbott and Costello picked up the theme in *Buck Privates*; Bob

Hope added *Caught in the Draft*. Even Walt Disney injected a hint of belligerence into *Dumbo*. In the film's closing moments, the baby elephant's giant ears inspire a breakthrough in military aviation: "Dumbombers for our defense!"[114]

Of all Britain's allies in Hollywood, Walter Wanger remained the most enthusiastic. But Britain could not always repay his devotion. Hitchcock recalled Sidney Bernstein gently explaining to Wanger that he could not be given exclusive film rights to the Nazi invasion of Britain.[115] The year 1941 brought a more serious strain on the MoI's romance with Wanger. Inspired by *London Can Take It*, Wanger proposed that he and the MoI cooperate to produce a documentary-feature on the newly formed Eagle Squadron. Wanger hoped that this would be "the greatest picture of aviation ever produced," but instead it showed the limits to which the documentary genre was subject during wartime. Work on Wanger's *Eagle Squadron* started well. The MoI agreed to cooperate so long as the film did not overlap with *A Yank in the RAF*. Wanger hired Harry Watt of the Crown Film Unit to direct and C. S. Forrester of BIS to write the fictional continuity scenes. By the summer of 1941, his production staff were en route for England. Then the problems began.[116]

The first problem involved Wanger's scenario. He hoped to tell the story of the Battle of Britain "through the eyes of the boys of Eagle Squadron," forgetting that the squadron was not operational until long after the end of the battle. But with the associate producer, Louis Huot, squandering the budget on lodgings in the Savoy, the problem of anachronism was a relatively small worry. A more serious threat came from the squadron's English commanding officer, who abhorred publicity and attempted to block the film—first by threatening to resign, and then by demanding that Harry Watt use only hidden cameras. The pilots proved hardly more enthusiastic. Initially they refused to be photographed, and then they demanded to be paid. Watt carried on regardless, and in the late summer of 1941 shooting began.

Watt soon became friendly with the pilots and built up a core group of spirited characters on whom he hoped to focus the film. To the chagrin of Wanger's associate producer, however, the squadron remained operational throughout filming. Thus, while Watt worked, the Eagles flew real missions and sustained real casualties. Six weeks into the film, nine airmen from the squadron were dead, including all six of the pilots selected to play the leads. Despairing, Watt informed Wanger that a documentary treatment had become "inappropriate" and added that the surviving pilots just didn't have the "character, appearance," or acting ability to communicate their own lives to a movie-going audience. Conceding the defeat of his original plans, Wanger promptly relocated the entire production to Hollywood and put Arthur Lubin in the director's chair. The MoI was furious that Wanger had abandoned ship, and the Air Ministry attempted to retain the footage for a previously unplanned documentary of its own; Wanger only received Watt's footage after Grierson, Wheeler-Bennett, and Halifax all applied pressure on the MoI.[117]

Wanger completed *Eagle Squadron* in the aftermath of Pearl Harbor. He rewrote the script, reedited the MoI footage, shot a wholly new story, and added an introductory tribute to the squadron by the journalist Quentin Reynolds. The British propagandists remained attendant at the film's rebirth. C. S. Forrester was credited for the story and John Wheeler-Bennett acted as a consultant. He pronounced the script "a grand story" that should be "a good boost for the cause." The MoI grudgingly provided technical advice and sound effects as required. But by its release the picture had become a studio-bound tale of an American volunteer's struggle to understand the British. By the end of the picture, he had earned a medal for his service as a pilot and had learned to cope with English reserve. With British characters acting out the myth of national regeneration and with a closing speech on the theme of Anglo-American cooperation, *Eagle Squadron* did promote the cause of Anglo-American relations. But the Eagle Squadron flyers themselves were unimpressed; several slipped out of the premiere. The appalled squadron leader forbade future film or press access to his base.[118]

Of all the major studios, MGM had—as of mid-1941—done the least to help the Allied cause. The studio took swift steps to remedy this, buying film rights to three of the year's British best-sellers: *Mrs. Miniver*, *Random Harvest*, and *Above Suspicion*.[119]

The transition of *Mrs. Miniver* from novel to screen bore out what BIS had long known—that the image of Britain presented by Hollywood and preferred by the American public bore little relation to reality. The United States seemed captivated by the quaint olde world of cottages and country houses and trips to town. Yet *Mrs. Miniver* also served to point up the process by which the American people "read" the Blitz, understanding the facts by projecting the experience onto their imagined world of British fiction. Although Struther's *Mrs. Miniver* was set in peacetime, Americans read the book with the sound of Mrs. Miniver's world being blitzed to rubble ringing in their ears. It seemed natural (and more dramatically appealing) for MGM to catapult the characters of the original into the midst of the Blitz.

In late August 1941, Louis B. Mayer summoned Sidney Bernstein of the MoI to his office. He announced his intention to film *Mrs. Miniver* and proceeded to act out highlights from the script. Bernstein agreed to help; although unable to persuade Mayer to use authentic British locations, he checked through early drafts of the script to ensure a modicum of authenticity. Mayer assigned the project to the able young director William Wyler. Filming began on November 11, 1941.[120] Despite Bernstein's efforts, the film carried the usual distortions. Struther's already slanted picture of English life became a saccharine caricature of rose-growing rustics and kindly aristocrats, with Greer Garson (as Mrs. Miniver) rising triumphant over all. Yet the film also drew together the strands of war mythology most appealing to Americans: Mrs. Miniver's pilot son denounces the class system, and her husband takes part in the Dunkirk evacuation. In the final moments of the film, a vicar stands in the bombed-out shell of his church and declares: "This is the people's war. It is our war. We are the fighters. Fight it with all that is in us. And may God defend the right!" "Onward, Christian Soldiers" melts into "Land of Hope and Glory," and RAF fighters fly overhead in V formation.[121]

When *Mrs. Miniver* finally appeared in 1942, it became an instant classic, sweeping seven Academy Awards. Roosevelt and Churchill are both said to have told Struther of their admiration for her creation; but the picturesque England depicted in the film infuriated the British Embassy and many old fighters in the British cause, including Dorothy Thompson. Eager to defend his contribution to the film, Sidney Bernstein commissioned George Gallup to investigate American moviegoers' responses to *Mrs. Miniver*, *Eagle Squadron*, and *This Above All*. In October 1942, Gallup polled large samples of residents in New York and Boston who had seen these films and other large samples of residents who had not, to determine their attitudes toward Britain. He found that 86.7 percent of those who had seen the films were favorably disposed to Britain, whereas only 59.2 percent of those who had not seen these films held this opinion. Even given the element of self-selection (Bund fascists were unlikely to pay to see *Mrs. Miniver*), the result was a testament to the power of film propaganda.[122]

Hollywood's increasingly militant partiality to the Allied cause did not pass unnoticed by the isolationists. In the summer of 1941, they struck back. On August 1, 1941, Senator Nye denounced Hollywood films as being cunningly contrived to "drug the reason of the American people" and "rouse war fever." That same day, Senator D. Worth Clark of Idaho announced his intention to conduct a formal investigation of the film industry. On September 9, Nye and Clark convened the first session of this "sub-committee of the committee on interstate commerce, United States Senate, regarding moving picture propaganda." Nye was both chairman of the committee and its first witness. He proceeded to recite a catalog of partisan film titles. He heaped particular scorn on Warner Brothers, alleging that the producers were bent on intervention because they were Jews. The interests of their race, he argued, were not necessarily the interests of U.S. foreign policy.[123]

As Nye fumed against Jews and British propagandists, Sidney Bernstein (who was proud to be both) rallied the defense. His biographer notes that he "spent considerable time in Hollywood trying to instill a sense of aggression, rather than guilt, in those liable to be called up" and helped persuade Wendell Willkie to act as the defense counsel. It was a master stroke. Willkie gave short shrift to the tired old men of

American isolationism, and the filmmakers rose to the challenge like
the seasoned stars of their own pictures. On September 25, 1941, Harry
Warner himself appeared before the committee. He refuted each charge
of war-mongering and, film by film, exposed his own patriotism and
Nye's ignorance. On September 26, the hearings adjourned in chaos.[124]
Attacks on the film industry persisted. In November, Representative
Karl Mundt of South Dakota attacked *March of Time*. By some ac-
counts, the Nye subcommittee planned to resume proceedings in
December and had subpoenaed Alexander Korda to take the stand on
December 12, 1941. Their examination doubtless would have proved
embarrassing to the British, but the events of December 7, 1941,
changed everything. The United States had joined Hollywood at war.[125]

The Reckoning: Pearl Harbor

> Everything was ready. From Rangoon to Honolulu every man was
> at battle stations . . . . This was the last act of the drama. The U.S.
> position had the simple clarity of a stone wall. One nervous twitch
> of a Japanese trigger finger, one jump in any direction, one overt
> act might be enough. A vast array of armies, of navies, of air fleets
> were stretched now in the position of track runners in the tension
> of the moment before the starter's gun . . . .
>
> *Time* magazine, December 8, 1941[126]

On the morning of December 7, 1941, an American professor and his
British wife were strolling on a Hawaiian beach. The professor became
voluble on the subject of America's readiness for war. Noting a wave of
aircraft passing overhead, he observed: "You see, we are constantly engaged in maneuvers. If only the British had been so well prepared."
Seconds later, he realized his mistake. The British Consul General in
San Francisco reported this story with amusement, but the professor's
observation was not entirely incorrect.[127] Most Americans were ready
for war and were unwilling to appease Japan. Lord Lothian had equated
America's isolationism of 1939 with British opinion during the Baldwin
years (1935–1937); in these terms, by December 1941, American opinion had certainly reached the Churchill phase. This cultural and
political readiness for war formed the background to—and arguably the
driving force of—the events of the final weeks of peace.

In October and November 1941, the Roosevelt administration still
hoped to maintain military support for the Allies in Europe while avoiding war in the Pacific. To serve the first end, FDR began to dismantle
the United States' neutrality legislation. To serve the second, the State
Department began talks with Japan, hoping to trade a Japanese withdrawal from China for an end to American economic sanctions. In the
event, failure in Asia brought success in Europe; but despite the argu-

ments of revisionist scholars, this need not have been a deliberate ruse on Roosevelt's part. The mood of the country at large pressed events toward such an outcome: the public sentiment that permitted the neutrality acts to be revised out of existence also made a genuine compromise with Japan impossible.[128]

The tide of interventionist films and writing was supplemented by the argument of events. FDR's convoy policy soon produced its first martyrs. On October 16, a German submarine attacked the convoy escort USS *Kearny* and left eleven sailors dead. Within twenty-four hours, Congress had voted by two-to-one to arm American merchant shipping. On October 31, 115 American seamen perished with the USS *Reuben James*. It was not the *Maine*, but it was quite enough to maintain the momentum of Roosevelt's policy. On November 13, 1941, the House passed revised neutrality laws by 212 votes to 194.[129]

With neutrality in tatters, the defeat of isolationism seemed virtually complete. Writing from its heartland, Graham Hutton reported that "The Isolationists are fighting a vocal and stubborn but hopeless rearguard action."[130] Public opinion polls reported that 72 percent of Americans now regarded "defeating Nazism" as "the biggest job facing their country," and 70 percent preferred war to an Allied defeat. Roosevelt's own press analysts told him that "The foreign policy issue is now settled."[131]

With this support, FDR was in no mood to listen to the half-hearted peace overtures transmitted by Japan on November 20, 1941—especially after U.S. intelligence intercepted a message from Tokyo's Foreign Ministry describing this note as an "absolute, final proposal." On November 24, FDR remarked that "the question" was now "how we should maneuver them into the position of firing the first shot without too much danger to ourselves."[132] The Japanese were already moving to this end. On November 25, the Japanese Imperial fleet sailed for Hawaii. On November 26, Roosevelt received word that Japanese troop ships were steaming south from Shanghai. An attack on Southeast Asia seemed imminent. After prompting from Chiang Kai-shek and Churchill, FDR authorized Hull to respond to the Japanese note with his own ultimatum, calling for a complete withdrawal from China. Tokyo saw no reason to call back its carriers. On November 27, Roosevelt issued a general war alert.[133] Dismayed by FDR's stand, the Japanese scrambled to find a modus vivendi; and by Friday, December 5, some observers in Washington thought they detected a lull in the crisis. Meanwhile, another issue had stolen the headlines.

On December 4, Senator Burton K. Wheeler and the *Chicago Tribune* shocked the country by publishing a secret Joint Chiefs of Staff document that included details of their chosen war strategy of "Germany first."[134] By one account, the responsibility for the episode lay not with an ill-disposed Senator but with William Stephenson. The least reliable authority on BSC has claimed that the document was a fake report compounded of genuine American plans already known to the Germans and disinformation planted to lead Hitler into error. Whatever the truth, the report certainly had this effect. The German Embassy seized on it as evidence of the United States' belief that the Reich could only be defeated by an invasion, and that 1942 would otherwise bring a German victory in the Soviet Union. The document must have encouraged Hitler to accept U.S. belligerence as a foregone conclusion and thus paved the way for his unilateral declaration of war against the United States on December 11.[135]

By December 6, intelligence reports on Japanese movements lay thick on the desks of Washington—probably too thick to be readily intelligible. The regular flow of British intelligence material added to the cluttered picture. On December 6, Ambassador Winant reported that, as of 3:00 A.M. London time, Japanese naval forces were off Cambodia and steaming toward the Kra Isthmus. The invasion of Malaya seemed at hand. By 9:30 P.M. Washington time, U.S. intelligence had decoded most of the Japanese response to Hull's memo of November 26. Roosevelt reportedly read the document, turned to Harry Hopkins, and said "This means war." In the early hours of December 7, 1941, his words were fulfilled.

It has been argued that the attack on Pearl Harbor came as no surprise to the British. A Royal Navy code-breaker later claimed that Churchill withheld vital information from Roosevelt and forced the Pearl Harbor debacle onto the Americans, to ensure U.S. belligerence and to protect his source.[136] Against this must be set the recollection of William Casey, who later served as director of the CIA, that "the British sent word that a Japanese fleet was steaming east to Hawaii."[137] Certainly the British made no sustained attempt to withhold intelligence specific to Pearl Harbor from the Americans. As John Toland has pointed out, in August 1941 a British double-agent named Dusko Popov (code-named TRICYCLE) arrived in the United States with a brief from German intelligence that included a request for details of the defenses at Pearl Harbor. His control at BSC, John Pepper, introduced him to the FBI; but despite Toland's arguments to the contrary, Hoover seems to have made little of TRICYCLE or his evidence of German interest in Pearl Harbor.[138] Given that, at this time, Hoover and Berle were treating all British intelligence material as "suspect," this may have been the price of BSC's wilder propaganda antics. Stephenson had cried wolf once too often. The U.S. Pacific fleet picked up the bill.

Although some signals from intelligence warning of the Japanese attack did reach Washington, no specific alert was sent to Hawaii. Yet given the disorganization of an American intelligence system still in its infancy, it is not difficult to see how vital messages might not have been decoded in time or might have been misdirected. Moreover, the decoded information fell on minds denied the historian's hindsight but displaying the prejudices of the era in full measure. Official, white,

America tended to see the Japanese as racially inferior and incapable of doing anything more damaging than mounting a *Captain America*-style sabotage raid in Hawaii. When General Short received a war alert on November 27, he ordered the aircraft stationed at Pearl Harbor to be drawn up in a tight anti-sabotage formation. Consequently the Japanese bombers found them lined up like bowling pins. As Admiral Ernest J. King put it, despite warnings and innumerable air-raid drills, "the basic trouble was that the Navy failed to appreciate what the Japanese could and did do." Hours after the attack, many still doubted; this in large measure enabled the Japanese to go on to destroy the U.S. air force stationed in the Philippines while it remained on the ground.[139] In the final analysis, it is most unlikely that either Roosevelt or Churchill would have contrived the attack on Pearl Harbor for propaganda purposes. With interventionism at high tide the President did not have to sink the U.S. Pacific fleet to secure U.S. entry into the war; he merely had to wait. Once the deed was done, however, the United States had an ideal starting point for its wartime propaganda campaigns.

The impact of the attack on isolationism was immediate. Colonel McCormick heard the news over Sunday lunch with Hutton's assistant, William Clarke, and a visiting British journalist. He rose from the table and declared: "The Japanese have bombed Pearl Harbor . . . I must leave my guests and write an editorial that will rally the nation against aggression."[140] As Senator Vandenberg put it, the Japanese attack "ended isolationism for any realist."[141] The next day, FDR asked for and received a declaration of war against Japan, and McCormick ran a special red, white, and blue war issue. Neither the President nor the colonel mentioned Germany or Italy. The German Embassy noted FDR's omission and suspected that he wished to avoid "worsening the situation in the Atlantic."[142] The Japanese attack had left the question of Germany unresolved. But American public opinion—the crowning glory of British propaganda policy—had already decided the outcome. It fell to Hitler to react.

By December 1941, Hitler had long abandoned any hope of preserving American neutrality, and he regarded American entry into the war as only a matter of time. On July 9, Admiral Raeder recorded that "The Führer" was "most anxious to postpone the United States entry into the war for another one or two months." In the course of the autumn of 1941, Hitler abandoned even this position and urged Japan to act quickly. He was not blind to the power of the United States, but he hoped that a quick attack might disrupt American aid to the Soviet Union and that an equally swift German declaration of war might enable the U-boats to press home their war against American shipping.[143]

Klaus Hildebrand has argued that Hitler worked throughout 1941 to tie Japan to the European war. A separate peace between Japan and the United States would have released American industry for the

European Theater alone. His declaration of war followed naturally from this policy. It fulfilled the Three Power Pact, and it gave him the initiative at a time when his troops faced a stalemate in the Soviet Union. By declaring war on December 11, 1941, Hitler claimed something inevitable as being his own creation. In so doing, he retained a measure of prestige and earned the right to press the Japanese for a reciprocal attack on the Soviet Union. But these considerations provided scant consolation. The United States was ready for war. The *Götterdämerung* of the Reich had begun.[144]

Epilogue:
British Propaganda in the United States after 1941

> To secure American collaboration in the defeat of the Axis
> was only one of our objectives. Unless we can also secure maxi-
> mum American collaboration in the conclusion of a satisfactory
> peace . . . our victory will be largely worthless . . . .
>
> Frank Darvall, December 13, 1941[1]

For some, the outbreak of war brought euphoria. At Princeton University, once an epicenter of isolationism, students built a massive
bonfire of books, furniture, and other college things they would never
need again, and danced around it into the small hours.[2] Meanwhile, BIS
New York planned a bonfire of its own. Sir Gerald Campbell had just received word of Adolf Berle's plans to open the BIS archives to public
scrutiny. On hearing the news, he panicked and telephoned the Ministry of Information in London to say that he was about to burn the entire archive. In the event, the files were spared the flames; but the
British remained sufficiently jumpy that, by one account, a rumor of an
approaching inspection sparked the administration to throw all the
sensitive documents into a taxi and whisk them into hiding at the New
York Consulate. Britain may have secured an ally, but the future of
British information and intelligence in the United States seemed bleak.
The British now faced the closure of its propaganda agencies and what
Wheeler-Bennett later called a "considerable public scandal . . . with
political consequences difficult to estimate." As the isolationist impulse
died, Berle's bill threatened to revive the anti-British propaganda
phobia, and in so doing poison the active Anglo-American military alliance at its birth.[3]

Despite Pearl Harbor, the British knew that they still required publicity in the United States, to ensure the smooth running of the alliance
and, more than this, to ensure American participation in the peace.
Fortunately the American internationalists who had worked for this

since Versailles now dominated the propaganda output of Washington, D.C., British protests against Berle's attack would receive a sympathetic hearing.

Berle proved a tenacious opponent, particularly after he heard that British Security Co-ordination had set an agent on his tail. He took pride in delivering a protest against the British action to Lord Halifax. He recorded in his diary that the only "dirt" unearthed by their agent—Paine—was the fact that he had two bathtubs in his home so that he and his wife could chat while soaking. This was hardly a secret. He had long since been nick-named "Two Bathtubs Berle." The agent had merely found the story in a newspaper.[4] But Paine's activities were only the beginning of the British rear-guard action. Both BIS and BSC mobilized their friends in Washington to defeat the new bill. Stephenson had little difficulty persuading Bill Donovan to act; after all, as he later put it, BSC supplied "the bulk of the COI's secret intelligence before Pearl Harbor and for several months thereafter." Donovan was thus defending his own umbilical cord. Meanwhile, BIS New York sent Isaiah Berlin to Washington to rally Britain's allies in the American press.[5]

In early January, the British Embassy began negotiating with the State Department over the future of British propaganda and intelligence in the United States. When a State Department official leaked full details of the dispute to Reuters, the crisis deepened further. Soon German propaganda crowed loudly over the split in the Allied camp. British concessions followed. When Berle claimed that, by addressing America's minorities in their own languages the Inter-Allied Information Committee violated America's "historic melting pot policy," the British happily transferred chairmanship of the IAIC to an American. They then offered to reorganize the BIS. By this proposed arrangement, Sir Gerald Campbell and the BIS administration would shift from New York to Washington, where they could keep in closer contact with the State Department.[6]

On February 10, the news came through. FDR had vetoed the McKellar bill. The President thereby formally endorsed the proposition that British propaganda could be useful, and the Congress now worked with the Roosevelt administration to redraft the bill in such a way as to allow continued British publicity while minimizing Soviet propaganda. As a testament to this, the Justice Department invited the British to help draft the replacement for the Foreign Agents Registration Act for themselves. H. Montgomery Hyde represented the BSC in this capacity, and Maurice Bathurst worked closely with Assistant Attorney General Jim Sharpe to ensure adequate loopholes for BIS. Finally, on May 1, 1942, Sir Gerald Campbell reported: "On April 30th 1942 the President signed [the] Foreign Agents Registration Bill which passed Congress without alteration of the form in which it had been drafted by the Department of Justice in consultation with us."[7]

Parallel talks between Lord Halifax, Berle, Attorney General Francis Biddle, and J. Edgar Hoover produced a modus vivendi on the matter of intelligence.[8] BSC was safe. The Anglo-American intelligence agreement of March 1942 marked the end of the war between Berle and Stephenson. With the bond between Donovan and Stephenson reinforced by their tussle with Hoover, Britain's part in the future development of the American intelligence establishment was assured. Stephenson continued to assist in the development of American covert warfare, becoming the darling of the American intelligence community. In 1944, the U.S. government thanked him with the Medal of Merit, and eventually even Berle softened. "It was," he later recalled, "impossible not to like Bill Stephenson." Hoover remained suspicious of British intelligence, but Anglo-American intelligence cooperation was now secure. It became a pillar of the postwar "Special Relationship."[9]

Once the crisis had passed, the British adapted their publicity machine to fit the new situation of coalition warfare. Brendan Bracken began his adjustments in the spring of 1942 by promoting Aubrey Morgan to the rank of Deputy Director-General of BIS, and head of the New York operation. With Sir Gerald Campbell now based in Washington, Morgan had tremendous freedom to direct operations as he saw fit. In May he amalgamated the BLI and BPS into one organization. Charles Webster resigned from the BLI in protest. Morgan knew exactly how he wanted the BIS to be run. On his return from London he summoned a meeting of all his staff and told them that he intended to build BIS on the same principles on which his grandfather built his famous Cardiff department store. BIS had to remember that "the customer was always right" and had to consider themselves "wholesalers of information."[10]

Morgan had even bigger plans. Sir Gerald Campbell had not performed well under pressure during the Berle crisis. Morgan now prevailed on the MoI to transfer Campbell to other duties. Robin Cruickshank in Bloomsbury agreed and, in Campbell's place, sent over Harold Butler, a regional director of home-front propaganda with a distinguished record of service with the International Labour Organisation. With the title of Minister of Public Relations and an office at the British Embassy in Washington, Butler presided over a new era of expansion in British publicity in the United States. BIS opened a branch office in San Francisco and sent information officers to the British Consulates in Boston and Seattle. New consulates opened in Kansas City and Denver and soon became part of the BIS network. The Los Angeles consulate acquired a BIS liaison officer and a film officer to look after British contacts with Hollywood; a full BIS branch followed under the veteran anti-appeaser, Victor Gordon Lennox.[11]

In the summer of 1942, Sidney Bernstein returned to the United States to serve as director of a new BIS Films Division. At this time, he concluded the so-called "Major Rosta Contract" between BIS and the eight major American film distributors. Under this agreement, each company agreed to distribute one feature and two short subjects each year made by or for the MoI. The scheme never quite worked properly. The MoI failed to produce suitable films in sufficient quantity, and it only released four features and sixteen shorts under the contract.[12] The BIS continued to exploit the propaganda themes developed during the battle against neutrality. The Foreign Office now formerly endorsed the idea of owning up to Britain's past errors and speaking of a national death and resurrection.[13]

The BIS continued to cultivate American unions, building Anglo-American relations at the grass roots and preparing public opinion for Britain's postwar reforms. Archie Gordon, Tawney's successor as British Embassy labor adviser, did much to advance the British case in Washington, while Chaim Raphael took command of the BIS initiative as the head of the Information Division's Economic Section. In Britain, the MoI American Division acquired a labor specialist. British officials traveled across the country, speaking at union meetings; and Raphael produced a journal entitled *Labor and Industry in Britain* and a string of pamphlets on British industry, including one with the unfortunate title *British Women in Labor*.[14] Other new BIS publications abounded. In 1942, the office launched its own magazine along the lines of *Reader's Digest*, entitled *Britain*; its circulation soon topped 27,000.[15]

In London, the arrival of American GIs in Britain increased the need for British domestic propaganda to ensure sound Anglo-American relations. A wave of "hands across the sea" feature films followed.[16] Meanwhile the BBC North American Service prospered. With branch offices in Chicago and across the United States, the whole corporation seemed enthusiastic not only at the prospect of meeting the need for publicity in the United States, but at the opportunity to introduce the best of the American style of broadcasting into Britain's domestic output.

The extraordinary level of cooperation between the American broadcasters in London and their British hosts reached its apogee in 1943, when Churchill offered Edward R. Murrow the co-director generalship of the BBC. Justice Felix Frankfurter urged Murrow to accept, seeing the offer as a unique opportunity to promote an Anglo-American postwar alliance. But Murrow suspected that the end of the war might bring conflicts of interest between Britain and the United States. He had no desire to divide his loyalties, and politely declined. Even without Murrow at the helm, the BBC achieved much during the remaining years of the war. In 1946, the corporation's adviser on American affairs reported that the North American Service had been perhaps "the most important single channel of mass communication between Britain and the United States" during the war. He noted that, by August 1945, some 450 American stations (approximately half the total number in the country) were rebroadcasting one or more BBC programs each week.[17]

Britain's greatest publicity successes, however, were its deeds. If British imperial policy remained a thorn in the flesh of America, other policies proved invaluable positive propaganda. As Halifax reported in February 1943, the Beveridge report on postwar social reform came as "one of the most effective pieces of British Propaganda for United States consumption for some time." He found evidence of this in the American language, since numerous American organizations that produced weighty documents now referred to these as their "Beveridge Report."[18]

From 1942 onward, the American government naturally carried the burden of war propaganda in the United States. The British supported this effort, working closely with the U.S. government's Office of War Information. The overlap was particularly obvious in the case of the Inter-Allied Information Committee, which prospered under its American chairman, Arthur Sweetser. Sweetser, who had served at Versailles and on the executive of the League of Nations in Geneva, saw the IAIC as a means to promote internationalism in the United States. He shifted the emphasis of IAIC publicity toward support for the ideals of the United Nations declaration of January 1942. Thus, in November 1942, the IAIC became the United Nations Information Organization (UNIO), and its journal became the *United Nations Review*. Sweetser stressed the importance of this work. In a UNIO meeting of December 15, 1942, he observed: "The United Nations had not only to consider the war against the aggressor powers but also to face the danger of individual nations withdrawing from common action and returning to isolationism when hostilities ceased. Unless the nations remained united, the sacrifices of this war would be in vain."[19]

Hoping to whip up public enthusiasm for the United Nations, the office publicized celebrations on the anniversary of the Atlantic Charter, promoted a "United Nations Day"; produced books, articles, and a syndicated strip cartoon (*United Nations Facts*); and even mounted a propaganda spectacular for the new medium of television. Few people had sets, but UNIO felt that the venture would attract enough press coverage to make it worthwhile. Throughout the process, UNIO monitored American opinion and noted the growing public commitment to a postwar international organization. Long before the San Francisco conference, UNIO officials knew that the battle had been won. There would be no repeat of 1919. UNIO duly became (and remains) the official publicity arm of the United Nations—a far cry from its origins as a British propaganda gambit in the autumn of 1940.[20]

There was poetic justice in the route of New York's VE Day parade. Following the course of Fifth Avenue, the parade passed through midtown Manhattan, the heartland of the press and propaganda world; past the offices of NBC; past the old site of the BLI; and past the windows of the BBC, UNIO, British Security Co-ordination, and British Information Services. High on the fifty-first floor of the Rockefeller Center, the junior staff of BIS joined in the ticker-tape shower with enthusiasm. They felt they had earned their part in the celebration. When the supplies of ticker-tape had been exhausted, they turned to the undistributed stacks of British propaganda material. Soon, torn-up pieces of propaganda began to float down onto the parade. Watching the procession from a lower floor, the BIS top brass were disturbed to recognize strips of BIS material floating past their window. Morgan's deputy, D'arcy Edmondson, immediately reached for his telephone. He left the staff in no doubt that, although the war was over, the BIS still had a job to do.[21] The Foreign Office agreed. It did not demolish the machinery of British publicity in the United States in 1945, but merely readjusted it to fit the new needs of peace.

The peace demonstrated the limits of publicity. Although the British campaign had grown out of a desire to cement an Anglo-American partnership and an English-speaking world order, the strategic realities of postwar power soon produced a very different international structure. The United States finished the war as the dominant partner in the Atlantic relationship. The British now needed American economic aid and a military commitment to Western Europe. The Foreign Office, which had taken control of the BIS and all overseas propaganda, sought to use propaganda to secure this end. The American Division of the MoI became an FO American Publicity Department at Carlton Terrace. Its efforts were rewarded by the Marshall Plan and the NATO alliance, but the aid came on America's own terms.[22]

Although the prewar vision of an equal Anglo-American partnership was now unrealistic, Atlanticism still had its part to play in British diplomacy: it gave Britain a unique position within the Western Alliance. Britain drew on its reservoir of wartime goodwill to maintain a place on the world stage appropriate to its former glory but far beyond its postwar capacity, and called it the Anglo-American "Special Relationship." Harold Macmillan's picture of Britain playing the role of Greece to the United States' Rome, was certainly not the vision that had inspired the Anglo-American set in 1919, but it was better than being France. As the British moved into strategic dependence on the United States and the Americans stepped into Britain's place on the world stage, BIS found itself ideally positioned to ease the transition.[23]

The personal relationships established during the war survived to underpin the "Special Relationship." The veterans of BIS played their part in this process. Ronald Tree committed his fortune to establishing the Ditchley Foundation, an Anglo-American think-tank housed in his stately home of Ditchley Park; and the Atlanticists launched a journal, *American Outlook*, with Graham Hutton as its London editor, Isaiah Berlin on the editorial board, and Ronald Tree on its board of directors.[24]

Aubrey Morgan was a casualty of the peace. The Foreign Office felt that he was "too big an elephant" for their stable, and his deputy inherited the administration of BIS New York. Morgan's experience did not go to waste, however. He served with distinction as personal public relations adviser to British Ambassador Oliver Franks. Eventually, he retired to live on his farm in Portland, Oregon, and died in 1984.[25]

John Wheeler-Bennett returned to his academic career at the end of the war. His writings included the official biography of George VI. He also attempted to write an official history of the BIS, but the Foreign Office considered the work far too sensitive to publish and buried it in their archives under a high security classification. He recorded many of his American experiences in memoirs published before his death in 1975.[26]

René MacColl found that his war work stood him in good stead for peace. C. V. R. Thompson, a senior correspondent from the *Daily Express* who admired his work in New York, recruited him to that paper. MacColl became a household name in postwar Britain as the *Express*'s roving foreign correspondent. One of his early assignments was a visit to the newly devastated city of Hiroshima. He died of cancer in 1971.[27]

William Stephenson was the only figure in the British campaign against American neutrality to attract public attention. As "The Man Called INTREPID," Stephenson acquired an international reputation. But some aspects of BSC haunted him. He spent his declining years in retirement on Bermuda, insisting against mounting evidence that his friend and BSC deputy Dick Ellis had not been supplementing his earnings by spying for Germany and for the Soviet Union.[28]

The American correspondents who covered the Blitz fared well in the postwar years. With Sevareid, Reston, and Middleton at the fore of American journalism, Britain could be sure of a sympathetic hearing. Ed Murrow moved from radio to become the first truly great journalist of the television age. He never forgot his contact with the BBC and remained committed to Lord Reith's vision of the educational power of broadcasting. He used the new medium of television to explore issues as varied as the desperate poverty of migrant farm workers, the dangers of smoking, and the poisonous demagoguery of Senator Joseph McCarthy. But his BBC ideals proved incompatible with the commercial priorities of CBS. The network pushed Murrow and his programs aside in favor of game shows and television Westerns. During the Kennedy years, he served as director of the United States Information Service. He died of lung cancer in 1963.[29]

Britain's best friend in Hollywood, Walter Wanger, led a checkered career. In 1951 he committed a "crime of passion" and found himself in jail for attempted murder. On his release, he immediately produced *Riot in Cell Block Eleven*, a feature exposing the need for prison reform. His other films continued to address foreign policy concerns. *Invasion of the Body Snatchers* warned of a mysterious enemy within; and his adaptation of Graham Greene's novel *The Quiet American* twisted Greene's original attack on American involvement in Southeast Asia into an anti-Communist propaganda piece. In 1962, his career ended in a spectacular flop—*Cleopatra*, then the most expensive film ever made. He ended his days as a tax exile in Britain. As his friend James Mason put it: "He always wanted to be a European."[30] In happier times, the British had made their gratitude to him clear. In November 1946, leading British film distributors, politicians, and journalists—including Wheeler-Bennett and Bracken—gathered at Claridge's to honor Wanger. Robin Cruickshank, who could not be present, sent his appreciation in writing. He praised the film producer as "a most noble and disinterested friend, advocate and protector of the good cause" and "an absolute hero" in Britain's "Valley Forge period." "We can't repay you for that," he wrote, "but we can at least show that we are conscious of the undischargeable debt."[31]

Of the British filmmakers, John Grierson eventually returned to Britain and pioneered the development of television documentaries. Powell, Pressburger, and Watt became stalwarts of the British film industry. Humphrey Jennings never fulfilled the promise of his wartime work. He died in a car crash in 1950.

Of the academics recruited to BIS, most slipped back into their careers. Isaiah Berlin became perhaps the most brilliant philosopher of his generation, earning a knighthood and the Order of Merit. He maintained a keen interest in Anglo-American relations, promoting trans-Atlantic academic links. Other BIS colleagues also played their part. Herbert Nicholas of the MoI and Frank Thistlethwaite and Dick Pear of BIS, pioneered the development of American Studies as an academic discipline in Britain. Chaim Raphael remained in the civil service, moving to the Treasury Information Department; he also wrote books on Jewish history and a series of mystery novels under the name of Jocelyn Davey, the first of which—*The Undoubted Deed*—was inspired by his American work, with Bill Ormerod clearly recognizable as the murder victim.[32]

Ormerod himself stayed on at BIS spreading his usual good cheer. He became a living legend among New York journalists, most of whom were convinced that he was the head of the BIS. One of his friends, Walter Cronkite, remembered him as "damn good salesman" for Britain and noted that the Radio and Television News Analysts Organization grew directly from the major's regular lunches with leading news commentators of the day. In 1960, to the delight of his colleagues, he received a knighthood in recognition of his service. Soon thereafter, Sir Berkeley Ormerod retired, embarked on a round the world cruise, met and married a fabulously wealthy widow, and settled in a villa in the Bahamas. He died in 1983.[33]

The BIS survives yet, with a skeleton staff but using technology undreamed of in 1939. Now, thanks to a satellite link to London, any American radio station with sufficient interest can call BIS over a special phone line and pick up broadcast-quality British policy statements and ministerial speeches moments after they are made. The enquiries continue to roll in: BIS handled some 67,000 requests in 1991 alone, including 12,000 from journalists and "other opinion formers." New desks reflect new priorities in British policy. BIS now includes an officer seconded from the Northern Irish civil service, whose job, in the words of the current director, is "explaining developments in Northern Ireland to Irish-Americans."

Much in Britain's wider approach to American opinion remains the same. Fifty years after the New York World's Fair, the British still make good use of royal visits, loans of Magna Carta, and subsidized exhibitions. American correspondents still get special briefings at the Foreign Office, and the Ministry of Defense remains the least forthcoming department in Whitehall. More significantly, the tide of trans-Atlantic cultural interchange continues to flow. The institutional descendants of the BBC North American Service now stand as by far the most important factor in forming American views of Britain. Each Sunday night, millions tune in to their public television station to watch the latest British costume drama on *Masterpiece Theatre*. America watches as a world of Bentleys and butlers, Spitfires and subalterns unfolds, and England is known.[34]

Conclusion:
British Propaganda and the Making of
American Foreign Policy, 1939 to 1941

> In retrospect, I believe more and more that unbeknown to most at
> home, we played a totally decisive part in making Americans, of-
> ficial and unofficial, realize that it was their war as well as ours.
> Sir Berkeley Ormerod, September 1966[1]

According to Joseph Goebbels, a propaganda campaign may be judged
by only one measure: success.[2] Goebbels's maxim holds particular importance for analysing a campaign in which one may be beguiled by the
artistry of Humphrey Jennings, the audacity of Bill Stephenson, or the
tenacity of Aubrey Morgan and John Wheeler-Bennett, and for which
Winston Churchill uttered some of the finest phrases ever wrought in
English with political intent. Regardless of the quality of this material,
the campaign can only be measured against its declared objective: to
create Anglo-American goodwill and, after the fall of France, to bring
America into the war.

The officers involved were themselves unsure of the value of their
work. Hermione MacColl, wartime head of registry at BIS and widow of
René MacColl, confessed that, although the effort undoubtedly secured
numerous free lunches for Major Ormerod, she suspected that it
"didn't make three ha'pence of difference" to the wider war. The events
of American entry into the war seemed a world away from Bloomsbury
or Fifth Avenue. Yet the cumulative achievement of the British effort
was tremendous. The British propagandists met with considerable success at each stage of their campaign. The efforts of the prewar planners
bore immediate fruit in the royal visit and the British pavilion at the
New York World's Fair of 1939. Their commitment to liberal broadcasting procedures ensured that London remained the clearinghouse for
American coverage of the European war, and that American broadcasters shared Britain's experience of the Blitz when it finally came. A
campaign that relied on news and American channels of communi-

cation could not have the shock impact of the World War I atrocity talk, but it was all the more effective for this. The American correspondents earned the credit for their war coverage; and by 1941, as contemporaneous polls demonstrated, the BBC had established a reputation for reliability that endures to this day.[3]

Of course, the American response to the news from Britain disappointed many in Whitehall. Neither the bombing of London (as predicted by Churchill) nor the relaying of that bombing, live, into the sitting rooms of America (as suggested by Ambassador Lindsay) drew an American declaration of war against Germany. This was a testament not to the weakness of British propaganda, but to the strength of American anti-interventionist sentiment. The British news had its impact, but the change took time.

The British propagandists understood that they were not creating opinion in a void, but building on existing tendencies in American political culture. The Foreign Office later compared the enterprise to gardening, with American political culture as a soil that was rich in a host of elements favorable to the growth of American sympathy for Britain (the bonds of a common language, political heritage, and literature), but that also contained material poisonous to such sympathy (the strains of isolationism, anti-imperialism, and anglophobia). In the Foreign Office metaphor, unless the soil was tended, the smallest seed of British provocation would produce an ugly crop of American anglophobia. Britain's job was therefore to cultivate the soil of America so as to encourage the right crop, and to bring that crop to fruit in time to help the war effort.[4]

Harry Hodson of the MoI Empire Division spoke of this process as one of sharpening the "incipient inclinations" of his audience: using propaganda to accelerate a natural development of public opinion. Being tied to existing political tendencies, such activities naturally appeared undramatic to observers and even to the audience itself. The British Information Services thrived on this approach. As Isaiah Berlin recalled, the BIS made no converts from the camp of anglophobia, but did much to "make friends friendlier."[5]

While sharpening the activities of Americans already sympathetic to Britain, the British publicists also worked to silence unsympathetic voices. The MoI and BIS provided answers to liberal critics of Britain, and their masters shaped high policy to help. The British engaged the isolationists through private intrigue and public openness. Their reputation for accuracy blunted German propaganda. Their tenacity under cover wrecked German covert operations. By late 1941, Britain had won the battle for U.S. intervention.

In his history of the BIS, John Wheeler-Bennett mourned the fact that the overall structure did not stabilize until early 1942, after months of "chaos, intrigue and frustrated hopes."[6] This should not be taken to negate the achievements to that date. Had the British neglected Ameri-

can public opinion in making high policy, or squandered the friendship
of resident correspondents in the same way as the French did, or as-
sailed the American public with the old school of propaganda in the
same way as the Germans did, pro-Allied feeling in the United States
would not have developed at the same pace.[7] Instead, the BIS and the
MoI provided a point of contact between the British government and
the American public. Before the war, the United States saw the British
government as a crumbling monolith, represented by crusty diplomats
who hid themselves away in their Massachusetts Avenue "compound."
The BIS changed this. It gave the British government a human face.
The British officials in the United States emerged as people whom you
could telephone, argue with, and invite to dinner, and who in return
would entertain you, confide in you, give you trips to England, and
supply you with complimentary feature articles by world-class journalists or interesting photographs of German atrocities in Poland. The
difference was fundamental.

While training Lord Halifax for the American circuit, his private
secretary suggested that he drop a certain story, playing on class dis-
tinctions, from his public repertoire. The story involved British troops
in World War I who chanced to capture a barrel of German beer. The
officers pronounced it undrinkable, but the mess sergeant asked if the
barrel might be handed over to the enlisted men. The following day, an
officer asked the mess sergeant whether the troops had enjoyed the
beer. The man replied that it was just perfect: had it been any better,
they wouldn't have been given it; and had it been any worse they
couldn't have drunk it.[8]

The development of British propaganda in the United States filled
a similarly narrow niche. To have done less to cultivate American
public opinion might have proved disastrous, because Britain could
not afford to squander one iota of American sympathy. Yet had the
British done more, had their effort peaked earlier, or had it sought to
bypass the trusted channels of the United States' own press and broadcasting system, Britain might inadvertantly have provided powerful
ammunition for the isolationists. As it happened, the isolationists were
unable to expose the full scale of the campaign. Their attack on film
propaganda came too late to make a difference, and the schemes of
the uncharitable Mr. Berle perished in the wake of Pearl Harbor.

The achievement of the British publicists cannot, of course, be
understood apart from the work of American internationalists or the
efforts of the President himself. This is not surprising, given that
Roosevelt, the American interventionists, and many of the key players
in British propaganda and diplomacy were all products of an inter-
linked Anglo-American elite. From the start, the British worked closely
with sympathetic Americans. The American press corps in London
cooperated closely with the British government.

Roosevelt himself, being committed to the Allied cause, subtly incorporated the British efforts into his own attempts to manipulate American opinion. He boosted the British cause by inviting the royal visit of 1939, he staged the Atlantic Charter, and he single-handedly thwarted enactment of a revised Foreign Agents Registration Act that might well have put the British propagandists out of business early in 1942. Roosevelt's role was uneven and his ardor cooled visibly as the 1940 election approached. But with the Presidency secure, FDR embarked on a great campaign to mobilize the United States. His fireside chats and press conferences were calculated to wring the maximum aid for Britain from his public; while the British, from Churchill down, worked to support his campaign with their reassuring refrain: "Give us the tools and we will finish the job." Yet for all his willingness to help the Allies, Roosevelt remained a prisoner of American public and Congressional opinion. The importance of external efforts to mobilize the public consent necessary for his foreign policy initiatives should not be underestimated. The President faced formidable opposition. The isolationists fought every advance in American aid, and Roosevelt won his victories only by the narrowest of margins. No component in securing that aid—let alone the role of British propaganda—can be dismissed. Once secure, that aid saved Britain. Without the material sent by Roosevelt and the boost to British morale that it provided, 1941 would have brought a British defeat.

The United States, of course, only joined the war after the Japanese attack on Pearl Harbor and Hitler's declaration of war, but even these acts were tied to the U.S. foreign policy that British propaganda promoted. The Japanese air force did not attack a sleeping giant, but a nation politically and industrially—if not quite militarily—prepared for war. Isolationism was already a spent force. Congress had thrown off the old neutrality laws, and the American public as a whole now embraced a new culture of war and global responsibility and held appeasement of an aggressor to be a cardinal sin. When Roosevelt took a hard line with the Japanese, he acted in accordance with the spirit of the public at large—a public that now counted the survival of Britain to be more important than American neutrality.

The United States joined a war that it knew principally through British eyes. During the critical years of 1940 and 1941, practically all of the United States' news about the war passed through London and was shaped either directly by the publicity and censorship structure of the British government or indirectly by the partiality of well-cultivated foreign correspondents. By 1941, this information had established the picture of a new dynamic Britain and a struggle based on moral issues. These same ideas were reflected and rearticulated in the domestic American press, redefining the United States' stand on the issue of war and its role in the world. Although British propaganda may not have changed the course of history, it certainly accelerated the process.

In a speech of February 1, 1938, Senator Borah raised the cry against the first stirrings of British propaganda in America, warning: "These things can not be whistled down the wind . . . . They are what make foreign policies . . . put nations into action . . . brought on the World War . . . . Our policy will be affected by them in spite of anything we may do."[9] He was right.

Notes

Abbreviations

BBC WAC: British Broadcasting Corporation, Written Archive Centre,
            Caversham Park, Berkshire.

BLEPS: British Library of Economics and Political Science,
            London School of Economics.

CRCC: Warren Kimball (ed.), *Churchill and Roosevelt:*
            The Complete Correspondence (Princeton, N.J.: Princeton
            University Press, 1984)

DBFP: *Documents on British Foreign Policy.*

DGFP: *Documents on German Foreign Policy.*

FDRL: Franklin D. Roosevelt Library (National Archives and
            Records Administration), Hyde Park, New York.

FRUS: *Foreign Relations of the United States.*

JCH: *Journal of Contemporary History.*

LoC: Library of Congress, Washington, D.C.

MoT: *March of Time* (American newsreel series).

NA: National Archives, Washington, D.C.

NA Ottawa: National Archives, Ottawa, Ontario.

NA:SMPB: National Archives, Sound and Motion Picture Branch,
            Washington, D.C.

POQ: *Public Opinion Quarterly.*

PRO: Public Record Office, Kew, England.

SHSW: Mass Communications History Center, State Historical Society
            of Wisconsin, Madison, Wisconsin.

SRO: Scottish Record Office, Edinburgh, Scotland.

Introduction

1. Charles Eade (ed.), *The War Speeches of the Rt. Hon. Winston S. Churchill*, Vol. 2 (London: Cassell, 1952), pp. 151, 202; Public Record Office, London (PRO) FO 954/29, Halifax to Eden, 24 February 1942; PRO PREM 4/27/9, p. 682.

2. For polls: William Manchester, *The Glory and the Dream: A Narrative History of America, 1932–1972*, Vol. 1 (Boston: Little, Brown, 1973), p. 277.

3. Interviews: Herbert Nicholas, Leonard Miall; PRO FO 371/22840, A7592/7053/45, Cowell and Gaslee, 31 October 1939.

4. For memoirs: Isaiah Berlin in II. G. Nicholas (ed.), *Washington Despatches* (Chicago: University of Chicago Press, 1981); Gerald Campbell, *Of True Experience* (London: Hutchinson, 1948); William Clark, *From Three Worlds* (London: Sidgwick & Jackson, 1986); Ronald Tree, *When the Moon Was High* (London: Macmillan, 1975); John Wheeler-Bennett, *Special Relationships: America in Peace and War* (London: Macmillan, 1975); Maurice Gorham, *Sound and Fury: Twenty-One Years in the BBC* (London: Percival Marshall, 1948). For the diplomatic background: David Reynolds, *The Creation of the Anglo-American Alliance* (London: Europa, 1981); On films: Michael Korda, *Charmed Lives* (New York: Random House, 1979); Anthony Aldgate and Jeffrey Richards, *Britain Can Take It: British Cinema in the Second World War* (Oxford: Oxford University Press, 1986). On the Secret Service: II. Montgomery Hyde, *The Quiet Canadian: The Secret Service Story of Sir William Stephenson* (London: Hamish Hamilton, 1962); and, notoriously, William Stevenson, *A Man Called Intrepid: The Secret War* (New York: Harcourt Brace Jovanovich, 1976).

Chapter 1

1. Vansittart, 31 December 1936, *Documents on British Foreign Policy* (*DBFP*) Second Series, Vol. 17 (London: HMSO, 1979), pp. 775–801.

2. *DBFP* Second Series, Vol. 17, p. 792.

3. *DBFP* Second Series, Vol. 17, p. 801.

4. *New York Herald Tribune*, 18 April 1921.

5. PRO FO 395/657, P974/151/150, Wilberforce to Leeper, 9 March 1939; Wayne S. Cole, "America First and the South," *Journal of Southern History* 44 (1956): 36–47; Interviews: Isaiah Berlin, Graham Hutton. For survey of isolationism: Manfred Jonas, *Isolationism in America* (Ithaca, N.Y.: Cornell University Press, 1969).

6. Cited in *New York Times*, 21 November 1938, AIPO poll: "Which European Country do you like best?"

7. Michael Hunt, *Ideology and U.S. Foreign Policy* (New Haven, Conn.: Yale University Press, 1987), pp. 78, 127.

8. Christopher Hitchens, *Blood, Class and Nostalgia: Anglo-American Ironies* (New York: Farrar, Straus & Giroux, 1990), pp. 63–97, 298–307; Penny Sumerfield, "Patriotism and Empire: Music-Hall Entertainment, 1870–1914," in John Mackenzie (ed.), *Imperialism and Popular Culture* (Manchester: Manchester University Press, 1984) p. 29; J. W. Wooster, *Edward Stephen Harkness* (New York: privately printed, 1949); Christopher Thorne, *Border*

Crossings (New York: Blackwells, 1988), p. 59; William Griffin, *Sir Evelyn Wrench and His Continuing Vision of International Relations During Forty Years* (New York: Newcomen Society, 1950); Robert D. Schulzinger, *The Wise Men of Foreign Affairs: The History of the Council on Foreign Relations* (New York: Columbia University Press, 1984), pp. 3–7, 14, 30–33, 98–99; D. C. Watt, "America and the British Foreign Policy-Making Elite, from Joseph Chamberlain to Anthony Eden, 1895–1956," *Review of Politics* 25 (1963): 3–33.

9. Bruce M. Russett, *Community and Contention: Britain and America in the Twentieth Century* (Cambridge, Mass.: MIT Press, 1963), p. 110.

10. Interview: Douglas Fairbanks, Jr.; Sheridan Morley, *Tales from the Hollywood Raj* (New York: Viking, 1983); Norman Riley, *999 and All That* (London: Gollancz, 1940), p. 108.

11. Thomas E. Hachey (ed.), "Winning Friends and Influencing Policy: British Strategy to Woo America in 1937," *Wisconsin Magazine of History* 55 (1971/72): 120–29.

12. Philip M. Taylor, *The Projection of Britain* (Cambridge: Cambridge University Press, 1981); C. Hartley Grattan, *Why We Fought* (New York: Vanguard Press, 1929), pp. 50–52; J. D. Squires, *British Propaganda at Home and in the United States from 1914 to 1917* (Cambridge, Mass.: Harvard University Press, 1935).

13. Sir Gilbert Parker, "The United States and the War," *Harper's* 136 (March 1918): 521–31; Walter Millis, *Road to War* (Boston: Houghton, 1935), pp. 62–72, 294.

14. For sample of 1920s propaganda scholarship: *Saturday Evening Post*, 15 June 1929, 29 June 1929, and 3 August 1929; Harold D. Laswell, *Propaganda Technique in the World War* (New York: Knopf, 1927); PRO FO 395/616, P2769/1157/150, Fletcher to FO, 21 September 1938; Clyde Miller, "For the Analysis of Propaganda," *Public Opinion Quarterly* 2 (1938): 133–34; *Propaganda Analysis* 1 (October 1937): 1.

15. PRO FO 395/437, P732/732/150, Fletcher to FO News Dept, 10 May 1929.

16. John Wheeler-Bennett, *A History of British Information in the U.S.A.* (New York: British Information Services, 1945), p. 4. This official history was compiled for the archives of the MoI, but it is currently classified and withheld from the PRO in London. I am grateful to BIS New York for making a copy available to me.

17. Wheeler-Bennett, *British Information in the U.S.A.*, pp. 4–5; B. J. C. McKercher, *The Second Baldwin Government and the United States, 1924–1929: Attitudes and Diplomacy* (Cambridge: Cambridge University Press, 1985), pp. 33, 119–27.

18. PRO FO 395/611, p. 329; Wheeler-Bennett, *British Information in the U.S.A.*, pp. 1–10; Interviews: Chaim Raphael, Hermione MacColl, Peggy Macmillan, Joan Galwey; FO 395/555, p. 18; PRO FO 395/437, P732/732/150, Fletcher to News Dept, 10 May 1929.

19. Asa Briggs, *The History of Broadcasting in the United Kingdom, Vol. 2, The Golden Age of Wireless* (Oxford: Oxford University Press, 1965), pp. 367–410.

20. Interviews: Miall, Alistair Cooke; Raymond Gram Swing, *Good Evening!* (New York: Harcourt, 1964), pp. 191–94; David Culbert, *News For Everyman* (Westport, Conn.: Greenwood, 1976), p. 102; Taylor, *Projection of*

Britain, pp. 74–77, and FO 395/523; British Broadcasting Corporation Written Archives Centre, Caversham, Buckinghamshire (BBC WAC) R28/174/1, 174/2.

21. Interview: Cooke; Briggs, *The Golden Age of Wireless*, p. 396.

22. Philip M. Taylor, "If War Should Come: Preparing the Fifth Arm for Total War 1935–1939," *Journal of Contemporary History* 16 (1981): 27–51; Temple Wilcox, "Projection or Publicity? Rival Concepts in the Pre-War Planning of the British Ministry of Information," *Journal of Contemporary History* 18 (1983): 97–116; Temple Wilcox, "Towards a Ministry of Information," *History* 69 (1984): 398–414; Robert Cole, "The Conflict Within: Stephen Tallents and Planning Propaganda Overseas Before the Second World War," *Albion* 12 (1982): 50–71; PRO PREM 1/272, report of 28 May 1938.

23. PRO FO 371/20651, A2378/2378/45, Eden to Lindsay, 10 March 1937.

24. PRO FO 371/20651, A2378/2378/45, Lindsay to Eden, 22 March 1937.

25. Hachey (ed.), "Winning Friends and Influencing Policy," *Wisconsin Magazine of History*, pp. 120–29.

26. John Harvey (ed.), *The Diplomatic Diary of Oliver Harvey, 1937–1940* (London: Collins, 1970), p. 73; Robert Rhodes James, *Anthony Eden* (London: Weidenfeld & Nicolson, 1986), pp. 187–89.

27. Interviews: Hutton, Helen Kirkpatrick Milbank. On Lothian, see: J. R. M. Butler, *Lord Lothian* (New York: St. Martin's, 1960).

28. Walter Harrison in *Editor and Publisher*, 1 October 1938 and 8 October 1938; Interviews: James Reston, Wallace Carroll.

29. Interviews: Janet Murrow, Eric Sevareid, Drew Middleton; S. J. Taylor, *Stalin's Apologist: Walter Duranty, The New York Times' Man in Moscow* (Oxford: Oxford University Press, 1990); Peter Kurth, *American Cassandra: The Life of Dorothy Thompson* (Boston: Little, Brown, 1990); Edward Bliss, Jr. (ed.), *In Search of Light: The Broadcasts of Edward R. Murrow, 1938–61* (New York: Knopf, 1967), pp. 3–4.

30. Interviews: Janet Murrow, Sevareid, Middleton; A. M. Sperber, *Murrow: His Life and Times* (London: Michael Joseph, 1986), chapter 3; R. Franklin Smith, *Edward R. Murrow: The War Years* (Kalamazoo, Mich.: New Issues Press, 1978), pp. 7–12.

31. Interviews: Hutton, Milbank; Helen Kirkpatrick, *This Terrible Peace* (London: Rich & Cowan, 1939); Helen Kirkpatrick, *Under the British Umbrella: What the English Are and How They Go to War* (New York: Scribner, 1939).

32. Interviews: Hutton, Milbank, Janet Murrow; Mrs. Murrow recalled that Murrow's British contacts included Sir Edward Grigg, Lady Milner, Lord Salisbury, Lord Cranborne, and Ronald Tree. Vincent Sheean, *Between the Thunder and the Sun* (New York: Harper & Row, 1943), pp. 30–33; Tree, *When the Moon Was High*, pp. 93–94.

33. PRO FO 395/616, P3423/1157/150, Warner, 23 December 1938; Robert Herzstein, *Roosevelt and Hitler: Prelude to War* (New York: Paragon, 1989), pp. 108–11, 114.

34. Interview: Fairbanks; Clayton R. Koppes and Gregory D. Black, *Hollywood Goes to War: How Politics, Profits and Propaganda Shaped World War Two Movies* (New York: Free Press, 1987), p. 124; Herzstein, *Roosevelt and Hitler*, p. 280.

35. Gregory La Cava (dir.), *Gabriel Over the White House* (MGM/ Wanger, 1933); William A. Wellman (dir.), *The President Vanishes* (Fox, 1934); William Dieterle (dir.), *Blockade* (Wanger, 1938); Walter Wanger, in Bernard Rosenberg and Harry Silverstein (eds.), *The Real Tinsel* (New York: Macmillan, 1979), pp. 80–99; Koppes and Black, *Hollywood Goes to War*, pp. 24–27; Walter Wanger, "120,000 American Ambassadors," *Foreign Affairs* 18 (October, 1939): 45–60; Ella Winter, "Hollywood Wakes Up," *New Republic* (12 January 1938): 284–97. For biographical details, see Wanger papers: Mass Communications History Centre, State Historical Society of Wisconsin, Madison, Wisconsin (SHSW).

36. Raymond Fielding, *March of Time, 1935–1951* (New York: Oxford University Press, 1978); "The Movies and Propaganda," *Propaganda Analysis* 1(6) (March 1938): 1.

37. Interview: Cooke; Fielding, *The March of Time*, pp. 90–95, 156, 221, 339; PRO BW 2/35, Joint Film Committee 1936–38; Forsyth Hardy, *John Grierson: A Documentary Biography* (London: Faber, 1979), p. 86; Harry Watt, *Don't Look at the Camera* (London: Elek, 1974), pp. 74–78; PRO FO 395/657, P2478/151/150, Fletcher to Embassy, 9 June 1939.

38. PRO FO 395/656, P325/151/150, BLI to Department of Trade, 18 January 1939; Only Alfred Hitchcock (dir.), *The Lady Vanishes* (Gaumont British, 1938) had obvious anti-Nazi content.

39. Interview: Fairbanks.

40. PRO FO 395/639, P1794/31/150, Evans (Los Angeles) to Department of Trade, 14 April 1939, etc.

41. Fielding, *March of Time*, p. 229; Michael Curtiz (dir.), *The Adventures of Robin Hood* (Warner Brothers, 1939).

42. PRO FO 115/3418/224, Mallet (Embassy) to Halifax, 20 January 1939; August Ogden, *The Dies Committee: A Study of the Special House Committee for the Investigation of Un-American Activities, 1938–43* (Washington, D.C.: Catholic University Press, 1943).

43. Jesse H. Stiller, *George S. Messersmith, Diplomat of Democracy* (Chapel Hill, N.C.: University of North Carolina Press, 1987), pp. 56–146; PRO FO 395/611, P2089/643/150, Lindsay to FO, 14 June 1938.

44. PRO FO 395/612, P2340, P2484, P3148/643/150; *New York Times*, 27 October 1938.

45. Ritchie Ovendale, *"Appeasement" and the English Speaking World* (Cardiff: University of Wales Press, 1975), pp. 199–200.

46. Reynolds, *The Creation of the Anglo-American Alliance*, pp. 44–45; Butler, *Lord Lothian*, p. 229; Scottish Record Office, Edinburgh (SRO) Lothian papers, GD40, Box 369, Lothian to Frank Aydelotte, 2 December 1938.

47. Harold Lavine and James Wechsler, *War Propaganda and the United States* (New Haven, Conn.: Yale University Press, 1940), p. 118; for similar sentiments in 1938: "The Munich Plot," *Propaganda Analysis* 2(2) (November 1938): 1–5.

48. Alec Douglas-Home, *The Way the Wind Blows: An Autobiography* (New York: Quadrangle/New York Times Book Co., 1976), p. 66; Iain Macleod, *Neville Chamberlain* (London: Muller, 1961), pp. 255–56.

49. Philip M. Taylor, "Film as Evidence," presentation to Institute of Contemporary British History summer school, London School of Economics, July 1989.

50. Ovendale, *"Appeasement,"* p.155; PRO FO 395/622, P2755/2645/150, Fletcher to Leeper, 28 September 1938; FO 395/656, P151/151/150, Wrench to Leeper, 6 January 1939, and Beith, 24 January 1939.

51. PRO FO 395/615, P1719/1157/150; FO 395/616, P2883, P3020 and P3262/1157/150; On Churchill: PRO FO 395/623, P3147/2646/150, Wilberforce to Leeper, 27 October 1938, and P3030/2645/150, Leeper to Lindsay, 18 October 1938; also Reynolds, *The Creation of the Anglo-American Alliance*, pp. 52–53.

52. *New York Times*, 10 December 1938; Tree, *When the Moon Was High*, pp. 79–81; Nigel Nicolson (ed.), *Harold Nicolson: Diaries and Letters: 1930–39* (London: Collins, 1967), p. 383.

53. PRO PREM 1/367, Murray/Roosevelt conversations, 16 and 24 October 1938.

54. Reynolds, *The Creation of the Anglo-American Alliance*, pp. 43–44; see also Harold Ickes, *The Secret Diary of Harold L. Ickes: Vol. II, The Inside Struggle, 1936–1939* (New York: Simon & Schuster, 1954), 29 January 1939, p. 571.

55. David Reynolds, "FDR's Foreign Policy and the British Royal Visit to the USA, 1939," *Historian* 45 (1983): 461–72.

56. PRO INF 1/15 and INF 1/17; also Taylor, *The Projection of Britain*, p. 275.

57. Taylor, *The Projection of Britain*, pp. 36–37; Richard Cockett, *Twilight of Truth: Chamberlain, Appeasement and the Manipulation of the Press* (London: Weidenfeld & Nicolson, 1989), pp. 82–85.

58. PRO FO 395/624, P2853/2853/150; Library of Congress (LoC): White Papers; *New York Sun*, 9 October 1939; Interviews: various.

59. PRO INF 1/20 and 719; Interviews: Hutton, Heather Harvey.

60. SHSW: NBC papers, Box 61/42, CBS, *Crisis: September 1938*.

61. PRO FO 395/656, P368/151/150, Fletcher to News Dept, 25 November 1938, "British propaganda in the U.S."; FO 395/616, P3423/1157/ 150; Taylor, *Projection of Britain*, p. 36.

62. British Library of Economics and Political Science (BLEPS): Charles Webster papers, 7/7, Minutes of ESU Private Group discussion, "The USA and the Post-Munich Situation," 1 February 1939; PRO FO 395/647, P2474/ 151/150, ESU Private Group Discussion, "The USA and the European Situation," 17 May 1939.

63. PRO INF 1/183, Lindsay to Leeper, 17 March 1939.

64. PRO INF 1/183, Leeper to Fass, 5 April 1939 etc; INF 1/719, "Channels of Publicity" Meeting 8, 4 April 1939, item 57; BBC WAC R61/2, "Transatlantic Broadcasting: Report of a Private Discussion Held at the ESU," 1 June 1939; FO 395/647, P2078/105/150, CID Sub-Committee on MoI: "Transmission . . . of Programmes for Broadcasting Overseas," Ryan, 25 May 1939.

65. PRO FO 371/22993, C3313/19/18, and FO 371/22966, C3102/15/18; Sidney Aster, *1939: The Making of the Second World War* (London: Deutsch, 1973), pp. 34, 75.

66. Manchester, *The Glory and the Dream*, pp. 240–41; PRO BT 60/52/4.

67. PRO BT 60/51/5. The British Council planned its exhibition in conjunction with the New York Museum of Modern Art; PRO CAB 24/288, CP 153 (39), Cabinet Memorandum: "Foreign Publicity," 10 July 1939; FO 395/613, P687/687/150; BW 63/9 and 10.

68. PRO BT 60/53/3 and FO 395/639, P148/31/150, P1865/31/45, and P2134/31/150, Wilberforce to Leeper, 22 May 1939; *New York Times Magazine*, 21 May 1939.

69. SRO Lothian papers GD 40/17/347; Lothian to Malcolm Macdonald, 2 November 1938; PRO CO 852/171/6; FO 371/22786, A472/18/45, Macdonald to Colonial Empire Marketing Board, DoT, India Office, etc., 14 January 1939; also CO 852/188/1, /2, and 118/3.

70. PRO FO 395/639, P1673, P2072, P2380, and P3472/31/150, Reports by McLean; Balfour, 30 August 1939; CO 852/244/1; *Oakland Tribune*, 28 July 1939; *Seattle Sunday Times*, 6 August 1939.

71. John Wheeler-Bennett, *George VI: His Life and Reign* (New York: St. Martin's, 1958), p. 380; Benjamin Rhodes, "The British Royal Visit of 1939 and the 'Psychological Approach' to the United States," *Diplomatic History* 5 (1981): 205.

72. *New York Herald Tribune*, 11 June 1939; Wheeler-Bennett, *George VI*, p. 387; Interview: Miall.

73. Wheeler-Bennett, *George VI*, p. 391; Reynolds, "FDR's Foreign Policy and the British Royal Visit," p. 469.

74. PRO FO 371/22800, A7769/7637/45, Lindsay to FO, 12 June 1939; FO 371/22801, A4443/27/45, Lindsay to Halifax, 20 June 1939; FO 371/22814, A4583/98/45, Butler to Scott, 3 July 1939.

75. PRO FO 115/3418/299, Mallet (Embassy) to Halifax, 28 April 1939; FO 115/3418/225, Dies Committee Press Release, 27 August 1939.

76. PRO FO 395/648, P3227/105/150, MoI Publicity Division Planning Section, Memo 271, "Report on the British Service of Information in the U.S. in Time of War," 20 July 1939; PRO FO 395/648, P3227/105/150, Memo 259, "Broadcasting to the U.S. in Time of War," 17 July 1939 and PRO INF 1/7, "Broadcasting in Wartime," 3 August 1939; also INF 1/29, Whyte to Waterfield, 4 August 1939, and INF 1/23, Memo by Waterfield, 30 August 1939.

77. PRO FO 395/648, P/2766/105/150, Mathews to FO, 15 June 1939; PRO INF 1/20/B; INF 1/29, Memo, 9 November 1939.

78. PRO INF 1/29; SHSW: NBC papers, Box 61/42, CBS, *Crisis: September 1938*; 18 September 1938. Interviews: various.

79. PRO INF 1/183, "Record of a meeting held at the Civil Service Commission on August 2nd, to discuss the relationship between persons broadcasting from London to the USA and the Censorship Authorities," 4 August 1939; also BBC WAC R61/2, Memo, Wellington, 30 August 1939, and American liaison, 3 September 1939.

80. PRO FO 395/648, P3227/105/150, MoI Publicity Planning Memo No. 271, 20 July 1939; FO 395/657, P3115/151/150, and FO 115/3418/225.

81. Wheeler-Bennett, Special Relationships, pp. 66, 74. Robert Bruce Lockhart, *Giants Cast Long Shadows*, (London: Putnam, 1960). Interviews: Miall, Berlin.

82. Wheeler-Bennett, *Special Relationships*, pp. 74–75; Anne Morrow Lindbergh, *The Flower and the Nettle: Diaries and Letters*, 1936–1939 (New York: Harcourt Brace Jovanovich, 1976); Anne Morrow Lindbergh, *War Within and Without: Diaries and Letters of Anne Morrow Lindbergh, 1939–44* (New York: Harcourt Brace Jovanovich, 1980), pp. 47–52; Lockhart, *Giants Cast Long Shadows*, pp. 71–72; *Life*, 11 August 1941; Kenneth S. Davis, *The Hero:*

Charles A. Lindbergh and the American Dream (Garden City, N.Y.: Doubleday, 1959), p. 407; Interviews: various.

83. Butler, *Lord Lothian*, pp. 229, 261; Reynolds, *The Creation of the Anglo-American Alliance*, pp. 44–45; Wheeler-Bennett, *Special Relationships*, pp. 66–68.

84. Interview: H. V. Hodson.

85. Edward R. Murrow, *This Is London* (New York: Simon & Schuster, 1941), p. 13.

Chapter 2

1. PRO FO 115/3419/585, Lothian to Halifax, 28 September 1939.

2. PRO FO 371/24227, A538/26/45, Darvall to Cowell, 18 December 1939; BBC WAC R61/3/1, "Service for American Broadcasts," circa late August 1939.

3. Wheeler-Bennett, *British Information in the U.S.A.*, p. 11.

4. PRO FO 115/3419/585, Lothian to Halifax, 28 September 1939.

5. Marian C. McKenna, *Borah* (Ann Arbor, Mich.: University of Michigan Press, 1961), p. 365.

6. Jerome Edwards, *The Foreign Policy of Col. McCormick's Tribune 1929–1941* (Reno, Nev.: University of Nevada Press, 1971), p. 147.

7. PRO FO 371/22816, A5981/98/45, Lothian to FO, 4 September 1939; Elliot Roosevelt (ed.), *FDR: His Personal Letters*, Vol. 3 (New York: Duell, Sloan, Pearce, 1950), pp. 278–79.

8. Asked by AIPO on 24 October 1939, "Do you think the present war in Europe is a struggle to defend Christianity, or do you think Christianity has little to do with it?" only 17% agreed; 74% said Christianity was "not an issue"; and 9% recorded a "Don't know" Hadley Cantril (ed.), *Public Opinion, 1935–46* (Princeton, N.J.: Princeton University Press, 1951), p. 1152.

9. PRO FO 371/24227, A540/26/45, Report by Tiltman, 7 December 1939.

10. LoC Borah papers, Box 513, Bliven to Borah, 10 July 1939.

11. PRO FO 371/24227, A701/26/45, Fletcher to Cowell, 8 January 1940; Lavine and Wechsler, *War Propaganda*, p. 145.

12. National Archives, Washington, D.C. (NA) RG165, Box 1240, 2327-B–226, 25; Porter Sargent, *Getting Us into War* (Boston: Sargent, 1941).

13. Lavine and Wechsler, *War Propaganda*, p. 119.

14. Saul Friedländer, *Prelude to Downfall: Hitler and the United States, 1939–1941* (New York: Knopf, 1967), pp. 53–65. *Documents on German Foreign Policy (DGFP)*, Series D 9, Thomsen to Foreign Ministry, 29 March 1940.

15. BBC WAC R61/3/2, Eckersley to Whyte, 18 April 1940; PRO FO 371/22839, A7052/7052/45, Lothian to FO, 5 October 1939; A7181/7052/45, Lothian to Halifax, 19 September 1939; *New York Times*, 14 September 1939.

16. Reynolds, *The Creation of the Anglo-American Alliance*, p. 317.

17. PRO PREM 1/416; PRO FO 371/24227, A2437/26/45, Whyte to FO, 30 March 1940.

18. PRO CAB 65/1, 54(39)10; CAB 65/6, 21(40)10; 29(40)6); *Foreign Relations of the United States (FRUS)*, 1939, Vol. 2, pp. 228–31.

19. PRO FO 371/24227, A539 and A1840/26/45, Lothian to FO, 20 February 1940; FO 371/22840, A8262/7052/45.

20. PRO CAB 65/5 27(40)2, 27(40)3, and 42(40)1.

21. PRO CAB 65/5, 50(40)1; CAB 65/8, 117 (40) Emergency Meeting No. 8; *FRUS*, 1939, Vol. 1, pp. 422–24, 541, 547; Walter Winchell, *Winchell: Exclusive* (Englewood Cliffs, N.J.: Prentice-Hall, 1975), p. 165; BBC WAC R61/6, NAR, 20 September 1940.

22. *Time*, 18 September 1939, 26.

23. Cedric Larson, "The British Ministry of Information," *Public Opinion Quarterly* 5 (1941): 416; Interview: Hodson.

24. Interview: Hodson; Tree, *When the Moon Was High*, p. 92; Cockett, *Twilight of Truth*, pp. 121–43.

25. NA Ottawa, Graham Spry papers, MG30/D297/44/7, "New Pills to Purge Melancholy . . ." For criticism of the MoI: Frank Gervasi, *The Violent Decade: A Foreign Correspondent in Europe and the Middle East, 1935–1945* (New York: Norton, 1989), pp. 200–206; Riley, *999 and All That*, pp. 68–72.

26. PRO PREM 1/439, "Censorship and the Reorganisation of the MoI"; NA RG 165/1085, 2270-a–62, Lt. R. A. Smith to War Dept, May 1940; PRO FO 371/22840, A7845/7052/45, Peake to FO, 8 November 1939.

27. Riley, *999 and All That*, p. 170; PRO INF 1/4, Divisional Progress Report, April 1940.

28. Interviews: Reston, Carroll; PRO INF 1/6, MoI Weekly Reports, 7 October 1939; FO 371/22840, A7845/7052/45, FO to Malett, 5 December 1939.

29. *New York Sun*, 9 October 1939; PRO FO 371/22839, A7052/7052/45, FO to Whyte, 2 November 1939.

30. PRO FO 371/2840, A7787/7052/45; FO 371/22841, A8608/7052/45.

31. PRO FO 371/22840, A8359/7052/45, Lothian to FO, 29 November 1939; minutes: Whyte and Monckton; SRO Lothian papers: GD40/17, Box 405, Lothian to Swoope, 22 March 1940.

32. BBC WAC R61/3/2, Eckersley, 21 March 1940; PRO FO 371/24228, A2622/26/45.

33. Gervasi, *The Violent Decade*, pp. 205–6. Interview: Larry Lesueur.

34. PRO FO 371/24227, A1073/26/45, Whyte to FO, 12 February 1940; PRO INF 1/6, MoI Progress Report: November 1939, Mathews to Whyte, 21 November 1939; Lavine and Wechsler, *War Propaganda*, p. 347.

35. BBC WAC R61/6, Rowse, 20 September 1939; R61/2, Memo, 24 January 1940.

36. Roger Eckersley, *The BBC and All That* (London: Sampson, Low, Marston, 1945); Roger Eckersley, *Some Nonsense* (London: Sampson, Low, Marston, 1945), pp. 12, 53.

37. BBC WAC R61/3/1, BBC American Liaison Division Memo, circa August 1939; R61/3/2, Eckersley memo: "Facilities for American Broadcasting . . . ," 25 January 1940; PRO INF 1/3, American Division Progress Report, April 1940, item 2.

38. BBC WAC R61/3/2, Eckersley to Whyte, 18 April 1940 and 27 March 1940.

39. BBC WAC R61/3/1.

40. BBC WAC R61/2, BBC Internal Memo "Arthur Mann's Ninth Recording," Johnson to Eckersley, 26 November 1939; Eckersley to Steele, 5 December 1939. On Mutual's bias: PRO FO 371/22840, A7970/7052/45, Cowell (FO), 16 November 1939.

41. BBC WAC R61/2, Eckersley to Darvall, 22 February 1940.

42. Interview: Cooke; Asa Briggs, *The History of Broadcasting in the United Kingdom, Vol. 3, The War of Words* (Oxford: Oxford University Press, 1970), p. 175.

43. SRO Lothian papers: GD40/17, Box 399, Cazalet to Lothian, 14 September 1939; Interviews: Carroll, Milbank.

44. Interview: Janet Murrow; Joseph E. Persico, *Edward R. Murrow: An American Original* (New York: McGraw-Hill, 1988), p. 167.

45. BBC WAC R61/2, Darvall to Madden, 27 October 1939; Murrow, *This Is London*, pp. 1–71.

46. Interview: Janet Murrow; Persico, *Murrow*, p. 160.

47. PRO FO 395/614, P1157/1157/150, Fletcher to News Dept, 21 February 1938; FO 371/24228, A2687/26/45; minute by T. North Whitehead; FO 371/24227, A538/26/45, Darvall to FO, 18 December 1939.

48. BBC WAC R61/1, Eckersley to MoI, 15 December 1939; PRO FO 371/22839, A8330/7053/45; FO 371/24227, A231/26/45.

49. PRO INF 1/756: Meeting at Chatham House, 27 June 1939; *March of Times*'s usual bias was evident in "The Battle Fleets of England," Vol. 6, No. 2 (September 1939), and privileged access to British footage was put to good use in "Britain's RAF," *March of Time*, Vol. 7, No. 2 (October 1940); PRO INF 1/3, MoI Progress Report, January 1940; INF 1/848, Whyte to Sir Kenneth Lee, Director General MoI, 22 January 1940.

50. PRO INF 1/568; PRO INF 1/6, MoI Weekly Report, 24 September 1939; PRO FO 371/24230, A3344/26/45; FO 371/22839, A7443/7052/45, Dudley to Whyte, 17 October 1939. Funeral footage was used in Humphrey Jennings (dir.) *Words for Battle* (Crown, 1941).

51. PRO INF 1/23, 81; INF 1/6, Report, November 1939; INF 1/3, Report, January 1940; INF 1/867, MoI Policy Committee, Programme for Film Propaganda, January 1940; and PRO T 162/994/E40318, as cited in Frederick Krome, "'A Weapon of War Second to None': Anglo-American Film Propaganda During World War II" (University of Cincinnati Ph.D. thesis, 1992), pp. 60–68. On Ball: Cockett, *Twilight of Truth*, pp. 9–11.

52. Caroline Moorehead, *Sidney Bernstein* (London: Jonathan Cape, 1984), pp. 113–21; Interview: Hodson.

53. Ian Dalrymple, "The Crown Film Unit, 1940–43," in Nicholas Pronay and D. W. Spring (eds.), *Propaganda, Politics and Film, 1918–45* (London: Macmillan, 1982), pp. 209–20; Humphrey Jennings, Harry Watt, and Pat Jackson (dirs.), *The First Days* (GPO Film Unit, 1939).

54. Stirling University, Grierson Archive, G4/24/153, Wright to Grierson, 27 August 1940; G4/24/154, Rotha to Grierson, 27 August 1940.

55. Stirling University, Grierson Archive, G3/7/2 and G3/15/86, Grierson to Fletcher, 7 September 1939; PRO FO 371/22839, A7100/7052/45, Lothian to FO, 13 October 1939; FO 371/22840, A7840 and A8192/7052/45; PRO INF 1/3, American Division progress report, January–February 1940; INF 1/598, Fletcher to Lothian, 15 October 1940.

56. PRO FO 371/22839, A7053/7052/45, Vansittart, 21 October 1939.

57. Stirling University, Grierson Archive, G3/15/88, Grierson to Tallents, 10 September 1939; G3/15/95, Grierson to Lothian, 19 September 1939; G3/8/3/1; Hardy, *Grierson*, pp. 99–100. The film became *Foreign Correspondent* and is discussed in Chapter 4 of this book, pp. 111–12.

58. Michael Powell, *A Life in Movies* (London: Heineman, 1986), p. 329; PRO INF 1/6, 23–30 October 1939.
59. Michael Powell, Brian Hurst, Adrian Brunel (dirs.), *The Lion Has Wings* (London/UA, 1939); PRO FO 371/22840, A7720, A7931, A7976, and A8060/7052/45; FO 371/22841, A9056/7052/45.
60. Michael Powell (dir.), *Contraband* (British National, 1940).
61. Roy Boulting (dir.), *Pastor Hall* (Grand National, 1940); Roy Boulting to author, 25 September 1987; Clive Coultass, *Images for Battle* (London: Associated University Presses, 1989), pp. 32–36.
62. Boulting to author; Interview: Stanley Wilson (son of Maurice Wilson); Koppes and Black, *Hollywood Goes to War*, pp. 32–33; James C. Schneider, *Should America Go to War?* (Chapel Hill, N.C.: University of North Carolina Press, 1989), pp. 93–94.
63. Interview: Fairbanks; Tree, *When the Moon Was High*, p. 126; Morley, *Tales from the Hollywood Raj*, pp. 165–66; SRO Lothian Papers: GD40/17, Box 405, Lothian to Vansittart, 24 September 1940.
64. Interview: Fairbanks; PRO FO 371/24228, A2687/26/45, Cavendish-Bentinck to Balfour, 15 April 1940; J. B. Priestley, *Britain Speaks* (New York: Harper, 1940), pp. 182–85.
65. *New York Times*, 19 March 1939, 30 April 1939, and 9 October 1939; PRO FO 395/565, P914/151/150, Evans (Los Angeles) to Embassy, 10 March 1939; Charles Chaplin (dir.), *The Great Dictator* (Chaplin, 1940); Anatole Litvak (dir.), *Confessions of a Nazi Spy* (Warner Brothers, 1939). Evans also hoped for sympathetic films from Paramount, but these did not appear.
66. PRO FO 371/24227, A638/26/45, Whyte to Balfour, 23 January 1940; Whyte to Lothian, 25 January 1940.
67. PRO FO 371/24230, A3581/26/45, Forrester, 20 May 1940; Fletcher to Huxley, 20 May 1940; Huxley to FO, 13 June 1940. The property was not filmed until 1951. Jack Warner also offered to make any film free of charge for the U.S. government, but not until August 1940: Richard W. Steele, *Propaganda in an Open Society: The Roosevelt Administration and the Media, 1933–1941*, (Westport, Conn.: Greenwood, 1985), p. 157.
68. PRO FO 371/22839, A7443/7052/45, Dudley to Whyte, 17 October 1939; Louis de Rochemont (dir.), *The Ramparts We Watch* (RKO, 1940); Fielding, *March of Time*, pp. 245–50; Fletcher School, Tufts University, Boston, Mass.: Murrow papers, Reel 17, Monckton to Watts (Newsreel Association), 18 April 1941; Stirling University, Grierson papers, G424/159/1; NA Ottawa, R2/5750/138.
69. PRO INF 1/6, Weekly Reports, especially 17 and 24 September 1939; PRO FO 371/26183, A161/118/45; FO 371/24228, A2656/26/45.
70. PRO INF 1/6, Weekly Report of American Division, 24 September 1939; "Who Started the War?" *Propaganda Analysis* 3(3) (15 December 1939): 33–39.
71. PRO INF 1/6, Memo by W. H. Stevenson, 8 December 1939.
72. PRO INF 1/6, Interim Report November–December 1939; INF 1/848, "Book Activities of General Division," 17 April 1940, and reports for January–April 1940; INF 1/3, Report January–February 1940.
73. PRO FO 371/24228, A2656/26/45, Cowell, 2 April 1940; PRO INF 1/848, Policy Committee Minutes, nos. 11, 15, and 17, for 5, 18, and 26 April

1940; Interview: Val Stavridi; Richards and Aldgate, *Britain Can Take It*, pp. 115–35; Graham Greene, *The Last Word and Other Stories* (London: Heineman, 1990), pp. 46–59; "Men at Work," *Spectator* (28 February 1941): 234–36; *New Yorker* (25 October 1941): 63–66.

74. PRO INF 1/6, MoI Weekly Reports, 16–23 October 1939; Interim Report, 24 November 1939.

75. PRO INF 1/6, MoI Weekly Reports, 23 October 1939, 11 December 1939, Interim Report: April 1939; PRO INF 1/3, Report on the MoI, February 1939, Religions Division; "Soldiers of the Lord," *Propaganda Analysis* 3(7) (1 April 1940): 61–72.

76. Ian McLaine, *Ministry of Morale: Home Front Morale and the Ministry of Information* (London: Allen & Unwin, 1979), p .168; PRO FO 395/653, A1133/120/150, Lindsay to Halifax, 17 March 1939; Interviews: Berlin, Raphael; FO 371/24230, A3436/26/46, Balfour, 24 June 1940; Chaim Weizmann, *Trial and Error* (London: Hamish Hamilton, 1949), pp. 521–22; Churchill did not begin to raise a Jewish Battalion until September 1944.

77. SRO Lothian papers: GD40/17, Box 399, Lothian to Cazalet, 11 March 1940; Lavine and Wechsler, *War Propaganda*, p. 204.

78. PRO FO 371/24228, A2364/26/45, Perlzweig to FO, 11 July 1940; Bernays (Chicago) to Embassy, 12 March 1940.

79. Interview: Hodson; PRO INF 1/848, E. H. Carr, "Principles and Objectives of British Propaganda in Foreign Countries," Policy Committee Meeting 10, 15 March 1940; INF 1/3, Monthly Reports, January and February 1940.

80. PRO INF 1/6, MoI Progress Report, 24 November 1939; PRO FO 395/648, P2990/105/150; FO 395/649, P3385/105/150.

81. PRO INF 1/6, MoI Weekly Report, 30 October 1939; PRO FO 371/24227, A1073/26/45, Whyte to FO, 12 February 1940; Lavine and Wechsler, *War Propaganda*, pp. 214–15. There is no evidence that these stamps originated in the MoI.

82. PRO FO 371/24227, A1852/26/45, Lothian to Whyte, 27 February 1940.

83. SRO Lothian papers: GD40/17, Boxes 398–406.

84. Lord Lothian, *The American Speeches of Lord Lothian* (Oxford: Oxford University Press, 1941), p. 47.

85. Lothian, *American Speeches*, pp. 1–19, 44–47; SRO Lothian papers: GD40/17, Box 398, Lothian to Amery, 9 January 1940; Box 405, "Speeches."

86. Lothian, *American Speeches*, pp. 47–63, 71–89, 104–10. Interview: Hodson.

87. Wheeler-Bennett, *Special Relationships*, pp. 77–79.

88. Wheeler-Bennett, *Special Relationships*, pp. 79–84; PRO FO 371/24227, A1852/26/45.

89. Wheeler-Bennett, *British Information in the U.S.A.*, p. 11; PRO FO 371/24228, A2047/26/45, 5 March 1940.

90. PRO FO 371/24227, A534/26/45, Fletcher to Cowell, 20 March 1940; Wheeler-Bennett, *Special Relationships*, p. 91.

91. Interview: Lord Harmsworth.

92. Interviews: Galwey, Lord and Lady Harmsworth, Hermione MacColl, Macmillan, Peggy Ratcliffe; PRO FO 371/22841, A9115/7052/45; FO 115/3420/1532, Lothian to Halifax, 20 December 1939; FO 371/24231, A3772/26/45,

minute by Scott, 12 August 1940. The office also monitored films, while the Baltimore Consulate undertook a detailed study of radio listening.

93. Interviews: Raphael, Berlin, Galwey, Frank Thistlethwaite. Ormerod obituary, *Times*, 3 November 1983; Wheeler-Bennett, *British Information in the U.S.A.*, pp. 29–30.

94. PRO FO 115/3419/585, Lothian to Halifax, 28 September 1939; FO 371/22840, A7713/7052/45; FO 371/24227, A585/26/45. FO 371/24229, A3154/26/45, Meeting at MoI, 2 May 1940; FO 371/22841, A8614/7052/45; Wheeler-Bennett, *British Information in the U.S.A.*, pp. 37–38.

95. PRO FO 371/24227, A774/26/45. In later years, Heath was skeptical of the benefits of his tour, and doubted whether Britain "had *ever* succeeded in influencing American public opinion." Edward Heath to author, 9 December 1987.

96. SRO Lothian papers: GD40/17, Box 402, Lamont to Lothian, 15 December 1939, etc.; PRO FO 371/22840, A792/7052/45.

97. PRO FO 115/3419/585, Lothian to Halifax, 14 December 1939.

98. PRO FO 371/22840, A8255/7052/45, Whyte, "Draft Note on Policy," 24 November 1939; *Washington Daily News*, 7 May 1940; Reynolds, *The Creation of the Anglo-American Alliance*, pp. 64–67.

99. *Chicago Daily News*, 26 October 1939; PRO FO 371/24227, A540/26/45, Report by Tiltman, 7 December 1939; FO 371/24228, A2256/26/45, Butler to Whyte, 12 March 1939; Lavine and Wechsler, *War Propaganda*, pp. 193, 281–324; Lothian, *American Speeches*, pp. 24–25, 57.

100. Clarence Streit, *Union Now* (London: Jonathan Cape, 1939); Jane Schwar, "Interventionist Propaganda and Pressure Groups in the United States, 1937–1941" (Ohio State University Ph.D. thesis, 1973); Lavine and Wechsler, *War Propaganda*, pp. 72–89; Sargent, *Getting Us into War*, pp. 71–72. The group included leaders of The Pilgrims, the Carnegie Endowment, and The Rhodes Trust. Eichelberger was chairman of the American Union for Concerted Peace Efforts, of which Shotwell (director of the Carnegie Endowment) was honorary vice-president; everyone sat on everyone else's board; SRO Lothian Papers: GD40/17, Box 402, Lothian/Lamont correspondence. These groups were also connected to the interventionist lobby of World War I. They shared aims, members, and funds from J. P. Morgan. Frederick Coudert and Henry Stimson played leadership roles in both committees: Grattan, *Why We Fought*, p. 117.

101. Lavine and Wechsler, *War Propaganda*, pp. 103–12; Interview: Fairbanks; Tree, *When the Moon Was High*, pp. 92–102; PRO FO 371/22819, A8548/98/45, Report by Tree, November 1939; SRO Lothian papers: GD40/17, Boxes 398 and 400.

102. Lavine and Wechsler, *War Propaganda*, pp. 271–81.

103. PRO FO 371/24227, A1358/26/45, BLI report No. 28.

104. SRO Lothian Papers: GD40/17, Box 514/43, Lothian to Long, December 1939.

105. PRO FO 371/24227, A538/26/45, Cowell to Fletcher, 15 February 1940; Dudley, March 1940; FO 371/22841, A8709/7052/45, Cowell, 12 December 1939.

106. Tree, *When the Moon Was High*, pp. 92–102; PRO FO 371/22819, A8548/98/45, Report by Tree, November 1939.

107. PRO FO 371/22840, A 8255/7052/45, Balfour to Whyte, 13 December 1939; FO 371/22841, A8710/7052/45, Tree to Butler, 12 December 1939; Whyte to Perth (FO), 21 December 1939; FO 371/24227, A710/26/45; Tree, *When the Moon Was High*, pp. 103–4.

108. PRO FO 371/24227, A538/26/45, Darvall to Cowell, 18 December 1939; A709/26/45, Whyte to Lothian, 1 January 1940 (emphasis in original); FO 371/22840, A8255/7052/45, Whyte, "Draft Note on Policy," 24 November 1939; FO 371/22841, A9115/7052/45.

109. Interview: Hodson; Michael Balfour, *Propaganda in War, 1939–1945: Organizations, Policies and Publics in Germany and Britain* (London: Routledge & Kegan Paul, 1979), pp. 61–62; PRO FO 371/25166, W532/532/49: "Propaganda Activities of MI7"; PRO INF 1/848, Ministerial Policy Committee 8, 1 March 1940. Monckton moved to the MoI as Deputy Director General; and all news was to be issued by the MoI or simultaneously by both the MoI and the military service departments. The service departments retained formal responsibility for their own news.

110. PRO INF 1/29, OEPEC paper 228, 20 Feb 1939 approves an extra specialist, senior assistant specialist, and typist; PRO FO 371/24228, A2413/26/45, Lothian to FO, 8 February 1940; A2114/26/45, Huxley to Scott, March 1940.

111. PRO FO 371/24227, A601/26/45, Darvall to Balfour, 14 January 1940 and A537/26/45, Darvall to Balfour, 18 January 1940; FO 371/24228, A2511/26/45, Scott (FO) to Whyte, 4 April 1940; Interview: Reston. After American entry into the war, it became standard practice for a U.S. OWI representative in London (Reston) to inform the MoI of areas of American misunderstanding of British policy so that suitable questions could be planted in the House of Commons and subsequently reported as though intended only for British ears.

112. PRO FO 371/22840, A7840/7052/45; *FRUS*, 1940 3, Kennedy to Hull, 12 June 1940, p. 37; PRO INF 1/3, American Division progress report, January to February 1940; McLaine, *Ministry of Morale*, pp. 263–71; David Reynolds, "Whitehall, Washington and the Promotion of American Studies in Britain During World War Two," *Journal of American Studies* 16 (1982): 165–88; K. R. M. Short, "Cinematic Support for Anglo-American Détente, 1939–43," in Philip M. Taylor (ed.), *British Cinema in the Second World War* (London: Macmillan, 1988), pp. 121–43.

113. PRO FO 371/24227, A1774 and A1073/26/45, Whyte to FO, 12 February 1940; FO 371/24228, A2242/26/45, North Whitehead, 21 March 1940.

114. PRO FO 371/24228, A2299/26/45, Reith to Halifax, 27 March 1940, Huxley, April 1940; FO 371/22841, A7190/7190/45 and A8764/7052/45.

115. PRO FO 371/24227, A538/26/45, Dudley in Fletcher to Cowell, 20 March 1940; A539/26/45, Darvall to Cowell, 14 January 1940; FO 371/24228, A2534/26/45, Dudley to Embassy, 19 March 1940.

116. PRO FO 371/24228, A2033 and A2256/26/45, Embassy to Whyte, 12 March 1939. This scheme came to nothing, but the strategy resurfaced in Churchill's phrase of 1941: "Give us the tools and we will finish the job."

117. PRO FO 371/24228, A2242/26/45, North Whitehead, 22 March 1940.

118. PRO INF 1/4, Divisional Progress Report, April 1940: British pictures led German by six to one in the South and by five to one in the Northwest;

General von Bötticher and Hans Thomsen to Foreign Ministry and Service Departments, 4 April 1940, *DGFP*, Series D, Vol. 9, pp. 73–75.

119. PRO INF 1/183, Townroe to Usborne, 19 September 1939.

120. PRO FO 371/24229, A3183/26/45, Darvall to Dudley, 4 April 1940; *Evening Standard*, 1 May 1940; *Daily Mail*, 2 May 1940.

121. PRO FO 371/24229, A3154/26/45, minutes, 2 May 1940.

122. Martin Gilbert, *Winston S. Churchill, Vol. VI, Finest Hour, 1939–1941* (London: Heineman, 1983), pp. 321–33, 356; Nigel Nicolson (ed.), *Harold Nicolson, Diaries and Letters, 1939–45*, (London: Collins, 1967), p. 86; Tree, *When the Moon Was High*, p. 118.

123. *FRUS*, 1940 1, pp. 184–216.

Chapter 3

1. Gilbert, *Churchill*, Vol. 6, pp. 468–69.

2. *FRUS*, 1940 3, Kennedy to Hull and FDR, 15 May 1940, pp. 29–30, and Roosevelt to Churchill, 16 May 1940, pp. 49–50.

3. PRO INF 1/848, Policy Committee: minutes for 14 May 1940; BBC WAC R34/473/1, Policy Committee, 17 May 1940.

4. Interview: Middleton; René MacColl, Diary for France 1940, 11–21 May 1940; Drew Middleton, *Our Share of Night* (New York: Viking, 1946), pp. 63–64; Nicholas Harman, *Dunkirk: The Patriotic Myth* (New York: Simon & Schuster, 1980), p. 242.

5. MacColl, Diary for France, 19–21 May 1940; Ben Robertson, *I Saw England* (New York: Knopf, 1941), p. 70.

6. *FRUS*, 1940 1, Kennedy to Hull, 27 May 1940, p. 233.

7. Harman, *Dunkirk*.

8. PRO PREM 4/25/8, Caldecotte to Churchill, 28 May 1940; Colville, 29 May 1940.

9. *New York Herald Tribune* 31 May 1940; Norman Gelb, *Dunkirk* (New York: Morrow, 1989), p. 285.

10. Gelb, *Dunkirk*, p. 285. These words soon became a part of British understanding of Dunkirk. As Angus Calder has noted, they were quoted on June 14 in a *War Illustrated* editorial; Angus Calder, *The Myth of the Blitz* (London: Jonathan Cape, 1991), p. 27.

11. PRO FO 371/24230, A3352/26/45, Lothian to Peake, 1 June 1940; Paul Gallico, *The Snow Goose* (New York: Knopf, 1941); William Wyler (dir.), *Mrs. Miniver* (MGM, 1942).

12. *FRUS*, 1940, Vol. 1, Kennedy to Hull, 16 June 1940, pp. 259–60; Sir John Colville, *The Fringes of Power: Downing Street Diaries, 1939–1955* (London: Weidenfeld & Nicolson, 1985): 18 June 1940, p. 164.

13. Interview: Middleton.

14. PRO CAB 65/8, 151 (40) 9, 1 June 1940.

15. Gilbert, *Churchill*, Vol. 6, p. 571; author's emphasis.

16. Colville, *The Fringes of Power*, 19 May 1940, p. 136.

17. Gilbert, *Churchill*, Vol. 6, pp. 471–72, 486; *DGFP*, Series D, Vol. 10, Hitler, 16 July 1940, p. 226.

18. Gilbert, *Churchill*, Vol. 6, pp. 332–33.

19. SRO Lothian papers: GD40/17, Box 399, Lothian to Cazalet, 1 July 1940.

20. Robert Dallek, *Franklin D. Roosevelt and American Foreign Policy* (New York: Oxford University Press, 1979), p. 243; *FRUS*, 1940, Vol. 3, memo by Welles, 23 May 1940, pp. 3–5, *FRUS*, 1940, Vol. 1, Hull to Kennedy, 14 June 1940, pp. 254–55; Philip Goodhart, *Fifty Ships That Saved the World* (Garden City, N.Y.: Doubleday, 1965), especially pp. 101–3; *New York Herald Tribune*, 26 May 1940; *New York Times*, 27 May 1940; LoC Clapper: Box 9, Robert Jackson interview, 27 May 1940. In fact, the Germans did not conduct sabotage operations in the United States: *DGFP*, Series D, Vol. 9, pp. 408–12, 491, 543.

21. University of Arizona, Tucson, Lewis Douglas Papers: AZ 290, Box 291/1; Schwar, "Interventionist Propaganda," chapter 7; also Mudd Library, Princeton, N.J., Committee to Defend America papers; PRO FO 371/24229, A3183/26/45, Chancery to FO, 3 June 1940; Walter Johnson, *William Allen White's America*, (New York: Holt, 1947), pp. 524–54.

22. SRO Lothian papers: GD40/17, Box 516, Miller to J. R. M. Butler; UA, Douglas papers: AZ 290, Box 265, Miller to Douglas, 5 June 1940; members included journalists Herbert Agar, Henry Luce, Ulric Bell, Joseph Alsop, and Elmer Davis; businessmen Lew Douglas and Whitney Shepardson; educators James B. Conant (Harvard) and Ernest Hopkins (Dartmouth); churchmen Henry Sloane Coffin and Henry P. Van Dusen (both of Union Theological Seminary, New York), and the historian of Great War interventionism, Walter Millis.

23. SRO Lothian Papers: GD40/17, Box 516.

24. Schwar, "Interventionist Propaganda," pp. 166–67.

25. Interview: Fairbanks; Goodhart, *Fifty Ships That Saved the World*, p. 112.

26. SRO Lothian papers: GD40/17, Box 516, Alsop to Butler, 28 June 1956. Lewis Douglas managed Century/White Committee liaison: UA, Douglas Papers: AZ 290, Box 291/1, "Van Dusen Group supper meeting," 11 July 1940.

27. Wayne S. Cole, *America First: The Battle Against Intervention* (Madison, Wis.: University of Wisconsin Press, 1953), pp. 10–14; Justus D. Doenecke, *In Danger Undaunted: The Anti-Interventionist Movement of 1940–1941* (Palo Alto, Calif.: Hoover Institution, 1990), pp. 6–9, 87–90; *New York Herald Tribune*, 8 June 1940.

28. *DGFP*, Series D, Vol. 9, pp. 339–40, 550–51, 558–59; Vol. 10, pp. 101–2, 250–51; Vol. 11, pp. 1–4, 243–44, 361–62; NA RG 165, 23227-a–39, Senator Clarke read the anglophobic Quincey Howe, *England Expects That Every American Will Do His Duty* (New York: Simon & Schuster, 1937) into the record.

29. SRO Lothian papers: GD40/17/399, Lothian to Brand, 25 June 1940.

30. PRO PREM 4/25/8, Halifax to Churchill, 8 July 1940.

31. PRO PREM 4/25/8; PRO CAB 65/8, 127(40)5.

32. PRO PREM 4/25/8, Morrison to Churchill, 4 July 1940; Churchill to Morrison, 5 July 1940.

33. *FRUS*, 1939, Vol. 1, Kennedy to Hull, 2 October 1939, pp. 499–500; PRO CAB 65/8, 142 (40), Churchill to Reynaud, 28 May 1940.

34. Gilbert, *Churchill*, Vol. 6, p. 579, Charles Eade (ed.), *Secret Session Speeches* (London: Cassell, 1946), pp. 8–16.

35. PRO PREM 4/25/8; PRO CAB 65/8, 159(40)8.

36. PRO FO 371/24230, A3464/26/45, Lothian to FO, 26 June 1940; PREM 4/25/8, Halifax to Churchill, 8 July 1940; CAB 65/8, 185(40); Colville, *The Fringes of Power*, pp. 173–76.

37. Churchill, *The Second World War*, Vol. 2, p. 201.

38. PRO PREM 4/25/8, Bevir to Hood (MoI), 7 July 1940.

39. Lothian, *American Speeches*, 97–115; PRO PREM 4/25/8.

40. SRO Lothian papers: GD40/17, Box 405, Van Dusen to Lothian, 2 August 1940; Box 398, Balderston to Lothian, 27 June 1940; LoC Balderston Papers, Box 2, Lothian to Balderston, 15 July 1940; Mark Chadwin, *The Hawks of World War II* (Chapel Hill, N.C.: University of North Carolina Press), pp. 55–56.

41. SRO Lothian papers: GD40/17, Box 405, Van Dusen to Lothian, 1 July 1940; Box 516, Miller to Butler; Chadwin, *Hawks of World War II*, p. 40; PRO FO 800/398, Lothian to Luce, 28 July 1940; Lothian to Shepardson, 28 and 30 July 1940.

42. SRO Lothian papers: GD40/17, Box 516, Alsop to J. R. M. Butler, 28 June 1956; *DGFP*, Series D, Vol. 10, pp. 456–57, 507–8.

43. PRO FO 371/24229, A3464/26/45, Lothian to FO, 3 June 1940; PRO PREM 4/25/8, Halifax to Churchill, 8 July 1940.

44. PRO FO INF 1/5, Divisional Progress Report, 27 May 1940; PRO FO 371/24229, A3197, A3183/26/45, Lothian to FO/MoI, 27 May 1940; FO to Lothian, 29 May 1940, and A3228, minutes as read to the War Cabinet on 18 May 1940.

45. PRO FO 800/398, Duff Cooper to Lothian, 18 June 1940; Lothian to Duff Cooper, 13 July 1940; SRO Lothian papers: GD40/17/399, Lothian to Brand, 25 June 1940.

46. PRO PREM, 4/25/8, Lothian to Churchill, 20 May 1940; PRO FO 371/24229, A3197/26/45.

47. PRO FO 800/398, Lothian to Duff Cooper, 13 July 1940; PRO INF 1/102, Darvall to Peterson, 24 August 1940; NA RG 59, Box 4789, 841.01B11/134, Embassy to State Dept; Interview: Lord Perth (formerly Viscount Strathallan).

48. PRO INF 1/102, Darvall to Peterson, responding to Monckton, 20 August 1940; PRO FO 371/24231, A3772/26/45, Childs to FO, 25 July 1940, and memo dated "July 1940."

49. Interview: Perth.

50. Interview: Perth.

51. PRO FO 371/24231, A4025 and A3772/26/45, "Memo. drawn by Mr. Childs after consultation with Lord Lothian," July 1940, discussed at MoI on 6 September 1940.

52. John Russell Taylor, *Hitch: The Life and Times of Alfred Hitchcock* (New York: Pantheon, 1978), pp. 143–44; Paul Tabori, *Alexander Korda* (London: Oldbourne, 1959), pp. 219–14; Korda, *Charmed Lives*, pp. 130–48; Christopher Andrew, *Secret Service: The Making of the British Intelligence Community* (London: Heineman, 1985); H. Montgomery Hyde, *Secret Intelligence Agent* (London: Hamish Hamilton, 1982), pp. 160–66, 245; Wheeler-Bennett, *Special Relationships*, p. 139.

53. Nigel West, *MI6: British Secret Intelligence Service Operations, 1909–45* (London: Weidenfeld & Nicolson, 1983), pp. 120–23; F. H. Hinsley and C. A. G. Simkins, *British Intelligence in the Second World War: Vol. 4, Security and Counter-Intelligence* (London: HMSO, 1990), p. 142; Montgomery Hyde, *The Quiet Canadian*, pp. 11–24; Andrew, *Secret Service*, pp. 358–59, 465.

54. Montgomery Hyde, *The Quiet Canadian*, pp. 25–26; Hinsley and Simkins, *British Intelligence*, Vol. 4, p. 143. On October 1, 1969, when interviewed by CIA historian Tom Troy, Cuneo denied this story. NA RG 263, Box 7/56, Troy interview notes; Franklin D. Roosevelt Library (FDRL), Hyde Park, New York, printed works collection: Thomas F. Troy, *COI and British Intelligence, an Essay on Origins* (Langley, Va.: CIA, 1970), pp. 31–37.

55. West, *MI6*, pp. 122–23, 239–44; NA RG 263, Box 7/57, Troy to Chief Intelligence Institute, CIA, 11 October 1974; Peter Wright, *Spy Catcher* (New York: Viking, 1988), pp. 325–29; NA RG 263, Box 7/56, Interview Bruce/Troy, 30 December 1972.

56. Hinsley and Simkins, *British Intelligence*, Vol. 4, p. 143; Montgomery Hyde, *Secret Intelligence Agent*, p. xv; Montgomery Hyde, *The Quiet Canadian*, pp. 2–5. Bill Donovan later said that Stephenson "taught us everything we know about foreign intelligence."

57. Montgomery Hyde, *The Quiet Canadian*, pp. 2–5; West, *MI6*, pp. 86, 201; Hinsley and Simkins, *British Intelligence*, Vol. 4, p. 144; Nigel West, *A Thread of Deceit: Espionage Myths of World War II* (New York: Random House, 1985), p. 131. In March 1940, the B ritish Purchasing Commission established its own anti-sabotage division (NA RG 59, Box 4700, 841.24/229); it was later absorbed into the BSC.

58. Stephenson, in Montgomery Hyde, *Secret Intelligence Agent*, p. xvii. There is an established story that Stephenson saw Donovan before his mission and suggested that Britain be "shown the red carpet" (Andrew, *Secret Service*, p. 466, and Anthony Cave Brown, *Wild Bill Donovan: The Last Hero* (New York: Times Books, 1982), pp. 147–49). CIA historian Tom Troy found a note on a document on OSS/BSC relations from 1944 in Donovan's own hand: "did not know S[tephenson] then [June 1940], only met him after return [from England]." Although Stephenson stuck to his story, Troy questioned "Stephenson's memory or honesty": NA RG 263, Box 7/55, Troy to CIA training, 16 February 1968.

59. Mowrer, *New York Herald Tribune*, 20–24 August 1940; David Stafford, *Camp X* (Toronto: Lester & Orpen Dennys, 1986), p. 14.

60. Montgomery Hyde, *The Quiet Canadian*, pp. 70–72.

61. PRO INF 1/29, "Function and Staffing of the American Division," 8 July 1940.

62. PRO INF 1/29, memo 8 July 1940, and OEPEC Paper 459, A/3/6, 31 July 1940.

63. Interview: Sevareid.

64. BBC WAC, Contributors file: Frederick Whyte, (1B), Whyte to Tallents, 4 September 1940; PRO FO 371/24232, A4224/26/45.

65. PRO FO 800/398, Whyte to Lothian, 4 September 1940.

66. PRO FO 800/398, Lothian to Whyte, 24 September 1940.

67. PRO INF 1/29, Darvall to Whyte, 14 August 1940; INF 1/102, Memo by Williams, 25 September and 10 October 1940; Darvall to Williams, circa 25 September 1940.

68. Michael Powell (dir.), *Forty-Ninth Parallel* (GFD/Ortus, 1941); Powell, *A Life in Movies*, pp. 329–87; Aldgate and Richards, *Britain Can Take It*, pp. 29–41.

69. BBC WAC R61/3/2, Eckersley to Whyte, 28 May 1940.

70. PRO INF 1/5, Divisional Progress Report, 27 May 1940; Briggs, *The War of Words*, pp. 404–6; Charles Rolo, *Radio Goes to War* (New York: Putnam, 1942), p. 184.

71. Rolo, *Radio Goes to War*, p. 184; BBC WAC E1/208/5.

72. Priestley, *Britain Speaks*, pp. 162, 232; Harwood L. Childs and John B. Whitton (eds.), *Propaganda by Short Wave* (Princeton, N.J.: Princeton University Press, 1941), pp. 113 et seq.; PRO INF 1/29, Darvall to Whyte, 14 August 1940.

73. Priestley, *Britain Speaks*, pp. 83–84.

74. Priestley, *Britain Speaks*, pp. 3–4, 33, 55, 71, 103–4, 118, 157–60; Calder, *Myth of the Blitz*, pp. 196–203.

75. *Times*, 6 July 1940; BBC WAC E1/438/1, Rendall, 23 June 1940; Childs and Whitton, (eds.) *Propaganda by Short Wave*, p. 111.

76. Stirling University, Grierson papers, G4/20/3/1, "Grierson, August 1940." He contrasted the power of the authentic voice over the radio with the sorry showing of British film. He implored the Films Division to "allow the people to emerge from behind the synthetic fog which now hides them."

77. Gorham, *Sound and Fury*, p. 112.

78. BBC WAC E1/208/2, Cock to BBC, 26 February 1941.

79. Interviews: Carroll, Kirkpatrick, Lesueur, Middleton, Reston, Sevareid. Biographical information: *Who Was Who*.

80. PRO FO 371/24230, A3352/26/45, Halifax to Eden, 5 June 1940.

81. PRO FO 800/398, Whyte to Lothian, 4 September 1940; PRO CAB 65/8, 236(40)6, 29 August 1940.

82. Sperber, *Murrow*, pp. 157–60; BBC WAC R61/3/2.

83. PRO FO 371/24230, A3352/26/45, Ridsdale to Monckton, 30 May 1940.

84. PRO FO 371/24230, A3561/26/45, memo by North Whitehead.

85. PRO FO 371/24230, A3464 and A3352/26/45, Halifax to Eden, 5 June 1940; Halifax to Sinclair, 14 June 1940.

86. PRO FO 371/24230, A3352/26/45, Lothian to Eden, 1 June 1940.

87. PRO FO 371/24230, A3352/26/45, Lothian to Sinclair, 26 June 1940 and 18 July 1940; Sinclair to Lothian, 13 July 1940; Vern Haugland, *The Eagle Squadrons: Yanks in the RAF, 1940–1942* (New York: Ziff Davis, 1979), pp. 31–32.

88. PRO FO 371/24231, A3961/26/45, Hopkinson to MoI, 17 August 1940.

89. Norman Gelb, *Scramble: A Narrative History of the Battle of Britain* (New York: Harcourt Brace Jovanovich, 1985), p. 172; PRO FO 371/24231, A3961/26/45, North Whitehead, 23 August 1940; Haugland, *The Eagle Squadrons*, pp. 31–32.

90. BBC WAC R61/46, American Liaison, annual report, 1941; Haugland, *Eagle Squadrons*, p. 32. RAF 71 (Eagle) Squadron was planned in June 1940 as an all-volunteer American unit formed from Americans already in the RAF. Training began September 19, 1940. Two further Eagle Squadrons followed: 121 and 133, in the spring and summer, respectively, of 1941.

91. Gilbert, *Churchill*, Vol. 6, p. 743.

92. PRO FO 371/24231, A3799/26/45, Halifax to Sinclair, 19 August 1940; PRO CAB 65, 228(40)2 and CAB 65/8, 228(40)2.

93. PRO FO 371/24231, A3799/26/45, FO to Lothian, 20 August 1940; Sinclair to Halifax, 21 August 1940.

94. British daily estimates were apparently exaggerated by an average of 55%; German daily estimates by 234%. Briggs, *The War of Words*, p. 288; Cantril (ed.), *Public Opinion*, p.1148, AIOP: 11 September 1940, "Recently

the English claimed that they shot down 387 German planes in one week and lost only 94 of their own. Do you think this report is accurate? Yes: 19%, No: 58%, Don't know: 23%," and "Recently the Germans claimed that they had shot down 427 British planes in one week and lost only 94 of their own. Do you think this report is accurate? Yes: 3%, No: 86%, Don't know: 11%."

95. PRO FO 371/24232, A4225/26/45, Alexander to Halifax, 13 September 1940.

96. Eade (ed.), *War Speeches*, Vol. 1, pp. 234–44; Gelb, *Scramble*, pp. 319–20; PRO FO 371/24231, A3964/26/45, North Whitehead, 19 August 1940.

97. Eade (ed.), *War Speeches*, Vol. 1, pp. 236, 243; PRO CAB 65/8, 225(40)5, 13 August 1940.

98. Raymond Clapper, "Let's Save the Children," *Washington Daily News*, 6 July 1940; *New York Herald Tribune*, 22 August 1940 and 8 October 1940; Angus Calder, *The People's War: Britain 1939–45* (London: Jonathan Cape, 1969), p. 129.

99. PRO FO 371/24229, A3197/26/45; FO 371/24231, A3993/26/45.

100. PRO FO 371/24231, A3993/26/45, Darvall to Whitehead, 19 October 1940; Gilbert, *Churchill*, Vol. 6, p. 793; Gorham, *Sound and Fury*, p. 117; Calder, *The People's War*, p. 129.

101. SRO Lothian papers: GD40/17, Box 400, Faulkner to Lothian, 23 February 1940; PRO FO 371/22788, A6404/18/45; FO 371/24225, A456 and A3356/8/45; FO 371/24228, A2603/26/45; FO 371/24229, A3154/26/45, meeting at MoI, 2 May 1940; PRO INF 1/4, Divisional Progress Report, April 1940; INF 1/5, Divisional Progress Report, 27 May 1940; FO 371/24232, A4877/26/45; *New York Times*, 22 May 1940.

102. PRO FO 371/24225, A4238 and A3526/8/45, Pickthall to Lothian, 13 July 1940; *New York Times*, 5–16 July 1940.

103. PRO BW 63/13-25.

104. T. S. Eliot, *The Complete Poems and Plays of T. S. Eliot* (London: Faber, 1969), p. 201; Monroe Wheeler (ed.), *Britain at War* (New York: Museum of Modern Art, 1941); Calder, *The Myth of the Blitz*, pp. 145–48; Roger Kojecky, *T. S. Eliot's Social Criticism* (London: Faber, 1971), p. 143.

105. PRO CAB 65/7, 141(40), 27 May 1940; Gilbert, *Churchill*, Vol. 6, pp. 643–44; PRO PREM 4/25/8.

106. *FRUS*, 1940, Vol. 3, pp. 64–79.

107. Eade (ed.), *War Speeches*, Vol. 1, p. 244.

108. PRO FO 371/24231, A4005/25/45, Survey, 23 August 1940; Goodhart, *Fifty Ships That Saved the World*, pp. 177–90.

109. PRO CAB 65/8, 245 (40) 5: 9 September 1940.

110. Stanley E. Hilton, *Hitler's Secret War in South America, 1939–1945* (Baton Rouge: Louisiana State University Press, 1981), p. 201; Joe A. Morris, *Nelson Rockefeller: A Biography* (New York: Harper, 1960), pp. 172–74.

111. Dallek, *Roosevelt and American Foreign Policy*, p. 249.

112. FDRL, PSF (Confidential), Box 9, State Department: Roosevelt to State, 28 May 1940; Berle to Roosevelt, 31 May 1940. FDRL, Cox papers, Box 61, Foreign Propaganda Activities, Control of, 19 June 1940.

113. NA RG 59/5361, 862.01 B 11/31, Fletcher Warren to Berle, 24 June 1940; NA RG 59/2946, 800.01B11/26, Division of Controls memo, 6 September 1940. In comparison, Japan and the Netherlands had 42 propagandists each; France, 36; and Italy, 33.

114. NA RG 59/2946, 800.01 B 11/19, memo by Flack, 26 June 1940. NA RG 59/2946, 800.01 B 11/19, memo by Joseph Green, 29 June 1940.

115. Stiller, *Messersmith*, pp. ix, 142–45; NA RG 59/2946, 800.01 B 11/19, undated memo by Berle.

116. Interview: Berlin; Jordan A. Schwarz, *Liberal: Adolf A. Berle and the Vision of an American Era* (New York: Free Press, 1987), pp. 130–31, 194–200.

117. FDRL, Berle papers, Box 211, Diary, 22 September 1939 (IV, 2, 139).

118. Schwarz, *Liberal*, pp. 178–79, 208; FDRL, Berle papers, Box 211, 8 March 1940, (V, 1, 130), 8 December 1939 (IV, 3, 76-7), Box 212, Diary, 7 December 1940 (VI, 2, 190-91). Pierrepont Moffat (U.S. envoy in Ottawa) also disliked British propaganda, as became clear in his negotiations with Canada on the opening of a propaganda bureau in the United States: Ottawa NA, RG 25/2924/2727.

119. NA RG 59/5361, 862.01 B 11/37, Berle to Hull, 28 August 1940; RG 59/2946, 800.01B11/26, Hull to Attorney General, 5 September 1940.

Chapter 4

1. Jennings and Watt (dirs.), *London Can Take It* (MoI, 1940).

2. Calder, *The People's War*, pp. 154–59; Churchill, *The Second World War*, Vol. 2, pp. 302–3.

3. Charles de Gaulle, *War Memoirs: The Call to Honor, 1940–1942* (New York: Simon & Schuster, 1955), p. 104.

4. PRO FO 371/24232, A4442/26/45, Peterson to Lothian, 24 September 1940; *FRUS*, 1940, Vol. 3, Kennedy to Hull, 27 September 1940, pp. 48–49; Gilbert, *Churchill*, Vol. 6, pp. 872–75, 877.

5. PRO CAB 65/8, 260(40)9, 27 September 1940.

6. Richard Collier, *1940: The World in Flames* (London: Hamish Hamilton, 1979), pp. 173–93; Calder, *The People's War*, pp. 159–60.

7. PRO CAB 65/8, 240(40)9; 267(40)2; Colville, *The Fringes of Power*, pp. 252, 256–57; Churchill, *The Second World War*, Vol. 3, pp. 440–41; CAB 65/8, 217(40), 1 August 1940.

8. Bliss (ed.), *In Search of Light*, pp. 29–31.

9. For a comparison between British coverage and American coverage, see Phillip Knightley, *The First Casualty* (New York: Harcourt Brace Jovanovich, 1975), pp. 234–35.

10. Wheeler-Bennett, *Special Relationships*, pp. 98–101.

11. Gilbert, *Churchill*, Vol. 6, pp. 778–79.

12. Kurth, *American Cassandra*, p. 318; Thompson, "The Example of England," *New York Herald Tribune*, 23, 25, and 27 September 1940.

13. Thompson, "These Crucial Days," *New York Herald Tribune*, 27 October 1941, as cited by Stephen John Sniegoski, "Intellectual Wellsprings of American World War Two Interventionism" (University of Maryland Ph.D. thesis, 1977), p. 170.

14. Bliss (ed.), *In Search of Light*, pp. 30–31, 18 August 1940.

15. Bliss (ed.), *In Search of Light*, pp. 30–31.

16. Interview: Sevareid.

17. BBC WAC R61/3/2, Eckersley, "Broadcasts to the U.S. . . . ," 21 May 1940. During May 1940, the three American chains made 208 broadcasts from

London: PRO FO 371/24230, A3288/26/45, Monthly Report, May 1940: CBS, 76; NBC, 114; Mutual, 18. By August, this leveled off at half the May figure.

18. BBC WAC R61/3/2, Eckersley to Brebner (News Dept, MoI) 19 June 1940. The new system required the permission of the Ministry of Home Security and the relevant military service department: memo by Eckersley, "Visits by the Americans to Air Raid Damage," 26 August 1940.

19. PRO FO 371/24230, A3352/26/45, Balfour, 7 July 1940.

20. BBC WAC R61/48, American Liaison Weekly Report, 22 July 1940; R61/47, Monthly Report, July 1940.

21. Interview: Janet Murrow.

22. BBC WAC R61/48, BBC American Liaison, Weekly Report, 5 August 1940; R61/3/2, Murrow to Eckersley, 14 August 1940; Interview: Sevareid.

23. Rolo, *Radio Goes to War*, p. 187.

24. Interviews: Sevareid, Janet Murrow; BBC WAC R61/48, Weekly Report 26 August 1940; CBS News 24 August 1940, University of Washington, Seattle, audio-visual section; Sperber, *Murrow*, p. 163; Gorham, *Sound and Fury*, p. 117.

25. BBC WAC R61/3/2, Darvall to Eckersley, 28 August 1940; MoI to Eckersley, 20 September 1940; R61/2, Eckersley to MoI, 26 September 1941. On taste: R61/55, Eckersley to Usborne, 14 and 23 November 1939.

26. Jennings and Watt (dirs.), *London Can Take It* (MoI, 1940).

27. Alexander Kendrick, *Prime Time: The Life of Edward R. Murrow* (Boston: Little, Brown), pp. 207–8; Sperber, *Murrow*, p. 174; Persico, *Murrow*, p. 173; Murrow, *This Is London*, pp. 179–81. Contrary to the assertion of both Kendrick and Persico, this historian found no evidence of any direct appeals by Murrow to Churchill for permission to broadcast.

28. Mollie Panter-Downes, *London War Notes: 1939–45* (New York: Farrar, 1941), p. 111; *New Yorker*, 27 October 1941; Interviews: Reston, Sevareid, Cronkite, Lesueur; BBC WAC, R61/47, BBC American Liaison Unit, Monthly Report, July 1940.

29. PRO CAB 65/8, 249(40)5; PRO INF 1/64, undated memo by Brebner; McLaine, *Ministry of Morale*, p. 92.

30. PRO CAB 65/8, 290(40), 18 November 1940. On myths that Churchill sacrificed Coventry to stimulate pro-British feeling in the United States see West, *A Thread of Deceit*, pp. 9–18.

31. BBC WAC R61/2/-, Murrow to Eckersley, 23 October 1940, and other material in file, especially Eckersley, Internal Circulating Memo, 2 October 1940.

32. BBC WAC R61/3/3, Eckersley to Darvall, 26 March 1941; Murrow to Eckersley, 9 October 1940.

33. Interviews: Carroll, Kirkpatrick, Lesueur, Middleton, Janet Murrow, and Sevareid.

34. Interviews: Carroll, Lesueur, Janet Murrow; Gorham, *Sound and Fury*, p. 95. In April 1941, the UP office was surrounded by time-bombs, and it moved into temporary quarters at the MoI.

35. Eric Sevareid, *Not So Wild a Dream* (New York: Atheneum, 1976), p. 179.

36. Interview: Phil Piratin; Calder, *The People's War*, p. 167.

37. *New York Herald Tribune*, 16 September 1940; *Chicago Tribune*, 16 September 1940; *New York Herald Tribune*, 17 September 1940.

38. Drew Middleton, *The Sky Suspended* (New York: Longmans, Green, 1960), p. 181; *New York Times*, 16 September 1940; Terence O'Brien, *Civil Defence* (London: HMSO, 1955), pp. 10, 199, 290, 392.

39. Interviews: Piratin, Lesueur; PRO CAB 65/9, 250(40)2; O'Brien, *Civil Defence*, p. 392.

40. Priestley, *Britain Speaks*, pp. 214–21.

41. Rolo, *Radio Goes to War*, pp. 186–88.

42. Imperial War Museum photographic collection; for a contemporaneous *Life* photographic anthology, see Allan A. Michie and Walter Graebner (eds.), *Finest Hours* (New York: Harcourt, Brace & Co., 1941).

43. *Life*, 23 September 1940, 27 January 1941; Cecil Beaton, *War Photographs, 1939–45* (London: Imperial War Museum, 1981), pp. 182, 189, and plates 13, 49; Hugo Vickers, *Cecil Beaton* (Boston: Little, Brown, 1985), pp. 239–44; Cecil Beaton, *The Years Between: Diaries, 1937–44* (London: Weidenfeld & Nicolson, 1965), p. 57.

44. Dalrymple, "The Crown Film Unit . . . ," p. 213; Moorehead, *Bernstein*, pp. 124–25.

45. Jennings and Watt (dirs.), *London Can Take It*.

46. Dalrymple, "The Crown Film Unit . . . ," p. 213; Moorehead, *Bernstein*, p. 130; Watt, *Don't Look at the Camera*, pp. 142–45.

47. Watt, *Don't Look at the Camera*, p. 145; Harry Watt (dir.), *Christmas Under Fire* (Crown Film Unit, 1940); PRO INF 5/75.

48. Interview: Janet Murrow.

49. Archibald MacLeish, *In Honor of a Man and an Ideal: Three Talks on Freedom* (New York: CBS, 1942), pp. 5–7.

50. Interviews: Sevareid, Reston, Lesueur, Janet Murrow, Middleton.

51. Interview: Middleton.

52. May 1940, 64% stay out, 36% risk war by aid; November 1940, 50% stay out, 50% risk war by aid; December 1940, 40% stay out, 60% risk war by aid; Manchester, *The Glory and the Dream*, Vol. 1, p. 277.

53. SRO Lothian papers: GD40/17, Box 398, Lothian to Nancy Astor, 27 November 1940; PRO CAB 65/8, 274 (40) 3, 21 October 1940; FO 371/24232, A5217/26/46, Ridsdale to Balfour (FO), 14 December 1940.

54. MacLeish, *In Honor of a Man . . .*, pp. 5–7.

55. SHSW NBC papers, 80/89.

56. PRO FO 371/24232, A5217/26/46, Ridsdale to Balfour (FO), 14 December 1940. By February 1942, Walter Wanger regarded the song as "passé": PRO INF 1/625, Bernstein/Wanger conversations.

57. Alice Duer Miller, *The White Cliffs* (New York: Coward-McCann, 1940), p. 70. K. R. M. Short, "The White Cliffs of Dover: Promoting the Anglo-American Alliance in World War II," *Historical Journal of Film, Radio and Television* 2 (1982): 3–25. The poem was unsuccessfully filmed later in the war.

58. SHSW Walter Graebner papers, Box 1/3, note by Churchill and draft by Walter Monckton, MoI, 9 October 1940.

59. Childs and Whitton (eds.), *Propaganda by Short Wave*, p. 117.

60. Alfred Hitchcock (dir.), *Foreign Correspondent* (Walter Wanger, 1940).

61. Leslie Halliwell, *Halliwell's Film Guide*, 7th ed. (London: Granada, 1990), p. 367.

62. John Ford (dir.), *The Long Voyage Home* (Walter Wanger, 1940).

63. *New York Times*, 10 August 1940; Michael Curtiz (dir.), *The Sea Hawk* (Warner Brothers, 1940).

64. Louis B. De Rochemont (dir.), *The Ramparts We Watch* (RKO/March of Time, 1940).

65. Irving Pichel (dir.), *I Married a Nazi* (Twentieth Century Fox, 1940); Archie Mayo (dir.), *Four Sons* (Twentieth Century Fox, 1940); Frank Borzage (dir.), *The Mortal Storm* (MGM, 1940); Mervyn Le Roy (dir.), *Escape* (MGM, 1940); Charles Chaplin (dir.), *The Great Dictator* (Chaplin, 1940); Koppes and Black, *Hollywood Goes to War*, pp. 31–33.

66. Michael Balcon (dir.), *Convoy* (Ealing, 1940); Carol Reed (dir.), *Night Train*, [aka *Gestapo* and *Night Train to Munich*] (Twentieth Century Fox, 1940). PRO INF 1/625, Wanger to Bernstein, MoI Films Division,28 March 1941.

67. Marcel Varnel (dir.), *Let George Do It* (Ealing, 1940); *Variety*, 23 October 1940; *New York Times*, 14 October 1940. The winter also brought Anthony Asquith (dir.), *Freedom Radio* (Columbia/Two Cities, 1941).

68. PRO FO 800/398, Lothian to Whyte, 24 September 1940.

69. Stirling University, Grierson papers, G4/26/20/3, Grierson to Elton (MoI Films Div.): late December 1940 calls for tabloid-style news film not documentary art—"We can take that up five years from now." He urged the MoI to aim for the guts rather than for the cerebellum: "encourage the attitude of the police reporter and shoot your export film for the *News of the World*."

70. Interview: Lesueur; BBC WAC R34/472/1, Stewart (MoI) to Controllers of Programmes and Home Service, BBC, 2 January 1941.

71. PRO INF 1/872, Lothian to FO, 25 November 1940.

72. Warren Kimball (ed.), *Churchill and Roosevelt: The Complete Correspondence (CRCC)*, Vol. 1, (Princeton, N.J.: Princeton University Press, 1984), pp. 80–81; PRO FO 371/24232, A4822/26/45, Whitehead, 12 November 1940; Williams to Ridsdale, 14 November 1940.

73. PRO INF 1/872, Tree to Duff Cooper, 20 November 1940.

74. PRO CAB 65/8, 299(40)4–7, 2 December 1940; *CRCC*, Vol. 1, pp. 87–111; Reynolds, *The Creation of the Anglo-American Alliance*, pp. 145–51.

75. Reynolds, *The Creation of the Anglo-American Alliance*, pp. 151–153; Interview: Berlin; Wheeler-Bennett, *Special Relationships*, pp. 112–13. For errors in Wheeler-Bennett's account, see David Reynolds, "Lord Lothian and Anglo-American Relations, 1939–1940," *Transactions of the American Philosophical Society* 73 (1983): 48.

76. PRO INF 1/872, Peake to Duff Cooper, 27 November 1940.

77. PRO FO 371/24232, A5006/26/45; PRO CAB 21/2021, Cabinet Memo by North Whitehead, 29 November 1940.

78. PRO PREM 4/25/7, Duff Cooper to Churchill, 29 November 1940; Churchill to Duff Cooper, 30 November 1940.

79. PRO CAB 65/8, 299(40)4–7, 2 December 1940; *FRUS*, 1940, Vol. 3, Churchill to Roosevelt, 7 December 1940, pp. 15–29.

80. PRO CAB 65/10, WM 297(40)5; CAB 66/13, WP(40)468, and Weizmann, *Trial and Error*, pp. 495–97.

81. *DGFP*, Series D, Vol. 11, pp. 624–27, 949–50.

82. BBC WAC R34/473/1, MoI Policy Committee, 30 May 1940, item 7; PRO FO 371/24229, A3009 and A3197/26/45, Lothian to FO, 28 June 1940, and Lothian to FO, 4 July 1940.

83. PRO FO 371/24229, A3197/26/45, Duff Cooper to Halifax, 2 July 1940; Halifax to Duff Cooper, 5 July 1940; FO to Lothian (draft) 4 July 1940.

84. Interviews: Stavridi, Jim Orrick; PRO FO 371/24229, A3197/26/45. For IAIC minutes: PRO INF 1/435.

85. PRO FO 371/24232, A4673/26/45.

86. PRO FO 371/24231, A4025/26/45, agenda and minutes of MoI meeting, 6 September 1940; PRO FO 371/26183, A118/118/45, minute by Williams, 4 January 1941, and A161/118/45, OPEC paper 606, February 1941.

87. PRO FO 371/24231, A4025/26/45, Lothian to MoI, 19 September 1940. Lothian's scheme was prefigured during the Munich Crisis, when Angus Fletcher arranged for small American papers to print BBC news (as furnished by Reuters) free of charge. This was appreciated, but he suggested at the time that any future service should be designed especially to be "more adequately suited to their purposes." PRO FO 395/656, P368/151/150, Fletcher to News Dept, 25 November 1938.

88. Wheeler-Bennett, *British Information in the U.S.A.*, p. 16; PRO FO 371/24231, A3772/26/45, Lothian to MoI, 15 August 1940; A4025/26/45, Childs to Scott (FO), 16 August 1940; Lothian to MoI, 19 September 1940.

89. Interviews: Thistlethwaite, Hermione MacColl; Wheeler-Bennett, *British Information in the U.S.A.*, pp. 19–23; PRO FO 371/24231, A4025/26/45, Lothian to MoI, 19 September 1940; SRO Lothian papers: GD40/17, Box 406.

90. PRO FO 371/24232, A4598/26/45, Childs to Scott, 8 October 1940, and circular, 21 October 1940. Childs's office was located in the Chancery Annex at 2433 Massachusetts Avenue, Washington, D.C. Interviews: Berlin, MacColl, Thistlethwaite, John Lawler; correspondence with "Mitch" Mitchell.

91. For BPS bulletins: Mudd Library, Princeton: Fight For Freedom papers, Boxes 7, 9, 77, and especially 11, 140, and 141; Wheeler-Bennett, *British Information in the U.S.A.*, pp. 18–22, 30; Chadwin, *Hawks of World War II*, pp. 138–39.

92. Mudd Library, Princeton: FFF Boxes 60 and 141/1; PRO T 188/300, Leith Ross papers, Treasury minute of 25 October 1940; Chadwin, *Hawks of World War II*, p. 138.

93. Wheeler-Bennett, *British Information in the U.S.A.*, p. 21.

94. PRO FO 371/24231, A4025/26/45, Balfour, 10 October 1940; Lothian to FO, 26 September 1940; PRO FO 371/26183, A976/118/45, North Whitehead, 28 February 1940.

95. PRO FO 371/24231, A4025/26/45, Lothian to Duff Cooper, 4 October 1940; Duff Cooper to Lothian, 13 October 1940; Lothian to Duff Cooper, 19 October 1940; Interview: Hermione MacColl; MacColl papers, Woodburn to MacColl, 30 September 1940.

96. Interviews: Hermione MacColl, Miall; René MacColl diary: November, December 1940; Miall papers, Morgan correspondence, 1970–1984.

97. PRO FO 371/24232, A5183/26/45, Lothian to MoI, 30 November 1940.

98. MacColl papers, MacColl diary, November, December 1940; PRO FO 371/24232, A5183/26/45, Duff Cooper to Embassy, December 1940. Interviews: Miall, Galwey, Hermione MacColl, Berlin.

99. Interview: Cooke.

100. Private information; PRO PREM 4/25/8. Embassy divisions over Lothian's illness do not figure in J. R. M. Butler's biography of Lothian. Coincidentally, the biographer was the brother of Neville Butler—the official who, in his own words, "did not insist on calling in a medical practitioner."

101. Lothian, *American Speeches*, pp. 132–44.

102. Borthwick Institute, York: Halifax diary, 12 December 1940.
103. NA RG 701/4111/1135 B.
104. PREM 4/25/8, Duff Cooper to Churchill, 14 December 1940.
105. PRO FO 954/29, Churchill to Roosevelt, 21 December 1940; Borthwick Institute, Halifax Diary, 20 December 1940, and Hickleton Papers, A4, 410 4–11, Churchill to Halifax, 18 December 1940.
106. David Dilks (ed.), *The Diaries of Sir Alexander Cadogan* (London: Cassell, 1971), p. 342.
107. George Catlin, *For God's Sake Go* (Gerrards Cross: Smythe, 1972), p. 242; MacColl diary, 22 December 1940.
108. PRO FO 371/24232, A5183/26/45, Scott, 24 December 1940.
109. Robert Sherwood, *Roosevelt and Hopkins: An Intimate History* (New York: Harper, 1948), p. 225; Colville, *Fringes of Power*, p. 322.
110. Dilks (ed.), *The Diaries of Sir Alexander Cadogan*, p. 344.

Chapter 5

1. Charles Eade (ed.), *The Unrelenting Struggle: War Speeches by the Right Hon. Winston S. Churchill* (London: Cassell, 1942), p. 63. ·
2. Dallek, *Roosevelt and American Foreign Policy*, pp. 256–59; George McJimsey, *Harry Hopkins: Ally of the Poor and Defender of Democracy* (Cambridge, Mass.: Harvard University Press, 1987), pp. 133–50.
3. Interviews: Berlin, Lord Inchyra, William Hayter, Lord Sherfield; *Chicago Tribune*, 1 and 2 February 1941; Lord Birkenhead, *Halifax* (London: Hamish Hamilton, 1965), pp. 477–79; *CRCC*, Vol. 1, p. 165.
4. Eade (ed.), *The Unrelenting Struggle*, pp. 54–63; BBC WAC R34/474, Williams, memo, 19 March 1940.
5. Interview: Berlin.
6. PRO FO 371/24232, A5183/26/45; Peake's report: PRO FO 371/26184, A3010/118/45, Peake Report, April 1941, pp. 65–95; Peake diary, January–April 1941; Interviews: Berlin, Hayter, Lady Peake.
7. Interviews: Berlin, Raphael, Richard Pear, MacMillan, Hermione MacColl, Berlin, Lord Harmsworth, Nicholas; PRO FO 371/26186, A4839/118/45, Campbell to Monckton, 14 June 1941; MacColl diary, 20 and 21 November 1940. At this time, the BLI and BPS employed a total staff of about sixty-four.
8. Interview: Galwey; MacColl diary, December 1940–January 1941.
9. MacColl diary: 10, 11, and 14 February 1941.
10. *PM*, 14 February 1941. *PM* is not mentioned in the weekly reports of the Polish Information Bureau in New York, and presumably this office had no part in publishing these pictures (see Polish Institute and Sikorski Museum, London, file A 10 1/9); however, all but one of the pictures may now be found in the archives this bureau, held at the Jósef Pilsudski Institute of America, New York. All the pictures eventually found their way to the Polish Ministry of Information in London and were published in the second "Black Book" of documents on German atrocities: Poland, Ministry of Information, *The German New Order in Poland* (London: Hutchinson, 1942).
11. Interviews: Galwey, Lord Harmsworth, Richard Miles, and Brenda Lawler interview and clippings collection; PRO FO 371/26184, A3010/118/45, Peake Report.

12. Interview: Berlin; Nicholas (ed.), *Washington Despatches*, p. ix.

13. Weizmann, *Trial and Error*, p. 522. On Jewish opinion: BLEPS, Webster papers, FRPS US Memoranda No. 68, 29 May 1941.

14. Interviews: Sir Maurice Bathurst, Miall, Lord Harmsworth; Wheeler-Bennett, *British Information in the U.S.A.*, p. 28.

15. Wheeler-Bennett, *British Information in the U.S.A.*, p. 29. Interview: Ratcliffe.

16. PRO FO 371/26183, A234 and A1149/118/45, Halifax to Monckton, 27 February 1941; PRO INF 1/435, IAIC, 17 June 1941; Interview: Stavridi.

17. PRO INF 1/435, IAIC Meetings, 11 March, 20 May, 3 June, 17 June, and 12 August 1941.

18. PRO FO 371/26184, A3010/118/45, Peake Report, April 1941; Wheeler-Bennett, *British Information in the U.S.A.*, p. 35.

19. PRO FO 371/26184, A3010/118/45, Peake Report.

20. PRO FO 371/26184, A3253 and A3631/118/45; Campbell, *Of True Experience*, p. 99.

21. In July 1940, Churchill formed Britain's Special Operations Executive (SOE) by amalgamating the sabotage unit of MI6 (Section D) with the War Office's guerilla warfare research unit (MI R) and the covert propaganda bureau Department EH. SOE was subdivided into three sections: SO.1 for propaganda; SO.2 for sabotage and "dirty tricks"; and SO.3 for planning: Charles Cruickshank, *SOE in the Far East* (Oxford: Oxford University Press, 1983), pp. 1–3, and M. R. D. Foot, *SOE: An Outline History of the Special Operations Executive, 1940–46* (London: BBC, 1984), pp. 9–25; Hinsley and Simkins, *British Intelligence*, Vol. 4, p. 144.

22. Montgomery Hyde, *The Quiet Canadian*, pp. 181–82; David Ignatius, "Britain's War in America: How Churchill's Agents Secretly Manipulated the U.S. Before Pearl Harbor," *The Washington Post* (Outlook Section: C), 17 September 1989, pp. 1–2; Eric Maschwitz, *No Chip on My Shoulder* (London: Herbert Jenkins, 1957); Bickham Sweet-Escott, *Baker Street Irregular* (London: Methuen, 1965); A. J. Ayer, *Part of My Life* (London: Collins, 1977), pp. 251–53; and Ivar Bryce, *You Only Live Once: Memories of Ian Fleming* (London: Weidenfeld & Nicolson, 1975), pp. 45–65. For establishment as submitted to the FBI: NA RG 59/2946, 800.01B11, Registration/1300, 1/2. (1944) and 800.01B11, Registration/1209 (1941).

23. BLEPS: Dalton II, Box 7/3; Montgomery Hyde, *The Quiet Canadian*, 187; PRO FO 898/106, Bowes-Lyon/Calder, 1942, 5C.

24. PR0 FO 898/103, Morrell, SO.1 Organisation, 10 July 1941. NA RG 263, Box 7/55, Cuneo to Troy, 13 November 1968; Box 7/56, Interview Troy–Cuneo, 2 September 1971; also Montgomery Hyde, *The Quiet Canadian*, pp. 199–204.

25. Tom Mahl has identified this agent as Sandy Griffiths: Thomas Mahl, "'Forty-eight land,' British Intelligence and American Isolation" (Kent State University Ph.D. thesis [pending] 1993).

26. PR0 FO 898/103, Morrell, SO.1 Organisation, 10 July 1941.

27. Private hands, MacColl diary: 7 December 1940; 3 January 1941; 10 February 1941; 14 February 1941.

28. PR0 FO 898/103, Morrell, 10 July 1941; PRO INF 1/435, Meeting 2, 22 October 1940.

29. Ignatius, "Britain's War in America."

30. PRO FO 898/103, Morrell, 10 July 1941.

31. PRO INF 1/872, Halifax to Duff Cooper, 1 January 1940.

32. Interviews: Berlin, Hayter; Wheeler-Bennett, *Special Relationships*, p. 120; *Nation*, 26 April 1941.

33. Interview: Berlin; Halifax Diary, 10 May 1941; *Time*, 19 May 1941; Birkenhead, *Halifax*, p. 506.

34. Peter Spence, "The BBC North American Service, 1939–1945," *Media, Culture and Society* 4 (1982): 364.

35. Interview: Hutton; Hutton papers; PRO INF 1/885, minutes of dinner, 19 February 1941; Monckton to Duff Cooper, 20 February 1941.

36. Interview: Wendy Reves; PRO INF 1/535; PRO PREM 4/25/7; Gilbert, *Churchill*, Vol. 6, p. 740; *New York Times*, 26 August 1941; *Saturday Review*, 27 February 1943; Emery Reves, *A Democratic Manifesto* (New York: Harper, 1942); Reves, *The Anatomy of Peace* (New York: Harper, 1946), and forward to Fritz Thyssen, *I Paid Hitler* (New York: Farrar & Rinehart, 1941); Obituary, *Times*, 7 September 1981.

37. PRO INF 4/25/4; Tree, *When the Moon Was High*, p. 169.

38. PRO FO 371/26183, A1041, A976; FO 371/26185, A4302/118/45.

39. Jonathan Dimbleby, *Richard Dimbleby* (London: Hodder & Stoughton, 1975), pp. 119–21; Charles Rolo, *Radio Goes to War*, pp. 188–89.

40. BBC WAC E1/207/1, Cock to BBC, 18 September 1940; R45/30, Rendall [Deputy Controller, Overseas Programmes, BBC] to BBC Glasgow, 21 February 1941. For its first year, the serial was written by Alan Melville and produced by John Robinson. The principal actors were Ernest Butcher and Nell Ballantyne; Gorham, *Sound and Fury*, pp. 106–7.

41. Spence, "The BBC North American Service," p. 367; BBC WAC E2/438/2, Gorham, 18 July 1941 and 5 August 1941; E1/208/1.

42. BBC WAC E1/208/1 and E1/207/1; R61/45 and E2/438/2, Ernest Davis to NAS Dir., 5 July 1940; Gorham, *Sound and Fury*, pp. 99, 132; Briggs, *The War of Words*, pp. 405–6; Interview: Cooke.

43. BBC WAC R62/54/Censorship/Air Raids, Madden to Gorham, 1 October 1941; R62/54/Censorship, Memo by De Lotbinière (Empire Service), 19 October 1941.

44. Rolo, *Radio Goes to War*, p. 189.

45. Interview: Cooke; Gorham, *Sound and Fury*, pp. 117–32; BBC WAC R61/54/Censorship/Air Raids, Gorham to Empire Service, 6 October 1941.

46. BBC WAC E1/191/Namesake Towns. The Sunbury broadcast was delayed until 17/18 January 1942.

47. BBC WAC R34/474, Williams, 3 April 1941; Watt, *Don't Look at the Camera*, pp. 146–53; Harry Watt (dir.), *Target for Tonight* (Crown, 1941); PRO INF 5/78; INF 6/335; INF 1/600; Moorehead, *Bernstein*, pp. 131–35.

48. David MacDonald (dir.), *This England* (British National, 1941). Other releases included Brian Desmond (dir.), *Dangerous Moonlight* (U.S. title, *Suicide Mission*) (RKO, 1941) and Anthony Asquith (dir.), *Cottage to Let* (U.S. title, *Bombsight Stolen*) (Gainsborough, 1941).

49. *Britain on Guard* (GPO, 1940); PRO INF 1/568, BLI report, 21 March 1941; PRO INF 6/327; Roy Boulting (dir.), *The Dawn Guard* (Charter, 1941); PRO INF 6/442; Roy Boulting, letter to the author.

50. PRO INF 6/331; INF 5/77; Humphrey Jennings (dir.), *The Heart of Britain* (Crown, 1941).

51. Kendrick, *Prime Time*, p. 234.

52. Humphrey Jennings (dir.), *Words for Battle* (Crown, 1941); PRO INF 6/338; INF 5/79.

53. Frank Sainsbury (dir.), *We Won't Forget* (MoI/Realist, 1941), as described in BLI Catalogue in FDRL, OF 73, file 5, (Motion Pictures), BLI to Early, March 1942; Tree, *When the Moon Was High*, pp. 163–64.

54. PRO INF 1/598, Fletcher to Lothian, 15 October 1940; PRO BW 63/2, and 63/4; INF 1/629; FO 371/26187, A6330 and A7269/118/45.

55. PRO INF 1/600. The MoI first discussed appointing a North American officer for the Films Division just after the fall of France.

56. PRO INF 1/600.

57. David Macdonald (dir.), *Men of the Lightship* (GPO, 1940); PRO INF 5/66, 67, and 68; also, INF 6/353. On U.S. release: INF 1/600, Cr. A. W. Jarratt RNVR, to DG MoI, 14 March 1941; Jack Holmes (dir.), *Merchant Seaman* (Crown, 1941).

58. PRO INF 1/568, BLI to MoI 21 May 1941, Col. Sir Norman Scorgie, 29 May 1941.

59. Stirling University, Grierson Archive, G/4/23/24, Grierson to Fletcher, 2 November 1939; Stanley Hawes (dir.), *Canada Carries On*, "Children from Overseas" (NFB/Columbia Canada, 1940); *World in Action*, "Churchill's Island" (NFB/UA, 1941).

60. NA Ottawa, T 1771/771/342, "Informal Meeting . . . to discuss Canadian Government Publicity in the U.S.," 8 March 1941; Fielding, *March of Time*, pp. 256–57; David Barker Jones, *Movies and Memoranda: An Interpetive History of the National Film Board of Canada* (Ottawa: Canadian Film Institute/Deneau, 1981), pp. 34–41; Hardy, *John Grierson*, pp. 120–21.

61. *CRCC*, Vol. 1, pp. 145–46.

62. Joseph P. Lash, *Roosevelt and Churchill, 1939–1941: The Partnership That Saved the West* (New York: Norton, 1976), p. 305; PRO INF 1/892, undated memo by Duff Cooper for Monckton.

63. PRO INF 1/892, minute by Hood, 11 March 1941; Empax No. 588, 12 March 1941, (Most Secret) General Distribution.

64. Interview: Middleton; PRO INF 1/892, Monckton to Radcliffe, 19 March 1941.

65. Robert Rhodes James (ed.), *Churchill Speaks: Collected Speeches, 1897–1963*, Vol. 6 (New York: Chelsea House, 1980), pp. 6378–84; Churchill, *The Second World War*, Vol. 3, 207; *CRCC*, Vol. 1, p. 179.

66. As sung by Karl Schwedler to the tune of "Daisy"; recording *Charlie and His Orchestra, Vol.1, German Propaganda Swing, 1940–1941* (Harlequin HQ 2058, 1987) B/2.

67. Calder, *The People's War*, p. 232; McJimsey, *Harry Hopkins*, p. 162.

68. Halifax papers, A4/410/4/11, Halifax to Churchill, 10 April 1941; William Langer and Everett Gleason, *The Undeclared War: 1940–1941* (New York: Harper, 1953), p. 456; Allan Winkler, *The Politics of Propaganda: The Office of War Information, 1942–1945* (New Haven, Conn.: Yale University Press, 1978), p. 21; Steele, *Propaganda in an Open Society*, pp. 15, 52, 64; Dallek, *Roosevelt and American Foreign Policy*, p. 336.

69. PRO FO 371/26145, A4072/3/45, Halifax to FO, Political Report, 28 May 1941.

70. LoC Ickes Papers, Box 247: "Propaganda Committee," November 1940; LoC MacLeish papers, Box 7, MacLeish to LaGuardia, 25 October 1941; MacLeish to Fletcher, 10 October 1941; Winkler, *The Politics of Propaganda*, pp. 22–23.

71. Schwarz, *Liberal*, p. 171; FDRL Printed Collection: Troy, *COI and British Intelligence*, p. 125.

72. NA RG 263 Box 2/16, memo Halifax/Welles, 16 June 1941; Box 2/19, Fleming to Donovan, 27 June 1941.

73. Ignatius, "Britain's War in America," p. C1; Briggs, *The War of Words*, pp. 405–6; BBC WAC E1/207/1.

74. Roosevelt to Churchill, 14 May 1941, *CRCC*, Vol. 1, pp. 186–87; McLaine, *Ministry of Morale*, p. 220.

75. PRO FO 371/26186, A4840/118/45.

76. NA RG 59/2946, 800.01B11/26, Report on Foreign Propaganda, 27 January 1941; FDRL PSF (Diplomatic) Box 74, Hull to FDR, re Polish propaganda, 4 October 1940.

77. NA RG 59/2946, 841.20211/23/(Confidential), Berle to Welles, 31 March 1941; NA RG 59/2946, 800.01 B 11 Registration/10390.

78. PRO FO 371/26184, A3010/118/45, Halifax to Duff Cooper, 25 April 1941.

79. PRO FO 371/26183, A976 and A2618/118/45, Halifax to FO, 9 April 1941; PRO INF 1/908.

80. PRO FO 954/29, Eden to Halifax, 15 April 1941; FO 371/26184, A3010/118/45, Halifax to Duff Cooper, 25 April 1941.

81. PRO FO 954/29, Eden to Halifax, 15 April 1941; FO 371/26184, A3506/118/45, Williams to Radcliffe, 27 April 1941.

82. Tree, *When the Moon Was High*, pp. 156–70; PRO FO 371/26183, A2896 and A3979/118/45, Tree to Eden, 23 May 1941.

83. PRO FO 371/26184, A3893/118/45, Beaverbrook, 20 May 1941, and North Whitehead, 22 May 1941.

84. PRO CAB 127/248, War Cabinet Defence Committee (Operations) DO (41), 19 May 1941.

85. PRO CAB 127/248, Beaverbrook to Cabinet, 22 May 1941; DO (41) 34th meeting, 23 May 1941; Churchill to Beaverbrook, 25 May 1941; Beaverbrook to Eden, 27 May 1941; Interview: Carroll.

86. PRO CAB 127/248, DO (41) 34th meeting, 23 May 1941; Churchill to Roosevelt, 23 May 1941, *CRCC*, Vol. 1, pp. 192–95.

87. PRO CAB 127/248, DO(41) 36th meeting, 29 May 1941; Reynolds, *The Creation of the Anglo-American Alliance*, pp. 203–4.

88. McLaine, *Ministry of Morale*, pp. 237–38, and hearsay reported to Victor Cazalet; Cazalet diary, 15 July 1941.

89. *Charlie and His Orchestra, Vol. 1*, B/7.

90. McLaine, *Ministry of Morale*, pp. 237–38; Interviews: Middleton, Nicholas.

91. PRO FO 371/26184, A4132/118/45, Halifax to Monckton, 30 May 1941; A4469/118/45, Halifax to Monckton, 31 May 1941; FO 371/26185, A4316/118/45, Churchill to Eden and Duff Cooper, 2 June 1941; PRO PREM 4/25/7; statement of 3 July 1941.

92. PRO FO 371/26186, A5028/118/45, Scott (FO) to Peterson (MoI), 29 June 1941; Wheeler-Bennett, *British Information in the U.S.A.*, p. 25. Campbell never used this money, and his successor at the helm of BIS allowed the fund to revert to the Treasury.

93. Wheeler-Bennett, *A History of British Information in the U.S.A.*, p. 30; Interviews: Bathurst, Berlin.

94. PRO FO 371/26183, A2618/118/45, Halifax to FO, 9 April 1941.

95. PRO FO 371/26186, A5028/118/45, Scott to Peterson MoI, 29 June 1941; OEPEC paper 830 revised; A4839/118/45, Campbell to Monckton, 14 June 1941; FO 371/30667, A636/399/45; Interview: Gizelda Fowler.

96. PRO FO 371/26185, A4155/118/45, Campbell to Monckton, 31 May 1941; A4679/118/45, minute by Evans, 18 June 1941; FO 371/26184, A4151/118/45; FO 371/26186, A5028/118/45, Scott to Peterson, 29 June 1941.

97. PRO FO 371/26184, A3343/118/45, Monckton to Cadogan, 6 May 1941; Scott, 7 May 1941; PRO FO 371/26186, A5346/118/45, Duff Cooper to Hutton, 8 July 1941; Interview: Hutton.

98. PRO FO 371/26185, A4679/118/45, Campbell to MoI, 20 June 1941; FO 371/26186, A5521/118/45; FO 371/26187, A6559/118/45; J. M. Winter (ed.), *R. H. Tawney: The American Labour Movement and Other Essays* (Brighton: Harvester Press, 1979), pp. xiii–xvi.

99. PRO FO 371/26183, A2586/118/45; Tree, *When the Moon Was High*, p. 168; Interview: Hutton.

100. PRO FO 371/26187, A6143/118/45, Campbell to Monckton, 2 August 1941; PRO PREM 4/35/7, 298; Vernon Bartlett, *Now and Tomorrow* (London: Chatto & Windus, 1960), p. 69.

101. PRO FO 371/26183, A2586/118/45, Halifax to FO, 9 April 1941; FO 371/26184, A3831/118/45, Cadogan to Fletcher, 3 June 1941; FO 371/26185, A4343/118/45, Fletcher to Cadogan, 5 June 1941; FO 371/26186, A4858/118/45; Interview: Lord Harmsworth.

102. BLEPS Charles Webster Papers, especially Webster diary 1941; Wheeler-Bennett, *British Information in the U.S.A.*, p. 26; Interview: Berlin.

103. Wheeler-Bennett, *British Information in the U.S.A.*, p. 25.

104. McDonnell diary, 6 and 13 May 1941; 1 and 3 November 1941; 17 February 1942.

105. McDonnell diary, 6–13 May, 17–25 July, and 1–3 November 1941; 17 February 1942; Halifax diary, 17–25 July 1941; Interviews: Berlin, Hayter, Inchyra.

106. Gorham, *Sound and Fury*, p. 10; PRO INF 1/568, BLI report, 24 June 1941.

107. PRO FO 371/26186, A4840 and A5002/118/45, Campbell to MoI, 12 July 1941; Halifax to FO, 2 July 1941; Duff Cooper to Campbell, 21 June 1940; Reynolds, *The Creation of the Anglo-American Alliance*, p. 205.

108. FDRL Berle Box 212, Diary 18 February 1941, (VI.3, 83–90).

109. FDRL PSF Box 71 (Diplomatic), Berle to Roosevelt, 26 June 1941.

110. FDRL PSF Box 71 (Diplomatic), Berle to Roosevelt, 26 June 1941; FDRL Hopkins papers, Box 307, Book 4/1; Berle to Hopkins, 7 July 1941, and Berle to Welles, 7 July 1941.

111. Theodore Wilson, *The First Summit: Roosevelt and Churchill at Placentia Bay, 1941* (Boston: Houghton Mifflin, 1969), pp. 75, 85, 237–38.

112. Churchill, *The Second World War*, Vol. 3, pp. 393–94.

113. Reynolds, *The Creation of the Anglo-American Alliance*, p. 215; PRO PREM 3/476/3, Churchill to War Cabinet, 24 August 1941.

Chapter 6

1. Samuel I. Rosenman (ed.), *The Public Papers and Addresses of Franklin D. Roosevelt, Vol. 10, 1941* (New York: Harper, 1950), pp. 384–92.

2. Dallek, *Roosevelt and American Foreign Policy*, pp. 287–88; Lash, *Roosevelt and Churchill*, p. 421; Rosenman (ed.), *Public Papers . . . of FDR*, Vol. 10, pp. 384–92.

3. Dallek, *Roosevelt and American Foreign Policy*, p. 288; Lash, *Roosevelt and Churchill*, pp. 417–21.

4. Thomas R. H. Havens, *The Valley of Darkness: The Japanese People and World War Two* (New York: Norton, 1986), pp. 80, 95, 102, 116–22; Akira Iriye, *The Origins of the Second World War in Asia and the Pacific* (New York: Longmans, 1987).

5. Dallek, *Roosevelt and American Foreign Policy*, pp. 274–75.

6. PRO FO 371/26188, A7667/118/45, Campbell to MoI, 19 September 1941; Doenecke (ed.), *In Danger Undaunted*, pp. 37–41.

7. PRO FO 371/26187, A6243/118/45, Sir Gerald Campbell (and Wheeler-Bennett), 30 June 1941.

8. PRO FO 371/26187, A6243/118/45, Campbell, 30 June 1941.

9. PRO FO 371/26187, A6662/118/45, MoI to Campbell, 1 September 1941, Part II.

10. Bartlett, *Now and Tomorrow*, p. 69; PRO FO 371/30667, A446/399/45, Campbell to Radcliffe, 10 January 1942.

11. PRO PREM 3/476/3, Smuts to Churchill, 29 August 1941; Churchill, 7 September 1941; Churchill to Winant, 10 September 1941.

12. PRO INF 1/102, Darvall to Establishment, 6 January 1941; Interviews: Galwey, Macmillan, Nicholas; Phyllis Bentley, *Here Is America* (London: Gollancz, 1942).

13. PRO FO 371/26183, A2932/118/45, Meeting, 25 April 1941; PRO INF 1/102, June–December 1941; Interview: Nicholas.

14. Interviews: Galwey, Macmillan, Ann Thoms.

15. Interviews: Nicholas, Galwey; SHSW Graebner papers, Box 1/2, Bracken to Graebner, 26 November 1941.

16. Interviews: Reston, Berlin, Nicholas, Galwey; Wheeler-Bennett, *British Information in the U.S.A.*, p. 26.

17. BLEPS, Webster diary, Winter 1941–42; PRO FO 371/26188, A8077/118/45, Radcliffe to Campbell, 19 November 1941.

18. Interviews: Hermione MacColl, Berlin, Thistlethwaite.

19. Interview: Miall; Wheeler-Bennett, *Special Relationships*, p. 122.

20. PRO FO 371/26184, A3010/118/45, Peake Report, May 1941; BLEPS, Webster papers, 9/1, BLI, Monthly Report, November 1941; Interviews: Wilson, David Daiches, George Forrest, Macmillan, Thistlethwaite, Lord Harmsworth. Later all information was work taken over by Jack Bennett (a scholar of medieval history from Cambridge University).

21. Interviews: Lord Harmsworth, Thistlethwaite. Correspondence: "Mitch" Mitchell; William Clarke, *From Three Worlds* (London: Sidgwick & Jackson, 1986), pp. 15–16.

22. BIS papers, BIS, New York, Barbara Hayes, statement of services, circa 1953: Interviews: Hermione MacColl, Macmillan, Pear, Wilson, Berlin, Hutton (and papers); BLEPS, Webster papers, 9/1, BLI, Monthly Report, November 1941.

23. Wheeler-Bennett, *British Information in the U.S.A.*, p. 29; PRO INF 1/102, Machell to MoI Publications Div., 20 June 1941; Interviews: Gizelda Fowler, Bathurst, Lord Harmsworth; *Britain*, 1943-45.

24. BLEPS, Webster papers, 9/1, BLI, Monthly Report, November 1941. November saw the publication of *Bulletins from Britain* issues 62–65; *Neptune* issues 16 and 17; *Britain Today* issues 60 and 61; issue 9 of the *Children's Letter*; a "Black List Amendment"; and the IAIC's *Inter-Allied Review*. For samples: FDRL F. C. Ward Propaganda Collection, 4/20 *Bulletins From Britain*, and 4/21 "BLI pamphlets"; FDRL Propaganda Collection Box 6, General.

25. PRO FO 371/26185, A4430/118/45, Fletcher to Childs, 28 May 1941, noted that the BLI mailing list was 35,000 and rising, and "NOT made up of the ESU type of sympathisers" but "a cross-section of the country"; also BLEPS, Webster papers, 9/1, BLI, Monthly Reports, November and December 1941.

26. Wheeler-Bennett, *British Information in the U.S.A.*, pp. 32–33; PRO FO 371/30667, A636/399/45, OEPEC paper 1126; Interviews: Raphael, Daiches, Cooke, Macmillan.

27. Interview: Hutton; Hutton appointment book, 1941.

28. Interview: Hutton; Hutton papers, Hutton to parents, 18 November 1941; BBC WAC R34/474, MoI Policy Committee, 8 January 1944.

29. Interview: Hutton.

30. Interviews: Hutton, George Ball; Hutton papers; Clarke, *From Three Worlds*, pp. 6–19.

31. Interview: Hutton; Hutton papers, Hutton to parents, 30 November 1941; 18 November 1941.

32. During absences by Whyte, Murrow served as chairman. BBC WAC E2/438/2; Gorham, *Sound and Fury*, p. 112.

33. PRO INF 1/435, IAIC meetings, 9 September 1941 and 7 October 1941; Interview: Stavridi.

34. PRO FO 371/24230, A3598/26/45, White, 14 July 1940; PRO INF 1/767, 1/768, 1/776, and 1/777.

35. PRO FO 371/26186, A5268/118/45, pp. 86–89: "Religions Division and the U.S.A.," Hugh Martin, 26 June 1940; FO 371/26187, A6013/118/45, Campbell to Martin, 28 July 1941.

36. McDonnell diary, 1 December 1941.

37. BLEPS, Webster papers, 9/1, BLI, Monthly Report, November 1941; Peter and Leni Gillman, *"Collar the Lot!": How Britain Interned and Expelled Its Wartime Refugees* (London/New York: Quartet Books, 1980), pp. 267–76, 318–19; Interview: Raphael.

38. Timothy Roger Dzierba, "Organized Labor and the Coming of World War II, 1937–1941," (State University of New York at Buffalo, Ph.D. thesis, 1983). The respective positions of the CIO and the AFL's Committee on International Affairs had long been ambiguous. Both had supported both the interventionist boycott of Japan and the isolationist Ludlow amendment. The AFL journal *American Federationist* was blatantly isolationist.

39. BLEPS: Webster papers, 7/7, Minutes of ESU Private Group discussion, "The U.S.A. and the Post-Munich Situation," 1 February 1939; PRO PREM 1/433; PREM 1/433, Lothian to Cadogan, 20 December 1939.

40. PRO FO 371/24230, A3383/26/45, Lothian to FO, 14 June 1940; North Whitehead to Citrine, 8 July 1940; Lothian to FO, 10 July 1940; Marion Dickerman and Ruth Taylor, (eds.) *Who's Who in Labor* (New York: Dryden Press, 1946).

41. PRO FO 371/24232, A4695/26/45, "Notes for Sir Walter Citrine . . . ," 30 October 1940; Walter Citrine, *My American Diary* (London: Routledge, 1941).

42. Churchill College, Cambridge, BEVN 2/1, Bevin to Churchill, 14 October 1940; BEVN 1 6/45; Diana Forbes-Robertson and Roger W. Straus, Jr. (eds.), *War Letters from Britain* (New York: Putnam, 1941).

43. BBC WAC E1/132, BPS New York survey, 17 June 1941; PRO FO 898/103, Morrell, "SO.1 Organisation," 10 July 1941.

44. BBC WAC E1/132, DIGESTION to MoI, 3 June 1941; Dzierba, "Organized Labor and the Coming of World War II," pp. 106, 124.

45. Interviews: Thistlethwaite, Raphael, Pear, Elvin; Winter (ed.), *R. H. Tawney: The American Labour Movement*, pp. xiii–xvii, 1–110. Tawney was eventually replaced by the affable Archie Gordon; Interviews: Berlin, Raphael, Bathurst.

46. Churchill College, Cambridge, BEVN 1, 6/45; Interviews: Berlin, Raphael.

47. Interviews: Berlin, Raphael. For writing, see James Carey, "Labor and Defense," *Executive Club News*, 18 April 1941.

48. Chadwin, *The Hawks of the World War II*, pp. 167, 183–84.

49. PRO PREM 4/25/6, Helen Rogers Reid/Willkie to Churchill, 27 June 1941; PRO FO 371/26187, A6302/118/45, Campbell to the MoI, 6 August 1941; FDRL: Ward collection, Box 4/21 (BLI Pamphlets), 'Jack Jones', 22 October 1941.

50. Churchill College, Cambridge, BEVN 6/58, Ulric Bell (FFF) and Luigi Antonini (American Labor Party) to Bevin, 5 June 1941. PRO INF 1/102, Divisional Plan, 18 December 1941; Lend-Lease Supply and Labour Relations: D'arcy Edmondson; Interview: Nicholas.

51. Churchill College, Cambridge, BEVN 6/58, Draft broadcast for 1 September 1941; Churchill College, Cambridge, BEVN 3/1, Bevin to Amery, 11 June 1941.

52. McDonnell diary: 14, 24, and 26 October 1941; 4 November 1941; Interview: Pear.

53. McDonnell diary, 4 November 1941; Halifax diary, 4, 5, and 10 November 1941; Birkenhead, *Halifax*, p. 285; *Time*, 17 November 1941. *Chicago Tribune*, 5 November 1941.

54. PRO FO 371/26186, A5891/118/45, Childs to MoI, 23 July 1941.

55. BBC WAC E1/158, Wellington to BBC, 23 October 1941.

56. Stevenson, *A Man Called Intrepid*, p. 325; Montgomery Hyde, *The Quiet Canadian*, pp. 194–96.

57. FDRL Berle, Box 213, Berle to Welles, 18 September 1941; Diary Vol. VII, 2, pp. 122–23.

58. Montgomery Hyde, *The Quiet Canadian*, pp. 121–29; W. N. Medlicott, *The Economic Blockade*, Vol. 2 (London: HMSO, 1959), p. 45.

59. Montgomery Hyde, *The Quiet Canadian*, pp. 121–29, and *New York Herald Tribune*, 31 August 1941; 2, 3, and 4 September 1941.

60. Donald Downes, *The Scarlet Thread* (London: Derek Verschoyle, 1953), pp. 59–62.

61. Montgomery Hyde, *The Quiet Canadian*, pp. 73, 88–93; *DGFP*, Series D, Vol. 13, p. 234.

62. Montgomery Hyde, *The Quiet Canadian*, pp. 73–74; Charles A. Lindbergh, *The Wartime Journals of Charles A. Lindbergh* (New York: Harcourt, 1970), pp. 550–52.

63. Montgomery-Hyde, *The Quiet Canadian*, pp. 188–91; Maschwitz, *No Chip on My Shoulder*, p. 145; Sweet-Escott, *Baker Street Irregular*, p. 147; Stevenson, *A Man Called Intrepid*, pp. 323–24, 343–47.

64. Eric Maschwitz, *No Chip on My Shoulder*, pp. 141–45; Lesley Storm, *Heart of the City* (New York: Dramatists Play Service, 1942). The play opened in early 1942.

65. BLEPS: Dalton II, Box 7/3, Dalton to Churchill, 24 September 1941.

66. Cole Blasier, "The United States, Germany, and the Bolivian Revolutionaries (1941–1946)," *Journal of Hispanic American History* 52 (February 1972): 26–54; Spruille Braden, *Diplomats and Demagogues* (New Rochelle, N.Y.: Arlington House, 1971), pp. 245–53; Montgomery Hyde, *The Quiet Canadian*, pp. 144–48.

67. Rosenman (ed.), *Public Papers*, Vol. 10, pp. 438–44; *DGFP*, Series D, Vol. 13, pp. 724–25; Friedländer, *Prelude to Downfall*, p. 302, note 5.

68. Franklin Roosevelt, *Complete Presidential Press Conferences of Franklin D. Roosevelt*, Vol. 18 (New York: Da Capo, 1972), pp. 260–61.

69. Montgomery Hyde, *The Quiet Canadian*, pp. 149–50; FDRL, President's Safe File (Box 3), Safe: Germany, Map *"Luftverkehrsnetz der Vereinigten Staaten Süd-Americkas Hauptlinien"* and key.

70. NA RG 263, Box 7/57, Troy to Chief Intelligence Institute, CIA, 11 October 1974; Ivar Bryce, *You Only Live Once*, pp. 62–64.

71. Montgomery Hyde, *The Quiet Canadian*, pp. 148–50; Stevenson, *A Man Called Intrepid*, pp. 297–98.

72. John F. Bratzel and Leslie B. Rout, "FDR and Secret Map," *Wilson Quarterly* 9 (1985): 167–73. The claim that Sandstede was murdered is also demonstrably untrue. Sandstede returned to Berlin in September 1941 and, after promotion, joined the Waffen SS; he was killed in action in March 1944.

73. Bryce, *You Only Live Once*, pp. 62–64.

74. Had Bryce wished to deceive his readers, he could easily have massaged his story to fit Montgomery Hyde's published version. It would seem that his recollection was at fault. On LATI, see Montgomery Hyde, *The Quiet Canadian*, pp. 144–49.

75. Bratzel and Rout, "FDR and the Secret Map," p. 171.

76. FDRL, Berle papers, Box 213, Berle to Hull, 5 September 1941, Diary Vol. VII, 1, pp. 226–27.

77. FDRL Berle, Box 213, Berle to Welles, 18 September 1941. Diary Vol. VII, 2, pp. 122–23.

78. FDRL, PPF Speech File, No.1389. Evidently, the COI had its own doubts about the authenticity of the map. *After* the President's speech, it launched a half-hearted investigation into this and related matters (including

the writings of the Nazi Party's favorite geopolitician, Karl Haushofer); the investigation turned up only a vaguely similar map in the *New York Daily Mirror* of August 25, 1941 (which may have been a BSC plant), and a bizarre map from 1911. FDRL, PSF (Diplomatic) Box 31, (Germany), Sterling to James, 3 November 1941.

79. Montgomery Hyde, *The Quiet Canadian*, p. 55; Dallek, *Roosevelt and American Foreign Policy*, p. 225.

80. BLEPS: Dalton II, Box 7/3, Dalton to Churchill, 24 September 1941.

81. FDRL Berle, Box 213, Berle to Welles, 18 September 1941. Diary Vol. VII, 2, pp. 122–23. "Elliott" is a misnomer for Dick Ellis.

82. NA RG 69, Finding aids: Purport list for 841.2021, 3 September 1941, purport for memo by Berle, notes "British intelligence tapped telephone wires of Musa, friend of Ambassador Henri Haye . . ." and adds "In U.S. memorandum regarding———and results of their findings being printed in the *New York Herald Tribune* J. Edgar Hoover of FBI reports that same done by the British without consulting anyone." NA RG 69, 861.20211/Musa.John.L. 1942.

83. Sumner Welles, *Seven Decisions That Shaped the World* (New York: Harper, 1951), p. 61; Montgomery Hyde, *The Quiet Canadian*, p. 67.

84. FDRL PSF Box 128 (Donovan/COI), FDR to Donovan, 13 October 1941.

85. Interview: Berlin; Wheeler-Bennett, *British Information in the U.S.A.*, pp. 49–51.

86. *Congressional Record*, Vol. 87, part 8, 8906, S.2060; *New York Times*, 18 November 1941; NA RG 59/2946, 800.01 B 11/33, Dunn and Atherton to Welles, 14 October 1941.

87. NA RG 59/2946, 800.01 B 11 Registration/1139 1/2, 17 November 1941, memo by Winthrop Crane, State Department Foreign Correlation section.

88. Montgomery Hyde, *Secret Intelligence Agent*, p. 179.

89. *New York Herald Tribune*, 5 September 1941.

90. *Master Comics*, No. 21, 1941.

91. Steele, *Propaganda in an Open Society*, p. 97.

92. *National Comics*, No. 7, January 1941, reproduced in Richard O'Brien, *The Golden Age of Comic Books, 1937–45* (New York: Ballantine Books, 1977); *Master Comics*, No. 21, 1941.

93. *Captain American*, No. 1, March 1941; No. 2, May 1941; No. 6, September 1941.

94. Robert H. Boyle, "A Champ For All Time!!!" *Sports Illustrated*, 19 April 1965, pp. 120–37.

95. Interviews: Berlin, Miall. Ron Goulart, *The Adventurous Decade* (New Rochelle, N.Y.: Arlington, 1975), p. 169. As Miall of the PWE New York recalled, later in the war BIS fed pro-British material to Fisher through the senior U.S. OWI officer, Lew Cowan.

96. Gallico, *The Snow Goose*; Murrow, *This Is London*; Ben Robertson, *I Saw England* (New York: Knopf, 1941); Arthur Donahue, *Tally-Ho! Yankee in a Spitfire* (New York: Macmillan, 1941); William Shirer, *Berlin Diary* (New York: Knopf, 1941); Douglas Miller, *You Can't Do Business with Hitler* (Boston: Little, Brown, 1941); Clarence Streit, *Union Now with Britain* (New York: Harper, 1941).

97. Harvey Klemmer, *They'll Never Quit* (New York: Funk, 1941), jacket notes; Cecil Roberts, "The Miracle of England," *Saturday Review of Literature*, 10 May 1941.

98. Klemmer, *They'll Never Quit*, pp. v, 8, 84, 120, 146–55, 290, 305.

99. Paul Fussell, "Writing in Wartime: The Uses of Innocence," in *Thank God for the Atom Bomb and Other Essays* (New York: Summit, 1989), pp. 53–81.

100. J. B. Priestley, *Britain Speaks*; Mollie Panter-Downes, *Letter from England* (Boston: Little, Brown, 1940); Forbes-Robertson and Straus, *War Letters from Britain* (New York: Putnam, 1941); Jan Struther, with Beatrice Curtis Brown (ed.), *Women of Britain* (New York: Harcourt, Brace & Co., 1941); Arthur Bryant, *Pageant of England* (New York: Harper, 1941); Archibald Wavell, *Allenby: A Study in Greatness* (New York: Oxford University Press, 1941); Phyllis Moir, *I Was Winston Churchill's Secretary* (New York: Funk, 1941); John Masefield, *The Nine Days Wonder* (New York: Macmillan, 1941); also, B. H. Bronson (ed.), *That Immortal Garland* (Berkeley, Calif.: Gillick & Co., 1941), an anthology of English literature sold in aid of the British War Relief Association of Northern California. I am grateful to Professor Paul Alpers, of the University of California at Berkeley for this reference.

101. Jan Struther (pseudonym of Joyce Maxtone Graham), *Mrs. Miniver* (New York: Harcourt, Brace & Co., 1940); *Saturday Review of Literature*, 17 August 1941, p. 15.

102. Winston Churchill, *Blood, Sweat and Tears* (New York: Putnam, 1941); James Hilton, *Random Harvest* (Boston: Little, Brown, 1941); Eric Knight, *This Above All* (New York: Harper, 1941); Paul Rotha (ed.), *Portrait of a Flying Yorkshireman: Letters from Eric Knight in the United States to Paul Rotha in England* (London: Chapman & Hall, 1952), p. 179.

103. Hilton, *Random Harvest* (1943 ed.); see p. 163 for flag-waving asides.

104. Knight, *This Above All*, p. 473; Rotha (ed.), *Portrait of a Flying Yorkshireman*, pp. 137–148, 178, 195. For the Hess story, see *Saturday Evening Post*, 20 December 1941.

105. PRO INF 1/848, memorandum by the Highets, 26 March 1940; Helen MacInnes, *Above Suspicion* (Boston: Little, Brown, 1941). For background: Ayer, *Part of My Life*, pp. 252–53.

106. Tabori, *Korda*, pp. 221–24; Powell, *A Life in Movies*, p. 363; Korda, *Charmed Lives*, pp. 148–55.

107. Alexander Korda, "Imagination vs. Microphone: Alexander Korda Cuts Shackles," *New York Herald Tribune*, 16 September 1940.

108. Alexander Korda (dir.), *That Hamilton Woman* (Alexander Korda, 1941); Tabori, *Korda*, pp. 221–24; Korda, *Charmed Lives*, pp. 148–55; PRO FO 371/26184, A3617/118/45, Ford to Fletcher, 23 April 1941.

109. Tabori, *Korda*, p. 229; Ernst Lubitsch (dir.), *To Be or Not to Be* (Ernst Lubitsch, 1942).

110. Henry King (dir.), *A Yank in the RAF* (Twentieth Century Fox, 1941); Halliwell, *Halliwell's Film Guide*, 7th ed., 1137; PRO INF 1/625, Bernstein to Wanger, 15 January 1941; Moorehead, *Bernstein*, p. 156.

111. Anatole Litvak (dir.), *This Above All* (Twentieth Century Fox, 1942); Carol Reed, *Young Mr. Pitt* (Twentieth Century Fox, 1940); Archie Mayo (dir.), *Confirm or Deny* (Twentieth Century Fox, 1941); Fritz Lang (dir.), *Man Hunt* (Twentieth Century Fox, 1941).

112. Lewis Seiler (dir.), *International Squadron* (Warner Brothers, 1941); Howard Hawks (dir.), *Sergeant York* (Warner Brothers, 1941); Vincent Sherman (dir.), *Underground* (Warner Brothers, 1941); PRO INF 1/600, Elton to Jarratt, 18 August 1941.

113. FDRL, Mellett papers, Box 5, White House 1940, Mellett (Office of Government Reports) to FDR, 23 December 1940, transmits Wanger's invitation and refers to him as "our friend." Mellett hoped that Roosevelt's speech might "clinch" plans for effective cooperation between Hollywood and the White House. FDRL, OF.73, Box 5, Motion Pictures, Release dated 27 February 1941; Koppes and Black, *Hollywood Goes to War*, p. 36.

114. Mitchell Leisen (dir.), *I Wanted Wings* (Paramount, 1941); Michael Curtiz (dir.), *Dive Bomber* (Warner Brothers, 1941); Arthur Lubin (dir.), *Buck Privates* (Universal, 1941); David Butler (dir.), *Caught in the Draft* (Paramount, 1941); Ben Sharpsteen (dir.), *Dumbo* (Disney, 1941).

115. Taylor, *Hitch*, p. 155.

116. PRO INF 1/625, Wanger to Bernstein, November 1940; Wanger to Bernstein, 19 December 1940; Wanger to Halifax, 10 June 1940, notes that his plan is for a nonfiction picture for later conversion to fiction if necessary; also SHSW: Wanger papers, Box 77/17, Wanger to C. S. Forrester, 21 April 1941; Bernstein to Wanger, 29 April 1941; Box 77/19, Contract Watt/Wanger, 13 June 1941.

117. PRO INF 1/625, Wing Co. Williams, Air Min., to Beddington MoI, 25 May 1941; Report by Watt, 17 October 1941; Grierson to Beddington, 23 December 1941; SHSW Wanger papers, 77/19, Watt to Wanger, 19 September 1941; Schoedsack (producer) to Wanger, 18 October 1941; Watt, *Don't Look at the Camera*, pp. 154–60; Wanger to Wheeler-Bennett, 1 December 1941.

118. SHSW Wanger papers 77/19, Wheeler-Bennett to Wanger, 6 February 1942; PRO INF 1/625, Bernstein to Wanger 20 April 1942; Arthur Lubin (dir.), *Eagle Squadron* (Universal, 1942); Watt, *Don't Look at the Camera*, pp. 154–60. Watt's actuality footage later received its own release as a documentary, *The Rendezvous*.

119. Mervyn de Roy (dir.), *Random Harvest* (MGM, 1942), starring Ronald Coleman and Greer Garson; William Wyler (dir.), *Mrs. Miniver* (MGM, 1942), starring Walter Pidgeon and Greer Garson; Richard Thorpe (dir.), *Above Suspicion* (MGM, 1943); Moorehead, *Bernstein*, pp. 132–35.

120. Moorehead, *Bernstein*, pp. 132–35; PRO INF 1/600, Elton to Jarratt, 18 August 1941; Mayer also promised to make *The Cargo of Innocents*, a tale of a Harvard boy on a destroyer, and the project eventually became Robert Z. Leonard (dir.), *Stand by for Action* (MGM, 1943). Axel Madsen, *William Wyler: The Authorized Biography* (New York: Crowell, 1973), pp. 212–18.

121. William Wyler (dir.), *Mrs. Miniver*, with screenplay by Claudine West, George Froeschell, and James Hilton, as preserved in the University of Southern California library.

122. Valerie Grove, in Jan Struther, *Mrs. Miniver* (London: Virago, 1989), especially p. xi); Kurth, *The American Cassandra*; Moorehead, *Bernstein*, pp. 142–44. Ironically, while her literary alter ego endured the Blitz on the screen, Jan Struther spent the war living on Manhattan's Central Park West, earning a lucrative living as lecturer.

123. Contrary to Wheeler-Bennett, *Special Relationships*, p. 140, and Korda, *Charmed Lives*, p. 154, the inquiry did not center on the unproduced *Mrs. Miniver*, but on films such as *Confessions of a Nazi Spy*, *A Yank in the RAF*, and Korda's *That Hamilton Woman*; Koppes and Black, *Hollywood Goes to War*, pp. 40–45; *Congressional Record*, Vol. 87, part 6, p. 6565.

124. Moorehead, *Bernstein*, p. 138; Rudy Behlmer (ed.), *Inside Warner Bros. (1935–1951)* (New York: Viking, 1986), pp. 188–91; Koppes and Black, *Hollywood Goes to War*, pp. 43–45; FDRL Mellett papers, Box. 1, Senate Sub-Committee Movie Investigation.

125. *Congressional Record*, Vol. 86 (Appendix), part. 5, A.5314; Korda, *Charmed Lives*, p. 154; Moorehead, *Bernstein*, p. 138.

126. *Time*, 8 December 1941.

127. PRO FO 371/34170, A6976/161/45, Fisher, San Francisco, to BIS, 5 July 1943.

128. Dallek, *Roosevelt and American Foreign Policy*, p. 302; Cordell Hull, *The Memoirs of Cordell Hull* (London: Hodder & Stoughton, 1948), Vol. 2, pp. 1054–94.

129. Dallek, *Roosevelt and American Foreign Policy*, pp. 291–93; Lash, *Roosevelt and Churchill*, pp. 428–29; Churchill, *The Second World War*, Vol. 3, pp. 459–61.

130. Hutton papers, Hutton to parents, 18 November 1941.

131. Cantril (ed.), *Public Opinion*, pp. 902–3. On November 19, 1941, AIOP asked: "Some people say that the biggest job facing this country today is to help defeat the Nazi Government; do you agree or disagree?" 72% agreed. Asked on September 17, 1941, "Which of these two things do you think is the more important—that this country keeps out of war, or that Germany be defeated?" 70% answered against Germany, and only 30% for isolation; also, Manchester, *The Glory and the Dream*, Vol. 1, p. 277; Steele, *Propaganda in an Open Society*, p. 102.

132. Dallek, *Roosevelt and American Foreign Policy*, p. 307.

133. Dallek, *Roosevelt and American Foreign Policy*, pp. 307–9; Robert Sherwood, *The White House Papers of Harry L. Hopkins*, Vol. 1 (London: Eyre & Spottiswoode, 1948), pp. 426–27; Hull, *Memoirs*, Vol. 2, pp. 1083–86.

134. FDRL Biddle papers, Box 1, Cabinet Meetings, 1941, 5 December 1941.

135. Stevenson, *A Man Called Intrepid*, pp. 298–300; John Toland, *Infamy: Pearl Harbor and Its Aftermath* (Garden City, N.Y.: Doubleday, 1982), pp. 287–89; *DGFP*, Series D, Vol. 13, pp. 950–51.

136. James Rusbridger and Eric Nave, *Betrayal at Pearl Harbor: How Churchill Lured Roosevelt into War* (New York: Summitt, 1991).

137. William Casey, *The Secret War Against Hitler* (New York: Kampmann, 1988), p. 7.

138. Toland, *Infamy*, pp. 258–61.

139. Rusbridger and Nave, *Betrayal at Pearl Harbor*, pp. 47–48, 250; Eric Larrabee, *Commander in Chief: Franklin Delano Roosevelt, His Lieutenants, and Their War* (New York: Harper & Row, 1987), p. 169. Gordon W. Prange, *At Dawn We Slept* (New York: McGraw-Hill, 1981), p. 736.

140. Clarke, *From Three Worlds*, p. 10.

141. Vandenberg (ed.), *Private Papers of Senator Vandenberg*, p. 1.

142. Interview: Hutton; Clarke, *From Three Worlds*, p. 10; *DGFP*, Series D, Vol. 13, pp. 978–79.

143. Friedländer, *Prelude to Downfall*, pp. 258, 313; Klaus Hildebrand, *The Foreign Policy of the Third Reich* (London: Batsford, 1973), pp. 114–15.

144. Friedländer, *Prelude to Downfall*, p. 309; Hildebrand, *The Foreign Policy of the Third Reich*, p. 114.

Epilogue

1. PRO INF 1/102, Darvall to Tree, 13 December 1941.

2. *Daily Princetonian*, 8 December 1941.

3. Tree, *When the Moon Was High*, p. 173 (placing the bonfire scare before Pearl Harbor). Wheeler-Bennett, *British Information in the U.S.A.*, pp. 48–56; Interview: Berlin; Correspondence: "Mitch" Mitchell to author, 9 February 1988.

4. Montgomery Hyde, *Secret Intelligence Agent*, p. 179; FDRL Berle papers, VII, 2, 50 et seq.; Schwarz, *Liberal*, p. 114.

5. NA RG 263, Box 8/63, Stephenson to Whitney Shepardson, circa 1960, "The early days of OSS"; Interview: Berlin.

6. NA RG 59/2946, 800.01/145-1/2. Berle to Hull, 26 January 1942; PRO FO 371/30667, A399, A630, A636, A1527, and A2701/399/45.

7. PRO FO 371/30667, A1346/399/45, Halifax to FO, 8 February 1942; A4205/399/45, Sir Gerald Campbell to MoI, 1 May 1942; FO 898/104, 10 February 1942; Interview: Bathurst; Montgomery Hyde, *Secret Intelligence Agent*, pp. 175–81.

8. *New York Times*, 10 February 1942, p. A7; NA RG 59/C 136, 841.20211/36, Confidential File, Berle to Welles, 4 March 1942; Minutes 5 March 1942; Montgomery Hyde misdates this meeting 2 March 1942, Montgomery Hyde, *Secret Intelligence Agent*, p. 181; NA RG 59/C 136, FW 841.20211/ 36, Confidential File, Berle Minute, 10 March 1942.

9. Donovan, Staff College lecture, November 1943 etc., NA RG 263 Box 1/4; NA RG 263, Box 3/24. FDRL Printed Collection: Troy, *COI and British Intelligence*, p. 27; Berle/Troy interview, 7 October 1969. BSC had a British rival for its covert propaganda role. In 1942, PWE established its own New York office under David Bowes Lyon, which assumed all liaison functions with the U.S. OWI. PRO FO 898/103-108; Interview: Miall; Wheeler-Bennett, *Special Relationships*, pp. 149–207.

10. Wheeler-Bennett, *British Information in the U.S.A.*, pp. 58–59; PRO FO 371/30667, A1789/399/45; Interviews: Berlin, Miall; Miall papers, Morgan to Miall.

11. *Denver Post*, 1 October 1942; Interviews: Bathurst, Hutton; Wheeler-Bennett, *British Information in the U.S.A.*, pp. 79–80.

12. Wheeler-Bennett, *British Information in the U.S.A.*, pp. 68–69; Moorehead, *Bernstein*, pp. 139–45; PRO INF 1/599.

13. PRO FO 371/26188, A9268/118/45, North Whitehead, 15 November 1941.

14. Interviews: Raphael, Berlin, Macmillan, Pear, Lionel Elvin.

15. Wheeler-Bennett, *British Information in the U.S.A.*, p. 75.

16. Interviews: Galwey, Thoms; Short, "The White Cliffs of Dover," pp. 3–25; Short in Taylor (ed.), *British Cinema in the Second World War*.

17. Interview: Miall; Sperber, *Murrow*, pp. 221–22; PRO FO 371/51627, AN464/4/45, Henry David (BBC) to Stafford Cripps (BoT), 5 February 1945.

18. PRO FO 371/34137, A1005/34/45, Report by Prof Alladyce Nicoll, WP (43) 59, 10 February 1943, and Halifax to Eden, 19 January 1943.

19. PRO INF 1/435, UNIB, 15 December 1942.

20. PRO INF 1/435, especially 19 May 1942. Interviews: Stavridi, Orrick; LoC Sweetser papers.

21. Interview: Macmillan.

22. Interviews: Nicholas, Macmillan; Eckersley, *The BBC and All That*, p. 157; Caroline Anstey, "Foreign Office Efforts to Influence American Opinion, 1945–1949," (London School of Economics and Political Science Ph.D. thesis, 1984); Caroline Anstey, "The Projection of British Socialism: Foreign Office Publicity and American Opinion, 1945–50," *Journal of Contemporary History* 19 (1984): 417–51.

23. Interview: Nicholas.

24. *American Outlook*, 1947 to 1948.

25. Interviews: Raphael, Miall.

26. Interview: Miall; Wheeler-Bennett, *Special Relationships*. The restricted report has been cited here as Wheeler-Bennett, *British Information in the U.S.A.*

27. Interview: Hermione MacColl.

28. I am grateful to Tom Troy for his advice on this point.

29. Interview: Janet Murrow; Sperber, *Murrow*; Persico, *Murrow*; Kendrick, *Prime Time*.

30. Don Siegel (dir.), *Riot in Cell Block Eleven* (Allied Artists/Wanger, 1954); Don Siegel (dir.), *Invasion of the Body Snatchers* (Allied Artists/Walter Wanger, 1956); Joseph L. Mankiewicz (dir.), *The Quiet American* (UA/ Mankiewicz, 1957); Joseph L. Mankiewicz et al. (dirs.), *Cleopatra* (Twentieth Century Fox, 1963). For a summary of Wanger's later years, see the biographical section of the Wanger papers: SHSW Madison. Wanger died in 1968. Other interventionists also moved into Cold War propaganda; De Rochemont and *March of Time* did much to promote the very term.

31. SHSW Wanger papers, 60/6, 5 November 1946; Box 30/6, Cruickshank to Bernstein, 2 November 1946.

32. Interviews: Raphael, Pear, Thistlethwaite, Nicholas.

33. Interviews: Cronkite, Sevareid, Fowler, Lord Harmsworth, Galwey, Daiches, Raphael; *Times*, 3 November 1983.

34. Interview: Cooke; BIS New York, clippings collection, especially Peter Innes (director, BIS) "British Information Services" in *The Bulldog Review* ("The newsletter of the British-American Chamber of Commerce"), November/December 1992, and private information.

Conclusion

1. Private hands, Alan Fowler papers: Sir Berkeley Ormerod to Mrs Gizelda Fowler, 19 September 1966.

2. Willi A. Boelcke (ed.), *The Secret Conferences of Dr. Goebbels: The Nazi Propaganda War, 1939–43*, (New York: Dutton, 1970), p. xvii.

3. Poll evidence in mid-1941 confirmed that British news was accepted with a relatively high degree of confidence by the American public. When asked "About how much of the news coming from newspapers and radio reporters in England, do you believe at the present time?" 27% registered a "high degree of confidence," 38.1% had a "medium degree of confidence." This compared with only 3.8% with "high" confidence in German news; 55.4% had "low confidence" or "no confidence" in German news. Cantril, Confidential report: "Public confidence in news from England and Germany," Office of Public Opinion Research, Princeton University, 9 October 1941: preserved in Mudd Library,

Princeton University, Harold W. Dodds papers. The results were: Britain: High, 27.2%; Medium, 38.1%; Low, 20.4%; None, 7.2%. Germany: High, 3.8%; Medium, 24.2%; Low, 39.4%; None, 26%. France: High, 4.7%; Medium, 25.1%; Low, 35%; None, 21.6%. Cantril summarized his findings: "There is noticeably more confidence in news from England than from Germany and France. People are as skeptical of news from France as Germany. Those who have more faith than others in British news and less in German, are more interventionist, less appeasement minded . . . ." I owe this document to Professor Richard D. Challener of Princeton University.

4. PRO FO 371/30670, A6581/399/45, R. I. Campbell to Neville Butler, 3 July 1942.

5. Interviews: Hodson, Berlin.

6. Wheeler-Bennett, *British Information in the U.S.A.*, p. 1.

7. Interviews: Middleton, Reston.

8. Birkenhead, *Halifax*, p. 507.

9. *Washington Herald*, 2 February 1938; McKenna, *Borah*, p. 353.

Bibliography

Manuscript Sources

British Archives (Government)

Public Record Office, Kew, PRO

Admiralty: ADM 1
Air Ministry: AIR 2
Board of Trade: BT 59, 60, 237
British Council: BW 2, 63
Cabinet Office: CAB 24, 64, 65, 66
Colonial Office: CO 852
Foreign Office: FO 115, 371, 395, 800, 898, 954
Ministry of Information: INF 1, 5, 6
Premier: PREM 1, 3, 4
Treasury: T 188
War Office: WO 165

British Information Services, New York

John Wheeler-Bennett, *A History of British Information in the U.S.A.* (BIS
      New York, 1946)
Clippings files: BLI 1920–1942 and BIS 1942–1993

British Archives (Private and Institutional)

Borthwick Institute, University of York

Lord Halifax (diary)

**British Broadcasting Corporation, Written Archive Centre, Caversham Park,
Berkshire (BBC WAC)**

Nos. E 1, E 2, R 28, R 34, R 51, R 61
Contributors files

British Library

John Masefield
Sir John Evelyn Wrench

British Library of Economics and Political Science, London School of Economics (BLEPS)

Hugh Dalton (collection I and II)
Sir Charles Webster
"Misc. papers"

Brotherton Library, University of Leeds
(Microfilm collection)

Anthony Eden
Lord Halifax
Cordell Hull
William Lyon Mackenzie King

Churchill College, Cambridge

A. V. Alexander
Ernest Bevin (collections I and II)
Alfred Duff Cooper
Philip Noel-Baker
Cecil Roberts
Lord Vansittart

John Grierson Archive, Stirling University Library

John Grierson

Polish Institute and Sikorski Museum, London

Polish Government, Ministry of Information files, A.10

Scottish Record Office, Edinburgh (SRO)

Lord Lothian, GD 40

Private Hands

Joan Galwey
Graham Hutton, c/o Hutton family
Lord King-Hall, c/o Miss Anne King-Hall
René MacColl, c/o Mrs. Hermione MacColl
Angus McDonnell, c/o The Honorable Hector McDonnell
Leonard Miall
Professor H. G. Nicholas
Charles Peake, c/o Lady Peake

United States Archives (Government)

National Archives, Washington, D.C. (NA)

Military Intelligence, RG 165
State Department, RG 59
Central Intelligence Agency, RG 263

Franklin D. Roosevelt Library (National Archives and Records Administration), Hyde Park, New York (FDRL)

President's Secretary's File (PSF)
Official File (OF)
President's Personal Papers (PPF)
Map Room File (MR)
Propaganda Collection (printed papers/misc.)
Private papers of
    Adolf A. Berle
    Francis Biddle
    Benjamin Cohen
    Oscar Cox
    Stephen J. Early
    Harry L. Hopkins (private papers and personal letters)
    Lowell Mellett
    Henry M. Morgenthau
    Eleanor Roosevelt
    James Roosevelt
    Whitney H. Shepardson
    F. C. Ward
    John Gilbert Winant

United States (Private and Institutional)

Columbia University (Butler Library), New York City

Nicholas Murray Butler
H. R. Knickerbocker
James T. Shotwell

Harvard School of Business (Baker Library), Cambridge, Massachusetts

Thomas W. Lamont

Harvard University (Houghton Library), Cambridge, Massachusetts

Jay Pierrepont Moffat
Oswald Garrison Villard

Hoover Institution, Palo Alto University, Stanford, California

America First Committee

British Library of Information
Private papers of
    Stanley K. Hornbeck

Library of Congress, Washington, D.C. (LoC)

Columbia Broadcasting System (CBS)
Private papers of
    John Balderston
    Hansen Baldwin
    William E. Borah
    Earl Browder (Microfilm Collection)
    Raymond Clapper
    George Fielding Eliot
    Felix Frankfurter
    Lillian Gish
    Harold Ickes
    Breckenridge Long
    Archibald MacLeish
    Key Pittman
    A. Philip Randolph
    Eric Sevareid
    Henry Stimson
    Clarence Streit
    Arthur Sweetser
    Raymond Gram Swing
    Robert Taft
    William Allen White

Mass Communications History Center, State Historical Society of Wisconsin, Madison, Wisconsin (SHSW)

National Broadcasting Company (NBC)
United Artists
Private papers of
    Walter Graebner
    H. V. Kaltenborn
    Walter Wanger

Princeton University (Mudd Library), Princeton, New Jersey

Committee to Defend America By Aiding the Allies (CDAAA)
Fight For Freedom (FFF)
Veterans of Future Wars
Private papers of
    Hamilton Fish Armstrong
    John Foster Dulles

Princeton University (Firestone Library), Princeton, New Jersey

America First Pamphlet Collection (bound)
Facts in Review
Whitehall Letter

Fletcher School, Tufts University, Boston, Massachusetts

Edward R. Murrow

University of Arizona, Tucson, Arizona

Lewis Douglas

University of Wyoming, Laramie, Wyoming

Louis B. De Rochemont
Richard De Rochemont

Private Hands

John and Brenda Lawler

Canadian Archives

National Archives of Canada, Ottawa

Department of External Affairs, RG 25
War Cabinet, RG 2
War Information Board, RG 26
Private papers of
    Loring Christie
    William Lyon Mackenzie King
    Lester B. Pearson
    Graham Spry
    Hume Wrong

Oral Sources

Interviews (with war service and interview date)

George Ball. Member, Committee to Defend America by Aiding the Allies, 1939–1941; later Assistant Secretary of State to Presidents Kennedy and Johnson (Princeton, N.J., 25 August 1993).

Sir Maurice Bathurst QC. Legal adviser, British Embassy/BIS (East Horsley, Surrey, 18 December 1987).

Sir Isaiah Berlin. BPS New York 1941–1942; head of BIS Survey, Washington, 1942–1945 (Oxford, 11 November 1985, and London, 29 September 1987).

Wallace Carroll. UP London 1938–1940; Office of War Information London and Washington, D.C., 1941–1945. (Winston-Salem, N.C., 16 July 1993).

Alistair Cooke. BBC/NBC broadcaster, U.S. correspondent for *Times* of London and *Manchester Guardian* (New York, 29 September 1990).

Walter Cronkite. UP war correspondent, Europe, 1942–1945 (New York, 13 January 1989).

David Daiches. Lecturer, University of Chicago and officer in BIS New York/Washington (Edinburgh, 31 January 1987).

Lionel Elvin. MoI American Division Labour Specialist, 1943–1945 (Cambridge, 26 May 1988).

Douglas Fairbanks, Jr. Film actor and pro-British activist (New York, 9 March 1990).

George Forrest. MoI Censorship, Liverpool, and BIS New York (Glasgow, 5 July 1988).

Gizelda Fowler. Advertising executive, J. Walter Thompson, New York, and widow of Alan Fowler, BIS New York (London, 7 January 1988).

Joan Galwey. BLI/BPS New York, 1939–1941; MoI London, 1941–1945, (Walberswick, Suffolk, 8 and 9 November 1987).

Lewis Jefferson Gorin. Princeton University class of 1936; National Chairman "Veterans of Future Wars" 1936; member, Kentucky League for a British Victory, 1940–1941 (Princeton, N.J., 7 June 1991).

Lord and Lady Harmsworth. BLI New York, 1939–1945. (Egham, Surrey, 12 October 1987).

Heather Harvey. Assistant to Arnold Toynbee, RIIA (London, 11 January 1988).

Sir William Hayter. First Secretary, British Embassy, Washington, from 1941 onward (Oxford, 28 February 1988, and correspondence).

Robert Heaney. British Passport Control Officer, New York, 1940–1943; British Consul, New Orleans (Greenwich, Conn., 9 March 1989).

Denis Hennessy. Archivist, British Embassy, Washington (Richmond-on-Thames, August 1986, and correspondence).

Alger Hiss. Lawyer for Nye Committee and State Department (New York, 24 April 1990).

Harry Hodson. Director of Empire Division, MoI, 1939–1940 (16 September 1987).

Graham Hutton. Foreign Office PID 1939–1941; Director of BPS Chicago 1941–1945 (London SW2, 6 June 1988, 13 June 1988, 21 June 1988, 11 July 1988, and 18 July 1988).

Lord Inchyra. Head of Chancery, British Embassy, Washington, under Lothian and Halifax (Perth, 5 November 1985).

Anne King-Hall. Daughter of internationalist, Stephen King-Hall, (Clapham Common, 20 October 1987 and 27 October 1987).

John and Brenda Lawler. Press Section, BIS New York (Briar Cliff Manor, N.Y., 31 October 1988).

Larry Lesueur. CBS London and Eastern Front (Washington, D.C., 31 March 1989).

Hermione MacColl. Head of Registry, BPS New York; widow of René MacColl (Wimbledon, 1 August 1987 and 8 August 1987).

Peggy Macmillan. MoI American Division and BIS New York (London, 2 November 1987).

Leonard Miall. BBC External Services, 1939–1942; PWE New York, 1943–1945 (Taplow, Buckinghamshire, 20 July 1987).

Drew Middleton. AP war correspondent, London and Europe, 1938–1945 (New York, 2 February 1989).

Helen Kirkpatrick Milbank. War correspondent, *Chicago Daily News* (Northampton, Mass., 5 August 1993)

Richard Miles. Royal Navy Officer; U.S. speaking tour, 1943, with later service in BIS/British Embassy, 1944–1945 (Kingston-on-Thames, 11 September 1987).

Janet Murrow. Widow of Edward R. Murrow, CBS. (New York, 14 November 1988).

Herbert Nicholas. RIIA Survey, Oxford, 1939–1941; American Division MoI, 1941–1946 (Oxford, 22 February 1988).

Jim Orrick. BIS/Inter-Allied publications section (Princeton, N.J., 29 November 1988).

Richard Pear. British Press Service (London, 17 July 1987).

Lord Perth. 'EH' Paris 1939–1940, MoI agent in United States, 1940; later with British Shipping Mission, Washington (London, 28 June 1988).

Phil Piratin. Communist Party counsellor for Stepney (later MP); leader of protests against poor air-raid provision (London, 1 May 1991).

Chaim Raphael. British Information Services, Information Division, from 1941 onward; head of Economic desk, editor of *Labour and Industry* (London, 18 June 1987 and 12 July 1988, and correspondence).

Peggy Ratcliffe. British Press Service, Survey Division, from 1939 onward (London, 13 October 1987).

James Reston. *New York Times*, London and Washington bureaus; Office of War Information, London (Washington, D.C., 30 March 1989).

Wendy Reves. wife of anti-Nazi publicist Emery Reves (by telephone, 5 September 1987).

Eric Sevareid. CBS London, 1937–1940 (Washington, D.C., 30 March 1989).

Lord Sherfield. Foreign Office Central Dept.; British Labour delegation in Washington, 1941; later Minister in British Embassy and Ambassador to United States (London, 10 December 1985).

Val Stavridi. MoI Greek Section, Inter-Allied Information Committee, 1941–1943. (London, May 1988).

Frank Thistlethwaite. British Press Service from 1940 onward (London, 23 September 1987).

Ann Thoms. Daughter of Sir Frederick Whyte; officer in MoI American Division, 1943–1945 (Aberdeen, 5 July 1988).

Stanley Wilson. British Library of Information, Information Dept. from 1941 (London, 3 September 1987).

Correspondence (with war service)

Roy Boulting. British filmmaker.

Thomas W. Childs. American lawyer and Grand Consul to the British Embassy in Washington during World War II.

The Right Honorable Edward Heath MP. Leader of Oxford Union Debating team, 1939 U.S. tour.

"Mitch" Mitchell. Telephonist, British Press Service, New York.

Audio-Visual

Radio

Firestone Library Audio collection, Princeton University, Princeton, New Jersey

British wartime radio broadcasts

National Archives: Sound and Motion Picture Branch (NA:SMPB), Washington, D.C.

Radio Collection: RG 200

University of Washington, Seattle, Audio-Visual Service

CBS News 1939–1945

Commercial Audio Records

Schwedler, Karl, et al., *Charlie and His Orchestra, German Propaganda Swing, 1940–1941* (Harlequin [HQ 2058], London, 1987).

Films

Newsreels

National Archives, Sound and Motion Picture Branch, Washington, D.C.

March of Time (U.S.A., 1935–1945).
Paramount (U.S.A., 1938–1941) (script only).
Universal (U.S.A., 1940).

National Archives of Canada, Moving Image and Sound Archives, Historical Resources Branch, Ottawa

Canada Carries On (Canada, 1940–1945)
World In Action (Canada, 1941–1945)

Select Documentary Filmography (held at Imperial War Museum, London)

Britain At Bay [overseas title: *Britain on Guard*] (GPO for MoI, UK, 1940).
Channel Incident, Anthony Asquith (dir.) (MoI, U.K., 1940).
Christmas Under Fire, Harry Watt (dir.) (Crown, U.K., 1940).
The Dawn Guard, Roy Boulting (dir.) (MoI/Charter, U.K., 1941).
Defenders of India (Bombay Talkies, India, 1943).
The First Days, Humphrey Jennings, Harry Watt, and Pat Jackson (dirs.) (GPO, U.K., 1939).
The Heart of Britain, Humphrey Jennings (dir.) (Crown, U.K., 1941).
Listen to Britain, Humphrey Jennings (dir.) (Crown, U.K., 1942).
Loföten, Tennyson d'Eyncourt (dir.) (Army/Crown Film Units, U.K., 1941).
London Can Take It, Humphrey Jennings and Harry Watt (dirs.) (Crown, U.K., 1940).
Men of the Lightship, David Macdonald (dir.) (GPO, U.K., 1940).
Neighbours Under Fire, Ralph Bond (dir.) (Strand, U.K., 1940).
Night Mail, Basil Wright and Harry Watt (dirs.) (GPO, U.K., 1936).
Ordinary People, Jack Holmes (dir.) (Crown, U.K., 1941).
Target for Tonight, Harry Watt (dir.) (Crown, U.K., 1941).
We Won't Forget, Frank Sainsbury (dir.) (MoI/Realist, U.K., 1941).
Why We Fight, Frank Capra et al. (dirs.) (U.S. Signal Corps, U.S.A., 1942–1945)
Words for Battle, Humphrey Jennings (dir) (Crown, U.K., 1941)

Select Feature Filmography

The Adventures of Robin Hood, Michael Curtiz (dir.) (Warner Brothers, U.S.A., 1939).

Casablanca, Michael Curtiz (dir.) (Warner Brothers, U.S.A., 1942).

Confessions of a Nazi Spy, Anatole Litvak (dir.) (Warner Brothers, U.S.A., 1939).

Confirm or Deny, Archie Mayo (dir.) (Twentieth Century Fox, U.S.A., 1940).

Contraband, Michael Powell (dir.) (British National, U.K., 1940).

Convoy, Michael Balcon (dir.) (Ealing, U.K., 1940).

Dumbo, Ben Sharpsteen (dir.) (Disney, U.S.A., 1941).

Eagle Squadron, Arthur Lubin (dir.) (Universal/Wanger, U.S.A., 1942).

Foreign Correspondent, Alfred Hitchcock (dir.) (United Artists, U.S.A., 1941).

Forty-Ninth Parallel, Michael Powell (dir.) (GFD/Ortus, U.K., 1941).

The Great Dictator, Charles Chaplin (dir.) (Chaplin, U.S.A., 1940).

Let George Do It, Marcel Varnel (dir.) (Ealing, U.K., 1940).

The Lion Has Wings, Michael Powell, Brian Hurst, Adrian Brunel, (dirs.) (London/United Artists, U.K., 1939).

The Long Voyage Home, John Ford (dir.) (Walter Wanger, U.S.A., 1940).

Mrs. Miniver, William Wyler (dir.) (MGM, U.S.A., 1942).

Night Train to Munich, Carol Reid (dir.) (Twentieth Century Fox, U.K., 1940).

Pastor Hall, Roy Boulting (dir.) (Grand National, U.K., 1940).

The Ramparts We Watch, Louis de Rochemont (dir.) (RKO, U.S.A., 1940).

The Sea Hawk, Michael Curtiz (dir.) (Warner Brothers, U.S.A., 1940).

Sergeant York, Howard Hawks (dir.) (Warner Brothers, U.S.A., 1941).

That Hamilton Woman, Alexander Korda (dir.) (Korda, U.S.A., 1941).

To Be or Not to Be, Ernst Lubitsch (dir.) (UA–Lubitsch/Korda, U.S.A., 1942).

Select Printed Sources

Published Documents

Berle, B., and Jacobs, T., eds. *Navigating the Rapids, 1918–1971: From the Papers of Adolf A.Berle* (New York: Harcourt Brace Jovanovich, 1973).

Bliss, Edward, Jr., ed. *In Search of Light: The Broadcasts of Edward R. Murrow, 1938–61* (New York: Knopf, 1967).

Butler, R.; Dakin, D.; Lambert, M.; et al., eds. *Documents on British Foreign Policy*, Second and Third Series (London: HMSO, 1949–1979).

Cantril, Hadley, ed. *Public Opinion, 1935–46* (Princeton, N.J.: Princeton University Press, 1951).

Colville, Sir John. *The Fringes of Power: Downing Street Diaries, 1939–1955* (London: Weidenfeld & Nicolson, 1985).

Dilks, David N., ed. *The Diaries of Sir Alexander Cadogan, 1938–45* (London: Cassell, 1971).

Doenecke, Justus D., ed. *In Danger Undaunted: The Anti-Interventionist Movement of 1940–1941 as Revealed in the Papers of the America First Committee* (Palo Alto: Hoover Institution Press, 1990).

Eade, Charles, ed. *Secret Session Speeches by the Right Hon. Winston S. Churchill* (London: Cassell, 1946).

Eade, Charles, ed. *The War Speeches of the Rt. Hon. Winston S. Churchill* Vols. 1–3, (London: Cassell, 1952).

Gallup, George H., ed. *The Gallup Poll: Public Opinion, 1935–71*, Vol. 1 (New York: Random House, 1972).

Kimball, Warren F., ed. *Churchill and Roosevelt: The Complete Correspondence*, Vols. 1–3 (Princeton: Princeton University Press, 1984).

Lothian, Lord. *The American Speeches of Lord Lothian* (Oxford: Oxford University Press, 1941).

Nicholas, H. G., ed. *Washington Dispatches 1941–45: Weekly Political Reports from the British Embassy* (Chicago: University of Chicago Press, 1981).

Perkins, E. R., ed. *Foreign Relations of the United States (FRUS)*, Vols. 1937–1942 (Washington, D.C.: Department of State, 1956–1958).

Pimlot, Ben, ed. *The Second World War Diary of Hugh Dalton, 1940–45* (London: Jonathan Cape, 1986).

Priestley, J. B. *Britain Speaks* (New York: Harper, 1940).

Rosenman, Samuel I., ed. *The Public Papers and Addresses of Franklin D. Roosevelt*, Vols. 1–5 (New York, Random House, 1938); Vols. 6–9 (New York: Macmillan, 1941?); Vols. 10–13 (New York: Harper, 1950).

Roosevelt, Franklin. *The Complete Presidential Press Conferences of Franklin D. Roosevelt*, Vols. 17–18 (New York: Da Capo, 1972).

Newspapers and journals as cited in the notes.

Select Contemporaneous Literary Sources

Churchill, Winston. *Blood, Sweat and Tears* (New York: Putnam, 1941).

Davey, Jocelyn [Chaim Raphael]. *The Undoubted Deed* (London: Chatto & Windus, 1956).

Eckersley, Roger. *Some Nonsense* (London: Sampson, Low, Marston & Co., 1946).

Eliot, T. S. *The Complete Poems and Plays* (London: Faber, 1969).

Gallico, Paul. *The Snow Goose* (New York: Knopf, 1941).

Greene, Graham. *The Last Word* (London: Heineman, 1990).

———. *The Tenth Man* (London: Heineman, 1985).

———. *Twenty-One Short Stories* (London: Heineman, 1977).

Hilton, James. *Random Harvest* (Boston: Little, Brown, 1941).

Knight, Eric. *Sam Small Flies Again: The Amazing Adventures of the Flying Yorkshireman* (New York: Harper, 1942).

———. *This Above All* (New York: Harper, 1941).

Lewis, Sinclair. *It Can't Happen Here* (Garden City, N.Y.: Doubleday, 1935).

Masefield, John. *The Nine Days Wonder* (New York: Macmillan, 1941).

Miller, Alice Duer. *The White Cliffs* (New York: Coward-McCann, 1940).

Storm, Lesley [Mabel Clark]. *Heart of a City* (New York: Dramatists Play Service, 1942).

Struther, Jan [Joyce Maxtone-Graham]. *Mrs. Miniver* (London: Virago, 1989).

Waugh, Evelyn. *Put Out More Flags* (Boston: Little, Brown, 1942).

Wheeler, Monroe, ed. *Britain at War* (New York: Museum of Modern Art, 1941).

Select Memoirs/Reportage

Ayer, Alfred J. *Part of My Life* (London: Collins, 1977).

Bartlett, Vernon. *Now and Tomorrow* (London: Chatto & Windus, 1960).

Braden, Spruille, *Diplomats and Demagogues* (New Rochelle, N.Y.: Arlington House, 1971).

Bryce, Ivar. *You Only Live Once: Memories of Ian Fleming* (London: Weiden-feld & Nicolson, 1975).
Campbell, Gerald. *Of True Experience* (London: Hutchinson, 1948).
Churchill, Winston S. *The Second World War,* Vols. 1–6, (London: Cassell, 1948–1954).
Clarke, William. *From Three Worlds* (London: Sidgwick & Jackson, 1986).
Cooper, Alfred Duff. *Old Men Forget* (London: Rupert Hart-Davis, 1953).
Daiches, David. *A Third World* (London: Chatto & Windus, 1971).
Downes, Donald. *The Scarlet Thread: Adventures in Wartime Intelligence* (London: Derek Verschoyle, 1953).
Eckersley, Roger. *The BBC and All That* (London: Sampson, Low, Marston & Co., 1946).
Eden, Anthony. *Facing the Dictators* (London: Cassell, 1962).
———. *The Reckoning* (London: Cassell, 1965).
Gervasi, Frank. *The Violent Decade: A Foreign Correspondent in Europe and the Middle East, 1935–1945*(New York: Norton, 1989).
Gorham, Maurice. *Sound and Fury: Twenty-One Years at the BBC* (London: Percival Marshall, 1948).
Halifax, [1st] Earl of. *Fulness of Days* (London: Cassell, 1957).
Hull, Cordell. *The Memoirs of Cordell Hull,* Vols. 1 and 2 (New York: Hodder & Stoughton, 1948).
Kirkpatrick, Helen. *This Terrible Peace* (London: Rich & Cowan, 1939).
———. *Under the British Umbrella: What the English Are and How They Go to War* (New York: Scribner, 1939).
Klemmer, Harvey. *They'll Never Quit* (New York: Funk, 1941).
Lockhart, Robert H. Bruce. *Comes the Reckoning* (London: Putnam, 1947).
———. *Giants Cast Long Shadows* (London: Putnam, 1960).
Maschwitz, Eric. *No Chip on My Shoulder* (London: Herbert Jenkins, 1957).
Middleton, Drew. *Our Share of Night* (New York: Viking, 1946).
Murrow, Edward R. *This Is London* (New York: Simon & Schuster, 1941).
Panter-Downes, Mollie. *Letter from England* (Boston: Little, Brown, 1940).
Powell, Michael. *A Life in Movies* (London: Heinemann, 1986).
Reynolds, Quentin. *The Wounded Don't Cry* (New York: Cassell, 1941).
Robertson, Ben. *I Saw England* (New York: Knopf, 1941).
Sevareid, Eric. *Not So Wild a Dream* (New York: Atheneum, 1976).
Sheean, Vincent. *Between the Thunder and the Sun* (New York: Random House, 1943).
Swing, Raymond Gram. *Good Evening!* (New York: Harcourt, 1964).
Tree, Ronald. *When the Moon Was High: Memoirs of Peace and War, 1897–1942* (London: Macmillan, 1975).
Vansittart, Robert. *The Mist Procession* (London: Hutchinson, 1958).
Watt, Harry. *Don't Look at the Camera* (London: Elek, 1974).
Weizmann, Chaim. *Trial and Error* (London: Hamish Hamilton, 1949).
Wheeler-Bennett, John. *Special Relationships: America in Peace and War* (London: Macmillan, 1975).

Select Monographs

Aldgate, Anthony, and Richards, Jeffrey. *Britain Can Take It: British Cinema in the Second World War* (Oxford: Oxford University Press, 1986).

Andrew, Christopher. *Secret Service: The Making of the British Intelligence Community* (London: Heinemann, 1985).

Balfour, Michael. *Propaganda in War, 1939–1945: Organisations, Policies and Publics in Britain and Germany* (London: Routledge & Kegan Paul, 1979).

Beaton, Cecil. *War Photographs, 1939–45* (London: Imperial War Museum, 1981).

Birkenhead, 2nd Earl of. *Halifax* (London: Hamish Hamilton, 1965).

Blum, John Morton, *V Was for Victory: Politics and American Culture During World War II* (New York: Harcourt Brace Jovanovich, 1976).

Briggs, Asa. *The History of Broadcasting in the United Kingdom*, Vols. 2–4, (Oxford: Oxford University Press, 1965–1979).

Brinkley, Alan. *Voices of Protest: Huey Long, Father Coughlin and the Great Depression* (New York: Knopf, 1982).

Brown, Anthony Cave. *Wild Bill Donovan: The Last Hero* (New York: Times Books, 1982).

Burns, James MacGregor. *Roosevelt: The Lion and the Fox* (New York: Harcourt, 1956).

———. *Roosevelt: The Soldier of Freedom* (New York: Harcourt Brace Jovanovich, 1972).

Butler, J. R. M. *Lord Lothian* (New York: St Martin's, 1960).

Calder, Angus. *The Myth of the Blitz* (London: Jonathan Cape, 1991).

———. *The Peoples War: Britain 1939–45* (London: Jonathan Cape, 1969).

Chadwin, Mark Lincoln. *The Hawks of World War II* (Chapel Hill, N.C.: University of North Carolina Press, 1968).

Cockett, Richard. *Twilight of Truth: Chamberlain, Appeasement and the Manipulation of the Press* (London: Weidenfeld & Nicolson, 1989).

Cole, Wayne S. *America First: The Battle Against Intervention* (Madison, Wisc.: University of Wisconsin Press, 1953).

———. *Roosevelt and the Isolationists, 1932–45* (Lincoln, Neb.: University of Nebraska Press, 1983).

Coultass, Clive. *Images for Battle: British Film and the Second World War, 1939–1945* (London: Associated University Presses, 1989).

Culbert, David H. *News for Every Man: Radio and Foreign Affairs in Thirties America* (Westport Conn.: Greenwood Press, 1976).

Dallek, Robert. *Franklin D. Roosevelt and American Foreign Policy* (New York: Oxford University Press, 1979).

Dimbleby, David, and Reynolds, David. *An Ocean Apart* (London: Hodder & Stoughton, 1988).

Divine, Robert A. *The Illusion of Neutrality* (Chicago, University of Chicago Press, 1962).

———. *The Reluctant Belligerent: American Entry in World War II* (New York: Wiley, 1965).

Fielding, Raymond. *March of Time, 1935–1951* (New York: Oxford, 1978).

Foot, M. R. D. *SOE: An Outline History of the Special Operations Executive, 1940–46* (London: BBC, 1984).

Friedländer, Saul. *Prelude to Downfall: Hitler and the United States, 1939–1941* (New York: Knopf, 1967).

Fussell, Paul. *Thank God for the Atom Bomb and Other Essays* (New York: Summit, 1989).

————. *Wartime* (New York: Oxford University Press, 1989).

Gelb, Norman. *Dunkirk* (New York: Morrow, 1989).

————. *Scramble: A Narrative History of the Battle of Britain* (New York: Harcourt Brace Jovanovich, 1985).

Gilbert, Martin. *Winston S. Churchill* Vols. 5–7 (London: Heinemann, 1977–1986).

Goodhart, Philip. *Fifty Ships That Saved the World* (Garden City, N.Y.: Doubleday, 1965).

Hardy, Forsyth. *John Grierson: A Documentary Biography* (London: Faber, 1978).

Harman, Nicholas. *Dunkirk: The Patriotic Myth* (New York: Simon & Schuster, 1980).

Harrison, Tom. *Living Through the Blitz* (New York: Schocken, 1989).

Heinrichs, Waldo. *Threshold of War: Franklin D. Roosevelt and American Entry into World War II* (New York: Oxford University Press, 1988).

Herzstein, Robert E. *Roosevelt and Hitler: Prelude to War* (New York: Paragon, 1989).

Hinsley, F. H., and Simkins, C. A. G. *British Intelligence in the Second World War: Vol.4, Security and Counter-Intelligence* (London: HMSO, 1990).

Hitchens, Christopher. *Blood, Class and Nostalgia: Anglo-American Ironies* (New York: Farrar, Straus & Giroux, 1990).

Hodgkinson, Anthony W., and Sheratsky, Rodney E. *Humphrey Jennings: More Than a Maker of Films* (Hanover, N.H.: Clark University Press, 1982).

Hosley, D. H. *As Good As Any: Foreign Correspondence on American Radio, 1930–1940* (Westport Conn.: Greenwood Press, 1984).

Hyde, H. Montgomery. *The Quiet Canadian: The Secret Service Story of Sir William Stephenson* (London: Hamish Hamilton, 1962).

Iriye, Akira. *The Origins of the Second World War in Asia and the Pacific* (London: Longman, 1987).

James, Robert Rhodes. *Anthony Eden* (London: Weidenfeld & Nicolson, 1986).

Johnson, Walter. *The Battle Against Isolation* (Chicago: University of Chicago Press, 1944).

Jonas, Manfred. *Isolationism in America, 1935–41* (Ithaca, N.Y.: Cornell University Press, 1969).

Kendrick, Alexander. *Prime Time: The Life of Edward R. Murrow* (Boston: Little, Brown, 1969).

Kimball, Warren F. *The Most Unsordid Act: Lend-Lease, 1939–1941* (Baltimore: Johns Hopkins Press, 1969).

Knightley, Phillip. *The First Casualty: From the Crimea to Vietnam: The War Correspondent as Hero, Propagandist, and Myth Maker* (New York: Harcourt Brace Jovanovich, 1975).

Koppes, Clayton R., and Black, Gregory D. *Hollywood Goes to War: How Politics, Profits and Propaganda Shaped World War II Movies* (New York: Free Press, 1987).

Korda, Michael. *Charmed Lives* (New York: Random House, 1979).

Kurth, Peter. *American Cassandra: The Life of Dorothy Thompson* (Boston: Little, Brown, 1990).

Langer, William L., and Gleason, S. Everett. *The Challenge of Isolation: The World Crisis of 1937–40* (New York: Harper, 1952).

————. *The Undeclared War, 1940–1941* (New York: Harper, 1953).

Larrabee, Eric. *Commander in Chief: Franklin Delano Roosevelt, His Lieutenants, and Their War* (New York: Harper & Row, 1987).

Lash, Joseph P. *Roosevelt and Churchill, 1939–1941: The Partnership That Saved the West* (New York: Norton, 1976).

Lavine, Harold, and Wechsler, James. *War Propaganda and the United States* (New Haven, Conn.: Yale University Press, 1940).

Leigh, Michael. *Mobilizing Consent: Public Opinion and American Foreign Policy, 1937–47* (Westport Conn.: Greenwood Press, 1976).

Lincove, David A. and Treadway, Gary R. *The Anglo-American Relationship: An Annotated Bibliography of Scholarship, 1945–1985* (Westport, Conn.: Greenwood Press, 1988).

McJimsey, George. *Harry Hopkins: Ally of the Poor and Defender of Democracy* (Cambridge, Mass.: Harvard University Press, 1987).

Mackenzie, John, ed. *Imperialism and Popular Culture* (Manchester: Manchester University Press, 1984).

McKercher, B. J. C. *The Second Baldwin Government and the United States, 1924–1929: Attitudes and Diplomacy* (Cambridge: Cambridge University Press, 1985).

McLaine, Ian. *Ministry of Morale: Home Front Morale and the Ministry of Information* (London: Allen & Unwin, 1979).

Moorehead, Caroline. *Sidney Bernstein* (London: Jonathan Cape, 1984).

Offner, Arnold A. *American Appeasement: United States Foreign Policy and Germany, 1933–38* (Cambridge, Mass.: Harvard University Press, 1969).

Ovendale, Ritchie. *"Appeasement" and the English Speaking World* (Cardiff: University of Wales Press, 1975).

Persico, Joseph E. *Edward R. Murrow: An American Original* (New York: McGraw-Hill, 1988).

Pronay, Nicholas, and Spring, D. W., eds. *Propaganda, Politics and Film, 1918–45* (London: Macmillan, 1982).

Quigley, Caroll. *The Anglo-American Establishment: From Rhodes to Cliveden* (New York: Books in Focus, 1981).

Reynolds, David. *The Creation of the Anglo-American Alliance, 1937–41: A Study in Competitive Cooperation* (Europa: London, 1981).

Richards, Jeffrey, and Aldgate, Anthony. *Britain Can Take It: The British Cinema in the Second World War* (New York: Oxford University Press, 1986).

Roberts, Andrew. *"The Holy Fox": A Biography of Lord Halifax* (London: Weidenfeld & Nicolson, 1991).

Rolo, Charles. *Radio Goes to War* (New York: Putnam, 1942).

Rusbridger, James, and Nave, Eric. *Betrayal at Pearl Harbor: How Churchill Lured Roosevelt into War* (New York: Summitt, 1991).

Russett, Bruce M. *Community and Contention: Britain and America in the Twentieth Century* (Cambridge, Mass.: MIT Press, 1963).

Sanders, Michael, and Taylor, Philip M. *British Propaganda in the First World War* (London: Macmillan, 1982).

Schneider, James C. *Should America Go to War?* (Chapel Hill, N.C.: University of North Carolina Press, 1989).

Schulzinger, Robert D. *The Wise Men of Foreign Affairs: The History of the Council on Foreign Relations* (New York: Columbia University Press, 1984).

Schwarz, Jordan A. *Liberal: Adolf A. Berle and the Vision of an American Era* (New York: Free Press, 1987).

Sherwood, Robert. *The White House Papers of Harry L. Hopkins*, Vols. 1–2 (London: Eyre & Spottiswoode, 1948).

Shulman, Holly Cowan. *The Voice of America: Propaganda and Democracy, 1941–1945* (Madison, Wis.: University of Wisconsin Press, 1990).

Smith, R. Franklin. *Edward R. Murrow: The War Years* (Kalamazoo, Mich.: New Issues Press, 1978).

Sperber, A. M. *Murrow* (London: Michael Joseph, 1988).

Squires, J. D. *British Propaganda at Home and in the United States from 1914 to 1917* (Cambridge, Mass.: Harvard University Press, 1935).

Stafford, David. *Camp X: SOE and the American Connection* (Toronto: Lester & Orpen Dennys, 1986).

Steele, Richard W. *Propaganda in an Open Society: The Roosevelt Administration and the Media, 1933–1941* (Westport Conn.: Greenwood Press, 1985).

Stevenson, William. *A Man Called Intrepid: The Secret War* (New York: Harcourt Brace Jovanovich, 1976).

Stiller, Jesse H. *George S. Messersmith, Diplomat of Democracy* (Chapel Hill, N.C.: University of North Carolina Press, 1987).

Taylor, John Russell. *Hitch: The Life and Times of Alfred Hitchcock* (New York: Pantheon, 1978).

Taylor, Philip M., ed. *British Cinema in the Second World War* (London: Macmillan, 1988).

———. *The Projection of Britain* (Cambridge: Cambridge University Press, 1981).

Taylor, S. J. *Stalin's Apologist: Walter Duranty, The New York Times' Man in Moscow* (Oxford: Oxford University Press, 1990).

Thorne, Christopher. *Allies of a Kind: The United States, Britain, and the War Against Japan, 1941–1945* (London: Hamish Hamilton, 1978).

———. *Border Crossings* (New York: Blackwells, 1988).

Thorpe, Frances, and Pronay, Nicholas. *British Official Films in the Second World War: A Descriptive Catalogue* (Oxford: Clio Press, 1980).

Toland, John. *Infamy: Pearl Harbor and Its Aftermath* (Garden City, N.Y.: Doubleday, 1982).

Troy, Thomas F. *COI and British Intelligence, an Essay on Origins* (Langley, Va.: Central Intelligence Agency, 1970).

Watt, Donald Cameron. *How War Came: The Immediate Origins of the Second World War, 1938–1939* (New York: Heinemann, 1989).

———. *Personalities and Politics: Studies in the Formation of British Policy in the Twentieth Century* (London: Longman, 1965).

———. *Succeeding John Bull: America in Britain's Place, 1900–1975* (Cambridge: Cambridge University Press, 1984).

West, Nigel. *MI6: British Secret Intelligence Service Operations, 1909–45* (London: Weidenfeld & Nicolson, 1983).

———. *A Thread of Deceit: Espionage Myths of World War II* (New York: Random House, 1985).

Willert, Arthur, *The Road to Safety: A Study in Anglo-American Relations* (London: Derek Verschoyle, 1952).

Winkler, Allan M. *The Politics of Propaganda: The Office of War Information, 1942–1945* (New Haven, Conn.: Yale University Press, 1978).

Select Articles in Academic Journals

Anstey, Caroline. "The Projection of British Socialism: Foreign Office Publicity and American Opinion, 1945–50," *Journal of Contemporary History* 19 (1984): 417–51.

Bratzel, John F., and Rout, Leslie B. "FDR and the Secret Map," *Wilson Quarterly* 9 (1985): 167–73.

Cole, C. Robert. "The Conflict Within: Stephen Tallents and Planning Propaganda Overseas Before the Second World War," *Albion* 12(1982): 50–71.

Hachey, Thomas E. "Winning Friends and Influencing Policy: British Strategy to Woo America in 1937," *Wisconsin Magazine of History* 55 (1971/72): 120–29.

Ignatius, David. "Britain's War in America: How Churchill's Agents Secretly Manipulated the U.S. Before Pearl Harbor," *Washington Post* (Section C), 17 September 1989, pp. 1–2.

Reynolds, David. "FDR's Foreign Policy and the British Royal Visit to the U.S.A., 1939," *Historian* 45 (1983): 461–72.

———. "Lord Lothian and Anglo-American Relations, 1939–1940" *Transactions of the American Philosophical Society* 73 (1983): 1–65.

Rhodes, Benjamin D. "The British Royal Visit of 1939 and the 'Psychological Approach' to the United States," *Diplomatic History* 2 (1978): 197–211.

Short, K. R. M. "The White Cliffs of Dover: Promoting the Anglo-American Alliance in World War II," *Historical Journal of Film, Radio and Television* 2 (1982): 3–25.

Spence, Peter. "The BBC North American Service, 1939–1945," *Media, Culture and Society* 4 (1982): 361–75.

Taylor, Philip M. "If War Should Come: Preparing the Fifth Arm for Total War, 1935–1939," *Journal of Contemporary History* 16 (1981): 27–51.

Watt, Donald Cameron. "America and the British Foreign Policy-Making Elite, from Joseph Chamberlain to Anthony Eden, 1895–1956," *Review of Politics* 25 (1963) pp. 3–33.

Wilcox, Temple. "Projection or Publicity? Rival Concepts in the Pre-War Planning of the British Ministry of Information," *Journal of Contemporary History* 18 (1983): 97–116.

Unpublished Dissertations and Presentations

Anstey, Caroline. "Foreign Office Efforts to Influence American Opinion, 1945–1949," *London School of Economics and Political Science* (Ph.D., 1984).

Brewer, Susan A. "Creating the Special Relationship: British Propaganda in America in World War Two," *Cornell University* (Ph.D., 1991).

Cull, Nicholas John. "A Fox Hunting Man Abroad: Lord Halifax as British Ambassador to the United States, 1941," *University of Leeds* (B.A., 1986).

———. "The British Campaign Against American 'Neutrality': Publicity and Propaganda 1939–1941," *University of Leeds* (Ph.D., 1991).

Dzierba, Timothy Roger. "Organised Labor and the Coming of World War II, 1937–1941," *State University of New York* (Ph.D., 1983)

Krome, Frederick James. "'A Weapon of War Second to None': Anglo-American Film Propaganda During World War II," *University of Cincinnati* (Ph.D., 1992).

Mahl, Thomas "'Forty-eight land', British Intelligence and American Isolation," *Kent State University* (Ph.D. [pending] 1993).

Schwar, Jane Harriet Dashiell. "Interventionist Propaganda and Pressure Groups in the United States, 1937–1941," *Ohio State University* (Ph.D., 1973).

Taylor, Philip M. "Film as Evidence," presentation to the Institute of Contemporary British History summer school, LSE, July 1989.

Index

Printed in the United Kingdom
by Lightning Source UK Ltd.
9711200001B/121